PAGANISM TO CHRISTIANITY
IN THE ROMAN EMPIRE

PAGANISM TO CHRISTIANITY IN THE ROMAN EMPIRE

By

WALTER WOODBURN HYDE

Philadelphia

UNIVERSITY OF PENNSYLVANIA PRESS

London: Geoffrey Cumberlege

Oxford University Press

1 9 4 6

TO

MY FORMER STUDENTS IN THE HISTORY OF RELIGIONS

ἀλλὰ τὰ μὲν προτετύχθαι ἐάσομεν ἀχνύμενοί περ,
θυμὸν ἐνὶ στήθεσσι φίλον δαμάσαντες ἀνάγκῃ.

Iliad, XIX, 65–66

CONTENTS

CONTENTS

INTRODUCTION

IN 1938 was celebrated the two-thousandth anniversary of the birth of Augustus Caesar, the founder of the greatest of empires, that of Rome. By the time of his death the Eternal City had conquered most of the countries in which the main current of history had theretofore run its course, for she then held under her sway all peoples, both civilized and barbarian, who dwelt in the broad zone extending from the Atlantic to the Euphrates and from the deserts of Africa and Arabia to the North Sea, and had thus become a world-state. Rome, in the middle of Italy, the central peninsula of the Mediterranean Sea, the theater of ancient history, through her geographical advantages, but more through her genius in war and in the organization of subject peoples, had first become head of Italy, and then of the world. Even before the close of the Republic during her great period of expansion (264–146 B.C.) she had begun to spread her Latin language and culture in the West and to unify the Graeco-Oriental culture of the East, and was soon to combine both into one great unity, the Graeco-Roman world. To establish and consolidate such an empire with its vast complex of ideas, customs and institutions and to assimilate them through organization and law so that the result was to last over a period of centuries was indeed a great work, "the greatest political work that any human being ever wrought" in the words of Merivale, the historian of Rome's first two centuries of prosperity. The Empire's importance culturally, religiously, and politically to modern times needs hardly be stressed, since out of it have come the political and religious ideas and, largely, the culture of our time. For the Roman Empire still lives on in our language, our laws, our municipal systems, our ideas of Church and State and, in many less obvious ways, still influences our lives. To quote J. G. Sheppard, the historian of its tragic passing: "As on Rome all ancient history converges, so from Rome all modern history begins."

After a century of civic disorder during which a series of supermen tried in various ways to cure Rome's ills—the Gracchi, Marius, Drusus, Sulla, Pompey, Caesar, Antony, Octavian—the dying Republic, following the battle of Actium in 31 B.C., yielded to a monarchy disguised in the interest of harmony under old Republican forms. Octavian—the future Augustus —conqueror of Antony and grandnephew of Julius Caesar, then became the first of a long line of emperors who directed the Roman State through all of the vicissitudes of the next five centuries.

Within its frontiers the Empire thus founded was a truly magnificent domain: "the fairest part of the earth and the more civilized portion of mankind," as Gibbon said in introducing his *Decline and Fall*. Under Trajan in the early second century, when it reached its widest extent, it stretched from York (Eboracum) to Thebes, and from Lisbon (Olisipo) to beyond the Tigris, and contained perhaps one third of the population of the corresponding areas in our day—the one time in history when civilized man of the West was under one rule.[1] For beyond her borders to the limits of earth lay only shadowy regions negligible to all save an Alexander or a Caesar. The ruler of this vast domain enjoyed both supreme civic and religious power, in the secular state, as Caesar; in the religious, as Pontifex maximus. In the words of the historian of the dissolution of the West:

> Even now a sovereign who should thus hold all the lands around the Mediterranean Sea . . . would be incomparably the strongest ruler in the world. . . . When Rome ruled she was not only the greatest, but practically the only Power of which the statesman and the philosopher took any cognizance.[2]

It had taken centuries to build and consolidate this empire, which fact should have warned the would-be world conquerors of later days of the futility of trying to erect a stable state in a day. Its great task, after the period of conquest was ended, was to assimilate its heterogeneous peoples, to complete the work of making the West Latin as the East was already Greek, to Romanize both, and to perfect its institutions especially its law. But, as the greatness of Athens was confined to less than a century and a half (479–338 B.C.), so the peak of Roman greatness lasted little more than a half century, roughly through the benign reigns of Hadrian and the Antonines (117–180). This Antonine Age has evoked the encomia of both ancient and modern writers. The contemporary Latin Church Father Tertullian *(ca.* 150–230) could say: "Each day the world becomes more beautiful, more wealthy, more splendid. No corner remains inaccessible. . . . Recent deserts bloom. . . . Forests give way to tilled areas. . . . Everywhere are houses, people, cities. Everywhere there is life." And Gibbon states forthrightly that "if a man had his choice he would prefer to have lived then than at any period since"; while Mommsen speaking more generally arrives at much the same conclusion:

> In its sphere which those who belonged to it were not far wrong in regarding the world the Empire fostered the peace and prosperity of the many nations united under its sway longer and more completely than any other leading power has ever succeeded in doing . . . and if an angel of the Lord were to strike a balance whether the domain ruled by Severus Antoninus was governed with the greater intelligence and greater humanity at that time or in the present day, whether civilization and national prosperity have since that time advanced or retrograded, it is very doubtful whether the decision would prove in favor of the present.[3]

It is a historical fact that no ruler who since has sat upon a European throne has attained the moral stature and Stoic adherence to the duties of high office reached by Marcus Aurelius, the finest spirit of all the emperors.

---

[1] Freeman says: "Her walls were no longer on the Tiber, but on the Danube, the Rhine and the German Ocean. Instead of an outpost at Janiculum her fortresses were at York and Trier. Many of the emperors after the first century were more at home in these and other distant cities than in the ancient capital, which they visited perhaps only two or three times in a reign for some solemn pageant. In these provincial towns the pulse of Roman life beat more strongly than in old Rome itself."

[2] Thomas Hodgkin in *Contemporary Review* (Jan. 1898), p. 53.

[3] *Provinces of the Roman Empire* (London, 1886), I, 9.

Despite obvious dark features of a civilization already static, the Romans were a fortunate people on whom the gods had showered many blessings. They had fertile provinces, fine cities adorned with splendid public buildings, safe roads radiating in trunk lines from the *miliarium aureum* in the Forum across intervening provinces to the uttermost confines of the State, varied industries, extensive commerce over the Mediterranean and along the coasts of the Atlantic and Indian oceans to the North Sea and the Far East. They also enjoyed humane laws whose spirit had been tempered by the moral ideals of Stoicism, in whose protection women, children, and slaves shared and which limited torture and recognized the rights of the accused. The jurist Ulpian in the reign of Alexander Severus proclaimed the sentiment that "all men are equal by a law of nature" and that slavery existed not by natural law as Aristotle thought, but only by the lower law of man. There were charities, public and private, asylums for orphans, free medicine for the poor and punishment for cruelty to domestic animals so that the latter received better treatment than they receive today in parts of the same area. Plutarch was unwilling to sell even an old ox, although Cato the Censor three centuries before had advised the selling of infirm slaves. There was equality between women and men before the law and a high ideal of marriage, both Seneca and Plutarch insisting for the first time on a single moral standard. There were libraries, schools, travel, and a government humane and strong enough to guarantee peace and security, even if through force. No such peace as the *pax Romana*, which endured with slight interruptions for two hundred years, ever existed before nor has existed since. And chief of all, men's sympathies were broadened by ethical philosophies, by Stoicism, which taught the doctrine of human brotherhood, and later by Christianity. Terence's line was the key:

humani nihil a me alienum puto.

Throughout the first two centuries of the Empire Rome because of her good government, uniform law, and ease of intercommunication became supreme in the minds of her citizens. Her ability to mold many races into one people came not so much through conscious effort as expressed in law, as through the unconscious desire of her people, much in the same way as different stocks are being absorbed in America today. Men from Britain, Africa, Greece, Moesia, and Syria were all Romans not only in culture but also in spirit, organically unified in their inner life, the provincials being brothers of those in the capital. Indeed, it was from the provinces that Rome drew many of her writers, philosophers, historians, generals, and some of her emperors.

With the passing of Marcus Aurelius in 180 and the accession of his unworthy son Commodus the prosperity of the Empire ended and its decadence was rapid and almost uninterrupted, reaching its lowest ebb in the third-century crisis caused by civil strife within and the barbarian menace without. During that crisis, especially between A.D. 235 and 284, the emperors became mere sports of the armies and the process of disintegration

ate into the very heart of the State, which offered the tragic spectacle of
a vast dying organization beset politically, socially, and economically by
forces it could not master, by anarchy, revolution, division, and the loss
of one-half of its territory, by plague, famine, taxation, and unremitting
pressure on the frontiers by the barbarians. Near the close of the century
Diocletian (284–305), the last of the "barrack" emperors and extravagantly
called by Ferrero "the last great man of antiquity," stayed the disintegration and inaugurated the first "scientific" constitution in the Empire's
history. But the State envisioned by Augustus three centuries before had
now disappeared and in its place there arose a centralized despotism of the
Oriental type, usually known as "the Dominate," in which one was "master" and the many were "slaves." It continued, however, for two centuries
longer in the West and, after Constantine the Great transferred the capital
from Italy to Byzantium on the Bosphorus which he rechristened *Nova
Roma,* it remained the ruler and the governmental pattern for many centuries longer in the East. This change was the result of the shift in the
center of political and commercial gravity from West to East. The immediate cause was the freedom of the new capital from the pagan traditions which were still so strong in Rome that the latter was unfit longer to
be the seat of Constantine's Christian state.

By now Christianity, one of two new forces (since the reign of Tiberius)
which were to change and destroy the Empire, had become so strong that
Constantine favored it largely in order to have its support in his political
schemes. With imperial favor it grew rapidly until at the end of the fourth
century it had become the sole official religion of the State. In the mean-
time the Germans, the other of the two new forces, began to menace the
Empire. The Visigoths were allowed to cross the Danube, defeating and
slaying the Eastern emperor Valens at Adrianople in 378, and later overrunning Greece and Italy, under their leader Alaric who sacked Rome in
410. They were followed by other tribes which again and again forced
their way across the Rhine and Danube until finally they had submerged
the Western Empire.

But patriotism outlived these momentous changes and was still strong
to the end of the fourth century as we see from the verses of the last of the
classical Latin poets, Claudian of Alexandria, who died under Honorius
(*ca.* 408):

> Rome, Rome alone has found the spell to charm
> The tribes that bowed beneath her conquering arm;
> Has given one name to the whole human race,
> And clasped and sheltered them in fond embrace;
> Mother, not mistress; called her foe her son;
> And by soft ties made distant countries one.
> This to her peaceful sceptre all men owe—
> That through the nations, whereso'er we go
> Strangers, we find a fatherland. Our home
> We change at will; we count it sport to roam

Through distant Thule, or with sails unfurled
Seek the most drear recesses of the world.
Though we may tread Rhone's or Orontes' shore
Yet are we all one nation evermore.[4]

The story of the last century of the Empire in the West, after Theodosius the Great at his death in 395 had divided the State between his two sons, is nothing short of a Greek tragedy—for its destruction became inevitable. For the western half collapsed eighty-one years later when German kings occupied the western provinces and, although the Eastern half, henceforth the Empire itself, lived on for a millennium it retained little of Rome, for it was an orientalized type of medieval state, Greek in organization, intelligence, and spirit. Gibbon has unduly maligned this later period in his summary account of the Byzantine or Greek Empire as "a uniform tale of weakness and misery," for, despite its welter of court intrigues, its treachery and deceit, conspiracies and fratricides, blindings and poisonings, and its exploitation of subject peoples, the dark history of the Byzantine Empire as we now know from the writings of later historians from Finlay to Vasiliev,[5] had its periods of glory and long remained the bulwark of Europe against the East. Moreover in it ancient Greece lived on long after Rome had passed in the West even though the latter has left a greater heritage to the peoples of western Europe. For while Roman culture as an entity passed as certainly as had that of the earlier Hittites, that of Greece endured in eastern Europe to the fifteenth century. Then all that was left of the Eastern Empire was the great capital on the Bosphorus which, after being protected for centuries by the massive walls of Theodosius II, finally fell to the Moslem Turks in 1453—the last remnant of antiquity projected into modern times. Since that date the Crescent has replaced the Cross over St. Sophia, the oldest surviving Christian church.

Among the various phases of the Roman Empire's life not the least interesting is the story of religion: how the ancient State-cult, having first added attractive doctrines of Greek philosophy and then various mystery-religions from the Near East, finally had to yield to Christianity. As early as the second century Christianity had become a potent factor in the life of

[4] On Stilicho's Consulship, Bk. III, XXIV, 150–59, tr. by T. R. Glover in his Life and Letters in the Fourth Century (Cambridge, 1901), chap. x.

[5] G. Finlay, History of Greece, B.C. 146–A.D. 1864, ed H. F. Tozer, 7 vols. (Oxford, 1877), especially II, "Byzantine Empire," pp. 716–1204, and III, "Greek Empire of Nicaea and Constantinople," pp. 1204–1461; J. B. Bury, History of the Later Roman Empire, A.D. 395–800 (London, 1889); History of the Eastern Roman Empire, A.D. 802–67 (London, 1912); ed. Gibbon, 7 vols., 5th to 10th eds. (London, 1928–38); A. A. Vasiliev, History of the Byzantine Empire; tr. by Mrs. S. Ragozin, 2 vols. (Madison, 1928–29); and see Bibliography in Cambridge Medieval History (cited hereafter as C.M.H.), IV (1927), 717–1053 (Leo III to Constantine XI). It has been computed that of the 107 rulers from 395 to 1453, 20 were assassinated, 18 blinded or otherwise mutilated, 12 died in monasteries or prisons, 12 abdicated, 3 died of starvation, 8 in battle or by accident, while the last, Constantine XI (1448–53), died a hero during the Turkish assault on Constantinople, May 29, 1453; see J. E. Harry, Americana, V, 709.

the Empire, foreshadowing its triumph in the fourth when the religion of Jesus superseded all rivals. Rome, especially after the conquest of Macedonia, Greece, and the Near East, struggled ineffectually to exclude certain of these mystery-cults by law, e.g. that of Bacchus by Senate decree in 186 B.C. and that of Isis-Serapis later, only to find that ideas cannot be fenced off by human decrees. At the beginning of the Empire, Augustus, partly as a political device in his plan to reëstablish Roman life as it had been before the debacle of the Republic since he recognized how intimately the ancient faith had been interwoven with the growth of Rome's greatness, and partly because of his sincere adherence to the ancient State-cult which he felt was menaced by these aliens, gave by his revival the last impulse of life to the old polytheism.[6]

But the vitality of the civic-cult, henceforth to be kept alive in part at least by the State, had largely disappeared; only the outward forms, the festivals and the public amusements which the State sponsored still attracted the masses who long since had surrendered to one or another of the alien mysteries, while the educated classes were now finding comfort in various philosophical systems. Although the Eastern cults collectively gave Rome an idea of the universality of religion and released a new spiritual force, they were no more destined to triumph than was Augustus' pagan revival or its official successor, the cult of the Caesars. It was Christianity, heir of the faith which Israel had learned through her prophets, which vanquished all other spiritual forces and became the sole religion of the Roman State.

As Rome's role in pagan history came to an end, she was destined to play another, a sacred one, in Christian history very like that of Jerusalem in Judaism. By the time of the Antonines men generally believed that Peter and Paul had founded the Roman Church—a question discussed below—and Rome's part in ecclesiastical history had begun; for Irenaeus, bishop of Lugdunum (Lyon) in Gaul, in his treatise *Against Heresies* (composed *ca.* 180), spoke of the Roman Church as

the very great, the very ancient, and universally known church founded and organized at Rome by the two most glorious apostles Peter and Paul. . . . For it is a necessity that every church should agree with this church, on account of its pre-eminent authority . . . inasmuch as the apostolic tradition has been preserved continuously. . . .[7]

Thus a Christian Rome, destined, like its pagan predecessor on the Palatine, to conquer a large part of the earth, gradually arose on Vatican Hill

[6] Long before, around the middle of the second century B.C., Polybius, the Greek historian, then living as a prisoner in Rome, had alluded to this Roman attachment to their old cult in his *Histories* (6:56, 6–7): "For I conceive that what in other nations is looked upon as a reproach, I mean a scrupulous fear of the gods, is the very thing which keeps the Roman commonwealth together."

[7] 3:3, 2; in the *Ante-Nicene Christian Library* (Edinburgh, 1868–69), Vol. I (The Writings of Irenaeus), 261.

whence one can look across the Tiber and see the hills of old Rome as the poet Martial said:

> *Hinc septem dominos videre montes*
> *et totam licet aestimare Romam.*

Here at the foot of the hill on the site of Agrippina's gardens was the former *Circus Neronis* begun by Caligula and later used by Nero for his chariot-races. To the north of it lay the shrines of Cybele and Mithra, known in later antiquity as the *Phrygianum* and *Vaticanum* respectively, and below them, Nero's gardens. Here in circus and gardens, according to Tacitus, the Emperor soon after the great fire of 64 staged the first persecution of the Christians, including perhaps the martyrdom of the Apostle Paul. The red granite obelisk, transferred by Caligula from Heliopolis in Egypt to adorn the *spina* of the circus, and removed to its present location in the center of the great Piazza of St. Peter in 1586 by Sixtus V, is the solitary surviving witness of Nero's revolting cruelties. While today the Palatine is in ruins, St. Peter's still draws worshipers from all parts of the world. Of the Christian conversion of Rome in the fourth century the historian Freeman said: "That Christianity should become the religion of the Roman Empire is the miracle of history; but that it did so is the leading fact of all history from that day onwards." But while the Empire became Christian, the Church became in part pagan. For it gradually assumed the Empire's monarchical form, and later the imperial gradations of rank and geographical divisions. By the eighth century the Bishop of Rome had become a temporal prince, so that the philosopher Hobbes could truthfully say of the Papacy that it was "the ghost of the Roman Empire, crowned and seated on the grave thereof." Still later, in our time, the Pope, having lost his temporal power, has gone further and has become, since 1870, virtually an absolute monarch over the spiritual lives of Roman Catholics.

It is the story of the transformation of Christianity into a secularized institution during its struggle with the pagan order of the Roman Empire which is outlined in the following pages. After a chapter on Roman religion including the later imperial cult, and one on the Eastern mystery-cults which influenced the old national religion, and another on Christianity's parent religion, Judaism, the succeeding chapters give an account of Jesus, both his person and teaching, and follow the development of the Church to the time of Theodosius the Great under whom it triumphed over all its pagan rivals. The subject is large, its modern literature vast, and its conclusions varied; the presentation of an informative account within a reasonable compass is obviously not only difficult, but venturesome and especially for a classical historian. The author has attempted to treat it in the spirit of critical historical scholarship of our time, which investigates the beginnings of Christianity as fearlessly as it would those of Mithraism or any other religion once powerful in antiquity.

ACKNOWLEDGMENTS

The writer is under obligations to a multitude of sources ancient and modern, too many to enumerate here, which have been freely used, as the footnotes disclose.

English citations from the Greek and Roman Classics are generally taken from the *Loeb Classical Library* (cited hereafter as *L.C.L.*), through the generous permission of its publisher, the Harvard University Press.

Chapter I

THE NATIVE RELIGION OF THE ROMANS

IN THE REPUBLIC

MUCH has been written in recent years on the religion of Rome so that its general history and characteristics are now well known although the religious feeling which it evoked among its followers is still difficult to appraise. While it never reached the spiritual heights of some religions, it did, however, with the help of alien borrowings—deities, rituals, philosophies and, in its later period, mystery-cults—satisfy the limited religious needs of a great people for over a millennium and, through the Christian Church, has left traces in European culture down to our time. To understand the conflict of religions during the Roman Empire and the victory of Christianity, it is necessary first to review the story of the native Roman religion in the Republic down to its revival under Augustus and the rise of its rivals in the Empire.

Since both Romans and Greeks had a common Indo-European heritage, Roman religion shared many of its features with its sister religion of Greece. Thus it too had no founder, reformer, prophet, nor inspired teacher, no initial revelation nor sacred books and little ethical content. Similarly it had no creeds nor dogmas and consequently was a matter of practice rather than of belief. Its priesthood, evolved out of the primitive medicine-man and purveyor of magic, was not hereditary and gave neither instruction nor exhortation but performed a body of accumulated ritual and ceremony in honor of various deities and in celebration of various human events. It was only gradually that the gods became personal and aware of men. They were not omnipotent, differing only a little from mortals, their human character shown by early ancestor worship and the latter's late offspring, the deification of men. But the Roman religion also disclosed differences from that of the Greeks. The Roman gods were ever regarded as abstract powers of nature which could influence men through the *ius divinum,* while those of Greece, for all their ideal forms, were full of individual life and activity. Nor were the Roman deities clothed with poetic imagination, being symbolized in their early stages in the most prosaic way—Jupiter by flint-stones, Mars by a lance, Vesta by a perpetual fire. Furthermore, the forms of Roman worship had little of the beauty of Greek, nothing like the colorful quadrennial Panathenaic festival at Athens. It had little of the Greek freedom from fear, perhaps the chief characteristic of Greek religion, and none of its joyousness. Certainly its idea of the hereafter was more barbaric and less spiritual.

9

The Romans believed that their religion began with the legendary King Numa [1] to whom they attributed many of the characteristic manifestations of their religion—the organization of the religious calendar, the institution of the three major *flamens* or special priests of Jupiter, Mars, and Quirinus, the virgin priestesses of Vesta, the colleges of pontiffs and augurs and other religious officials, the worship of such gods as Terminus, the god of boundaries, and the erection of the first shrine to Janus, the god of all beginnings. Some of these institutions certainly antedated the foundation of Rome while others were later in origin than King Numa's time—some of them, such as augurs and pontiffs, being borrowings from the Etruscans.

It was the type of religion which we should expect of an essentially practical and unimaginative people like the Romans, for it was prosaic, aristocratic, and political, adapted more to public life than to individual sentiment, a religion of the State rather than of the individual. It was a class-religion for it was not until the close of the long-drawn out struggle in the early Republic between patricians and plebeians that the plebeians were allowed a part in public worship. Thus that conflict which ended with the passage of the Licinian Rogations in 367 B.C. was not only political, but religious in character. The priests were always State officials, temples and altars were supported by State moneys, ceremonies were supervised by the State and religious law administered in State courts. From the first it emphasized the virtues of the family, for every family formed a tiny church on whose pattern the State religion was fashioned. Prayer and sacrifice remained public ceremonies, the former being little more than a magical formula, the latter no more than a primitive rite. So long as men did not fail of their specified duty to the gods they might expect favors in return; a tacit contract of *quid pro quo* as when in time of war or pestilence promises of victims (*votum publicum*) were made *pro rei publicae salute* by the consuls who took office January first. While plebeians were largely excluded from the public ceremonies the aristocratic leaders of Rome remained loyal to their religion for centuries, even after their belief in it had waned, since it was interwoven in their privileges. Thus Roman religion remained to the end the formal faith of the State rather than the expression of individual belief.

Its outstanding external characteristic was its hospitality to alien influences which it assimilated and in doing so religion changed its character and outlook just as the Roman people changed theirs in the process of assimilation in other fields. Livy (1:8, 5–6) recounts the legend of how Romulus opened an asylum on the saddle between the summits of the Capitoline Hill for the turbulent rabble, both free and slave, of neighboring peoples. Thus early Rome learned the secret of how to treat conquered peoples and territories. Similarly, at the threshold of her career she opened her religion to the outer world becoming in religion, as in letters, art, and science, a large-scale borrower, although, like the Greeks, she stamped all

[1] See J. B. Carter, *Religion of Numa, and other Essays on the Religion of Ancient Rome* (London, 1906).

she took with her own imprint and made it Roman. During her long career from the conquest of the neighboring villages of the plain of Latium down to the time of Trajan, Rome continually accepted influences from all the peoples whom she successively subdued—Latins, Etruscans, Greeks, and later, Gauls, Spaniards, Britons, and the various peoples of the vast area between the Mediterranean and the Euphrates.

Because of such successive influences with their consequent changes it is difficult to define Roman religion as a whole beyond its being a formal polytheism characterized by ritualistic ceremonies, but it is easy to differentiate various stages of development and decline. These stages included: primitive animism and magic; the beginning of the personification of spirits and powers of nature during the late regal period; the humanizing of these spirits following contact with Latins, Etruscans, and Greeks during the Republic, a process completed after the Hannibalic War in the identification of Roman with corresponding Greek deities; the corruption of orthodoxy as a result of the increasing scepticism ushered in by Rome's foreign wars; the revival of the ancient faith on a political basis under Augustus, and lastly, the long decline during the Empire when Caesarism, later Greek philosophies, Oriental mystery-cults, and Christianity, all hostile to the old polytheism, held sway. It was this last stage which formed the rich heritage of cult and ceremony which was Rome's religious gift to the Church. The evolution of Roman religion thus extended over many centuries and its period of degeneration extended over as many more.

The chief inner characteristics of Roman religion of the Republic were its polytheism and ceremonialism. In the course of time it developed a vast number of guardian deities who presided over all the needs and conditions of human life. Few religions, if any outside India, have more falsely divided the godhead.[2] A good example of this tendency is afforded by the various deities who, according to Varro and other writers, watched over the life of the infant: Parca, the fate who presided at birth; Rumina (from *ruma,* teat), who watched over its suckling from a temple at the foot of the Palatine near the fig-tree, the *Ficus Rumina* of Ovid (*Fasti* 2:412), under which Romulus and Remus were suckled by the she-wolf; Levana who raised the infant from the ground; Fabulinus who helped the baby to talk; Potina who taught it how to drink and Edusa how to eat; and Cuba or Cunina who protected it in the crib. Besides an array of higher deities there were few abstractions which were not deified in the course of time. Among them were Metus (Fear); Febris (Fever), who had three temples at Rome; Bona and Mala Fortuna (Good and Bad Luck); Fortuna muliebris; Fors Fortuna (Lucky Chance), to which Servius Tullius dedicated a temple on the Tiber below Rome; Salus (Health), afterward given the attributes of the Greek Hygieia (Prosperity), who had had a temple erected on the Quirinal in 367 B.C.; Pax (Peace), later identified with Greek Irene; Con-

2 Cf. G. Boissier, *La religion romaine d'Auguste aux Antonines* (4th ed.; Paris, 1892), I, 1f.; E. Renan, *Lectures on the Influence of the Institutions, Thought, and Culture of Rome on Christianity* (4th ed.; London, 1898), Lecture I, pp. 10f.

cordia (Harmony), whose earliest shrine dated from 367 B.C., invoked also at the festival of the *Caristia* with Salus and Pax; Pudicitia (Modesty and Chastity), first worshiped by patrician matrons and later by plebeians; Honor and Virtus, frequently mentioned together and with temples built by Marcellus in 212 B.C.; and many others. Of all such deified abstractions the greatest was *Respublica* or *Res,* the Roman State—the safety of the Roman people—personified. What Petronius in his *Satyricon* (17) has the Cumaean Quartilla, a devotee of Priapus, the deity of fertility, of fields and herds, say of the welter of divinities among the Greeks of South Italy was equally true of the Romans:

> The gods walk abroad so commonly in our streets
> that you can more easily find a god than a man.

Ceremonialism was so elaborate and the various rites carried out with such meticulous regard for accuracy that some critics have seen in Roman religion merely a body of formalities with little or no religious feeling. Every major event in human life from birth to death, the seasons, days of the week, family meals, occupations, everything had its appropriate ceremony. Nothing of a public or private nature was undertaken at Rome except with the sanction of religion for the Romans believed that divine influence was at work everywhere in human affairs. Each deity had its festival or holiday (*feriae*) commemorated with detailed ceremonies. Different offerings were made to male and female deities—such as white victims to the gods above (*Di superi*) and black to those below (*Di inferi*). In all these sacrifices and prayers the formulae were so exact that a mistake of the officiating priest might destroy the efficacy of the entire ritual. Such scrupulous attention to the letter of the ritual is shown by the legend of the death of Numa's successor Tullus Hostilius who during his last illness performed the rites (from Numa's lost calendar) of Jupiter Elicius ("he who is called down by incantation") only to be struck dead by lightning because of a mistake he had made in the performance of the ritual. To Ovid, last of the Augustan poets, in his *Fasti,* we are indebted for a description of the astronomical phenomena and rituals of the Roman festivals.[3] Long after Roman faith had passed and the Roman Empire was no more, the emotion called forth by many of these festivals remained so potent and deeply ingrained that the Christian Church had no alternative but to accept them, albeit under changed names.

The early Roman calendar, like the Greek, was merely a priestly device to mark the recurring festivals. The primitive Latin calendar began in March, its ten months' year still recalled by the names of the last four months of our year, and was first transformed, as was believed, by Numa

---

[3] Only six of his intended twelve books, one for each month from January to July, have survived complete. No ancient writer mentions the last six. They were either lost at Tomi during the poet's exile or his literary executors suppressed them as unfinished. That they were composed is clear from Ovid's *Tristia* (2:549). On the *Fasti,* see Sir J. G. Frazer's ed. in *L.C.L.* (1931), pp. xvii and xix, and F. Peeter's *Les Fastes d'Ovid* (Bruxelles, 1939) based on the study of the MSS.

into a lunar year of twelve months and 355 days.[4] The earliest surviving religious calendar dates, however, not from Numa, but from 304 B.C., in which forty-five days are noted as sacred to the gods, both fixed or "stated" annual festivals (*feriae stativae*) and many "movable" ones (*feriae conceptivae*) arranged by priests and magistrates on changing days. Besides this and the Julian calendar fragments of thirty others have survived which regulated the religious ceremonies of as many festivals.

Of the prehistoric beginnings of Roman religion we can recover something from philology, archaeology, the study of comparative religions, especially those of Greece and India, and survivals of earlier phases in the historic period. During the second millennium B.C. successive waves of Indo-Europeans from the Danubian grasslands crossed the Balkan and Alpine chains into the Mediterranean land. The Achaeans entered Greece and the isles of the Aegean prior to the thirteenth century (*ca.* 1400–1300 B.C.) and perhaps as early as 1700 B.C., and amalgamated with the native Pelasgians, while later hordes of Hellenes from the northern mountains followed and destroyed the Mycenaean culture described by Homer. Italians or *terramara*, "fertile-soil," peoples and their kin the Villanovans entered Italy; the latter is a conventional name given by archaeologists to designate a group of tribes which exhibited a fairly unified civilization in the Early Iron Age at the beginning of the twelfth or eleventh century B.C., receiving their name from their peculiar funerary urns first found in the cemeteries at Villanova near Bologna and later in Etruria and Latium. The culture of the Italians developed differently and more slowly than that of their Hellenic relatives since the latter came into immediate contact with the older advanced Aegean civilization while the former met only barbarism. For long the Italians remained in the fishing and hunting stage and only slowly became agriculturists and then urban dwellers. By the dawn of history they had spread over much of north and central Italy, the Latins forming a small group with related Sabines, Umbrians, Samnites and others. From them sprang the Romans who ultimately controlled all Italy.

The primitive Latin religion down almost to the close of the regal period at Rome was animistic, i.e., the worship of objects believed to contain intangible spirits or wills (called *numina* by the later Romans). The Latins filled their world with these vague and undefined potencies. They had no temples, idols, or religious monuments, but only fetiches. Their *loca sacra* were individual trees or groves, springs, mountain-tops, and the hearths, thresholds, and even the cupboards of their dwellings which were believed to guard various aspects of nature and life. Thus although the

---

4 This was later adjusted to a solar one of 366½ days by the pontiffs who introduced a four-year cycle with two intercalary months of twenty-three and twenty-five days respectively inserted into February every second and fourth year. This imperfect calendar was corrected to the true solar one of 365¼ days by Julius Caesar with the help of the Greek astronomer Sosigenes in 46 B.C.—"the last year of confusion" having fifteen months —the calendar which with the final adjustment under Pope Gregory XIII in 1582 serves us yet.

early Latins shared with the Greeks in the common Indo-European inheritance, in Italy no wealth of beautiful mythology developed as in Greece where myths had accumulated in the Mycenaean period of fusion between Aegeans and Achaeans.

Such impersonal guardian spirits hardly distinguishable from the objects in which they dwelt, without personification or ethical character but mere functionaries, some friendly, others to be won over by propitiatory rites of magic, by sacrifice and prayer, formed "the protoplasm of primitive religion" to use a phrase of Warde Fowler. Out of such spirits vague in form and thought was slowly evolved the State-cult of Rome with its pantheon of anthropomorphic deities having their origin in feelings of awe and fear, feelings called by the Romans *religio*—however much the connotations of its derivative have been changed. Among such spirit guardians of prehistoric origin were the household deities Vesta, the Penates, Lares, and Genius, and the *Di agrestes* or spirits of the fields, such as Tellus, Faunus, Silvanus, which survived throughout later antiquity.

Vesta, the chief female spirit of early times, was at first guardian of flocks and herds but continued ever after as the beautiful symbol of the hearth largely uncontaminated by later anthropormorphic features such as altered the evolution of her Greek counterpart, Hestia. The rudimentary nature of both Greek and Italian civilization is reflected in her worship which originated in the difficulty of preserving fire in primitive times. From this difficulty arose the custom of keeping a perpetual fire for the community long after the need of it had passed. It was early kept by the daughters of the Latin chieftain in his hut—as it is still among the primitive Australian aborigines and until recently among the Natchez and Chippewa Indians. Thus every dwelling became Vesta's home since the hearth in the *atrium* was the center of the Roman house around which the family assembled for the common meal (*cena*), having cast a salt-cake offering into the embers.

Later when the sacred flame had become a goddess she received a public shrine (hardly a temple) in the Forum near the *Regia*.[5] It was a circular edifice preserving in stone the form of the original chieftain's hut. Here there was no statue, but only fire, the symbol of the spirit. It became the most sacred spot in Rome since here the citizens felt themselves united into a common family. The fire, traditionally brought with the Penates from Troyland by Aeneas, was attended by the Vestal Virgins, originally four and then six in number, who dedicated themselves in childhood to a thirty-year service during which they were considered to be as stainless as the fire itself. Once a year only, and then under the inspection of the Pontifex maximus, they extinguished the fire and rekindled it on March first, the ancient Latin New Year's Day. In the innermost part of the shrine one of the two *Palladia* or images of Athena was kept. It was also believed to have come from the Trojan citadel with Athena and was simi-

---

[5] The latter was on the site of the chieftain's house and later became the official residence of the Pontifex maximus.

larly claimed to be in the possession of various other cities of Italy. The Vestals lived in the splendid *Atrium Vestae,* southeast of the Forum on the northwest foot of the Palatine.[6]

The *Di Penates,* the two tutelary house-spirits of the storeroom (*penus*), also received libations and sacrifices at the domestic hearth. Later they were enshrined in the Forum near Vesta. The Lares, also house-spirits, as well as the guardians of various localities, were believed to be spirits of the dead who still hovered about their former dwelling-places. This belief gave rise to the early Roman custom, not abrogated till the time of the "Laws of the Twelve Tables" (451 B.C.), of burial inside the house to have the dead near the living. Originally genii of the fields they had shrines at crossroads (*compita*) where the lands of various families joined and were honored in an annual festival, the *Compitalia,* near the winter solstice. At meals the family also cast bits of food onto the hearth in honor of the *Lares familiares* whose images stood nearby in a small shrine, the *lararium.* Thus Penates and Lares guarded the household in the relation of our house and home. Finally there was the Genius, the invisible companion of every man, and especially of the *paterfamilias.* Later in the cult of the Caesars the Genius of the State was personified in the person of the emperor.

Magic was widespread in the primitive religion if we may judge by its many survivals in later antiquity. For Roman religion, like all others, was conservative and reluctant to surrender any of its past (just as the ideas of a global flood and a Garden of Eden still cling to Christianity). The "Twelve Tables" show that by the fifth century, however, "black" or malevolent magic was severely punished but sympathetic or "homeopathic" magic—mimicking of the effect desired in order to produce it—was allowed. A typical example of the latter was the *aquaelicium,* i.e., means to produce rain.[7] During a drouth Roman matrons and magistrates carried in procession the *lapis manalis* or "pouring-stone" from outside the Porta Capena near the temple of Mars through the city to the altar of Jupiter Elicius to whom a solemn prayer for rain was addressed. The stone was probably hollow and when filled with water spilled over the brim thus imitating rain overrunning the sky. A stranger survival occurred at the ancient festival of the *Lupercalia* celebrated on February fifteenth in the grotto of the Lupercal at the base of the Palatine in honor of Lupercus surnamed Februus. Two priests, *Luperci,* girded with goatskin strips ran around the base of the hill and struck with thongs women who had delib-

[6] It was burned 191 B.C., rebuilt by Hadrian (117–38), destroyed by Gratian in 382, and excavated in 1883–84, its discovery revolutionizing our knowledge of Vesta. See H. Jordan, *Der Tempel der Vesta und das Haus der Vestalinnen* (Berlin, 1886); R. Lanciani, *Ancient Rome in the Light of Modern Discovery* (Boston and New York, 1888), chap. vi, pp. 134f. (especially pp. 158 f.) with illustrations. Cf. Tacitus *Annales* 2:86. The round temple nearby was discovered in 1489 and destroyed 1549.

[7] As Paulus Diaconus calls it in his eighth-century abridgment of the work of the second-century grammarian Festus.

erately placed themselves in their way in the belief that the blows were a charm against barrenness.[8]

There were many taboos, too, against the magical influence supposed to emanate from certain objects and animals which rendered them dangerous. Examples of such taboos are found in the restrictions on the *flamen Dialis* (of Jupiter), the chief of the three early major *flamens*, the other two being *Martialis* (of Mars) and *Quirinalis* (of Quirinus). He must always appear in public with the insignia of his office, a white conical cap (*apex*), a woollen toga (*praetexta*), a sacrificial knife, and accompanied by a lictor. Though being freed from all civil and political duties he must not leave Italy, or even Rome for more than two nights in the year, must not look at soldiers, must not labor, touch horse, goat, dog, raw meat, corpse, or grave. He could not wear an unbroken ring or walk beneath a vine and must cut his hair and nails with an iron knife. Rome also, like Greece and Babylonia before her, had various superstitions, lucky days (*dies felices*) such as January first and such unlucky ones (*infelices*) as the anniversary of her defeat by the Gauls at the Allia in 390 B.C. The unlucky days were also called *atri* (black), but only because they were marked with a coal on the religious calendar.

In Numa's lost calendar there were still "spirits" without anthropomorphic features but their functions were already defined. There were as yet neither temples nor idols but only the ancient *loca sacra* although the worship now reflected the spirit of the forms of change from an agricultural to an urban politico-military community at Rome. The State-cult was already functioning and in it three spirits were emphasized above the others— those of Jupiter, Mars, and Quirinus. Jupiter was the Indo-European sky-divinity worshipped as the spirit of light and sunshine, rain and storm, his will revealed by thunder, lightning, and the flight of birds. In prayers he was invoked second only to the purely Italian spirit Janus, and his *flamen*, highest of all, ranked after the latter's priest.[9] The Latin towns from time immemorial had celebrated annually a tribal festival in honor of Jupiter Latiaris, the guardian spirit of their confederacy, in a grove on the Alban Mount, on whose lower slope stood Alba Longa. It was traditionally built by Aeneas' son Ascanius three hundred years before Rome and destroyed by Numa's successor and never rebuilt, its inhabitants being transferred to Rome. Jupiter was impersonal, the sky itself, even the title *Diespiter* signi-

---

[8] From the verb *februare* ("to purify") February was named the month of "purification" in the calendar by the Decemvirs.

[9] Janus with his counterpart Jana at first represented the sun and moon but later their names were associated with *janua* (door), so that Janus became the spirit of all beginnings and was invoked first in all undertakings, civil, religious, and military. Numa dedicated to him a four-arched covered passageway in the Forum where, later, money-changers and merchants displayed their wares. There were many other arches of Janus in Rome (Ovid *Fasti* 1:257, and Livy XLI, 27). Duilius, after his naval victory over Carthage in 260 B.C., built his temple near the theater of Marcellus (Tacitus *Annales* 2:49) with two doors opposite each other which were closed in peace and opened in war—the former only three times in antiquity.

fying only the lord of the heavens, but betraying no real fatherhood any more than the same title of Zeus, his Greek counterpart, did in the Homeric period.

Mars, of Umbro-Sabellian origin, became in time the chief Italian deity after Jupiter, being regarded as the ancestral god of Rome, and not until centuries later (in 138 B.C.) was he identified with Ares, Greek god of war. Early he received the surname Gradivus, "the Strider," and was not connected with war but rather with agriculture and woodland, flocks and herds, becoming confused with the old Latin deity Silvanus. As protector of Rome he became identified with Quirinus the protector of the Sabines before their fusion with the Romans. The first month of the Latin calendar, Martius, was sacred to him as the fertilizing spirit of spring. As the god of war Numa gave him a *flamen* and a college of twelve dancing *Salii* who worshipped him in a procession in which three of them carried a small oval shield (*ancile*).[10] They sang hymns in obsolete Latin which, in Quintilian's day at the end of the first century, were "scarcely understood by their own priests." For long Mars had altars only at Rome, one of which was in the Campus Martius where he was regarded as patron of martial exercises. Another, outside the walls, was dedicated to him in 388 B.C.

The name Quirinus, the Sabine spirit of the Quirinal Hill, was first used adjectivally of Mars (he of the spear—Sabine *quiris*).[11] When Mars became the Roman war-god, Quirinus, as such, became obscured and the name was given to the legendary Romulus, to Janus, and centuries later poetically to Augustus and Antony.

Influences

The first major influence to alter native Roman religion came from the Etruscans during their brief conquest of Rome—the only people who conquered the Romans till the close of antiquity.[12] Their somber religion which permeated all their affairs, public and private, was receptive to Greek ideas. They used Greek builders and artists and reproduced Greek statuary, pottery, and jewelry, acting as intermediaries between the Greek

---

[10] The original one was believed to have fallen from the sky. On its preservation that of Rome depended.

[11] It was believed by some to be the derivation of the title *Quirites* (originally the Sabines), as opposed to *Romani*. Servius (on Vergil, *Aeneid* 7.710; cf. Livy 1.13) says that after the Sabines and Romans were united under Romulus the Romans called themselves Quirites in a civil capacity but retained the name Romans in a political and military sense. Servius derives the name from the Sabine town of Cures rather than from *quiris*.

[12] Of Anatolian origin and reaching Italy in the early ninth century B.C. they soon spread over North and Central Italy from the Alps to Capua but later were confined to Etruria proper along the Tyrrhenian (Etruscan) seaboard. Their race and, despite the survival of thousands of inscriptions in early Greek characters, their language still remain unsolved puzzles. They took Rome in the latter half of the sixth century B.C., the last three kings being supposedly of Etruscan origin. It is possible that Rome received its name from the word *ruma* (suckling breast) which may be Etruscan. Under them a stone wall was built around the city and the ancient cemetery in the Forum no longer being used was now included within the *Pomerium* or open space left free of buildings which limited the city auspices, in which no burials were allowed thereafter.

colonies of South Italy and the Romani. They taught the Romans their perverse art of divination or interpretation of the future by the flight of birds (augury) and by the inspection of the entrails of animals (haruspicy), as well as by portents, prodigies, and omens, all of which overlaid native Roman divination and lasted for centuries. As late as 408, when Alaric and his Visigoths menaced Rome, Etruscan experts offered their services to save the city. Warde Fowler has called their arts of divination "the fruitless arts of the most unfruitful of Italian peoples." [13]

It was the Elder Tarquin who taught the Romans to make the transition from animism to anthropomorphism, i.e., from spirits to gods, by showing them how to interpret their *numina* as personalities with temples and cult-statues. Having introduced Minerva from Falerii he formed a triad of Minerva, Jupiter, and Juno, the three corresponding to the Etruscan Menfra, Tinia, and Cupra. Soon a temple was erected in their honor on the Capitoline which henceforth for half a millennium remained the focus of Roman religion.[14] Here were kept Jupiter's bolts—*lapides silices* (flint-stones)—used by the *fetiales* or guardians of the public faith when declaring war and peace whence arose the solemn oath *per Jovem lapidem iurare*. This, then, was the shrine of Jupiter *Optimus Maximus*, a title far above that of *Latiaris*. Now for the first time a Roman "spirit" was represented by a statue, Jupiter having a bearded face like the Greek Zeus. But he did not become the general subject of plastic art until long afterward in the Graeco-Roman period.

It is probable that in side-aisles of this temple there were crude images of Juno and Minerva. Juno was merely an extension of Jupiter like Dione or the "etymological" wife of Zeus before he espoused Hera. She was evolved to care for women, presiding thereafter over marriage and childbirth; her month, *Junonius*, was regarded as the most favorable time for marriages as June still is. Her worship as a separate Roman goddess reached Rome from Etruscan Veii after the dictator Camillus took the city in 396 B.C. She was given a sanctuary on the Aventine where her festival *Matronalia*, the greatest for Roman women, was celebrated on March first. She, like Saturn, was also a guardian of finance and, under her name *Moneta*, had a temple on the Capitoline to which was attached the Roman mint whence the late Latin word *moneta* and English "money" are derived. Minerva also came independently from Veii and in Rome became Jupiter's

---

[13] *The Religious Experience of the Roman People* (London, 1911), p. 309.

[14] It was the work of Greek builders, tradition having it that the building was vowed by Tarquinius Priscus and a beginning made under him; the walls were raised by Servius Tullius, completed by Tarquinius Superbus, and dedicated the third year after the expulsion of the kings, or in 507 B.C., by the Republican consul Horatius. It was a magnificent structure of native tufa faced with stucco. It became incredibly magnificent through the donations of successive consuls, its bronze gates covered with gold and its marble interior filled with works of art. It was destroyed by fire four centuries later in 83 B.C. but its restoration was begun by Sulla who placed a chryselephantine cult-statue of the god Jupiter within it. The restoration was completed in 69 B.C. by the consul Catulus who had jointly triumphed with his colleague Marius over the Cimbri. It was again destroyed in A.D. 69 (the "Year of Four Emperors") and rebuilt for the last time by Domitian more magnificently than ever before.

daughter, the patroness of the arts, trades, and crafts, and protector of men in war. Thus she was easily identified later with Athena, Greek virgin goddess of wisdom and war. Before 207 B.C. she had her own temple on the Aventine in which the guilds of craftsmen, including poets and actors, met. Her festival began March nineteenth, i.e., on the fifth day after the Ides, and hence was called *Quinquatrus,* according to Varro.[15] At first it lasted for only one day, but later because of an incorrect explanation of the name, for five days.

The Romans, through commercial contact with neighboring towns and peoples, now began to borrow many alien deities. First from the Latin towns, which with the Etruscans they had defeated at Lake Regillus in 498 B.C., came Heracles, the greatest of Greek heroes (from Tibur), and Castor (from Tusculum). Such Greek deities had already become widely diffused among the Italian peoples through Etruscan influence. In Rome Hercules had only altars, the principal one being the *Ara Maxima* in the Forum Boarium, or cattle-market, which he was believed to have founded. Here, as was customary at all altars, supplicants placed themselves under the hero's protection, and violence against such refugees was regarded as violence against Hercules. Castor with Pollux had a temple by 484 B.C. near the Forum erected in gratitude for their help at Lake Regillus; a temple in which the Senate often sat. Diana came from Latin Aricia, an old Italian rather than Greek spirit of the woods worshiped with savage rites on the borders of the Lake of the Woods (*Lacus nemorensis,* the present Lake Nemi). Her cult was connected with Lucina, goddess of light, which became a surname of Juno also since both presided over births like the Greek Ilithyia. She was also guardian of hunters. Servius Tullius was believed to have erected the first Roman shrine to Diana within which was a wooden statue of the goddess. The shrine later became the sanctuary of the Latin League. In Rome Diana gradually took over the attributes of Artemis and Hecate until she had become "the huntress chaste and fair" of the late Latin poets, but her fusion with Artemis was not officially completed till 179 B.C.

The greatest of all influences exerted on Roman religion was Greek for it changed its entire nature. It came, for the greater part, indirectly through contact with the Greek colonies of South Italy, Magna Graecia. From them the Romans took deities, religious usages such as the *Graecus ritus,* and myths, a process not completed till late in the second century B.C. when an almost complete fusion of Greek and Roman deities had been effected resulting in a different religion, the Graeco-Roman, which Augustus later visioned as the faith of the Empire. This Greek influence had already begun through Etruscan mediation as we have seen but was accelerated at the beginning of the Republic by the Sibylline Books whose

---

[15] *De lingua Latina* VI, 14. *Quin* in the calendar, properly the name of one day, was later taken to mean five (March 19–23). The word *quinquatrus* means the "fifth black (ater)" day from the Ides of March.

oracles introduced Greek elements and whose authority the Senate acknowledged in crises over a period of centuries.

In these books were garnered Greek oracles in hexameter verse originating largely in Anatolia and brought to Cumae, the oldest of the colonies of Magna Graecia. Traditionally they were acquired from the Cumaean Sibyl or prophetess of Apollo by Tarquin the Younger whom she compelled to pay the exorbitant price for three books which she originally demanded for nine, six being destroyed in the interim. They were kept in the vaults of the Capitoline temple, at first in charge of the patrician college of *duo viri sacris faciundis;* soon after 367 B.C. in that of the decemvirs; later under Sulla and still later in that of the *Quindecimviri.* Thereafter this "farrago of nonsense," as Sir James Frazer has called it, was consulted for the Senate in crises to discover means, through proper religious rites, by which to avert danger from the State.[16] However, the date assigned in antiquity for their appearance in Rome is too early and certainly Vergil's version that they were consulted by Aeneas in the Sibyl's grotto on the shores of Lake Avernus, before his descent into the infernal regions, is too early. Their first recorded interference in Roman affairs was in 496 B.C. when, during a corn-famine, they demanded the introduction of Demeter, the Greek "corn-mother" whose cult was then introduced with the allied ones of Dionysus, god of viticulture, and Persephone, queen of the lower world. The three were later identified with the Roman Ceres, goddess of plant-life, and Liber, Italian deity of planting and fructification, and his sister Libera respectively. Already in 493 Ceres had a temple at the base of the Aventine near the Tiber in the plebeian quarter of Rome whence most of her devotees came. That her early Roman worship was important is also shown by the fact that the plebeian *aediles* (servants of the tribunes since 494 B.C., who received their name from her temple or *aedes* which they administered) imposed the fines levied on criminals in her temple. There also the confiscated property of traitors was stored as well as the Assembly *plebiscites* and the later *senatusconsulta.* But her ritual and personality were slowly modeled after the Greek goddess, while her rites were carried out in Greek by Graeco-Roman matrons. Once more in the same century, in 431 B.C., the Books demanded that Apollo, already known to the last Tarquin, who was the first Roman to consult the oracle at Delphi, receive a temple as god of healing. The *Ludi Apollinares* followed two centuries later in 212 B.C. during the agony of the Hannibalic War.

Again in 399 B.C. during Camillus' siege of Veii [17] (a poor summer at Rome) the Books recommended that the Greek festival, *Lectisternia,* should be introduced at Rome. Then for the first time this device was seen by Romans when portable images of three pairs of Greek deities were dis-

---

[16] For their fragments, see H. Diels, *Sibyllinische Blätter* (Berlin, 1890); G. Wissowa, *Religion und Kultur der Römer* (2nd ed.; München, 1912), pp. 534f.; and cf. J. P. Postgate, *Selections from Tibullus and Others* (2nd ed.; London, 1910), Appendix B.

[17] It was the chief of the twelve confederated Etruscan towns and had had fourteen wars with Rome over a period of three and one-half centuries until it fell in 396 B.C.

played on couches at a banquet [18] on the assumption that the gods were regaled by food like men.   It was used again in 366–365 B.C. when a *Lectisternium* was celebrated during a pestilence and *Ludi scenici* were introduced, as Livy tells us (7:2, 2).   In all, this tawdry device was used on six occasions in Rome, the last after the battle of Lake Trasimene in 217 B.C. during the Hannibalic War (Livy 22:1, 19) when six pairs of Graeco-Roman deities were displayed showing the fusion of the two religions.   Such a festival was generally followed by what the Romans called a *Supplicatio* also sponsored by the Sibylline oracles, a Greek rite of public prayer or thanksgiving similar to the English "day of public humiliation," such as was ordered during a malignant fever in the summer of 1658.   Then men, women, and children crowned with laurel marched to the strains of the lyre from Apollo's temple to various altars and shrines where they prostrated themselves before the images of the gods, kissing their hands and feet, while members of the college in charge of the Books performed the rites with prayers.   It was first performed in 396 B.C. after the fall of Veii (Livy 5:33, 3) and many times thereafter.   It was also used for thanksgiving after great military victories lasting in later times for forty or forty-five days instead of the original three.   In 293 B.C. Asclepias (Roman Aesculapius) was brought from his great shrine at Epidaurus in Greece and was given a temple on the isle in the Tiber, the first we hear of the medical art as distinct from healing in Rome.

The fusion of Roman with Etruscan or Greek gods and heroes continued, the Greek being further examples of the *Di novensides,* "newly settled" or alien gods as opposed to the older *Di indigetes,* or "indigenous" ones, i.e., those who once had lived on earth and were worshiped after death such as Aeneas, Romulus, Latinus, and others.   Thus Mercury, originally the Etruscan deity Turms now with a Roman name, the Roman deity of commerce, took on the attributes of the Greek Hermes; the Roman Neptune, appearing in Etruscan art as Nethuns, though probably not genuinely Etruscan in origin, long the god of rivers and springs but later, after the Romans had become seafarers, god of the sea and husband of Salacia, deity of salt water, became merged in the Greek Poseidon while Salacia was identified with the latter's wife, the Nereid Amphitrite.   Saturn, whose name comes from *sero* (to sow), became the Greek Cronus, son of Uranus and Gaea, who overthrew his father and became sovereign of the world himself.   There is little resemblance, however, between the two, but more between Saturn and Demeter.   Legend had Saturn come to Italy during the reign of Janus and found a village on the Capitoline at whose foot his temple in which the Republican treasury was housed was later to stand. As king he was believed to have taught the Italians agriculture and the arts of civilization and under him Italia or Saturnia enjoyed a golden age. Pliny the Elder says that his hollow statue was filled with oil, thus symbolizing olive-culture in Latium, and that woollen fillets around his feet kept him from running away.   As agriculture is the source of wealth, his

---

[18] Cicero *De oratore* 3:19 *fin.*

wife became Ops, patroness of agriculture and identical with Terra. The *Saturnalia* celebrated in Saturn's honor became Rome's greatest festival. The god became so overlaid with Greek attributes in the course of time that little was left of the Roman deity.

Sometimes the fusion was difficult, as in the case of Venus-Aphrodite. While Aphrodite, of Oriental-Greek origin, was a very human deity of sensual love as well as a nature power on earth, sea, and in the air, the Italian Venus was at first only the spirit of gardens, flowers, and spring-time like the Italian Flora and so unimportant. Her Roman cult went back to the regal period when she had shrines near the Capitol, one of which was ascribed to Ancus Marcius, grandson of Numa. Her fusion with Aphrodite overlaid her, like Ceres and Saturn, with Greek attributes. Aphrodite *Erycina* from Mt. Eryx in western Sicily reached Rome at the beginning of the Second Punic War when she had a temple on the Capitoline. To Venus *Verticordia*, "turner of men's hearts," another was erected in 114 B.C. at the behest of the Sibylline Books. Caesar exalted her worship as Venus Genetrix, a cult founded by Scipio Africanus, since Caesar traced his descent from Aeneas, reputed son of Venus. April, as the beginning of spring, was sacred to her and recalled her early Italian functions, both Greek and Latin ideas being blended in the splendid apostrophe to Venus Genetrix with which Lucretius began his *De rerum natura,* in which he pictures her as the creative source of nature and life. Such amalgams continued throughout the second century B.C. Thus in 191 B.C. Juventas, Roman deity of youth, was merged in Greek Hebe, goddess of eternal youth as well as handmaiden of the Olympians. She represented the eternal youth of the Eternal City and had a chapel on the Capitoline in Minerva's court and later a temple in the city below. To her and to Jupiter, Roman boys prayed on assuming the *toga virilis* as the sign of having reached their sixteenth year. We add one more identification, that of the Greek Hades or Pluto, transliterated into Latin as Pluto or translated as *Diespiter* (Divine Father) a title originally given to Jupiter, and poetically, but not in cult, to Orcus, the spirit of oaths who punished perjury, and later, exclusively, to Pluto. He had been introduced at the command of the Sibylline Books in the early Republic and had a chapel near the altar of Saturn and another, a subterranean one, beneath the Campus Martius, which he shared with Proserpina. The Greek Hades was also the name of the abode of the dead—the "invisible place" in the depths of the earth where men became incorporeal shadows which, while retaining the outward form of the living, were without mind or consciousness, their speech unintelligible gibberish like the squeaking of bats. King Hades was a favorite figure of the later Roman poets, especially Vergil, who, in the sixth book of the *Aeneid,* tells how Aeneas, like Odysseus in the *Odyssey,* descended to the lower world through a cave beside Lake Avernus near Naples where he conversed with his father and had a prophetic vision of Rome's future glory.

But these ideas did not supplant the native Roman ones of the hereafter, also a cheerless abode below where "deified" spirits of the dead, *Di*

Manes, euphemistically called the "good ones" (from *manus,* "good"), but not gods in the proper sense, dwelt in unindividualized masses. It was also believed as in Greece that the dead before passing below might hover around the tomb,[19] which gave rise to special rites at the tomb based on the belief that the dead continued their ghostly participation in the family life above. In the *Comitium,* a space near the Forum used till the second century B.C. for meetings of the Assemblies (*Comitia*) and law-courts, was a pit regarded as an entrance to the world below (*mundus*) closed by a stone, the *lapis manalis* or *Manes'* stone (rather than the "pouring-stone" already discussed as used in magic). Three times a year this was lifted on days sacred to the infernal gods when it was possible for the Manes to appear and fruits were thrown into the pit. And the Roman, like the Greek, also believed [20] that if the solemn rites of sepulture were not duly observed, the spirit of the dead man would not be accepted among the shades but would wander over the earth. In February, from the thirteenth to the twenty-first, there was also a public festival (the *Parentalia*) in honor of deceased relatives ending in the Feast of the Dead (*Feralia*), the Roman equivalent of the Catholic Feast of All Souls in November. Then, as Ovid says (*Fasti* 2:563–64), the temples were closed and no incense was burned on the altars nor fires made on the hearths. It was followed on the twenty-second of February by the *Caristia,* a banquet of thanksgiving for the survivors, celebrated by families in honor of the family gods, when feuds were laid aside (*Fasti* 2:617f.).

The possibility of a future life was left in doubt throughout the Republic and Early Empire. A Roman could believe what he wished about the future of his soul if only he fulfilled his obligations at the tombs of his ancestors. He was not like the Greek who could believe and say what he wished privately but must not promulgate views discordant with those of the State religion, nor like the Christian who believes in a future life but has not rationalized its location. Only with the extension of Oriental cults, all of which, like Christianity, assured a life hereafter, and the adoption of their various deities did the Roman masses form definite views of immortality.

Some Greek religious institutions, however, were not acceptable at Rome. A good example was the *Bacchanalia,* the Roman name for the Greek *Dionysia,* which was banned in 186 B.C., after one of the worst scandals of the Republic, if we may believe the detailed account of it left by Livy in Book 39 of his *History.* Since his account was composed nearly two centuries after the event and is most certainly overdrawn it is hard to know definitely what happened. A quack Greek priest of Dionysus had introduced the rites into Etruria where they were held three times a year in daylight and were seemingly innocent enough, though later both there and in Rome they became scandalous, accompanied by immorality, drunk-

---

[19] This idea probably originated in disease caused by plague-infected corpses which led to cremation both in Greece and Italy.

[20] As Tertullian tells us, in his *De anima* (56), the earliest work on Christian psychology composed soon after 200.

enness, and frenzy. At first only women were admitted, the priestesses being Roman matrons. One of these at some time admitted men and changed the celebration from day to night and its occurrence from three to five times a month. The promiscuity of the sexes under the license of darkness opened the way for unheard of debaucheries and even for the hatching of political conspiracies. Their real nature finally reached the ears of the consuls who, armed with Senate approval, made an investigation. Livy mentions a *multitudinem ingentem* of members, some seven thousand, and the investigation ended in the imprisonment or death of thousands although the rites continued sporadically in South Italy long afterwards.[21] The real reason for their banning at Rome, however, was doubtless political rather than religious since the Senate regarded them as a conspiracy against the State; Rome was ever apprehensive of secret political associations.

During the latter part of the process of Graeco-Roman fusion scepticism accompanied by superstition grew because of lack of faith in the old gods and their rituals. This was largely the result of the influx of richer Greek religious ideas derived from the Sibylline Books which showed the Romans the relative crudeness of their native gods and myths. But it was accelerated by the third century wars, those with the Samnites ending in 290 B.C., with Pyrrhus 275–270 B.C., and two with Carthage 264–241 and 219–201 B.C., especially the Second when Rome's military reverses at the hands of her most ruthless enemy Hannibal shook faith in the belief that their gods, if they existed at all, were angry so that the old *pax deum* could not be restored merely by the old methods of prayer and sacrifice. Fear then rose to fanatical heights. In the First Punic War with Hamilcar the consul Claudius Pulcher when attacking the Punic fleet off Drepanum in western Sicily in 249 B.C., neglecting the warning of his *pullarius* in charge of the sacred fowl (*pulli*) that they would not eat (a bad sign), had them thrown into the sea, an act to which his defeat was attributed. He was later impeached and condemned.

The acid test of faith, however, came in the Second Punic War, the worst fought in Roman antiquity, comparable with the Peloponnesian War in Greece. After the defeat at the Trebia in 218 B.C. many prodigies appeared, Livy recording one of an ox climbing a third-story building in the cattle-market and casting itself down. To allay anxiety the Senate had recourse to the Books, purified the city and celebrated a *Lectisternium* in honor of Juventas and a *Supplicatio* at Hercules' altar. Before the battle of Lake Trasimene in 217 B.C. more portents appeared in consequence, it was believed, of Flaminius, the consul, having ignored the auspices on leaving the city to take command. To this oversight his defeat, the practical annihilation of his army, and his death were laid (Livy 21:63). Then recourse was had to a *Ver sacrum* (sacred spring), when in great crises it was usual to vow the products of the succeeding spring, crops and fruits;

---

[21] The bronze tablet containing part of the Senate decree against them was discovered in Calabria in 1640 and is now in Vienna; *C.I.L.*, I (1863), No. 196; Livy 39:8–19.

in earlier times even children were expatriated. The rite, however, now proved ineffective. Fabius Maximus, named pro-dictator by the unanimous voice of the people, restored the old rites although it was rather his method of "delay" which saved Rome from destruction. The *Ludi magni*, at the order of the Books, were now added to the old *Ludi Romani* believed to have been founded by Tarquinius Priscus in honor of Jupiter, though both Cicero and Dionysius of Halicarnussus refer them to the victory at Lake Regillus. Another *Lectisternium* and *Supplicatio* were celebrated in which Greek gods appeared on the couches, thus ending the exclusiveness of the old *Di indigetes*, and showing the near culmination of the Graeco-Roman fusion.

After the defeat at Cannae in 216 B.C. fear became hectic and prodigies and portents increased. Two Vestals were found to be incontinent, one of whom committed suicide while the other was immured alive in the *Campus Sceleratus* (Polluted Field) under the city-wall by order of the Pontifex maximus in conformity with an ancient law, and their seducers were scourged to death. Fabius Pictor, Rome's first historian, although he wrote in Greek, was sent by the Senate at the recommendation of the Books to Delphi to inquire about the issue of the war and ways by which the angry gods might be appeased. A Gallic man and woman and likewise a Greek couple were buried alive in the Forum Boarium once said to have been the scene of human sacrifice.[22] Prodigies so multiplied in 213 when Hannibal was trying to take Tarentum that Roman religion collapsed almost completely. In the words of Livy:

And now not only in secret and within the walls of private houses were Roman rites abandoned, but in public places also, and in the Forum and on the Capitoline there was a crowd of women who were following the custom of the fathers neither in their sacrifices nor in prayer to the gods,[23]

since they felt their own gods had forsaken them.

Marcellus, called "Sword of Rome" and five times consul, who took Syracuse in 212 B.C., was accustomed to ride in a closed litter in order not to see unfavorable omens.[24] In that year, when Hannibal came in sight of Rome, the ancient Latin oracles in Saturnian verse used in early harvest songs in Saturn's honor were placed beside the Sibylline Books in the temple of Jupiter, this again marking the fusion of the Graeco-Roman religions. Hasdrubal's crossing of the Alps into North Italy in 207 B.C. to effect a junction with his brother caused renewed panic. But after his defeat and death at Sena, near the Metaurus, twenty-seven maidens were ordered by the consuls to celebrate the victory by dancing through the streets of Rome chanting the victory hymn of Livius Andronicus and a three-day *Supplicatio* helped to restore for a time the belief that the *pax deum* was once more in force.

[22] Livy's words "then alien to the Roman spirit" may refer either to its being a Greek rite or more likely to its being out of date in Rome.
[23] 25:1, 7, *L.C.L.*, VI (1911), 44.
[24] So Cicero *De divinatione* 2:36, 77.

It was in the year 204 B.C. and again on the advice of the Sibylline Books that the Senate, in order to drive Hannibal out of Italy,[25] took the most momentous step yet taken in the development of Roman religion by introducing the cult and the black-stone fetich of the Great Mother (Cybele) from Pessinus in Galatia. She came with her Oriental priests (the *Galli*) and was received into the Roman pantheon. By 191 B.C. she had a temple on the Palatine. She was the harbinger of a host of other mystery-religions from Greece and the Near East.

While Etruscan influence had helped to divert the native trend of Roman religion that of the Greeks helped to destroy Roman morality. As soon as Jupiter took over the amatory adventures of Zeus, morality almost disappeared from Roman religion and became, as it always had been in Greece, a social rather than a religious problem. Still, religion at Rome retained some connection with morality since oaths, treaties, and leagues remained in Jupiter's province. Thus Vergil pictures Aeneas as kept in the path of duty (*pietas*) by Jupiter—a reflection of the thought of the poet's own time.[26]

It was during this period of scepticism that Plautus, Rome's greatest comic poet, ridiculed on the stage the transformation of Roman deities into Greek including all the latter's frailties, as Euripides and Aristophanes had done with various Greek gods centuries before in Athens. In his one burlesque, the *Amphitruo,* produced just after the Hannibalic War and based on the union of Zeus and Alcmene, Jupiter and Mercury appeared in the dramatis personae. Similarly, Ennius, "father of Roman poetry," who came to Rome from Calabria in 204 B.C., in his lost Greek tragedies did the same if we may judge from the two surviving lines of his *Telamo* in which he asserted that the gods took no interest in human affairs—the viewpoint of the later Lucretius. Ennius also translated the late fourth-century B.C. *Sacred History* of Euhemerus—both the translation and original are lost—in which the Greek writer recounted his visit to the capital of the fabled isle of Panchaea in the Erythraean Sea where in a temple to Zeus he saw a column inscribed with the births and deaths of various gods. From this he argued that the gods in general were merely mortals revered after death for their good deeds to men. Such writings tended to increase the prevailing scepticism and to undermine the divinely sanctioned morality.

[25] The Books cryptically referred to the ousting of a foreign enemy from Italy, officially identified with Hannibal, who then retreated into Bruttium and the next year left Italy for Carthage.

[26] The question whether religion and morality were originally separate elements, though inextricably joined in Christianity, has long been discussed, Edvard Westermarck favoring their original distinction and A. E. Crawley believing that they were always fused and indistinguishable elemental interests of mankind, morality being evolved from the religious impulse. Westermarck, *The Origin and Development of Moral Ideas* (2nd ed.; London, 1906), I, chap. i, 3; Crawley, *The Tree of Life: a Study in Religion* (London, 1905), chap. xix, pp. 287f. In any case Dean Stanley was right in saying: "The one great corruption to which all religion is exposed is its separation from morality," and in asserting that its absence in both Greek and Roman religions was one of their major deficiencies. See his *Lectures on the Jewish Church* (2nd ed.; New York, 1899), I, 3, 98.

Scepticism continued through the second century B.C. beginning with Rome's eastern wars, those with Philip V of Macedon (200–196 B.C.) and Antiochus the Great (192–188 B.C.). In 193 B.C., according to Livy (34:55) the Roman people became so weary of expiatory rites over earthquakes—which had become so frequent that the Senate could not perform its duties properly since the consuls who presided were busy with religious rites—that the Decemvirs again consulted the Books. In consequence of the prevailing scepticism a *Supplicatio* was ordered and the consuls issued a most curious decree: that on any one day when religious rites had been ordained because of an earthquake "no person should report another earthquake on that day."

Hellenistic Philosophies

It was during this decadent period that Roman religion was first influenced by two Hellenistic philosophies, Stoicism and Epicureanism. Their influence was toward practical morality rather than metaphysical speculation for they tried to teach men how to secure happiness in their present life—thus affecting the inner life of individuals and furthering the prevailing scepticism. While the tendency of Greek religion toward increasing its pantheon and cult-practices had been arrested by philosophical thought which succeeded in subordinating polytheism to rationalism by ridding it of its mythology and by insisting that the Olympian gods must be exponents of morality, Roman religion had undergone no such metamorphosis heretofore. This was largely due to the practical temperament of the Romans and to the fact that their time and thought, after the Punic Wars, had been actively devoted to building a world-power. Thus the ancient cult-ceremonies still remained the expression of their faith. Later on in the Empire with the extension of the Oriental mystery-cults emotionalism rather than rationalism resulted. Roman religion had now degenerated into little more than the perfunctory performance of rituals and had little hold on the masses and less on the educated classes. The latter now found comfort in the new philosophies.

Stoicism, which had become identified with the extension of Greek culture everywhere and was the standard of Greek ethics, reached Rome under Panaetius of Rhodes [27] and Epicureanism had come a little earlier. While the former with its elementary theology and stern ethics favored religion in general by explaining man's place in the universe, his relation to the godhead, and how to live in peace here, the latter was subversive of all religion and so fed the prevailing doubts. Stoicism was the first appeal to the Roman conscience, since Roman religion had known nothing of an individual sense of right and wrong but regarded "sin" as a scruple about the omission or wrong interpretation of ritual. It was, moreover, the last pagan attempt to present a logical world and man's relationship to God before the advent of Christianity since its adherents similarly asserted, as

---

[27] He was later head of the "Porch" at Athens. He had been invited in 144 B.C. by Scipio Aemilianus Africanus Minor, conqueror of Carthage in 146 B.C., to share his home and to give private and public lectures at Rome.

we see from Cleanthes' *Hymn to Zeus* in part quoted by St. Paul in his speech in Athens (Acts 17:28), that "we are also his offspring," i.e., parts of the Divine Reason. Its ascetic character of indifference to all externals, pain or pleasure, poverty or wealth, illness or health, and its severe ethics found less appeal among the Greeks with their easy-going morals than among the Romans, since its emphasis on the achievement of virtue as the aim of life and on living in conformity with nature coincided with the Roman standards of manhood, courage, and honesty. Hence it impressed some of the noblest men of the late Republic, such as the Younger Cato, and of the early Empire such as Persius, Epictetus, Seneca and, above all, the Emperor Marcus Aurelius [28] as well as such great women as Arria, wife of Caecina Paetus.[29] It was, in the words of Bertrand Russell, a "free man's religion."

Its influence waned before rising Christianity first as a philosophy and then as a religion although it continued to interest the thoughtful well into the sixth century over eight hundred years after Zeno, its Semitic founder, had first taught it in Athens. Its cosmopolitan character made it easy for Christianity to absorb some of its ethical spirit although its static spirit of acquiescence and resignation and its condemnation of the virtues which result from identifying God with love were in opposition to the latter's dynamic character.

It, consequently, brought a new idea of religion to Rome far in advance of Graeco-Roman polytheism but one capable of compromising with that polytheism if only the latter's mythology were rationalized. Most Stoics of the Roman period believed the gods could be worshiped as manifestations of the Divine Reason, though Zeno himself had regarded temples, statues, sacrifices, prayers, and the entire *cura et caerimonia* of religion, as Cicero called it,[30] as futile. But all agreed in believing that peace and wisdom resulted only from living in harmony with the Divine Reason. Stoicism humanized Roman life and law [31] although it never completely won over the Roman nature. Its philosophical teachings were far above the grasp of the common man for identifying God and man was an intellectual problem of which only trained minds were capable. Thus it alienated the ordinary Roman who was now being inoculated with the virus of Near-East mystery-religions.

By destroying human emotions which the Stoics believed were mere fancies from which the wise man should be free,[32] the ordinary man was repelled. Moreover, the system discouraged scientific investigation and overemphasized morality as the main interest of humanity. It preached

---

[28] His priceless book of *Meditations* in Greek has fortunately survived, and has been translated into all civilized tongues. It has influenced many great men of our time.

[29] When her husband, ordered by Claudius to destroy himself, faltered, she stabbed herself and handed him the dagger saying, *"Paete, non dolet."* As the result of many such examples of fortitude, "stoic" today means what it did to Epictetus and Seneca, indifference to suffering and the unfailing performance of duty.

[30] *De inventione* 2:161.

[31] The Stoic spirit is disclosed throughout Hadrian's *Edictum perpetuum.*

[32] So Cicero *De finibus* 3:10, 35.

no individual conscious life beyond the grave, deified neither God nor gods and encouraged no philanthropy since the Stoic regarded his fellow-man as inherently bad and impossible of redemption. The Stoic even denied to women a share in the Divine Reason. In a word Stoicism lacked warmth, emotion and sympathy, things which should be in any religion or ethical system. Of its great exemplar, the Emperor Marcus, it has been well said: "He was essentially a soldier left to hold a fort, surrounded by overpowering hosts of the enemy. He could not conquer nor drive them away, but he could hold out to the last and die at his post." [33] Stoicism, however, helped the fusion of races, customs, and creeds, and hence was an appropriate doctrine at the time when after Alexander civilizations were fusing and a new rule of life was needed which would outlive national decay and guide men in a world of change. For the Stoics were all "citizens of the world" and so aloof from local ties. Thus Seneca said "I know my country is the world," [34] and Marcus said "An Antonine my country is Rome, as a man it is the world." [35]

If Stoicism could make some compromise with Roman religion Epicureanism could not. Its founder had long warred on superstition and its great Roman expositor Lucretius—and Stoicism shows no comparable figure [36]—eulogized Epicurus as a savior for having discovered a rational plan of life. Tradition has wrongly made Epicurus an atheist and lover of pleasure although he did not deny the existence of the gods but only their interest in men's affairs and, like Socrates, he took part in the civic cult at Athens teaching not "pleasure" but tranquility of mind (*ataraxia*) as life's aim. He even believed that the gods' contemplation of their own perfection far away in the intermundia of space influenced men for good, one of the really religious features of the system. Certainly Cicero's stricture that Epicurus, "in abolishing divine beneficence and divine benevolence, uprooted and exterminated all religion from the Roman heart," [37] is unjust.

At first unpopular at Rome [38] it enjoyed a transient popularity after Lucretius and Cicero had interpreted it, the one in a scientific and sympathetic spirit, the other in that of hostility in his *De finibus* and *De natura deorum*.[39] But its popularity soon passed and only a few thereafter were known as its devotees.[40] Under Nero, however, its perverted form which

---

[33] Fowler, *op. cit.*, p. 375.

[34] *De vita beata ad Gallionem* 20; it is addressed to his brother, proconsul of Achaea in 52.

[35] *Meditations* 6:44.

[36] His *De rerum natura* has its nearest counterpart in *Paradise Lost* whose author was more akin to him than to any other poet because of his moral earnestness and sense of the beauty of nature.

[37] *De natura deorum* 1:44, 121, *L.C.L.* (1933).

[38] Athenaeus says Epicureans were banished from Rome in 175 (or 155 B.C.) "because of the pleasures they introduced."

[39] Cicero had been an auditor of Phaedrus (*ca.* 70 B.C.) when the latter was head of the "Garden" in Athens.

[40] Such as Pomponus Atticus, Cicero's friend, Horace, Pliny the Younger and Lucian.

encouraged sensual pleasures became the fashion among *la jeunesse dorée* of the Emperor's court under the leadership of Petronius, whence our words "epicure" and "epicurism" acquire their invidious connotations. Trajan, at the solicitation of his wife Plotina, reorganized it in the next century. After his time the School became a defence against superstitious trends, but by Julian's time (361–63) it had practically disappeared before popular mystic beliefs.

Lucretius' poem, one of the great masterpieces of Latin letters, explains in stately hexameter verse and archaic language not only the Epicurean psychology and ethics but the atomic and evolutionary doctrines of Democritus—the indestructibility of matter, the changelessness of the universe, material and infinite, the constancy of the law of cause and effect. It thus began the reign of inductive reasoning still used in all experimental science. He denounced the vices of contemporary society enmeshed in sensual emotionalism, ascribing them to superstitious belief in the gods and unreasoning fear and hope resulting from a false appreciation of reality. He offered his master's message as the remedy, an example of reason aimed at freeing men from unseen terrors.[41] But the attempt to destroy the two most harassing fears of humanity, the vengeance of God and death, on material grounds, set his system outside the pale of religion as then understood, as did his assertion that there is no life beyond the grave since the soul at the death of the body was dissolved into the atoms which composed it.

Cicero was repelled by its materialism and morality as we still are and by its egoistic ethics divorced from civic obligations, leaving no place for the social virtues. In his ridicule of the system as well as the meaningless religious ceremonies of his day he said in true Catonian style: "It seems astonishing that one augur does not laugh when he sees another, and more astonishing that you [Epicureans] can refrain from laughing among yourselves." [42] While the Stoic emphasized duty as the highest virtue the Epicurean found his "in the absence of pain." Thus both systems reached the same goal, happiness, by different routes and both taught virtue but for different reasons, the one as the aim of life, the other as the means to that end. This, in the case of Epicureanism, meant aloofness from the *Sturm und Drang* of existence, an independence of externals. For the Epicurean

---

[41] Four lines, twelve words in Greek, found among the fragments of two books of Epicurus' lost *De natura* over a century ago in Herculaneum summarize Epicurus' diatribe against the popular religion. They have been thus translated:

> There is nothing to fear in God.
> There is nothing to feel in Death.
> What is good is easily procured;
> What is bad is easily endured.

First published by J. C. Orelli, *Fragmenta librorum ii et xi De Natura* (Lipsiae, 1818). See also Achilles Voghano, *Epicuri et Epicureorum scripta in herculanensibus papyris servata* (Berolini, 1928).

[42] *De natura deorum* 1:26, 71. Cf. the similar and more often quoted jibe of Cato the Censor in Cicero's *De divinatione* 2:24, 51, his surprise "that a soothsayer does not laugh when he sees another soothsayer."

was anti-political, accepting the State only as a makeshift, and anti-marital, accepting marriage likewise as a makeshift, and the wise man should involve himself neither in political nor domestic activities. The great defect of the system was that it regarded religion and its doctrine of immortality as illusions and so it in no sense could be a substitute for religion or ethics.[43] No wonder, then, that Epicureanism played little part as a substitute for the decaying religion of Rome. It has been well said that "since the Garden of Eden was closed to our first parents, happiness has not been the lot of any considerable community for any considerable time," [44] and assuredly neither Stoics nor Epicureans advanced it far in the degenerating state of Roman religion. Philosophy did not stay the latter's decay, since that religion continued its course of disintegration through the last century of the Republic. Philosophy had taught the Romans that their gods were little more than figures of speech.

Religion, already in the second century B.C., had begun to be regarded as a restriction on political advancement. Such restrictions were especially felt by the high religious dignitaries such as the *flamens*. Since these and others were appointees of the Pontifex maximus they had to serve even if it meant their political extinction. Two examples cited by Livy (37:51 and 41:42) will show how religious officials felt that the interests of public life were more important than those of religion. In 189 B.C., Q. Fabius Pictor, praetor and *flamen Quirinalis,* was kept from going to his province Sardinia after his praetorship was over since as *flamen* he could not leave Italy. But after debates in the Assembly and Senate he was ordered to keep his religious office from which he had tried to resign. Again in 180 B.C., L. Cornelius Dolabella, one of the board of *duo viri navales,* appointed to equip a fleet, was named *rex sacrificulus,* ancient high-priest of sacrifice, and told to resign his civil office as incompatible with his religious duties. He was saved from so doing only by an unfavorable omen which caused the court of appeals to adjourn. Such restrictions were felt later so strongly that the office of *flamen Dialis* instituted for Jupiter by Numa and burdened, as we have seen, with many exacting ceremonies, remained vacant for three-fourths of the first century B.C. from Sulla to Augustus (87–11 B.C.) since no one wanted to be barred from political advancement by holding it. And that of the *rex sacrificulus* was sometimes unfilled. The sacred colleges of immemorial antiquity—pontiffs, augurs, *flamens, fetials*—now enjoyed only social prestige.

Although the old State-cult continued to exist officially, with its ceremonies and machinery of worship strictly observed, it had lost all semblance of reality. For now prayer-formulae were merely mumbled; sacrifices had no inner meaning; lustration or purification of temples, houses, and indi-

---

[43] It effected one good at Rome, however, for it helped to purge Roman religion of its crass mythology and also, like Stoicism, to prepare the way for something better to follow, Christianity.

[44] S. R. Maitland, *The Dark Ages* (2nd ed.; London, 1889), p. 14.

viduals was only a spectacle; the ancient *votum* or tacit compact between gods and men was invalid; priests meddled in politics; temples were empty and falling into ruin; and the religious calendar was neglected. No wonder that Varro, "the most learned of the Romans," who died in 28 B.C. at the very threshold of the Empire, feared "lest the gods might perish not from enemy invasion, but neglect of the citizens." [45] It seemed that Roman religion was not only moribund but dead—the empty shell of what had once been the motive power of Roman greatness. Only one part of it, the oldest—the spirits of the household and those of field and harvest—still kept the reverence of the common man. Thus Horace, himself an Epicurean, tells a country-girl that her vines, crops, and cattle, will prosper if only she raises her

upturned palms to heaven each time the moon is born again . . . if with incense, with grain of this year's harvest and with a greedy swine she appeases the Lares, and if her pure hands have touched the altar . . . they appease estranged Penates even by sacred meal mingled with the crackling salt.[46]

Still, despite its meaningless formalism, Roman religion or what was left of it remained the expression of religious feeling. Cicero who condemned its conventions praised the reality behind them when he wrote that *"in religione, id est cultu,* the Romans were superior to all other peoples." [47] And when, in a speech before the Senate, he asked "who . . . can fail to be convinced that it is by its [divinity's] power that this great empire has been created, extended, and sustained," and added: "in piety, in devotion to religion, and in that special wisdom which consists in the recognition of the truth that the mind is swayed and directed by divine disposal, we have excelled every race and every nation." [48] Sallust and the Augustan poets, especially Vergil, echoed the same sentiment.

IN THE EMPIRE

Roman religion had fallen into such decay that it is literally a matter of wonder that it could have come to life again and have continued over a period of centuries, changed, of course, but retaining some of its past splendor. This was due in part to its politico-national character, but far more to the efforts of one great Roman, Augustus Caesar, the founder of the Empire. For he made Romans return for a season to their old religious fealty.

The Augustan Revival

As we have seen the Roman world had grown weary and sceptical as a result of the wars of conquest and civil strife of the late Republic. It longed for the return of a settled social and economic life under the *pax Romana* which now began—the first real peace since Alexander's conquests

[45] Quoted by E. Aust, *Religion der Römer* (Münster, 1899), p. 80.
[46] *Odes* 3:23, *L.C.L.* (1919).
[47] *De natura deorum* 2:3, 8.
[48] *De haruspicum responsis* 9:9, *L.C.L.* (1923).

three centuries before. Peace was to start with the official revival of the ancient faith, which is not only the outstanding event in the history of Roman religion but such a revival is unique in the history of religion. It is a tribute to Augustus' statesmanship that, although he was a free-thinker like his grand-uncle Julius, he could see the advantage to which he could put the universal spirit of thanksgiving to effect a renaissance of the State-cult, to make the *ius divinum* once more effective, to give a new lease of life to the faith that had made the Republic strong and, at the same time, to strengthen his political position.[49] Constantine, over three centuries later, when standing on the threshold of yet another epoch in the history of Europe, was still interested in Augustus' work, as was Julian to an even greater degree a few years later. In fact the last fragments of Augustus' revival were extinguished only in the fifth century by Theodosius II, when he forbade even the ancient family worship of the Penates, Lares, and the Genius of the State.[50]

His revival, more political than religious in aim, was part of his general plan of reform intended to recall the Roman people to the practice of their ancient virtues, and was meant especially to bind them to his new order, and to impress on them the stability of his one-man rule. Thus he could conceal his real position as dictator in order to foster loyalty to himself and to bring unity to the State—the forerunner of the alliance of throne and altar in later Europe. For he believed, as had Ennius nearly two centuries before, that

moribus antiquis stat res Romana virisque,

and attributed the debacle of the last century of the Republic to the decline of religion. He focussed popular attention not on the State as an abstract institution, but rather on his own person, a plan under which Rome took the initial step along the way, taken long before by the Hellenistic Greeks, which led to the deification of his successors.

He hoped to revitalize the outworn fabric by new meanings and thus to win popular interest and, at the same time, to wean the people from the attraction of the Oriental mystery-religions which had now begun to grow menacingly in strength. To this end he made Apollo (his tutelary deity at Actium in 31 B.C.) the center of the new Graeco-Roman religion. In 28 B.C. he dedicated a temple to him in the grounds of his palace on the Palatine, i.e., in *solo privato*,[51] thus making the Greek god the equal of

---

[49] For an estimate of his life and character, see W. W. Hyde, "The Bimillennium of the Birth of Augustus Caesar," *Scientific Monthly* (July 1941), pp. 38–50. A very different view of Augustus as "the original stuffed shirt" and to his enemies a "whited sepulchre" is that of C. R. Cochrane in *Christianity and Classical Culture* (Oxford, 1940), p. 127, n. 1. As seducer, adulterer, and sensualist in private life, see Suetonius' *Life of Augustus*, chaps. 69, 71.

[50] *Codex Theodosianus* 16:10, 2. Cf. Sir Samuel Dill, *Roman Society in the Last Century of the Western Empire* (2nd ed.; London, 1919), Bk. I, chaps. i, iv.

[51] See Suetonius, *Life of Augustus*, chap. 29, 3. The biographer here adds that the emperor joined the temple colonnades with Latin and Greek libraries, and that in his old age he often held meetings of the Senate here and revised the jury lists.

the Roman Jupiter ensconced five centuries before on the neighboring Capitoline. Just prior to this on his return from Egypt he had assumed the office of augur and had become a member of the college of *Quindecim-viri*, but did not take the religious title of Pontifex maximus until the death in 12 B.C. of Lepidus, his former colleague in the Triumvirate, who held it. This gave to his person a halo of sanctity so great that all his successors, pagan and Christian down to Gratian (367–373), assumed it as the sign of their headship of the State religion.

In 17 B.C. he restored the *Ludi saeculares* with great pomp on the basis of a new *saeculum* of one hundred and ten years. We still have the made-to-order *Carmen saeculare* which Horace composed for its celebration, its most-enduring monument if not as Guglielmo Ferrero has called it "a magnificent poem." [52] In it the court poet, despite being an Epicurean, deplored the waning of religion and asked for legislation to revive it, thus disclosing the Emperor's belief that the future of Rome still depended on religion and morality as much as on the fertility of men, beasts, and crops and on good government. It was sung before the shrines of Apollo and Jupiter by choruses of boys and girls respectively. Games, held from May twenty-sixth to June third, marked the division between the "old" and the "new" eras. [53] They were not genuinely Roman since they rested on an oracle in the Sibylline Books, as Horace tells us; were celebrated outside the *pomerium* (that the infernal gods might not be brought within) and in honor of Greek gods. Thus the whole celebration proclaimed the cosmopolitan character of the revived religion.

We learn about the revival chiefly from Suetonius' *Life of Augustus* (chaps. 31, 75, 93) and from ten words in the Emperor's official account of his reign published after his death by his stepson Tiberius which began with the famous words *Rerum gestarum divi Augusti* still to be read on the walls of the ruined temple of *Roma et Augustus* in the Turkish capital Ankara, the ancient Ancyra in Galatia. We quote these words: "duo et octaginta templa deum in urbe decreto senatus refeci," [54] which caused Livy to call him (4:20, 7) *templorum omnium conditor ac restitutor*. Among these temples were the ancient shrine of Jupiter *Feretrius* on the Capitoline supposed to have been built by Romulus and the recent temple of Cybele (the only Oriental deity accepted by the Emperor) on the Palatine which replaced the older one burned in A.D. 3. He increased the number of the priesthood, their privileges and allowances, notably those of the priestesses of Vesta for which deity he erected a new shrine on the Palatine; restored disused religious offices, notably those of the *flamen Dialis* and the

---

[52] *Greatness and Decline of Rome* (New York, 1907–1909), V, 93.

[53] We know about them from the excavations in 1890 on the Tiber embankment where they took place and where mutilated inscriptions, a letter of Augustus, decrees of the Senate and records of the *Quindecimviri* were found: *C.I.L.*, VI, No. 3232–33, 3237–44; H. Dessau, *Inscriptiones Latinae selectae* (Berolini, 1892, 1902, 1906 and 1914–16), II, 1, No. 5050, 582.

[54] Th. Mommsen, *Res gestae divi Augusti ex monumentis Ancyrano et Apolliensi* (2nd ed.; Berolini, 1883), IV, 17. For the copy in Pisidian Antioch, see D. M. Robinson, *Res gestae divi Augusti, as recorded on the Mon. Antiochenum* (Baltimore, 1926).

rex sacrorum, and so increased sacrifices that an epigram on the column of Marcus Aurelius still standing in the Piazza di Colonna fits Augustus better than the later emperor: "The white cattle to Caesar, greeting. If you conquer there is an end of us." He restored the ancient priesthood of the twelve Arval brothers who long before had offered sacrifice for the fertility of the fields (*arva*) to Dea Dia, an ancient Roman "corn" deity, and had himself enrolled as a member. They now made the old vows and sacrifices on January third to the Emperor's family, a custom continued to the time of Theodosius I.[55]

Suetonius also records that in 12 B.C. Augustus burnt some two thousand rolls of Greek and Roman prophecies preserving only "the genuine Sibylline Books" copies of which were then removed from the Capitoline vaults to Apollo's shrine on the Palatine where they were kept for the next four centuries in two gilded cases in front of the pedestal of the god. In 29 B.C. on the spot in the Forum where Caesar's body had been displayed to the people he had dedicated the *Aedes Divi Julii,*[56] thus making Caesar the first dead emperor to become a god. Later, in 2 B.C., due to a vow made at Philippi in 42 B.C. and as a special act of *pietas,* he erected a temple to Mars Ultor, or "Avenger" of Caesar in his own Forum Augusti, Mars being the traditional ancestor of the Julian *gens.* It was a splendid temple described by Ovid,[57] which marked the apogee of the glorification of his family.

While in 27 and 23 B.C. Augustus had refused to accept deification and in 13 B.C., on his return from Spain, had declined an altar in the *Regia* or official residence of the Pontifex maximus, in 9 B.C. he accepted an altar of Peace, and later so associated his name with religion that the Senate recognized his divinity. In the East, provincials had been accustomed during the Hellenistic Age to venerate not only their sovereigns as gods but even Roman magistrates in charge of provinces. This latter custom began with Flamininus in 196 B.C. (after his defeat of Philip V at Cynoscephalae the year before) when he was worshiped in Greece together with Apollo and Heracles.[58] He was followed by others, including Scipio Africanus who was regarded as superior to ordinary men,[59] Caecilius Metellus Pius, proconsul of Spain under Sulla, Verres in Sicily, Marius Gratidianus the legate of Quintus Cicero in Asia, and Pompey—all without official authorization from Rome. Cicero when governor of Cilicia (52–50 B.C.) refused

---

[55] A series of ninety-six *Acta,* or minutes, of their meetings inscribed on stone and dating from Tiberius to Gordian III (14 to 241) were found between 1570 and 1869 on the site of the ancient grove of Dia between Rome and Ostia: Mommsen, *History of Rome* (5th ed.; New York, 1905), I, Bk. 1, chap. xv.

[56] Cassius Dio XLVII, 18, 19.

[57] *Fasti* 5, 550f. On Augustus' renewal of *pietas,* see R. Bloch, "L'Ara Pietatis Augustae," *Mélanges d'arch. et d'hist. de l'école française de Rome,* LVI (1939), and V. W. Scramuzza, "Livy on the Ara Pietatis Augustae," *Classical Philology,* XXVIII (1943), 240–45.

[58] Plutarch, *Life of Flamininus,* 16:4. On this subject, see E. Fiddes, "The Beginning of Caesar-Worship," *Owens College Historical Essays* (London, 1902), I, 1–16 (from Flamininus to Caesar).

[59] Livy 26:19.

such an honor [60] although he took the permanent title of *imperator* [61] and aspired to a triumph for subduing the Cilician pirates. Julius Caesar had enjoyed an Eastern cult,[62] as Augustus had also.[63]

Finally Augustus allowed his name to appear with *Roma* in an eastern cult and on finding it could be used as a symbol of patriotism let it be so used in the West, although not in Italy. Tacitus [64] recounts how certain Spaniards asked permission to erect a temple to him at Tarraco (Tarragona) where he had wintered in 26 B.C. after his Cantabrian campaign, and says that in this way "a precedent was given for all the princes." Suetonius (chap. 57) says he would only accept a temple in a province "jointly in his own name and that of Rome" and adds that he melted down statues of himself in Rome. In Vienna (Vienne) in Gaul a temple was dedicated to him and his wife Livia by Claudius which from the fifth century to 1793 was the Church of Notre Dame de Vie.

The cult of Augustus and Rome finally reached Italy but only as an Oriental one being served by six Oriental freedmen—the *Seviri*—who became annual *Augustales* (*sc. viri*) devoted to the Emperor in binding State and cult together. In 29 B.C. the Senate had decreed a libation to his *Genius* to be poured at private and public meals and in 7 B.C. he associated himself with the two *Lares Compitales,* "of the crossroads," by having a statue of his *Genius* placed beside them in their chapels, Ovid saying that Rome had "a thousand Lares and the Genius of the chief, who handed them over to the public; the parishes worship the three divinities." [65] Every man had his *Genius* but Augustus out of the throng of such private ones had raised himself above ordinary men. His surname Augustus, i.e., "revered," conferred on him by the Senate in 27 B.C. also elevated him to the rank of divinity. While, then, he had no temple in Italy erected to him as a god but only shrines to his *Genius,* in many ways he helped to institute the imperial cult followed by his successors.[66]

With Augustus' revival, Roman religion proper ends. For that revival, centering in his person, from the first contained elements of self-destruction, not only in its obsolescence and its competition with mystery-religions which better suited popular religious needs, but above all in its encouragement of the tendency to Caesar-worship which superseded it officially. It

---

[60] *Epist. Ad Atticum* 5:21, 7, and *Ad Quintum fratrem* I:9, 26. In the latter he says "he allowed neither statues nor shrines."

[61] The cognomen *imperator,* first assumed by Caesar and accepted by Augustus, was not used by Tiberius, Caligula, nor Claudius but was taken by Nero and, beginning with Vespasian, became permanent.

[62] See J. F. Toutain, *The Economic Life of the Ancient World* (New York, 1930), Bk. I, pp. 26f.

[63] W. Dittenberger, *Orientis graeci inscriptiones selectae* (Lipsiae, 1903), II, 458.

[64] *Annales* 1:78.

[65] *Fasti* 5:145–6; Augustus had created two hundred and sixty-five parishes (*vici*) in Rome and each had a shrine of the *Lares Compitales,* Ovid's one thousand being an exaggeration.

[66] See Lily R. Taylor, "The Worship of Augustus in Italy" in *Trans. Amer. Philological Ass'n,* Vol. LI (1920); and *The Divinity of the Roman Emperor* (Middletown, 1931).

was not to be the real religion of the Empire although with Senate support some of its outer forms were preserved down to the time of the Carthaginian dynasty of the Severi (193–217), since Augustus' successors found it to their advantage to maintain it together with the imperial cult. Some of its power, as we shall see, lasted to the close of the fourth century and even later. But the official religion of the Empire from Tiberius to Diocletian nearly three centuries later was to be something quite different: the imperial-cult or Caesarism.

Rome had become a vast imperial domain throughout the Mediterranean area in whose every part the consuls of the Senate were effective. The need of a universal religion to be a common bond uniting all the varied peoples and interests of the State was universally felt. There was no religious unity in Augustus' revival of the multiple Graeco-Roman deities to match the political unity of Roman rule. Many were soon drawn away from the revived polytheism in the quest of some more unifying and protective power. Thus during Augustus' own lifetime there began a contest between the old and the new for religious mastery of the Empire.

Where better could unity be found than in the person of the Emperor himself, the visible symbol of Roman stability, the wielder of more power than any man had ever possessed? In the Emperor the people felt security such as had not been known for centuries past. After Actium, the temple of Janus was closed as a sign of peace for the third and last time in Roman history and the *pax Romana* was so firmly established over the civilized world of the West that it was to last for the next two centuries, the longest cessation of war in the story of man. Understandably Augustus and his successors were regarded as earthly providences who dispensed peace and prosperity so that their apotheoses seemed only natural. Thus it came about that the imperial master sat on the throne of the old gods and his cult became official.

Starting with the oath of allegiance (*sacramentum*) sworn to the Genius of Augustus and of the Roman people, augmented by the Eastern process of deification, the progress of the new cult was certain despite the reluctance of Augustus and his stepson Tiberius to accept divine honors. For Tiberius also refused temples in his honor although, curiously, he furthered the cult of *Divus Augustus*. Tacitus [67] records how, before the Senate, he answered a Spanish delegation which had come to Rome for permission to erect a temple to him in Spain with these words: "*Ego me, patres conscripti, mortalem esse . . . testor,*" adding that he was content to perform the duties of the highest office. He allowed his statues, however, to be placed among those of the gods and in 27 allowed the province of Asia to dedicate a temple in his honor, although two years later he refused to permit the province of Baetica in southern Spain to erect one there. He also, like Augustus, was hostile to the Oriental cults. [68]

Immediately after Augustus' death the Senate declared him a god and

[67] *Annales* 4:38.

[68] On one occasion, as noted later, because of a scandal in high life he had the priests of Isis crucified like slaves, her temple dismantled, and her statues cast into the Tiber.

introduced his worship into Italy. A new college (*Augustales*) of priests
with suitable functions and powers and the Augustal games were instituted in the service of the imperial god in A.D. 15. Tacitus says twenty-
one prominent Romans were selected by lot for the first panel of priests.[69]
In the provinces where the imperial-cult was almost without exception
enthusiastically accepted regular hierarchies from high priest down were
established, forming the pattern for later Church rule. All must conform
to, and share in, the imperial ritual and must burn incense before the
Emperor's statue and offer obeisance to it. The only people to refuse
were the "outlaw" Christians and this was one of the major causes of the
persecutions which stained imperial history from Nero to Diocletian. The
title of divinity was regularly given by the Senate to all the emperors after
their death except to such evil ones as Caligula, Nero, Domitian, and Commodus.[70] But the new cult, somewhat like Shintoism in modern Japan,
was largely a test of loyalty to the State and the Emperor. It had waned
by the end of the second century though it lasted a century more officially.
Constantine's favor to Christianity finally ended it though remnants of it,
like those of the cult of the old Roman gods, continued as a social power.[71]
The Roman masses, however, while willing to conform with the imperial-
cult and outwardly with Augustus' revived polytheism, needed something
more emotional to satisfy their religious cravings. This they readily found
in the various Near-East mystery-cults.

Near-East Mystery Cults

With the accession of Tiberius' successor Caligula (37–41) a new type
of religion with a very different appeal, which had long lain dormant in
Rome, began to grow strong—that of the Near-Eastern mystery-religions
which changed the whole religious outlook of many Romans and has left
traces in the Christian Church. It was these religions (and one might
belong to more than one) all of which were opposed to the official imperial
cult and to Graeco-Roman polytheism, and Christianity, their common
enemy, which formed the real religion of the Empire. Some few, such as
that of Cybele, were accepted officially into the Roman pantheon but
most of them existed only through imperial favor. They, with kindred
philosophies—both to be discussed in the following chapter—formed a
background to the Christianity which eventually vanquished them.

To understand how such cults arose in the East and finally reached
Rome and the West it is necessary to revert to the new order established
by Alexander the Great. The six centuries from his conquest of Persia
(330 B.C. f.) to Constantine the Great (A.D. 330f.) have been rightly re-

---

[69] *Annales* 1:54; he states that Tiberius, Drusus, Claudius, and Germanicus were
added. He says the college was patterned on the ancient priesthood founded by Titus
Tatius, King of the Sabines, of which nothing is known.

[70] See E. R. Bevan in Hastings' *Encyclopedia of Religion and Ethics* (New York,
1908–22), IV, 529–32. Cited hereafter as *E.R.E.*

[71] On Caesarism, see especially J. Iverich in *E.R.E.*, III, 50–56, and the literature there
listed.

garded by historians as of momentous importance in the history of religion. Those who regard Alexander only as a conqueror who invaded the territories of Persia without cause are mistaken since he was something more, a great statesman as well who accelerated a movement which became a turning-point in history comparable with those of the Renaissance and Reformation.[72] Constantine's espousal of Christianity which started it on its world mission as the religion not only of Rome but of Europe, marked another turning-point, that from the ancient to the medieval world.

Alexander paved the way for Rome's adoption of the Eastern mystery-cults and of Christianity itself by his destruction of national provincial barriers and the particularism of the ancient world. He made man international and cosmopolitan, a process which centuries later reached its height in the Roman Empire. He displaced Aramaic, long the language of diplomacy and trade from Egypt to Mesopotamia, by a simplified form of Greek intelligible to all Greeks and easily acquired by foreigners, a koiné in which men could converse from Macedonia southward to the cataracts of the Nile and eastward to the Tigris. Out of his vision of the mixture of races, the "marriage of East and West," came also religious syncretism or theocrasia, which for centuries thereafter was an important phenomenon in the religious history of Greeks, Romans, and Jews, for it became universal, the similarity of ethnic deities naturally following that of different peoples. It also led to eclecticism in philosophy. Through syncretism the Oriental cults as well as Christianity grew strong in the Western world. We must not omit, however, one great evil, subversive of both religion and morality, which grew out of Alexander's work—the deification of the conqueror and his immediate successors.

During the succeeding centuries and especially the first three Christian ones, with which latter we are here concerned, religion became the great motive power of life which lasted, to quote Ernest Barker, for a millennium after Constantine's death, during which

the basis of human organization is the religious motif, and human society is ecclesiastical in its primary inspiration.[73]

For after Alexander's time men everywhere were seeking a religion of redemption and a satisfying worship. As Francis Legge has said:

there has probably been no time in the history of mankind when all classes were more given up to thoughts of religion, or when they strained more fervently after high ethical ideals,[74]

and Sir Samuel Dill had already written in the same vein:

[72] It must be emphasized that while his empire proved ephemeral—soon fulfilling the prophecy of Daniel (11:4) that "his kingdom shall be broken, and shall be divided toward the four winds of heaven"—the results of his work have affected all political and religious history since.

[73] In Cyril Bailey's Legacy of Rome (Oxford, 1933), p. 77.

[74] Forerunners and Rivals of Christianity: Being Studies in Religious History from 330 B.C. to 330 A.D. (Cambridge, 1915), I, xlix.

The world was in the throes of a religious revolution and eagerly in quest of some fresh vision of the Divine, from whatever quarter it might dawn.[75]

We see this religious ferment especially in the spread over Mediterranean lands of the various Near-East religions which emphasized everything that Roman religion did not, and even more in the spread of Christianity later.

As a result of Alexander's conquests religion in Western Asia, Egypt, and Greece fell to a low level chiefly due to the destruction of Persian provincial nationalities and the consequent decay of national religions. Alexander's immediate successors, the Seleucids of Asia and the Ptolemies of Egypt, put little in place of these defunct religions beyond their own decaying Greek cults and such new ones as that of Tyche (goddess of Fortune, now regarded as the tutelary city-deity of such centers as Antioch) and the imperial cult. In the second century B.C., however, there was a reaction against Hellenic polytheism in Western Asia and Egypt, and native deities—Cybele, Isis, Mithra and others even including the Jewish Yahweh at the time of the Maccabees—became important. In the Far East Buddhism, the Protestant form of older Brahmanism with its central doctrine of salvation from sorrow and existence, ousted the Greek deities of the princes of Bactria and northwest India. At this point the mystery-religions emerged from obscurity as populations became more cosmopolitan and Roman armies accepted recruits from all over the Near East, for these in coming westward brought their own gods and rites with them. Such cults reached Greece for the most part after Alexander's time and there became inwoven in the fabric of Greek polytheism; they first reached Italy and the West after the Second Punic War through Rome's conquests in Greece and Western Asia, at the very time when Roman religion had become moribund.

Various circumstances in the West favored their popularity, notably the decay of the Graeco-Roman civic-cults which had been bound up with the city-state type of government which collapsed in Greece at Chaeronea in 338 B.C. and in Italy still later. The revival in Greece and Greek South Italy during the third and following centuries B.C. of sixth-century mystic Orphism (a cult originating in the Thrako-Phrygian rites of Dionysus Zagreus), also helped their acceptance since this offered an alternative to the gloomy Hades of the Homeric period and so aroused much interest in Rome. Orphism was a lofty system and had influenced many prominent Greeks in its earlier period—Pythagoras, Heraclitus, Plato. It shifted interest from this world to one beyond with its central doctrine that the soul was entombed in the body and longed to regain its former celestial abode. As a system it lasted a thousand years in Greece and Rome and its doctrines of regeneration and redemption have never been lost.

The Romans through contact with the Near East had learned that they also had something new to experience in religion. While the West had

[75] *Roman Society from Nero to Marcus Aurelius* (London, 1911), p. 82. Cf. also T. R. Glover, *Greek Byways* (New York, 1932), p. 219; and A. D. Nock, *Conversion: the Old and the New in Religion from Alexander the Great to Augustine of Hippo* (London, 1933).

always been active politically, the East had ever been contemplative. Its civilizations had always remained sacerdotal, as that of the Middle Ages was to be in Europe, the only learned men being the priests and the only schools, the temples. Whatever discoveries were made were always attributed to the gods, learning and faith ever going hand in hand. The Orient put faith above reason as its guide while the Greeks had long since rationalized their mythologies through the influence of philosophy which made their religious thought independent of faith. Metaphysics had destroyed the vitality of Greek polytheism and the later Hellenistic philosophies helped to undermine the polytheism of Rome. The Romans were too practical to be much attracted by metaphysical speculations, concentrating their efforts instead on human conduct. But the time had come when Oriental priests were to teach Romans about supernatural matters. While the semi-civic Graeco-Roman priests gave no sacerdotal mediation, had no parishes, used no exhortation, and earned their livelihood largely from civic work, the Oriental priests devoted their entire time to the duties of their office and so aroused devotion in their initiates. They were unlike the Roman priests, too, in that they believed, without any self-deception, in the reality of the things they taught.

There were many of these mystery-religions and they show great diversity of character and outlook. Most of the Greek cults, however, played relatively little part in the religious experience of Rome. Apart from Orphism there were in the Greek world the Andanian mysteries of Messenia in honor of Demeter, Apollo, Persephone, and the Cabeiri, which were older than the Spartan conquest of Messenia, but are known to us mainly through an inscription of 91 B.C.[76] which speaks of a sacred drama in which married priestesses impersonated the goddesses. There were further also secret rites in honor of the Cabeiri, a group of four underworld powers of fertility identified by the Greeks with Hephaestus, Dionysus, Demeter, and Kore, which were celebrated on the North Aegean island of Samothrace. They were pre-Greek in origin but had been thoroughly Hellenized by the time of Alexander. Another Greek mystery-cult was that of the *Dionysia* celebrated in Athens and Thebes and the oldest of all were the mysteries celebrated in September-October at the village of Eleusis near Athens in honor of Demeter and Persephone. The excavation of the site of the *Telesterion* or "Hall of Initiation" here by the Greek Archaeological Society has shown that they were prehistoric.[77]

At first the Eleusinian mysteries were simple agrarian rites to increase fertility, but gradually, as they were drawn into Greek anthropomorphism, they became actuated by higher motives, the relation of man to the Deity

---

[76] See H. Collitz, *Sammlung der gr. Dialekt-Inschriften* (Göttingen, 1884f.), III, 2, No. 4689.

[77] Founded either in the Minoan-Mycenaean period or, perhaps more in harmony with the archaeological finds, posterior to the arrival of the Hellenes in the Middle Helladic period; see A. W. Persson in *Archiv für Religionswiss.* XXI (1922), 202, 308; and M. P. Nilsson, *The Minoan-Mycenaean Religion* (London, 1927), pp. 387f., 402f. For the excavations, see D. Philios, *Eleusis, her Mysteries, Ruins and Museum* (London, 1906).

and the assurance that Persephone, queen of the lower world, could protect her votaries hereafter as we see in the seventh-century B.C. Homeric *Hymn to Demeter.* Dionysiac and Orphic elements modified the rites still more in the sixth-century B.C. when Iacchus (a form of Dionysus) was admitted as a third deity and the mysteries were more directly concerned with life hereafter. Last of all, rites of retribution and individual immortality were added through the influence of philosophers and poets. Sophocles and the painter Polygnotus believed that the initiates of this cult had an advantage over others in receiving future blessings; Cicero said Athens produced nothing better in reference to civilizing life and in assuring hope of the hereafter; [78] and Clement of Alexandria centuries later speaks of the mystic drama in honor of the goddesses.[79] Grave-reliefs indicate the hope thus inspired, as when in an Athenian epitaph we read that a hierophant or initiating priest found "death was not an evil but a blessing." [80] These mysteries lasted throughout the historic period, being notably prominent in the Empire under Julian (361–363) and especially esteemed by the Neo-Platonists. The edict issued by Valentinian I and Valens (364–375) against secret societies did not molest them. They ended only with the destruction of Eleusis by fanatical Christian monks in the train of Alaric's invasion of Greece (A.D. 395–96). The wild and mystic rites of the *Dionysia* under the Latin name *Bacchanalia* were banned in Rome as already told.

Thus it was not the Greek mysteries but those from Asia and Egypt which chiefly captivated Rome. Like the Greek ones these were secret, but their orgiastic ecstasy and psychical aberrations were generally more violent. This ecstasy—Plato's "divine frenzy"—accompanied them all for they were emotional rather than doctrinal. It was induced by various means such as pageantry, delirious dances, music, physical mortifications, abstinence, silence, and in some cults by a sacred drama which pictured with great realism the earthly sufferings, death, and resurrection of their human-like deities analogous to the medieval miracle plays. While the votaries mourned the death of their deities like mortals, in every case grief was changed to joy during the course of the festival at the god's rebirth. On first consideration it seems strange that unemotional Romans should have accepted such fervid worships, barbarian in origin and retaining much of their original savagery. And in fact they did at first arouse government disapproval and their members remained largely Oriental slaves, artisans, and soldiers. They were supported by voluntary contributions like modern churches, which excluded all idea of gain in the initiates. Their exacting austerities were derided by the thoughtful and their appeal to individualism was foreign to the entire Graeco-Roman idea of civilization:

Greek and Roman society was built on the conception of the subordination of the individual to the community, of the citizen to the state; it set the safety of the commonwealth, as the supreme aim of conduct, above the safety of the individual

---

[78] *De legibus* 2:14.

[79] *Protrepticon* (hortatory address to the Greeks), 12.

[80] In *Ephemeris archaiologiké* (Athens, 1883), p. 81.

whether in this world or in the world to come. Trained from infancy in this un-
selfish ideal, the citizens devoted their lives to the public service and were ready
to lay them down for the common good; or if they shrank from the supreme sacrifice, it never occurred to them that they acted otherwise than basely in preferring
their personal existence to the interests of their country. All this was changed by
the spread of Oriental religions which inculcated the communion of the soul with
God and its eternal salvation as the only objects worth living for, objects in comparison with which the prosperity and even the existence of the state sank into
insignificance.[81]

But they contained elements to counterbalance such drawbacks. Gus-
tav Anrich in his work on their influence on Christianity [82] has tabulated
five main reasons which brought them success in the West: their immemorial antiquity; their symbolism in which the initiate found religious
truth; their doctrine of ultimate union of man and deity; their response
to a sense of sin and sacramental cathartic; and their offering an assurance
of immortality. And Franz Cumont, our chief authority on the subject,
has estimated their varied appeal in these words:

These religions gave greater satisfaction, first of all, to the senses and emotions, in
the second place to the intelligence, and finally and chiefly to the conscience.
They offered, in comparison with previous religions, more beauty in their ritual,
more truth in their doctrines, and a superior good in their morality. . . . They
refined and exalted the psychic life and gave to it an almost supernatural intensity,
such as the ancient world had never known before.[83]

That they brought consolation to countless initiates cannot be denied
since it is attested by many ancient writers as well as by the opposition of
Christian apologists down to St. Augustine. While today there is difference of opinion about their value most writers on the subject (Gruppe, Cumont, Anrich, Dill, Loisy, Bigg, Inge, Angus) agree that with their obvious
defects the mystery-cults had, nevertheless, many redeeming qualities, offering a blend of higher and lower elements all the way from spirituality
to sensuousness. They all had the same aims as Christianity, *soteria* (salvation), the worship of a pure God, the living of a pure life, and the culti-
vation of brotherly love, features absent from the revived Graeco-Roman
religion.

The greatest lack of Roman polytheism had been that of any assurance
of immortality, although the Orphics and the Eleusinian mysteries had
supplied it for centuries to the Greeks. Even before the Augustan revival
few Romans of standing believed that their gods interfered with human
affairs [84] and, as to the hereafter, Rome had evolved as yet nothing higher

[81] Sir James Frazer, *Golden Bough*, 1 vol. ed. (New York, 1922), p. 357.
[82] *Das antike Mysterienwesen in seinem Einfluss auf das Christentum* (Göttingen,
1894), pp. 35f.
[83] *Oriental Religions in Roman Paganism* (Chicago, 1911), pp. 28, 44. See also the
great work of J. F. Toutain, *Les cultes païens dans l'empire romaine* (Paris, 1911), I, 20.
[84] Cf. W. Warde Fowler, *Roman Ideas of Deity in the Last Century of the Republic*
(London, 1914).

than the wretched cult of the *Di Manes* already discussed. Even this belief had long been abandoned by the educated classes, although Lucretius
shows by his opposition that it was still believed by the common man. A
few representative examples from the late Republic and early Empire will
show the absence of belief in a life hereafter. Cicero, although he denounced the Epicureans in favor of the Stoics, remained basically agnostic,
like his friend the jurist Servius Sulpicius Rufus, as we may see from the
latter's letter of consolation addressed to the orator from Athens in 45 B.C.
on receiving Cicero's lament at the death of Tullia.[85] Caesar held the
Epicurean doctrine that "death ends all mortal ills and leaves no room for
sorrow or pity." [86] Sallust, who died 34 B.C., in the passage quoted, said,
"Beyond the grave there is no opportunity for either anxiety or joy." Catullus, Rome's greatest lyric poet who died 54 B.C., said to his Lesbia: "For
us, when the short light has once set, remains to be slept the sleep of one
unbroken night." [87] Lucretius, who died 55 B.C., and the Epicureans generally gloried in the belief that death ended all. And in the early Empire,
Pliny the Elder, who died in his zeal for science during the eruption of
Vesuvius (A.D. 79), said: "neither body nor mind possesses any sensation
after death" and called such thoughts the "fictions of childish absurdity." [88]
Around the close of the first century Rome's great castigator of vice, Juvenal (?60–140), said that not even boys then believed there were "manes and
kingdoms below ground, and punt-holes, and Stygian pools black with
frogs, and all those thousands crossing over in a single bark." [89] In sepul-
chral inscriptions from the early Empire doubts are frequently expressed.[90]
Many more such examples could be cited against the belief in a future life
which has been called "the noblest single offering that human Reason has
yet laid on the altar of human hope." [91] It is, then, no wonder that Romans of lesser mold readily went from the cold religion of the State to the
eschatological mystery-cults all of which, like Christianity, taught that life
here conditioned life hereafter.

Thus we have seen that the paganism of the Roman Empire included
various paganisms which existed side by side with the old State-cult revived
by Augustus and the imperial one which officially superseded it. Throughout the Empire the old Graeco-Roman gods, long over-shadowed by foreign
mystery-cults, philosophies, and Christianity, still lived on but, after a final
show of power under Julian, with ever diminishing prestige—"a mosaic to

[85] *Ad familiares* 4:5, 6. Here Rufus questions "if there be any consciousness even
among the dead." Similarly, in Cicero's lost treatise *De consolatione,* he tried to persuade himself for a time that his daughter still lived in the world of spirits.
[86] Quoted by Sallust *Catiline* 51:20.
[87] 5:6; tr. by F. W. Cornish, *L.C.L.* (1935).
[88] *Historia Naturalis* 7:188.
[89] *Satires* 2:149f.; tr. by G. G. Ramsay, *L.C.L.* (1918).
[90] E.g. Nos. 191 (from Mutina), 214 (from Aquileia), 428 (from Stabiae); Carmina
Latina epigraphica of the *Latin Anthology,* ed. by Fr. Bücheler (Lipsiae, 1885–96), Vol.
II; cf. Fowler, *op. cit.,* p. 26, n. 2.
[91] Sir William D. Geddes, *The Phaedo of Plato* (2nd ed.; London, 1885), pp. xxvii–
xxviii.

which traditions, superstitions, poetry, and a general inquiry lend their share." [92]

Its final intellectual refuge was in a small group of aristocrats, chiefly at Rome, who still clung to it in the face of Christian victory, since it was part of the classical heritage to which they were still devoted. The old titles "augur" and "quindecimvir" were still kept like those of "consul" and "tribune" but with little of their former meanings left. Once supreme over the late Republic and early Empire Graeco-Roman polytheism was vanquished, like the Oriental cults and Greek philosophies, by Christianity when Constantine favored the latter. It had, indeed, received deathblows when Aurelian (270–275) installed the Palmyrene *Sol invictus* on the Capitoline as "protector of his Empire" with its pontiffs and priests rivalling those of the Roman gods, and when Diocletian and his former colleagues in 307 erected an altar in the ancient Celtic town of Carnuntum on the Danube to Mithra as "protector of their Empire." These two events marked not only the culmination of Oriental influence at Rome, but also the doom of what was left of the ancient Roman religion. Still the subsequent edicts of Constantine and Constantius, which denounced Roman rites of sacrifice, divination and magic, temples and altars, show that there was still some life in the indigenous faith, decrees kept up even after Theodosius had thought he had destroyed it. Later remnants of the ancient polytheism, reduced to superstition, survived among the countryfolk as a sort of cryptic Christianity. For the Italian peasants still observed in addition to the Christian rites some of the pagan ones. They still revered haunted springs, groves, and mountain-tops, kept some of the old festivals, especially those connected with husbandry, and worshiped the old guardians of hearth and home even as their distant ancestors had done, quite irrespective of imperial decrees. Many of these festivals proved recalcitrant to the advancing Church which was compelled to accept them. A good example was the festival of the *Lupercalia* in honor of Faunus (under the name Lupercus), perhaps the oldest in Rome and revived by Augustus. It was transformed after a long struggle into the Christian Festival of Purification in 494 by Pope Gelasius I.

[92] W. K. Boyd, *Ecclesiastical Edicts of the Theodosian Code* (New York, 1905), p. 54.

Chapter II

MYSTERY-RELIGIONS AND KINDRED PHILOSOPHIES

MYSTERY-RELIGIONS entered Italy in such numbers that Juvenal [1] said that "the Syrian Orontes poured into the Tiber," and he might have added the Nile, Halys, and Euphrates as well, since the cults came not only from Syria, but from Egypt, Anatolia, and Persia. Out of the many which came Romeward we shall discuss only four of the more important: the Great Mother of Phrygia, Cybele; Isis of Egypt; the Syrian Goddess or Atargatis and, most important of all, Mithra, the Persian god of light. As there were few native Roman mysteries these mystery-religions were in no sense an evolution from Roman religion, but represent rather the yielding of the old Roman spirit to superior Oriental thought and practice. In the words of Josef Strzygowski, the Viennese historian of art, "the West expires in the embrace of the East." [2]

CYBELE

The first Oriental religious invader of Italy was the Anatolian fertility goddess Cybele, "mother of the gods," whose rites from immemorial antiquity had centered at Pessinus in the southwestern corner of Galatia on the frontier of Phrygia. There, legends of her and her love for Attis had long been current. Her wild worship was celebrated on the wooded mountain-tops by her attendant *Corybantes,* and when the tempest roared it was believed to be the sound of her chariot being drawn by lions and panthers. On her way westward she became identified among the Greeks of Asia Minor with Rhea, another "mother of the gods," a deity of Cretan origin localized also on mainland Greece. Accompanied by her frenzied priests, the Galli, Cybele reached Rome in 204 B.C. when Hannibal, still unbeaten, was making a stand in the mountain-fastnesses of Bruttium. P. Cornelius Scipio Nasica, judged by the Senate to be "the best citizen in the State," and matrons of Rome received her black-stone fetish at Ostia and with great ceremony carried it to Rome and ensconced it in the temple of Victory on the Palatine. She thus became the earliest alien deity allowed within the city. Thereupon the crops became plentiful and the following year Hannibal left Italy to meet Scipio Africanus at Zama (202 B.C.) in Numidia and Cybele was accepted officially as a part of the Roman pantheon. By 191 B.C. she had her own shrine on the Palatine and her own festival, the *Megalensia,* commemorative of her adoption. Her orgiastic, un-Roman rites, however, were soon found to be a menace to morality, and

---

[1] *Satires* 3:62.
[2] *Kleinasien, ein Neuland der Kunstgeschichte* (Leipzig, 1903), p. 234.

her worship became isolated and citizens, for a time, were forbidden to become her priests or even to participate in her mysteries.

Her cult, as it developed in Rome, included that of Attis, another Asia Minor deity, the two symbolizing the male and female elements in nature. In the legend current at Pessinus, Attis had been unfaithful to the goddess who drove him mad so that he mutilated himself beneath a pine tree into which his spirit passed while his blood was transformed into violets (the aetiological explanation of why a pine log wreathed with violets was carried in Cybele's procession by the "Tree-bearers" or *Dendrophori*). Catullus' "Lament of Attis" (LXIII) is the chief important surviving Latin literary work inspired by Cybele's worship. It presents a vivid picture of the frenzy engendered by her rites, the swing of the "galliambic" verses (50–75) —the meter supposed to have been used by the chanting Galli—replete with alliterations, repetitions, and strange compounds impressing even the Latinless auditor of the present day. We also have a picture of the goddess' Roman procession during the spring celebration of the *Megalensia* in Lucretius' poem (2:66–632), in which he speaks of her image being carried along to the music of cymbals, flutes, and horns, and her path bestrewn with flowers, while largesses of silver and copper were made to her priests.

Her worship, as is attested by epigraphical and numismatic evidence,[3] spread over Italy, North Africa, Spain and Gaul, and especially along the Rhine and Danube frontiers of the Empire. Her final shrine in Rome, the *Phrygianum,* was across the Tiber near the site of the present Basilica of St. Peter. Claudius was the first emperor to release the restrictions placed on her cult over two centuries before and then, like other such Eastern religions, it came under the supervision of the college of *Quindecimviri* in charge of the Sibylline Books, while her cult affairs were under the immediate management of an *archigallus* and a high-priestess. The Senate now defined the cult's privileges allowing citizens to become its priests, and Cybele henceforth became one of the chief objects of imperial worship and a rival of Christianity. During the third-century crisis her worship remained strong and continued important through the fourth—the last appearance of her processions at Rome occurring in 394 under the usurper Eugenius. At the beginning of the fifth century it still flourished in Carthage where the youthful Augustine saw her processions of priests with "dampened hair, whitened faces and affected gait." In all, the cult of Cybele flourished in the West for some six centuries.

Her annual festival was held in March, when the legend of Attis was rehearsed in a passion-play. On the Ides a bull was sacrificed and a procession, led by the *archigallus* and "Reed-bearers" or *Cannephori,* passed through the streets in commemoration of Cybele's finding of Attis. After a week's intermission, on the twenty-second, a pine tree was felled and the log, prepared with woolen fillets and violets to represent a corpse, was carried by the *Dendrophori* to Cybele's temple. On the twenty-third the log was buried and great lamentation followed, accompanied by the blaring of

³ For the latter, see H. Mattingly and E. A. Sydenham, *Roman Imperial Coinage* (London, 1923–38), IV, Pt. 2.

trumpets, commemorative of Attis' death.   On the twenty-fourth (*dies san-guinis* or "day of blood") the high-priest drew blood from his arm over the altar while the inferior priests in a frenzied dance flagellated themselves and gashed their bodies with knives to show their participation in the sorrows of the god.   Perhaps, although the evidence is not clear, certain of the initiates may have then followed Attis' example by sacrificing their virility.[4]   On the following night, the twenty-fifth, Attis' tomb was found to be empty and then the joyous *Hilaria,* a carnival of license and merry-making, ensued in honor of the god's resurrection, i.e., the rebirth of spring. The emotional strain of two days of lamentation and joy made the twenty-sixth a day of rest (*requietio*).   On the following day the festival closed with Cybele's silver statue carried in procession on an ox-cart through the Porta Capena to its *lavatio* in the brook Almo below the city walls where the *Quindecimviri* bathed image, cart, and cult-articles and then brought them back to her temple.   The remainder of the day was given over to a joyous carnival.   Of the splendor of the mystic drama of Attis' death and rebirth A. D. Nock has said that "the drama of nature's death and life has nowhere found a more moving expression in ritual." [5]

While the rites of initiation were mostly secret we know the characteristic one, communion with the deity through a bath in bulls' blood.   This was the impressive *taurobolium,* a rite of rejuvenation and symbolic baptism which cleansed the initiate from sin and caused him "to be born again," and one whose performance was so costly it was borne by the brotherhood in common.[6]   Its Anatolian background is obscure, Cumont deriving it from the Cappadocian cult of Ma or that of Anahitá, the latter identified with the Roman Bellona, a war-like deity revered by soldiers,[7] while H. Hepding has derived it from Phrygia.[8]   The earliest Italian appearance of the *taurobolium* was in the cult of Juno Caelestis, a Romanized version of the Phoenician Astarte which was introduced into Carthage long after the Third Punic War, while its first mention in Western Europe is an inscription from Puteoli dated A.D. 134.[9]   In connection with Cybele it was celebrated in honor of Antoninus Pius (138–161) at Lugdunum (Lyon) in Gaul.   Prudentius, the first important Christian poet, of the fourth century, in his *Peristephanum* gives us an extended account of the ceremony of which he seems to have been an eyewitness.[10]   Prudentius detested the rite because of its affinity in a redemptive way to Calvary of

[4] Reasons for such emasculations have been discussed by H. J. Rose, *Classical Quarterly,* XVIII (1924), 11f., and A. D. Nock, in his "Eunuchs in Ancient Religion," *Archiv für Religionswissenschaft,* XXIII (1925), 25f.

[5] *Cambridge Ancient History,* XII, 423.   Cited hereafter as *C.A.H.*

[6] *Corpus Inscriptionum Latinarum,* XII, No. 4321.   Cited hereafter as *C.I.L.*

[7] *Textes et monuments figurés relatives aux mystères de Mithra* (Bruxelles, 1896–99), I, 194f.

[8] *Attis, seine Mythen und sein Kult* (Giessen, 1903), p. 201.

[9] *C.I.L.,* X, No. 1596.

[10] X, 1011f.   For an account of Prudentius, see Glover, *Life and Letters of the Fourth Century,* chap. xi.

which he imagined it was a travesty, while some modern writers, e.g. Dill [11] regard it as the nearest pagan approach to Christianity. According to Prudentius a trench was dug over which a platform of planks perforated with holes was laid, on to which a garlanded bull was led and slaughtered, its blood drenching the initiate below who, clad in toga and covered with fillets and ornaments, was symbolically buried in a pit. He later emerged, his sins now washed away and (to carry out the idea of his rebirth) he was given milk, like a child, to drink.[12] The efficacy of the baptism lasted twenty years when it might be reënacted and the initiate became *in aeternum renatus*.[13] Sometimes the *taurobolium* alternated with a *criobolium* or "ram's baptism." The last *taurobolium* at Rome occurred in the *Phrygianum* in 396.

Cybele's cult, despite its un-Roman and even revolting practices, enjoyed a special position among other Eastern religions during the Empire since it was under political control and officially accepted as part of the civic cult, its holidays having a place on the pontiffs' calendar.[14] In the West its bloody rites were transformed into a symbol of spiritual redemption. But one of its worst features seems to have been retained, the simulation of a sacred marriage when the catechumen was bodily united with Cybele. The great appeal of the cult was the idea of the rebirth of a god who has died which it brought to the Romans for the first time. In addition there was appeal in the figure of a goddess who was a merciful mother bringing to her votaries the assurance that they, like Attis, would live again. At the beginning of the *Hilaria* the priest anointed the lips of the initiate with oil and chanted the sacred Phrygian hymn: "Be of good cheer, ye mystae of the god who has been saved: to you likewise there will come salvation for your trouble." [15]

ISIS

The great religious gift of Hellenistic Egypt to Rome was the associated cult of the three gods: Serapis, official god of the Greek rulers and center of the State worship at Alexandria; Isis, a survival from the ancient Egyptian priestly caste to whom many ancient religious ideas were attached; and her son Harpocrates (the older Horus) god of the peasant fellaheen, the three forming a triad. Their interrelated worship was spread rapidly over the Roman Empire by Egyptian commerce and became one of its chief Oriental faiths. The cults of the two deities, Isis and Serapis, reached Italy simultaneously and they were often worshiped in the same precincts and their priests taught similar doctrines.

[11] *Op. cit.*, p. 555.

[12] S. Sallustius in his *De diis et mundo*, composed under Julian: tr. by G. Murray in *Four Stages of Greek Religion* (New York, 1912), pp. 185f.

[13] *C.I.L.*, VI, Nos. 510, 512.

[14] In Philocalus' calendar of the middle of the fourth Christian century (discussed in Excursus I, below), the opening day of the festival was marked *canna* (reed) *intrat* and the twenty-second of March as *arbor* (tree) *intrat*.

[15] So Firmicus Maternus *De errore profanum religionum*, p. 22. It was addressed to Constantius and Constans.

Curiously we know little that is certain about the origin of Serapis, but more about that of the older Isis.   His name is non-Egyptian and probably Babylonian,[16] though it bears a superficial resemblance to Osorapis (User-hapi), the Greek name for Apis, the bull deity whose mummies were entombed for centuries in huge monolithic granite sarcophagi at Memphis (excavated by Mariette in 1851).   His worship was intended to enlist the common homage of Greeks and Egyptians, but the element Osiris in the worship of Serapis (through the probable agency of Osorapis) led to the latter's eventual replacement in Egypt by Serapis.   Some scholars have appealed to later inscriptions to show that the name Serapis was a corruption of Osiris-Apis, Osiris being the ancient Egyptian deity of the underworld to whom Apis was assimilated, and especially to a bilingual one of the time of Ptolemy Philopator (221–205 B.C.),[17] although U. Wilcken has contended that the parallel appearance of Serapis and Osorapis in inscriptions means an independent origin for each.[18]

Both Plutarch [19] and Tacitus [20] recount how Ptolemy Soter, founder of the Greek monarchy in Egypt, was told in a dream to fetch the colossal statue of Hades from Sinope on the Black Sea to Alexandria.   There it filled the *cella* of the Serapeum built to receive it and was pronounced by the committee, composed of the Egyptian priest-historian, Manetho, and the Eumolpid, Timotheus of Eleusis, appointed to fuse ideas in the formation of a new deity, to be the equivalent of the revered Egyptian bull-god the dead Apis, assimilated to Osiris, king of the lower world.   Thus the creation of Serapis as a political device of the clever Ptolemy to unite his people, Greek and Egyptian, is of interest in the history of religion as a man-made deity.   Others, however, have regarded Serapis as older than Ptolemy since Plutarch [21] and Arrian,[22] late biographers of Alexander, mention for the first time a temple of Serapis in Babylon consulted alone, according to the authentic court diary, on behalf of the conqueror during his last illness, a temple which his general Ptolemy must have seen.   This may have been either a "traveling" shrine, which followed Alexander to Asia and was later ascribed to Serapis, or one of a similarly named Chaldean deity Serepsi, i.e., the Babylonian Ea, King of the Deep Sea and father of Marduk,[23] but it only adds difficulty to the problem of why, in Ptolemy Soter's vision, the god had to reach Alexandria from Sinope.

Whatever the origin of Serapis the cult spread rapidly over Egypt since Aristides, a Greek rhetorician of the second century, says (45:32) that there were in his day forty-two shrines of the god, the chief ones at Alexandria,

---

[16] H. P. Weitz in W. H. Roscher's *Ausführliches Lexikon der gr. und röm. Mythologie* (Leipzig, 1889–1937), *s.v.* "Serapis."

[17] *Inscriptiones Graecae*, No. 4969.   Cited hereafter as *I.G.*

[18] In *Archiv für Papyrusforschung*, III (1906), 249f. ("Sarapis und Osiris Apis").

[19] *De Iside et Osiride*, chap. 28, 361F–362B.

[20] *Histories*, IV, 83f.

[21] *Life of Alexander*, chap. 76.

[22] *Anabasis of Alexander*, 7:26.

[23] See C. F. Lehman, "Sarapis contra Oserapis" in *Klio, Beiträge zur alten Geschacite*, IV (1904), 396.   Cited hereafter as *Klio.*

Memphis, and Abydos. The ruins of the Serapeum at Alexandria have been found in the mound now marked by Diocletian's Pillar—wrongly called Pompey's—in the oldest part of the city (Rhacotis). It was the center of a congeries of buildings in connection with the great Museum.[24] The Egyptian form of the worship had a beautiful ritual and many devotees, but apart from teaching immortality had little to recommend it. In Greece and Rome Serapis became syncretized with many deities, G. Dietrich calling such syncretism the chief event in ancient *theocrasia*.[25] But Ptolemy's new religion, like his attempt to Hellenize Egypt, did not last long since the religious ideas incorporated into Serapis were soon absorbed in Egyptian ideas and by the third Christian century the Greek colonists in Egypt were thoroughly fused with Egyptians. Thereafter the Egyptian deities again came into their own.

Here we are more interested in Serapis' consort Isis, Egyptian Ese, most famous of Egyptian goddesses, already known from the "Pyramid" texts as sister-wife of Osiris and sister of the evil Set (Typhon), power of darkness who slew Osiris. She, in great grief, searched for her husband's body and buried his scattered limbs, the search symbolizing the struggle between civilization and barbarism, as Plutarch's story (*op. cit.*, chap 27:361D) shows. Her cult absorbed all other feminine cults of Egypt during the New Kingdom (beginning 1580 B.C.). Herodotus, in the middle of the fifth century B.C., called her Demeter and still in his day the most revered deity in Egypt. In later times her chief center in the Delta was at Bubastis (Tell Basta) on the Pelusiac branch of the Nile, where she was worshiped as the deity of motherhood and queen of the dead. But her chief temple in the Ptolemaic and Roman periods was on the island of Philae in the Nile in Upper Egypt which was founded by Ptolemy Philadelphus and his wife Arsinoë in 286 B.C. and remained one of the last refuges of paganism in Egypt to the middle of the fifth century,[26] and was not closed till the time of Justinian in the sixth, long after her Roman worship was banned. She was identified by the Greeks and Romans with a bewildering number of other goddesses.

Her worship entered the ports of Asia Minor, the Aegean Isles, Greece and Italy. It reached Syracuse in Sicily in the reign of Agathocles who died in 289 B.C., and Puteoli in South Italy by the close of the second century B.C. This was the chief Italian port in Hellenistic and early imperial days where St. Paul later landed on his way to Rome. She had temples in Pompeii, Herculaneum, and Stabiae (Castellamare) near Naples. In the ruins of Pompeii skeletons of her priests who could not escape Vesuvius in 79 have been found. The earliest Isiac *collegium* in Rome dates from the time of Sulla (80 B.C.). The cult, like that of Cybele, long remained obscure, the Senate vainly trying to check its advance because of its loose morality and un-Roman emotionalism. Thus, in the decade 58–48 B.C.,

[24] See G. Botti, *L'Acropole d'Alexandrie et le Serapéum* (Alexandria, 1906).
[25] *Kleine Schriften* (Leipzig, 1911), p. 159.
[26] *I.G.*, III, 4945–46.

its altars and statues were repeatedly overthrown by the consuls, but set up again by her votaries. In 43 B.C., the triumvirs, to curry favor with its worshipers, planned a temple at Rome,[27] which was not built till eighty years later under Caligula on the Campus Martius, i.e., outside the *pomerium*.

Tibullus, the lyric poet, when on his way East with his patron Messala in 30 B.C. fell ill at Corcyra and wrote his Delia in Rome to intercede with Isis on his behalf. He mentions the baths and propitiatory rites of her worshipers, their robes of linen and their sleeping apart in her temples, listening to the peculiar metallic rattle (*sistrum*) of the priests, and reciting her praises night and day.[28] His is the earliest Roman account of the cult. It was in the same year that Augustus destroyed all Serapea within the walls, and two years later the Senate decreed that Isis should have no shrine within the *pomerium*. Tiberius in A.D. 19 destroyed her temple and crucified her priests,[29] but his successor Caligula established her cult in his palace, in whose ruins Isiac decorations have been found.[30] Josephus says the Emperor donned female garb when participating in the mysteries.[31]

Soon there were shrines wherever Roman armies went. Traces of them have been found from Africa to Britain and from Spain to the Black Sea. The Flavians, under whom her real importance in the West began, Hadrian, Commodus, Caracalla, called "lover of Serapis," and Diocletian all favored Isis and Serapis. The burning of the Serapeum in Alexandria in 391 was a severe blow to the cult of Serapis as well as of Isis in Egypt and elsewhere. Isis had her last procession at Rome three years later, the same year which witnessed the last one of Cybele. Rufinus, chief minister of State under Theodosius the Great and his son Arcadius, boasted that he had destroyed *caput ipsum idolatriae*. Isis had influenced the Greek world for eight centuries from her first appearance in the Piraeus in the early fourth century B.C. and, with Serapis, the Roman Empire for five.

While Isis' mysteries perished with her last initiates we may recover some idea of the devotion her cult aroused from Book XI of *The Golden Ass* of Apuleius [32]—ten days of ascetic preparation, baptism, and processions during November and again in March—the winter festival being a mingling of grief at Osiris' death and joy at the finding of his body, the spring (*navigium Isidis*) marking the opening of navigation. The descriptions of the rites seem to have been based on those which the author had seen performed near Corinth. He describes how a certain Lucius, who had been turned into an ass by an enchantress, was restored to human form by the

---

[27] Cassius Dio, *Roman History*, 47:15.

[28] 1:3, 23f.

[29] Suetonius, *Life of Tiberius*, chap. 26.

[30] Cumont in *Revue d'histoire et de littérature religieuse*, New Series, CXIV (1936), 127.

[31] *Antiq.*, XIX:1, 5.

[32] *Metamorphoseon seu de asino aureo*, XI, 9–16, *L.C.L.* (1915). It is a second-century humorous and romantic satire on the hypocrisy and debauchery of Oriental priests and frauds of magicians and jugglers.

aid of Isis whose priest he finally became.   One moonlight night on the shore at Cenchreae (port of Corinth) he prays to the "Queen of Heaven," falls asleep and is visited by a venerable form with her hair wreathed in flowers and a *sistrum* in her hand, which rises from the sea.   She repeats her various names—substantiated by a late inscription from the island of Ios (Nio) in the Cyclades—ending with what she calls her true name "Queen Isis." [33]   She then tells how she had created heaven and earth, laws and justice, and in short everything beautiful in the life of mortals.   Plutarch (9:354C) also mentions an inscription in her temple at Sais on the Rosetta branch of the Nile wherein she boasts: "I am all that has been, is, and shall be, and my veil no mortal yet has lifted."

Thus, like Serapis, Isis is an excellent example of *theocrasia* which borrowed not only rituals such as the *taurobolium* but myths and symbols from various cults.   The Greeks and Romans finally imagined that all foreign pantheons contained the same deities as their own, the names alone being different.   Thus the *Corpus Hermeticum* of the Hermetic cult, an amalgam of Egyptian, Greek, and Chaldean religions, cosmologies, and philosophies, reflects all ideas and practices of the Graeco-Roman period ranging from spirituality to magic, Hermes Trismegistus, Egyptian Thoth (or Tehuti), being a depository for all magical knowledge.

At Isis' November festival a mystical drama, the "Finding of Osiris," was enacted in Rome as it had been for ages at Abydos on the Nile.[34]   It pictured Osiris' murder, Isis' grief and wanderings in search of his body, Horus' triumph over Set and the resurrection of Osiris, as we learn from Plutarch's account (*op. cit.* 12–20:355D–358E) which Egyptian monuments confirmed.   The mourning of priests and initiates turned to joy when Isis succeeded in her quest, the joy expressed in banquets and games. Osiris became the ideal of manhood, and by reverencing his rites under the name of Serapis mortal men would also live hereafter, not as tenuous shades in Hades, but in possession of mind and body in heaven.   It was this doctrine of immortality that principally helped Egypt for a time to conquer Rome religiously.   Isis, at first, in Italy was so indulgent to human frailty that Juvenal could speak of *Isiacae sacraria lenae*,[35] in reference to youths frequenting her shrines in quest of amatory adventure.   But later on she became the exemplar of virtue, exacting of her devotees strenuous penances, some of which Juvenal mentions (6:522f.), such as breaking the ice on the Tiber on a winter morning, plunging into its waters, and crawling naked and shivering on bleeding knees back to her temple on "the field of Tarquin" (i.e., the Campus Martius).   He adds that, if Isis so ordered, her followers would journey to the confines of Egypt and fetch water even from Meroë (in Aethiopia) with which to sprinkle her chapel.   He also adds that her priests—who personified her dog-faced attendant Anubis,

[33] *The Golden Ass*, XI:4.   For the 2nd or 3rd century inscr. from Ios, *I.G.*, XII, 5, 1, No. 14.   A long list of syncretic names is found in an invocation to her in *Oxyrrhynchus Papyri* ed. by Grenfell and Hunt (London, 1898–1929), XI, No. 1380.

[34] H. Schaefer, *Die Mysterien des Osiris in Abydos unter König Sesostis III* (Leipzig, 1904).

[35] *Satires* 6:489.

messenger of the goddess to guide the souls of the dead to the lower world like the Greek *Hermes Psychopompos* (the two names combined forming the hybrid *Hermanubis*)—ridiculed the Romans for mourning Osiris. Her women devotees kept their initiation robe for a burial shroud in which to meet the judgment of Osiris.

It is not difficult, then, to understand why the Romans, at first repelled by the strange rites of Isis, were later attracted by them; the ordinary woman, by the splendid processions and the novelty of what she saw; the educated, by the antiquity and impressiveness of the ritual, the beautiful drama, the tenderness of Isis, her rigorous rules of abstinence and purification, communion with deity, separation of her clergy from the world, and especially the final judgment and promise of a blissful hereafter with her, here emphasized more than in any other of her sister religions. She, as the "universal woman" and "queen of heaven" also attracted men as well as women. Her ritual bore a marked resemblance to that of early Christianity, as Sir James Frazer has pointed out:

Indeed the stately ritual with its shaven and tonsured priests, its matins and vespers, its tinkling music, its baptisms as aspersions of holy water, its solemn processions, its jewelled images of the mother of God, presented many points of similarity to the pomp and ceremonies of Catholicism.[36]

Isis was, then, the *mater dolorosa* of paganism who sympathized especially with mothers in their sorrows and afflictions. In his prayer Lucius says:

[Thou] by thy bounty and grace nourishest all the world, and bearest a great affection to the adversities of the miserable as a loving mother. . . . Thou art she that puttest away all storms and dangers from men's life by stretching forth thy right hand . . . and appeasest the great tempests of fortune. . . .[37]

It is, then, only natural that some students have seen her influence as "mother of sorrows" and "mother of Horus," in whom the Greeks saw their grief-stricken Demeter searching for her daughter Persephone raped by Pluto, on the Christian concept of Mary. The motif of mother and child appears in many statuettes which have been found in her ruined shrines on the Seine, Rhine, and Danube, and which the early Christians mistook for the Madonna and Child, and little wonder since it is still difficult to differentiate between the two types.

The epithet "Mother of God" (*Theotokos*) as applied to Mary seems to have been used at first by Alexandrian theologians at the close of the third century, although it does not appear in any extant writing of that period. It became common in the fourth, being used by Eusebius, Athanasius, Gregory of Nazianzus in Cappadocia and others; Gregory saying that "the man who does not believe Mary was the *Theotokos* has no part in God." [38] Epiphanius, bishop of Constantia on Cyprus (367–403), in his *Panarion* (Breadbasket), a sort of "medicine chest" of remedies for the eighty heresies

[36] *Adonis, Attis and Osiris* (2nd ed.; London), p. 347.
[37] *The Golden Ass*, XI, 25.
[38] *Orat.* LI, 738.

listed in it,[39] was the first to denounce Christian women for making a goddess of Mary and offering cakes to her on the altar. By about 427 the name *Theotokos* became the center of a dispute between Orthodox Christians and the followers of Nestorius, bishop of Constantinople (428–431). He denied her divinity and declared that there were two persons fused in Jesus Christ—God the Son (or "Word") and the man Jesus who died on the Cross who alone was Mary's son, while ordinary Christians believed God and man were fused in one person with two natures. In a sermon delivered about 430 Proelus, patriarch of Constantinople, spoke of Mary as "the holy Virgin" and "Mother of God," and at the opening of the Council of Ephesus in 431 Cyril of Alexandria spoke of her as "mother and virgin." The matter was debated at that Council when Mary was officially declared "Mother of God" and Nestorius was deposed. The title meant that Mary was the "mother" not of the godhead, but only of one "Person" in it, who is also God. Even Mary's epithet, *Stella maris* revered by sailors, has been derived from Isis' *Navigium*, in which she was fused with Artemis Dictynna, "of the nets," whose cult ultimately goes back to a Minoan origin. Despite Isiac similarities to the deified Mary, it seems better, however, to explain them not as borrowings, but as parallel beliefs.

ATARGATIS

Rome was also indebted to Syria for several deities. The religion of Syria never displayed the unity of those of Anatolia, Egypt, or Persia, and her unorganized deities reflected the political disunity of the country where for centuries Canaanites, Hittites, Aramaeans, Philistines, Phoenicians, Hebrews, and others remained more distinct than in other Near-East areas, and all tenaciously kept their cults intact. After being subject to Assyria, Chaldea, Persia, and Macedonia, Syria finally extended its name over the vast area of the Seleucids who, from their capital at Antioch in the distant West, built by the founder of the dynasty, Alexander's general Seleucus Nicator (312–280 B.C.), ruled for a time over most of the conqueror's Asiatic domain. We know relatively little of these Syrian religions in which male deities generally took precedence over female, until they began to move westward in the late Republic and added characteristic features to Roman paganism.

The first Syrian deity to reach Greece, Italy, and the West was the fish-goddess Atargatis of Hierapolis, formerly Bambyce (Mabus or Membidj) near the Euphrates, along with her consort, the "storm" baal Hadad, a Syrian deity adored as Rimmon at Damascus and also known as Addu Rammon in Syria and Babylonia.[40] Again we have no direct evidence

---

[39] Based on Irenaeus and the lost heresies compiled by his pupil Hippolytus of the early third century.

[40] The compound Hadadrimmon appears as a place-name in the valley of Canaanite Megiddo in Zechariah (12:11), where the prophet speaks of a "lamentation." While older writers connected this with the death of Josiah who was there slain by Necho of Egypt in 609 B.C., it is now more generally referred to Adonis or Tammuz, the allusion being to mourning common at his festivals. Again, it may merely be connected with the pomegranate (*rimmon*).

that her cult—although it was favored by certain emperors, Suetonius telling us that Nero was an initiate into her mysteries, the one Oriental religion which he favored but soon abandoned [41]—ever became a part of the
State-religion of Rome.　But there is ample evidence that two Syrian baals
stood at the top of the Roman pantheon for short seasons as we shall note
later.　The Greeks, notably Lucian, usually called her "the Syrian Goddess" (Latin *Deasura*).　The etymology of the name Atargatis is a compound of two Syrian deities, Athtar (contracted into Atar), the Aramaic
name for Phoenician Astarte, Babylonian Ishtar and Old Testament Ashtoreth, and the Palmyrene Athe ("opportune time").　This has led to con-
fusing her with these goddesses, especially with Astarte, but only the names
and not the personalities were identical, since Astarte and Atargatis had
separate shrines at Ascalon.　With the waning of Semitic power and the
cult of Ishtar-Astarte, the leading features of the latter, life-giving power of
water and fecundity of fish, were transferred to Atargatis who replaced her.

One of her two main shrines in Syria was at Philistine Ashkelon (Ascalon) where her temple stood near a lake.　This is the town in which Herodotus (1:105) places the temple of Heavenly Aphrodite which may have
been a successor to that of Atargatis.　The second shrine was at Hierapolis
which Lucian called the largest and wealthiest in Syria for it attracted
pilgrims from all over Western Asia.　In connection with both temples fish
were sacred.　At Ascalon the goddess was represented as a mermaid according to Lucian,[42] with the body of a woman ending in the tail of a fish.
According to the historian Diodorus [43] Derceto—a modified form of Atargatis—cast herself in shame into the water because, through Aphrodite's
inspiration, she had fallen in love with a youthful devotee by whom she
became mother of the Assyrian queen Semiramis, and was changed into
a fish; but Hyginus, fabulist of Augustus' time,[44] says she was saved by a
fish from drowning.　Her bathing-place was shown at the source of the
Chaboras (the Khabur canal),[45] a Mesopotamian tributary of the Euphrates,
where also fish were sacred to her.　All such myths were merely aetiological explanations of Syrian abstinence from fish-eating.

Atargatis was worshiped as the founder of social and religious life,
goddess of generation and fertility, and she and Hadad were regarded as
protectors of communities.　By the combination of various such powers
she ultimately became a great nature goddess like Cybele.　Her great
temple at Hierapolis, restored by Nicator's second wife Stratonice (according to Lucian, chaps. 28–29, 39–41), harbored within its precincts domestic
and wild animals.　In the court there was a row of huge *phalli*, symbolic
of her generative powers, while inside the temple there was a statue of the

[41] Suetonius, *Life of Nero*, chap. 56.
[42] *De dea Syria*, chaps. 14, 25.
[43] In his *Historical Library*, 2:4.
[44] In his *De astronomia* 2:30.　This work, based on Eratosthenes, is an abridgment of
the original, made in the late second century.
[45] The Chebar of the book of Ezekiel (1:1, and *passim*).

goddess standing on lions, its head covered with jewels (32). Her priests, like Cybele's *Galli*, were eunuchs and her temples, like those of Aphrodite with whom the Greeks identified her, were defiled by sacred prostitution and the sacrifice of both adults and children until the practice was banned by Hadrian.

About all we know of the cult comes from the essay of the Syrian satirist Lucian, *De dea Syria*, who knew of it personally (53), and from the *Golden Ass* of Apuleius already mentioned (8:25f.). The latter called her "all-powerful" (*omnipotens*) and "all-productive" (*omniparens*) and describes her priesthood. But neither the Greek nor the Roman writer fully understood her rites. Lucian records (50–52) how on festal days her eunuch-priests, "painted youths," formed processions along the roads near her temples with the statue of the goddess riding in a car and how they shrieked and whirled in the dance to the music of flutes until they swooned, and how in their frenzy they scourged each other and cut themselves with knives, their blood bespattering the curious onlookers. However, he pictures them sane enough to accept food and money and adds that they eked out their livelihood by thievery and prophesying.

We first hear of the worship of Atargatis in Italy from the prisoners taken in the war with Antiochus the Great (192–188 B.C.) and sold into slavery. This was also, probably, the earliest appearance in Italy of Chaldaei, the Babylonian priests who practiced astrology. After the downfall of Corinth in 146 B.C. and the waning of her commerce there was a regular traffic in Syrian slaves at Delos and it was through such slaves and merchants that the Greeks and Romans learned to know the goddess. The first Servile Revolt in Sicily (134–132 B.C.) centering at Enna and Tauromenium was led by a Syrian religious mystic who gathered some 200,000 slaves under his banner before they were finally beaten by the consul P. Papirius. This indicates the hold of the cult on the alien countryfolk of that island. During the Empire such slaves worked in the fields and houses of well-to-do Romans, and Syrian merchants were to be found in various Mediterranean ports, especially in Ostia, Naples, and Puteoli. A temple was dedicated to Atargatis on the Janiculum across the Tiber which stood until the close of antiquity and in whose ruins inscriptions of Hadad have been found.

Fish were also sacred to Dagon, the fish-god of Gaza and Ashdod in Palestine, worshiped by the Philistines supposedly in the form of half-man and half-fish,[46] and thus the counterpart of Derceto. He may have been identified with Oannes described in a fragment of Berosus' *History of Babylonia* (Bk. 2) as half-man and half-fish, but endowed with reason, who was believed to have emerged in early times from the Persian Gulf to teach the Babylonians civilization. Oannes may also be identified with the Babylonian god Ea conceived in human form but wearing a fish-skin

---

[46] Judges 16:23. His statue is mentioned in I Sam. 5:2f. It is the belief of some that the name comes from *dag*, "fish," although the Assyro-Babylonian Dagan is not etymologically so connected, since *"nun"* (not *dag*) signifies fish.

garment. Various ancient writers mention the taboo against eating fish,
a custom still observed in Roman days near Dolichene in Commagene (a
district of northeast Syria), in Tripoli (Tarabulus near the coast of Phoe-
nicia), and in Asia Minor. Modern travelers have reported that the Anatolian peasants of today rarely eat fish, an example of totemic prohibition
based on hygiene. Sir William M. Ramsay and his party in 1891 fell ill
from eating them from a stream in the Taurus Mountains.[47] Here the inhabitants believed that the fish contained evil spirits; similarly in antiquity
it was believed that Atargatis caused tumors in those who disregarded her
ban, and only priests and initiates could eat fish at her mystic banquets
in the belief that they were eating the goddess herself. Out of such superstitions the Greek word for fish, *ichthys,* became an early Christian symbol,
its Greek letters forming an anagram which is made up of the initials of
"Jesus Christ, Son of God, Savior." [48] But the sacred fish of the goddess
had nothing to do with the Eucharist, the propagation of the symbol merely
having been extended by the popular fish-cults of Syria.

Certain Phoenician and Syrian baalim also reached Greece and Italy.
One of these was Adonis, the favorite of Aphrodite, whose festival spread
from Byblus (Jebel) where it originated to Babylonia where he was worshiped as Tammuz (Ezekiel 8:14), and later to Greece, Alexandria, and
South Italy. Its celebration at Alexandria as a women's festival is described in detail by the great nature poet Theocritus in his Fifteenth Idyll.
Other baalim came from interior Syria, notably Dolichenus, a war-god
identified with Jupiter, who was brought to Rome by Syrian artisans in
Vespasian's reign (A.D. 69–79). Two others replaced Jupiter in the Empire for a time, one from Emesa (Homs) under the Syrian boy-emperor and
priest Elagabal (218–222), the other under Aurelian (270–275), discussed in
chapter vii below.

It is difficult to understand why the Romans accepted Syrian cults with
their worship of animals (fish), inanimate objects (axe of Dolichenus), and
heavenly bodies (heliolatry). And even more difficult, why they allowed
sacred prostitution in their temples, even in that of Aphrodite Erycina,
i.e., Atargatis, in western Sicily (San Giuliano), a wholly un-Roman practice which was brought to Rome at the beginning of the Second Punic War.
Similarly the immolation of men, women, and children, which endured
longer in the cult of Atargatis than in any other even lasting clandestinely
after Hadrian's ban [49] was wholly un-Roman. For despite Voltaire's ridicule in the eighteenth century of scholars who believed such accounts,
there are too many well-attested examples of such practices now to admit of
doubt. Cumont explains temple prostitution as an outgrowth of exogamy,

---

[47] *Impressions of Turkey during Twelve Years of Wandering* (London and New York,
1897), pp. 288f.

[48] See S. Reinach, *Cultes, mythes et religions* (2nd ed.; Paris, 1908), III, 431; and the
exhaustive work of F. J. Dolger, *Ichthys, das Fischsymbol in frühchristlicher Zeit als
Kurzung des Namen Jesu* (Münster, 1922–28).

[49] Porphyry *De abstinentia* 2:56; Tertullian *Apology,* 9.

while Frazer finds it a relic of primitive communism. Nor could the doctrine of immortality have been the great attraction to the Romans since in the cult of Atargatis it was emphasized less than in others. Cumont, therefore, has found the cause of the attraction of the Syrian deities among the educated Romans in their "scientific" astrology, characteristic of them all. The Elysian fields of the blessed were not below, but above the earth and stars. The priests, no longer the caricatures of Lucian, were experts in astral lore and Chaldean fatalism. To them the Sun was the cosmic guide and the soul of life, which latter was determined by the stars. At death the soul ascended and the priests alone knew the way through the planetary spheres. This Syrian belief in the omnipotence of the Sun approached monotheism more nearly than any other Near-Eastern religion with the exception of Judaism. But for all this the Syrian cults never appealed to the Roman imagination like those of Cybele and Isis.[50]

MITHRA

The most popular of the Near-Eastern cults was that of Mithra which spread over the West at the beginning of our era, reached its zenith in the third century, and ended with Theodosius' repressive legislation at the close of the fourth. Mithra had his origin in Zoroastrianism, for a time the religion of the Persian Empire. Because of its great similarities in organization and doctrines Mithraism became the rival of Christianity among the Eastern religions in the latter's long struggle with Roman paganism. Its appeal was varied: its human qualities of fraternity, democracy, and faith, its antiquity and impressive ritual, its clerical organization, its doctrine of purification from sin, its high system of ethics and, following Zoroastrianism, its doctrine of antagonistic powers of good and evil ever struggling for mastery in the world, and especially its final judgment and clear promise of a blessed hereafter. Furthermore, it was freer of sex impurities than its sister religions. As most of its features are found in Christianity, when the latter became victorious, Mithra's followers easily passed into it or into Manichaeism, which has been called "the final assault made by Persia on the Occident," the heretical faith which assimilated the adoration of Zoroaster with that of Christ, and which reached Italy at the end of the third century and Africa in the fourth, where the youthful Augustine for a season was interested in it. Again, we have no definite evidence that Mithraism became a part of official Roman paganism before the middle of the third century at least, but there are numerous proofs that it enjoyed imperial favor for centuries.

Some scholars have regarded the struggle between Christianity and Mithraism as a crucial one, the decision between them hanging in the balance till Constantine extended his favor to the former and Theodosius banned the latter. Such scholars agree with the oft-quoted statement of Renan: "If Christianity had been checked in its growth by some deadly

[50] See H. A. Strong and J. Garstang, *The Syrian Goddess* (2nd ed.; London, 1913).

disease, the world would have become Mithraic." [51] However, a truer estimate is that of Cumont:

> It [Christianity] performed the miraculous feat of triumphing over the ancient world in spite of legislation and the imperial policy, and the Mithraic mysteries were promptly abolished the moment the protection of the State was withdrawn and transformed into hostility. [52]

Remains of the struggle are found in two institutions adopted from its rival by Christianity in the fourth century, the two Mithraic sacred days, December twenty-fifth, *dies natalis solis,* as the birthday of Jesus, and Sunday, "the venerable day of the Sun," as Constantine called it in his edict of 321.

When Mithraism reached Italy in the first century B.C. its roots already ran far into the past, going back to a time even anterior to the separation of Iranians and Hindus, since Mithra appears not only in the Persian Avesta but in the earlier Indian Vedas. In the former, after the reorganization of the ancient Iranian religion by Zoroaster (*ca.* 600 B.C.), Mithra is a figure secondary to Ahura-Mazda (Persian, Ormazd) who dwelt in the realm of heavenly light, while Ahriman (Angra-Mainu) reigned in darkness. For here Mithra was only a *yazata* or demigod, created by Ahura-Mazda to help in fighting evil, a warlike figure as he was in later Mithraism. Zoroaster (Persian Zerdusht) simplified the ancient faith by relegating the former gods to the positions of *daivas* (daemons) and by teaching the purificatory quality of fire, and of the plant *haoma* from which a sacred drink was brewed. We see his ritual in the *Gathas,* the oldest part of the Avesta or Persian Bible, canonized under the Sassanid kings of later Parthia in the third century and lasting until the extinction of the dynasty by the Saracens in the seventh. Most of the survivors—those left in Persia were ironically called by the Moslems, Guebers or Ghebers (infidels)—fled to India where their descendants, the fire-worshiping Parsis of the Bombay district, still cleave to the ancient dualism. Zoroaster's evangile, summed up as "good thoughts, good works, and good acts," is the earliest to offer man a choice between good or evil, Ahura-Mazda or Ahriman. He regarded world history as the continuous struggle between these two, but prophesied that ultimately the good would prevail.

With the Persian conquest Zoroastrianism spread through the Euphrates valley and in Babylon became modified by contact with Chaldean astrology and the worship of Babylonian Marduk. Here Mithra was identified with the Sun-god Shamash, god of righteousness and order, just as later

---

[51] *Marc Aurèle et la fin du monde antique* (4th ed.; Paris, 1899), p. 579: cf. a similar statement in his *On the Influence of the Institutions, Thought and Culture of Rome on Christianity and the Development of the Catholic Church,* tr. from the French by Charles Beard (London and Edinburgh, 1880; 4th ed., 1898), p. 35.

[52] *The Mysteries of Mithra* (2nd ed.; Chicago and London, 1910), p. 199. This work is Pt. 2, of Vol. I of his *Textes et monuments figurées relatifs aux mystères de Mithra,* which contains 931 pages, 50 illustrations, and 9 photogravures, thus forming a complete descriptive and critical collection of texts, inscriptions, references, and monuments, the standard work on the subject. The translation is by T. J. McCormack.

through contact with the Ionian Greeks he became identified with the Greek Sun-god, Helios. After the collapse of Persia, many "fire-lighters" or *magi* lived in obscurity in Pontus and Cappadocia where they taught the advent of a savior-god. Some of these were doubtless "the wise men of the East"—translated *magi* in the Vulgate—who were present at Jesus' birth (Matt. 2:1). It was in Asia Minor, perhaps during the religious ferment started by Alexander, that the new religion, Mithraism, took the definite form which we know in its Roman period when Mithra was the supreme Sun-god *invictus,* identified by the Romans with Sol or its Genius, the main actor in the creation and rejuvenation of the world, protector of heroes and soldiers here and hereafter, and mediator between this world and the one beyond. The ritual in Asia Minor was no longer in Persian but largely in Aramaic, the language of countries west of the Tigris until it was gradually superseded by Greek. The new cult retained many features of the old, its sacrifices, prayers, offerings, and general background. Thus by the time of Jesus, Mithraism had spread and was the great faith of Western Asia as Buddhism was of Eastern. It influenced Judaism and through the latter Christianity with the old Iranian dualism, belief in Satan, angels, and the hereafter.

Rome had her first knowledge of Mithraism during the Mithradatic Wars in Asia Minor (88–63 B.C.) when the Latin West came into direct contact with the Near East. Nearly two centuries later, when Trajan carried Roman arms eastward to the Tigris and southward to the Persian Gulf (115–116) and captured the Parthian capital Ctesiphon, Rome and New Persia (Parthia) became neighbors and the active propaganda of the Mithraic mysteries began in the West, especially in Rome. There Mithra became the deity of bravery and fidelity, a soldier's religion. A few votaries had already reached Italy in the form of pirates captured by Pompey in 67 B.C.[53] Lactantius Placidus, in his notes on the *Thebais* (I:719–20) of the poet Statius, says the cult passed from Persia to Phrygia and thence directly to Rome passing over the mainland Greeks, the hereditary enemies of Persia. Oriental soldiers in Roman armies, as well as merchants, carried it along the European and African frontiers of the Empire into the Danubian provinces of Pannonia, Moesia, and Dacia and the Rhenish provinces of Upper and Lower Germany, and especially into the *agri decumates,* the wedge between the two rivers, where Mithraic ruins are most plentiful. Thus at Heddernheim, a suburb of Frankfort, three ruined *mithraea* have been found, in Hesse three more, and others at Neuenheim near Heidelberg, and all along the Rhine from Basel Augst to Xanten in northwest Germany.

Statius (*ca.* 45–96) is the first Roman writer to refer to the typical Mithraic bas-relief (in the *Thebais*), while the oldest Mithraic inscription found in Italy is of the time of Vespasian. Nero entertained the Mithraic king Tiridates who, ousted from his Armenian throne, had come to Italy (in 66) with a large retinue to receive it back. He claimed that he saw in Nero

---

[53] Plutarch, *Life of Pompey*, chap. 94.

an emanation of Mithra.[54]   A century later Lucian parodied the cult,[55] but by the close of the second it was firmly ensconced in all military posts, Cumont having traced its progress from the Black Sea to Scotland and from the Sahara to the northern frontiers.   Commodus was the first emperor to be publicly inducted into the mysteries.   By then it had become popular with the Roman aristocracy and no longer the despised faith of immigrants. It reached its climax under Valerian (253–260), who had been initiated in a cave at Sirmium in Pannonia.   He established a college of priests at Rome and placed the words *Sol dominus imperii romani* on his coins. Beginning with Aurelian, Mithraism was officially absorbed in the Syrian solar pantheon, which by then had become reconciled with science and philosophy.   But the loss of Dacia in 275 was a severe blow, for now the German barbarians destroyed the *mithraea* along the Danube frontier.

Diocletian upheld sun-worship as is shown by the fact that he, Galerius, and Licinius at a conference held in 307 at Carnuntum on the Danube, one of the oldest centers of European Mithraism, restored a *mithraeum* there and dedicated an altar to Mithra as "protector of their Empire." [56] Diocletian's colleague Maximian had already dedicated a *mithraeum* at Aquileia *Deo Soli*.[57]   But Diocletian's erection of an *iseum* and *serapeum* in Rome shows he was not a whole-hearted Mithraist.   Constantine kept Mithraism from becoming supreme not by persecution, but by his Edicts of Toleration (in 311 and 313).   Indeed, the un-Roman imperial cult reflected Oriental heliolatry since the Sun was considered the patron of the emperor.   After a short revival under Julian, Gratian in 382 banned Mithraism and all other pagan cults in favor of Catholicism.   We last hear of it at Rome in 394 when it, with the worship of Cybele and Isis, was banned, but Mithraism, like them, continued clandestinely in the recesses of the Alps and Vosges until well into the fifth century, while in the Asiatic countries of its origin its vigor continued to the time of the Moslem conquests.   It had lasted at Rome over four and one-half centuries.   Many western *mithraea* were destroyed by Christian zeal, the Christian fanatics killing and burying the priests in their ruins.   That the struggle was savage is shown by the condition of such ruins.   One at Dieburg in Hesse, discovered in 1896, shows it was thus destroyed and one at Saarburg in the Rhineland disclosed the shackled skeleton of a priest.[58]

Archaeology, with the aid of notices by Greek and Roman writers and by the Church Fathers such as Tertullian [59] and Justin,[60] has unearthed many Mithraic monuments—sixty *mithraea* alone in Rome, among them the largest known, in the Baths of Caracalla, discovered in 1912; seventy-

[54] For his journey, see Cassius Dio *Epit.* LXIII, 2f.
[55] In his *Deorum concilium* 9 and *Jupiter Tragoedus* 8.
[56] Its recovered inscription reads: *D[eo] s[oli] i[nvicto] M[ithrae], Fautori imperii sui.*
C.I.L., III, 1, No. 4413, p. 552; Dessau 1, No. 659, p. 150.
[57] *C.I.L.*, V, 1, No. 803, p. 9.
[58] Pictured by Cumont, *Mysteries*, fig. 46, p. 204: *Textes*, II, 519.
[59] *De praescriptione haereticorum.*
[60] *Apologia.*

five typical sculptures, and over 100 dedicatory inscriptions. For Rome became the center of western Mithraism since there were large garrisons there, veterans who had won their *honesta missio,* Eastern merchants and slaves. Five *mithraea* were also found at Ostia, all of the second and third centuries. They were all subterranean chapels simulating caves, lighted by candles, containing a perpetual fire and supplied with a purificatory water-system. At the entrance was a colonnaded *pronaos* which opened on a descending stairway, flanked by sacristies or supply rooms, at the base of which was a vestibule which opened into the main hall always oblong in shape and furnished with benches along either side for the worshipers, while the aisle between was reserved for the mystic rites. They were uniformly small, the one at Sarmizegethusa in Dacia accommodating about a hundred men, while most held no more than fifty. This seems to preclude congregational worship on any large scale, but shows rather that they were ordinarily used for initiations since soldiers and slaves could not be present in numbers at fixed times. At the far end of the hall was an altar before which stood a carved altar-piece of *Mithra Tauractonus,* i.e., slaying the bull, the chief event in his earthly life. Its unveiling was doubtless the solemn moment of the entire ritual.[61]

Copies of this relief, always of mediocre workmanship, first modeled by a sculptor of the Pergamene School after the relief of Nike slaying a bull which is still on the balustrade of the latter's temple on the Acropolis, are found in many European museums. The god is represented as a beautiful youth clad in a streaming mantle and conical "Phrygian" cap. Kneeling on the bull's back he pulls its head back with one hand and plunges a knife into its throat with the other. On either side stand attendant spirits—the mysterious *cautes* and *cautopates,* evidently the *dadophori* of inscriptions, since each holds uplifted inverted torches. Beneath the bull's belly are a scorpion biting off its genitals to be placed in a sacred vessel—the *kernos*—and carried to the moon-goddess for fructification and thus representing birth; a serpent lapping up the blood, representing growth; and a dog springing toward the wound, representing death. On most reliefs there are also representations of the Sun and his messenger the raven, a lion, and a fig-tree. The whole relief is enclosed in a frame made of panels in relief showing scenes from the god's career. One from Osterburken,[62] midway between Heidelberg and Würzburg, is the basis of Cumont's reconstruction of two groups, one illustrating the origin of the god, the other his otherwise lost legend, the final scenes representing the god and the vanquished Sun reconciled at a last supper and mounting a fiery chariot which crosses the sea.

[61] The altar and bas-relief are represented as restored in the interior of St. Clement's *mithraeum,* hewn from the rock of the Capitoline at Rome (discovered in 1869), in *Dictionnaire d'archéologie chrétienne et de liturgies* (Paris, 1934), II, Pt. 2, p. 1547, fig. 8209 (taken from *Comptes-rendues de l'Academie des inscriptions et belles-lettres* [1915], fig. 2, p. 208).

[62] Cumont, *Mysteries,* No. 240.

Mithraism was organized religiously as a fraternity like a modern masonic lodge, its members being similarly bound by ties of secrecy and fraternity, and before the law like a church, having the right to hold and to manage its property. Its priests, evolved out of the *magi,* were not a professional class but merely taken from the *patres* or highest order of members—the *pater patrum* at the top exercising jurisdiction over the initiates, to whom he gave the oath of secrecy.[63]

The theology of Mithraism is reconstructed largely from the panels mentioned since all Mithraic literature is lost. Behind all is "Boundless Time," the older *Zervan akarane* of the *magi,* called in the West *Aeon* or *Saeculum,* Kronos or Saturn, the ultimate creator. It is represented in art as a sexless being in the form of a human monster with a lion's head, its body encircled by the coils of a serpent, and covered with zodiacal signs and seasonal emblems. It had four wings to represent the swiftness of time and held the keys of heaven in either hand, a scepter in the left and a thunderbolt on its breast. Its offspring were Heaven and Earth which begat Ocean, thus forming a triad, the progenitors of other gods including Ahura-Mazda and Ahriman. Ahriman tried to dethrone the former, but was cast back into hell only to escape to harass mankind. The chief deity was Mithra, represented as born from a rock in full manhood with a torch and a knife in his hands, who reigned in the aether as god of all life. His first tasks were to show his strength in a struggle with the Sun, whom he later vanquished and made his ally, and then with a divine bull created by Ahura-Mazda, this act being the central feature of the myth. He dragged it into a cave whence it escaped, but Mithra, warned by a crow, the Sun's messenger, caught it again and slew it. From its blood sprang useful plants and animals. In Italy its soul became Silvanus, the Roman deity of flocks. Thus the bull's death was the birth of life. Meanwhile man was created and remained under the protection of Mithra, for Ahriman sent deluges, floods, and pestilences against him.

His labors over, Mithra ascended with the Sun to heaven, but the struggle between good and evil continues among men, most of whom were on the side of the former. Purity was the righteous goal, sensuality was to be avoided, lustrations and absolutions were used to get rid of evil, Mithra became mediator between this world and heaven, and he was unconquerable (in Persian, *nabarze,* in Latin, *invictus,* in Greek, *aniketos*). At the allotted time a second bull will appear, Ahriman will be destroyed and Mithra will call the dead from their tombs, separate the good and the evil,

---

[63] His title recalls that of the Roman bishop—*papa*—whose tiara, or pointed beehive headdress in three sections or diadems, came from the Byzantine court costume, being first mentioned in the life of Pope Constantine (708–715) and in the *Liber Pontificalis* as the *camelaucum,* and again in the eighth-century forgeries known as the Donation of Constantine. It is a papal non-liturgial ornament, the miter being used instead at all liturgical functions. The name *tiara* for the headdress of the Persian kings, mentioned by various Greek writers (Herodotus 1:132 and elsewhere; Aeschylus *Persae* 661; Xenophon *Anabasis* 2:3, 23), may well be a Persian word, its character sovereign rather than sacral like the diadem of the Pope mentioned.

the former to dwell above, the latter to be annihilated. Thus the dead do not descend into Hades but, as in the cult of Atargatis and in Christianity, ascend. The four elements—earth, air, water, and fire—were sacred, and the Sun, Moon, and planets were worshiped.

The ritual was secret and what we know of it comes from hostile and hence unreliable witnesses, i.e., churchmen.[64] The number of grades of initiates is uncertain, although St. Jerome says that in his time, i.e., in fully developed Mithraism, the *sacratus* (mystic) must pass through seven stages corresponding with the seven planetary spheres traversed by the soul in its final ascent: *corax* (raven), *cryphius* (hidden), *miles* (soldier), *leo* (lion), *Perses* (Persian), *heliodromus* (courier of the Sun), and *pater* (father).[65] Inasmuch as all were "soldiers," some have reduced the number to six.[66] On occasions masks and appropriate garb were worn to represent the grades and the actions of birds and beasts were simulated as in mimetic representations in other cults, a primitive survival from the time when deities in the East had animal forms. Porphyry[67] says the first three grades were preparatory to the real initiation or *sacramentum* when the oath of secrecy was taken, and adds that children might take them.

Absolutions and ordeals accompanied the successive grades to show the initiate's courage and faith. Tertullian says[68] that the *miles* was offered a garland, but cast it aside with the words "Mithra is my crown," and that the initiate then was burned on the forehead with a red-hot iron. Porphyry[69] speaks of baptism by immersion, passing through flames with hands tied and eyes blindfolded, and of "simulating" death. Lampridius[70] relates that Commodus during his initiation actually slew a man. With the grade of *leo* initiates became participants since then they partook of the sacrament of bread and water or wine—the latter replacing the *haoma* drink which was unknown in the West—thus commemorating Mithra's last banquet, a rite which imparted immortality. St. Jerome says "the devil had by way of imitation introduced the very [Christian] solemnity into the mystery of Mithra." The *summus pontifex*, as Tertullian called the *sacerdos* or *antistes*,[71] was in charge of the ritual, held office for life, and could marry

[64] A. Dietrich, in *Eine Mithrasliturgie erläutert* (3rd ed.; Leipzig, 1922), has published a Mithraic liturgy of Egyptian origin written in Greek, which shows the magical formulas, invocations, and prayers used by the priests after A.D. 100 readapted to magical use about 300.

[65] *Epist.* CVII *Ad Laetam*, p. 292. Cumont, however, has shown that *cryphius* was not in the MS of Jerome but was inserted there from two Latin inscriptions found at Rome, *C.I.L.*, VI, Nos. 751, 753. M. Rostovtzeff, in an article "Das Mithraum von Dura," *Römische Mittheilungen*, XLIX (1934–35), 180–207, has (p. 206) replaced it with *nimphus*, found twelve times inscribed in the ruins at Dura.

[66] E.g. W. J. Phythian-Adams, "The Problem of the Mithraic Grades," *Journ. Rom. Stud.*, II (1912), 53–64. Celsus in Origen's *Contra Celsum* 6:22 gave eight.

[67] *De abstinentia* 4:16.

[68] *De corona* 15.

[69] *De antro nympharum* 15.

[70] *Life of Commodus*, chap. 93; *Scriptores historiae Augustae*, ed. D. Magie, L.C.L., I, 105.

[71] *De praescript.* 40.

only once, as do the priests of the Orthodox Church in our time. He had charge of the three-fold daily worship and that of the planet which governed each day, and kept the perpetual fire. The chief festival was on December twenty-fifth, the rebirth of the winter sun, and the sixteenth of each month was a festal day. On Sundays there were special services of prayer, sacrifice, and the chanting of a litany.

Mithraism had no cult drama to portray the earthly experiences of the god, since he did not die annually and return like Attis, Adonis, and others. It is doubtful if the *taurobolium* was celebrated at Mithraic services although some believe it was borrowed from Cybele's ritual.[72] Furthermore, for some unknown reason, it had no women devotees, although these predominated in most of the Oriental mysteries as they do in the modern Church and were the only ones in some, e.g. that of Adonis. For women appear in no inscriptions as initiates, priestesses, or benefactresses. One advantage resulted from this exclusion of one-half of the population, for it freed Mithraism from all sensual associations which were present in the cults of Cybele, Atargatis, and Isis. The loss was in part compensated for by the wives and daughters of Mithraists attaching themselves to the more feminine cults, especially to that of Cybele whose temples were frequently near the *mithraea*, e.g. on the Vatican Hill, an association doubtless originating in Asia Minor. It is known that women did not have so high a status in early Christianity as men. Paul, while he said Christ had blotted out the distinction between male and female, required women to come veiled to service,[73] but this hardly because of inferiority but of his own perverted ideas of modesty.

Resemblance between Mithraism and Christianity and the supposed influence of the former on the latter have aroused more interest in Mithraism than in any other Near-East religion. Members of both were "brothers," a term used also in other cults, e.g. in that of Jupiter Dolichenus where they were called *fratres carissimi,* long before the term was used in the New Testament in a religious sense; both had legends of shepherds coming with gifts to adore the newborn Mithra and Christ—although how this could be in Mithraism, since Mithra was born before the creation of man, is hard to see; both had legends of a global flood, with only one family surviving in an ark, and of a final conflagration; both taught that heaven was above and not below and unrelenting warfare on evil with the final victory of the good; both had a sacred meal, although such a common feast is as old as humanity; baptism and an elevated system of ethics—the Mithraic being lost unfortunately but it appears to have emphasized abstinence and continence and inculcated asceticism and bodily mortification. The deity of both systems was a mediator between this world and the next and both taught he would return, awaken the dead, judge the good and the evil and give immortality to one and annihilation to the other. Moreover,

---

[72] Sir Samuel Dill, *Roman Society from Nero to M. Aurelius,* pp. 556–609; F. Legge, *op. cit.,* II, 259. But it is denied by Cumont, *Textes* I, 334, and by others.
[73] I Cor. 11, 5–6: 14:34–35; I Tim. 2:11–12; etc.

both reached the West almost simultaneously and were diffused under similar conditions and largely for the same reasons—the unity of the Empire and its moral depravity. Each drew its members from the lower classes, and each felt the rivalry of the other and that final victory meant the religious leadership of the Empire.

Such resemblances intensified mutual animosity, the Christians accusing the Mithraists of stealing their rites. Thus Justin imagined that their whole system [74] was the devil's trickery to mislead the Christians. Doubtless the Mithraists accused the Christians similarly but their polemical literature is lost.[75] Some modern writers have even imagined that such similarities show that Christianity was either an adaptation of Mithraism or, at least, the outcome of the same background.[76] If there was any such borrowing it doubtless would have been on the Christian side since Mithraism was the older. But there were also just as striking differences between the two systems. An important one was the relationship of each to the Roman State-cult. Mithraism and its kindred philosophies compromised with it in establishing their monotheism without combatting polytheism, while Christianity not only steadfastly opposed Mithraism and all its sister religions but the imperial and civic cult of Rome. Christianity was free of the nature worship of the past with which Mithraism was inextricably linked. But the chief difference of all was the object of adoration: while the Mithraists worshiped a mythical creation of the imagination, the Christians worshiped Jesus who, whatever the Church made of him later as the Christ, was a historical figure instinct with human sympathies, whose personality was even greater than his teaching.

Mithraism did not make its appeal through colorful processions nor a divine drama. Its success was rather due to its ethics, the outgrowth of Zoroastrian dualism which, like the ethics of Christianity, produced action. While all these Near-East mystery-religions taught salvation, final justice, and immortality, only Mithraism and Christianity fought a holy war against evil. Its apotheosis of "Boundless Time" and of the Sun with its manifestations of heat and light were philosophical concepts which attracted the educated. But its expansion in the Western world after all only kept pace with the extension of Oriental immigrants there. It finally perished,

not only because it was encumbered with the onerous heritage of a superannuated past, but also because its liturgy and its theology had retained too much of its Asiatic belief.[77]

Cumont adds that the triumph of Roman Mazdeism

[74] *Apologia* 1:66.

[75] Similarly the Spanish *conquistadores* in Mexico and Peru in the sixteenth century regarded certain native rites as parodies of Christianity, a phenomenon with many parallels in religious history.

[76] So J. M. Robertson, *Pagan Christs* (1903). See W. R. Halliday, *The Background of Early Christianity* (Liverpool, 1925), Lecture X, "Similarity of Christian and Pagan Ritual," pp. 312–23.

[77] Cumont, *Mysteries*, V.

would not only have preserved from oblivion all the aberrations of pagan mysticism, but would have perpetuated the erroneous doctrine of physics on which its degradation rested.

Thus Mithraism, like her sister cults, failed and Christianity triumphed, and this despite their antiquity, authority, pageantry, symbolism, and allegories. When all non-essential features are removed there was little left beside myth, legend, and superstition, instead of theology and spirituality. Samuel Angus has said:

Christianity offered a more profound and spiritual message than the mysteries to the theosophic mind of the Orient, the speculative mind of Greece, and the legislative mind of Rome.[78]

Influences on Christianity

In closing this inadequate account of the Oriental mysteries we should touch briefly upon the question of their influence on Christianity which has been discussed ever since the appearance of Lobeck's *Aglaophamus* [79] over a century ago. There is still little unanimity among scholars. As for direct influence in borrowing, as some of the Church Fathers believed, this could only have been insignificant for there was only hostility between Christianity and the mystery-cults. Whatever influence was exerted, therefore, must have been indirect, i.e., through the general atmosphere diffused by them. As a group they formed a sort of *praeparatio evangelica*, a smoothing of the way for the spread of Christianity. The Synoptics certainly have nothing in common with them, since Jesus' work was public and confined to Palestine, while the message of the hierophants was secret and expressed all over the Empire. In early Christianity there is no indication of communions, purifications, or other ceremonies and little about the life to come, which, as we shall see in chapter v, was confused by Jesus with a millennial order on this earth. But in the Fourth Gospel and in the Letters of Paul the case is different, and it is essentially with the latter that diversity of opinion about borrowings exists. Some scholars, notably R. Reitzenstein [80] and A. Dietrich,[81] have found strong Mithraic influences in Paul's terminology and concepts, while others have been more moderate.[82] It would seem only natural that Paul, reared in Tarsus, a Mithraic center, should have been influenced by Mithraic ideas, e.g. his use of the word "rock" (I Cor. 10:4), although this example is too

---

[78] *The Mystery-Religions and Christianity* (New York, 1925), p. 270.

[79] Königsberg, 1829.

[80] First in his *Poimandres* (Leipzig, 1904), and later in his *Die hellenistischen Mysterienreligionen; ihre Grundgedanken und Wirkungen* (2nd ed.; Leipzig, 1920; 3rd., 1927). Here he discusses such expressions as *Krieger Christi, gnosis, pneuma, Abendmahl* as influenced by the mysteries; pp. 8f., and n. 8, on pp. 71–88; pp. 48f., and n. 47, on pp. 135–88; pp. 55f., and n. 44, on pp. 188–244.

[81] In his *Mithrasliturgie* mentioned.

[82] See C. Clemen, *Der Einfluss der Mysterienreligionen auf das älteste Christentum* (Giessen, 1913) and *Primitive Christianity and its non-Jewish Sources* (Edinburg, 1912); P. Gardner, *The Religious Experience of St. Paul* (London, 1911); K. Lake, *The Earlier Epistles of St. Paul* (London, 1911); H. A. A. Kennedy, *St. Paul and the Mystery Religions* (London, 1913). For bibliography, Clemen, *Religionsgeschichtliche Erklärung des Neuen Testaments* (Giessen, 1934), pp. 62f., 1192f.

common a metaphor to be pressed. Paul says little of heaven or hell, future rewards and penalties so prominent in the mysteries, but usually follows Jesus' idea, which also appears in Mithraism, of the annihilation of the wicked rather than their relegation to a place of torment. In I Corinthians (2:6–7) he speaks of "God's wisdom in a mystery, even the mystery that has been hidden" as an advanced stage in Christian instruction "for the mature" which points to a knowledge of the mysteries. In two passages of Colossians (2:8–10; 16–22) he even warns the Colossians against infringing upon the apostolic message of Christ's place in redemption by introducing oriental mystic notions.[83] But we quote E. R. Goodenough, an extreme opponent of the idea of Paul's borrowing:

In view of the character of Paul, it is at once incredible that he should from such sources [Mithraism] have taken over practices and ideas directly and *de novo* to weave them into his new faith.[84]

It is better, then, to derive technical terms, names, and ideas from the common Hellenistic milieu. In an age of *theocrasia* it was inevitable that one religion should unconsciously influence another. That Catholicism, however, owes many of its practices and ideas to the mystery-religions is clear. It is summarized by Dean Inge as

the notion of secrecy, of symbolism, of mystical brotherhood, of sacramental grace, and, above all, of the three stages in the spiritual life [of the Mysteries], ascetic purification, illumination and epopteia [the highest grade, or "salvation"] as the crown.[85]

When we add, as shown later on, that the Christian concept of the hereafter as we have it now was not that of Jesus or Paul, but entered Christianity in the post-Apostolic Age and was largely taken from the mysteries—we can easily gauge the later influence exerted on our religion by the mystery-cults.

We have already noted in Chapter I the well-accepted fact that the early Church was compelled to accept certain beliefs and practices of its converts in accommodating itself to its ever-widening environment, such assimilations following a natural process, and we have mentioned the Christian "Festival of Purification" as an example. The Venerable Bede in England (673–735) preserves a letter of Gregory I dated 601 in which the Pope's British adviser, the abbot Mellitus, is quoted as recommending that pagan temples should not be destroyed but

altered from the worshiping of devils into the service of the true God (that the people) may forsake their error of heart and be moved with more readiness to haunt their wonted places to the knowledge and power of the true God.[86]

The fifth-century Church historian Socrates calls the Christian Easter a per-

[83] See discussion by J. Moffatt, *The Thrill of Tradition* (New York, 1944), pp. 15f.
[84] *By Light, Light* (New Haven, 1935), p. 10.
[85] *Christian Mysticism* (London, 1899), p. 354.
[86] *Ecclesiastical History of the British Nation* (A.D. 731). *L.C.L.* (1930), I, chap. xxx.

petuation of an ancient usage "just as many other Christian customs have been established." [87]   And Bede elsewhere says that Easter there was "the old festival worshiped with the gladness of a new solemnity." [88]   He means that the British festival in honor of the Norse divinity of Spring, Anglo-Saxon Eastra or Ostara,[89] was changed into the festival long celebrated by the Christians in honor of the Resurrection, but in a new spirit.

One of the few notices of Easter or Passover in the New Testament occurs in I Corinthians (5:7–8) [90] where Paul says "For our passover also hath been sacrificed, even Christ," meaning the Christian Passover from the Old Dispensation of the moral law to the New through Christ's death.   We first hear of the dispute about the date of its observance in the Quartodeciman Controversy (*quarto-decima s.v. dies lunae*) in the second century between the Eastern and Western churches.   The controversy was concerned with the relative importance of the *date* or the *day* of observance.   The Quartodecimans maintained that their custom of observing the festival on the date of the Jewish Passover, the fourteenth of Nisan (April), when the Jews slaughtered the Passover lamb, irrespective of the day of the week on which the fourteenth day of the moon might fall, should be continued, while their opponents believed that their custom of celebrating Easter always on a Sunday, the day when Jesus was believed to have risen and appeared to his disciples, should be strictly kept, as we learn from Eusebius.[91]   As the Christian Sunday sometimes coincided with the Passover the latter deprecated as un-Christian the celebrating of their festival on the same day as the Jewish one.   Thus the date of the Passover of the Jewish calendar determined Easter for one group of churches while the moon's course determined it for the other.   Bishop Victor I of Rome (*ca.* 190–202) excommunicated all the churches of Asia Minor, but the controversy smouldered under his successors until it was finally settled for the universal Church at Nicaea in 325, when it was decreed that Easter should be solemnized on the first Sunday after the full moon following the vernal equinox, the date varying from March twenty-second to April twenty-fifth.   Socrates repeats part of the decree "that none thereafter should follow the blindness of the Jews." To the bishops of Alexandria, then the metropolis of science, was given the task of computing the date on the basis of the Metonic cycle of nineteen years, discovered about 432 B.C., corrected by Callippus in 330 B.C. and later used by Ptolemy in observing eclipses, after which the new moon returns to the same date as before.[92]

[87] *Hist. Eccles.* (A.D. 306–439), 5:2.

[88] *De temporum ratione* 15.

[89] He gives it dialectically as Eostra, a name connected with "east," whose sacred month April he equates with the *mensis paschalis* of the Jewish Passover (Hebrew *Pesach*) commemorative of the Israelites leaving Egypt (Exod. 12).

[90] In Acts 12:4 only the A.V. mentions "Easter," corrected in R.V. as "Passover"; in Hebr. 11:28 "Passover" is also mentioned.

[91] *Historia Ecclesiastica* 5:23–25.   Cited hereafter as *H.E.*

[92] But their "paschal cycles" were inaccurate over a long term of years and were not accepted by all churches.   Now Easter is the first Sunday after the paschal full moon, i.e., on the fourteenth day of the calendar or full moon which matures on or next after March twenty-first and, if on a Sunday, on the first Sunday thereafter.

LATE GREEK PHILOSOPHIES

During the Empire philosophy again played a part in Roman religious experience but in the direction of Oriental mysticism rather than, as in the late Republic, in that of practical morality. Now arose two semi-Oriental schools: the Neo-Pythagoreans who claimed to have revived the teachings of the ancient Pythagorean brotherhood and the Orphics, although the new literature consisted of little more than commentaries on the older doctrines; and the Neo-Platonists who claimed to have obliterated the ravages of scepticism in polytheism by propounding the theory that knowledge transcended reason, a mystical transformation of Platonism through the speculations of a series of non-Greek thinkers beginning with Plotinus and expanding over a period of three centuries. The doctrines of both schools were allied to those of the mystery-religions since they likewise spread the spirit of otherworldliness in their efforts to do what Graeco-Roman polytheism had failed to accomplish.

The Stoic Posidonius of Syria who spent his later life in Rome, in the first half of the last century B.C., had reëmphasized the duality of matter and spirit, body and soul, and taught the Orphic doctrine that real life began only with the death of the body. He first brought to the Romans the idea that knowledge of the godhead transcended reason. Cicero was influenced by his doctrine of the hereafter in his "Dream of Scipio" at the close of the *Republic* (6:9–26), which was composed in 54–53 B.C. In it he extends life beyond the human span into the universe and eternity and has the soul, freed from the body, soar into the aether. He presents a similar thought also in Book I of the *Tusculan Disputations* written in 45 B.C. Neo-Pythagoreanism was introduced into Rome principally by Cicero's friend Nigidius Figulus, but only became prominent in the first Christian century. It tried to bring a new spirit into both philosophy and religion, which were then mere formalisms, by teaching belief in a future life for which present-day life was a preparation, and that salvation could be attained only by freeing the soul of its earthly impurities, "the muddy vesture of decay," through a life of asceticism such as had been followed by the Pythagoreans centuries before, and through belief in the Orphic doctrines that had been incorporated into the systems of both Pythagoras and Plato. He coupled Plato's "real" ideas, which he found to be only mental, i.e., existing in the mind of God, with non-mental matter, thus forming a dualism suggestive of Oriental influence, even if already known to Greek thought. Oriental ideas were joined to the Pythagorean ascetic trend, based on ethical dualism and reminiscent of the Stoic tradition.

Its chief representative was Apollonius of Tyana, "the sage of Cappadocia," who lived through most of the first century, dying at the age of one hundred under Domitian, after having traveled eastward as far as India to learn about Oriental mysticism and westward as far as Rome and later to Spain, as we learn from his romantic biography by Philostratus.[93]

[93] See his *The Life of Apollonius of Tyana*, tr. by F. C. Conybeare, 2 vols., *L.C.L.* (1912).

In it he is represented as having magical powers of casting out devils, raising the dead, e.g. a Roman girl (4:19), healing the sick and claiming authority to reform the world, all of which recall similar passages in the Gospels. While some have regarded this miraculous *Life* as that of an imaginary character and even as "a religious work of fiction," F. C. Baur long ago attempted to prove it was a pagan answer to New Testament history.[94] He was probably self-deceived rather than an impostor. By connecting Orphic, Pythagorean, and Platonic thought with Stoicism, neo-Pythagoreanism forged the viewpoint with which Neo-Platonism later attacked Christianity. Thus, in a sense, the revival was merely an early stage of the later more original system of Neo-Platonism with its similar doctrines of divine and mortal, God an abstraction, intermediate spirits, asceticism, and disregard of the world of the senses.

Neo-Platonism was the mystical philosophy which transformed Platonism as taught by Plotinus and his successors. It was the last ancient attempt to explain the dualism of appearance and reality in which speculation passed beyond the natural thought of Stoics and Epicureans and reached a high degree of mysticism, influenced by the Oriental mystery-cults and Christianity, and directed to the godhead and man's relation to the universe. Since by philosophy we mean rational thinking it was a failure as such, although it played a role in later Roman paganism. Since it produced no further developments outside the School and because of its syncretism of the doctrines of the Academy, Oriental mysteries, and Philo's attempt to reconcile Greek thought with Judaism, it has been called "the clearing-house" of ancient philosophy and religion, both "their consummation and dissolution" and, in Windelband's phrase, "the mummification of Greek thought." Such a system in which the speculative faculty alone enables man to vision the godhead, naturally affected only the intellectuals, for its understanding was far beyond the average intelligence of the later Empire, the so-called "Dominate" (284–476). It originated in Alexandria under Ammonius Saccas who left no writings behind, but as a system culminated in his pupil for ten years, Plotinus. Alexandria, with its mixture of races, was favorable to such a fusion of philosophy and religion. Because of his acquaintance with all preceding systems from which he took whatever supported his thesis, especially identifying doctrines of the Academy and Lyceum, he was, as pointed out by K. O. Müller a century ago, as much a Neo-Aristotelian and neo-philosopher as strictly a Neo-Platonist.[95]

In Rome, Plotinus, an Egyptian born in 204 or 205 at Lycopolis (Assiut) in Middle Egypt, probably of Roman colonial parentage but Greek in outlook, taught a quarter century until his death (244–270). His Roman lectures were delivered during the height of the third-century crisis

[94] *Apollonius von Tyana und Christus,* ed. by E. Zeller (Tuebingen, 1832 and Leipzig, 1876).
[95] *Geschichte der griechischen Literatur bis auf das Zeitalter Alexanders* (Breslau, 1841; London, 1888).

but in the words of Dean Inge, "he ignored the chaos which surrounded his peaceful lecture room," [96] since it was his belief that a man should attach no importance either to the loss of position or the ruin of his country; [97] and in reading him no one would suspect that he taught when the Roman Empire had reached the depth of its political and social degradation. The Emperor Gallienus and his wife Salonina were his hearers for a season, which helps us to correct in part the wrong opinion of that emperor handed down by ancient historians.

Plotinus assumed a principle above reason (*nous*), the "One" of Plato, which he called "Primal Being," the "Good," as first cause and source of all being, identified with the godhead, an essence not to be characterized since it is beyond comparison, that which "neither thinks, wills or desires." While incomprehensible, it is the only reality in a world of illusion which is a transcription of the real world. The supreme aim of philosophy is elevation to the godhead, a spiritual union to be brought about through an inner intuition or creative faculty produced by intense contemplation or ecstasy. Porphyry tells us that during his six years as his pupil (262–268) Plotinus attained such union only four times, while he himself later attained it only once when he was sixty-eight years old! It was a state which could not be reached permanently in life due to the human soul not being free of the earthly, but could be achieved only after the death of the body. In a lost treatise, *On Immortality*, Plotinus followed Plato's idea that the soul was incapable of dissolution. By a series of emanations from the "One," came Reason which contains within it the ideal world; from it came the "World Soul" which gives to matter its forms and qualities, the visible world being a transcript of it; and from the latter came the soul of man, preëxistent before its descent into the body, but retaining a recollection of its former life and a longing to return to it, from which longing comes our hope of final union. The soul's return is helped not by sense perceptions, but by reflection and especially by love and the idea of the beautiful. Plotinus accepted the four "political" virtues—prudence, courage, temperance, and justice—above which he placed the "purifying" ones beyond contamination by the body, these latter attained by avoiding the sensual; and he taught that elevation to the godhead was helped by these, reproduced on a higher plane than that of the "political" ones.

He discussed evil and how to avoid it, basing his reasoning on Zoroastrian-Mithraic dualism. While Greek thinkers generally had regarded evil as the contamination of the soul by corporeal appetites and found the only remedy, regulation, Plotinus taught that the body must be destroyed. To quote a famous passage: "The sensuous life is a mere stage-play, all the misery in it is only imagination, all grief a mere cheat of the players. The soul is not in the grave, it looks on while nothing more than the external phantom weeps and laments." Neo-Platonic ethics reached their height in Julian's attempt to restore "Hellenism," and again at Alexandria in the persons of the mathematician-astronomer Theon and his more famous

---

[96] *Philosophy of Plotinus* (2nd ed.; London and New York, 1923), I, 277.
[97] *Ennead* 1:4, 7.

daughter Hypatia. The latter was head of the "mother" school there till her assassination (about 415) by a frenzied mob of Christian monks, a deed, if not instigated by Archbishop Cyril, the inevitable sequel of his violent speeches and acts. She has remained, because of her sex, beauty, and fate, philosophy's most reverenced martyr.

Plotinus' chief disciple was Porphyry (233–304) who published his master's fifty-four treatises in nine books or the *Enneads* [98] and wrote his biography. His sole aim was the "saving of souls" and to that end he vigorously preached asceticism and abstention from meat and sexual indulgence. He was a violent opponent of Christianity and defender of paganism as we see in his *Adversus Christianos* (1–15), which was publicly burned by Theodosius II in 435. Another distinguished pupil was Iamblichus who died about 330, the chief representative of the Syrian School. He gave Neo-Platonism a mystical coloring, his speculations including miracles and theurgy, for he peopled the world with a throng of supernatural beings who influenced natural events. He claimed to possess knowledge of the future teaching that such beings were accessible through prayer. In the attempt to justify polytheism he coördinated all the cults except Christianity but his mysticism marks the beginning of the waning of Neo-Platonism. The last great representative of the school lived a century later, the polymath Proclus of Lycia, called *Diadochus* or "successor," i.e., of Plato's genuine doctrines. He taught (450–485) in the Academy at Athens, the logical final refuge for the system. By then it was no longer a philosophy but rather a religion, since he recapitulated all classical religions and philosophies on a logical basis, although his ideas were tinged with mysticism. After his death Neo-Platonism was still taught as a theory together with other systems in the schools of Athens until they were all closed in 529 by the infamous decree of Justinian.

This brief account of Neo-Platonism, the last ancient attempt to oppose Stoic and Epicurean materialism, gnostic supernaturalism, and Christian universalism, shows that it influenced Christianity more than it did paganism. Its dissolution was due not only to the extreme speculations of Iamblichus who reduced it to theurgy and magic, but more to the power of Christianity. It failed to meet the requirements of the times although it influenced various Christians, such as St. Augustine, the Pseudo-Dionysius the Areopagite [99] and Scotus Erigena of the ninth century. But Augustine condemned its theurgy, as in his oft-quoted statement that "any old woman of the Christians is wiser than these philosophers." Our interest in it here is its championship of all forms of pagan thought arrayed

[98] First known through Ficinus' Latin version (Florence, 1492; reprinted at Basel, 1580 with Petrus Perna's Greek text).

[99] Named from the Athenian converted by Paul's speech in Athens (Acts 17:34) whose name became attached to a fifth-century body of writings containing Greek, Oriental, Jewish, and Christian elements of unknown origin and authorship, but all going back to Neo-Platonic principles. They also influenced medieval Christian thought; see Migne, *Patrologia Graeca* (cited hereafter as *P.G.*), Vols. III, IV; and the Latin version by Erigena, *Patrologia Latina* (cited hereafter as *P.L.*), p. 122.

against their common enemy Christianity, when the Roman State-cult, the mysteries, and philosophies joined in a common crusade against it.[100]

In connection with these philosophies a word should be added about astrology or astralism, the pseudo-religious science based on the assumption that there is a mystical sympathy between the stars and man, and its ally magic, called a "bastard sister of religion." Astrology, which was present in all the mysteries, had a sacerdotal origin in Sumeria whence it passed to the Babylonians and thence to the Persians, the latter giving it a role in Zoroastrianism. Its antiquity and boasted scientific method spread it westward after Alexander's conquests until it reached Italy with Stoicism which had accepted it in part. It was taught there by Posidonius. It became a highly specialized art at Rome in the hands of Oriental priests, driving out Roman augury and haruspicy, not yet banned by the State. It came via Greece which had been overrun by Chaldaei or *mathematici*, i.e., astrologers, who later, in Rome, became so obnoxious that they were exiled in 139 B.C.[101] But Nigidius had made them again popular and the taking of horoscopes became a common practice, reaching its height under Tiberius when the poet Manilius is supposed to have composed his *Astronomia* (Bks. 1–5) which, despite its title, had more to do with astrology than with astronomy. But astrology is no more religion than modern palmistry and while it played a role in Stoicism, the later philosophies and mysteries, it was unimportant in the religious experience of the Empire since its speculations transcended the imperial religious bounds. Those who practiced it were those who were dissatisfied with Etrusco-Roman divination. Tacitus' famous condemnation of it in six words:

genus hominum potentibus infidum, sperantibus fallax,[102]

is as true today as it was in the early second century, as is also his further remark that this race "will always be both forbidden and retained." Its one advantage was that it favored monotheism.

Its ally magic, the "black art," was practiced by the Egyptians, Syrians, Jews, Greeks, and Romans, and became as universally feared in antiquity as it was in the later Middle Ages. It was a lucrative business in Rome despite stringent regulations and drastic penalties. That the Jews were especially addicted to it is shown by the story in Acts of Simon Magus, who tried with money to buy Jesus' power of healing to add it to his own. In Italy it had less vogue outside the mystery-cults which taught it as an escape from the fatalism and determinism of astrology. Roger Bacon in the thirteenth century, in his letter on "The Nullity of Magic," first showed its

---

[100] For Neo-Platonism, see W. Windelband, *History of Ancient Philosophy* (New York, 1899); and Charles Bigg, *Neo-platonism* (London, 1895).

[101] Valerius Maximus *De factis dictisque memorabilibus* 1–9, 1; 3, 3. The term later was applied to the philosophical "Dogmatists," e.g. in Sextus' *Adv. mathematicos* (i.e., physicists).

[102] *Histories* 1:22: "a race of men untrustworthy for the powerful and fallacious for the hopeful."

fallacy, although he felt the impossibility of changing men's belief in it or in any other superstition since on his death-bed he said: "I repent of having given myself so much trouble to destroy ignorance." [103]

It may be added in general that philosophy can exhort men to a virtuous life, but it cannot free them from one of vice. Luther said: "precepts show us what we ought to do, but do not give us power to do it." Not even Stoic ethics, the best that paganism offered, could rival the Christian reverence for Jesus' simple message. Moreover, while pagan ethical systems were all parts of philosophy, that of Jesus was the essence of Christianity. Philosophy may comfort the reflective, but it is beyond the ordinary man who needs the emotional warmth of religion rather than dry logic. This he found at Rome, as already noted, in the mystery-religions and Christianity. To quote one of the latest historians of Greek religion:

Die Religion der Polis war vorbei; man suchte und fand in Syncretismus eine Welt-Religion zu der auch das Christentum gehört.[104]

In that syncretism Christianity played the part that Neo-Platonism did in philosophy. It similarly accepted contributions from all the religions that preceded it.

---

[103] See F. Cumont, *Astrology and Religion among the Greeks and Romans* (New York and London, 1912); his "Le mysticisme astral dans l'antiquité," in *Académie royale de Belgique, classes des lettres* (1909), pp. 256–87; and "Fatalisme astral et les religions antiques," in *Revue d'histoire et de lit. religieuse*, N. S. (Nov. 1915).

[104] O. Kern, *Die Religion der Griechen* (Berlin, 1926–38), Vol. III: *Von Platon bis auf Julian.*

Chapter III

JUDAISM AND THE OLD TESTAMENT

ANOTHER Near-East religion to reach Rome, but not a mystery cult except, perhaps, in part during the Alexandrian period, was Judaism, the post-exilic faith of the Jews.

While Roman paganism, largely through the mystery-religions, influenced early Christianity, Judaism influenced it more than all other religions combined since it was its parent stock. While playing an inglorious role politically the Hebrews of antiquity developed a unique faith in God and desire for fellowship with him, a faith based on the ethical idea of God's holiness demanding holiness in his worshipers. This faith they kept for centuries although with many lapses due to the influence of neighboring religions. Later, through the reinterpretation of Jesus and Paul, it became the basis of Christianity through which Rome influenced the Western world and which, through its influence on Islam, has influenced the Eastern as well.[1] Thus, the influence of the Jews on the world has been largely religious, as Ernest Renan long ago said: "What Greece was as regards intellectual culture, and Rome as regards politics, the nomad Semites were as regards religion."[2] Consequently the appearance of the Jews in world history during the Greek period beginning with Alexander, and their activity lasting to Hadrian's war of extermination in the early second century, have been of great importance in the story of religion. Even before Alexander they had influenced Egyptians, Syrians, Babylonians, Assyrians, Chaldeans, and Persians and were influenced in turn by most of these, especially by the Babylonians and Chaldeans through astrology and magic and by the Persians through Zoroastrianism. Judaism during the later Roman Empire spread far from Palestine. With the exception of Christianity and a few remnants of Zoroastrianism in India, it alone has survived to our time still remaining what it was largely in antiquity, an ethnic faith. Since Ezekiel's time during the Babylonian Captivity Jews have regarded themselves as "the chosen of God" who after their exodus from Egypt protected them from their enemies, led them in battle and conquest, punished their transgressions and gave them their law, claims made by no other ancient people.

[1] C. H. Toy, *Judaism and Christianity* (London, 1920); F. C. Burkitt, "The Debt of Christianity to Judaism," and A. Guillaume, "The Influence of Judaism on Islam," both in *The Legacy of Israel,* ed. by E. R. Bevan (Oxford, 1928); C. C. Torrey, *The Jewish Foundation of Islam* (New York, 1933).

[2] *History of the People of Israel* (Boston, 1894–95), I, 22; cf. a similar estimate by E. A. Freeman, *The Chief Periods of European History* (London and New York, 1886), p. 66.

Their history begins with Abram, later changed to Abraham (Gen. 17:5), "the Hebrew" (14:13) who, according to the "priestly" account (P) in Genesis migrated from Babylonia (Ur of the Chaldees) to Palestine some five or more centuries before the exodus out of Egypt, and was followed by Isaac, Jacob (surnamed Israel) and the latter's sons whose names after the Egyptian sojourn headed the twelve tribes of Israel. Inscriptions recently found at Mari on the Middle Euphrates confirm the tradition that he came, perhaps in the nineteenth century B.C., from Haran where the Creation, Garden of Eden, Deluge, Tower of Babel and other early incidents centered.[3]

The ancient story of the Hebrews is mainly that of the evolution of their religion from Sinai after their centuries-long sojourn in Egypt where they had lived an alien people with their own organization and customs in the northeastern Delta in the midst of the Egyptian world as recounted in Genesis and Exodus. Thanks to archaeological and topographical data we need no longer treat with distrust early Israelite traditions because of their legendary details. The historicity of the Egyptian oppression is fully shown by the familiarity of the authors of Genesis and Exodus with Egyptian conditions.[4] But the long-contested date of the Exodus is still under dispute, centering chiefly around two periods separated by over a century and a half. Some have placed it near the middle of the fifteenth century (ca. 1447 B.C.), in the reign of Amenhotep II, a date which agrees closely with the only clear statement about it in the Old Testament (I Kings 6:1), that it occurred 480 years before Solomon began the Temple in the fourth year of his reign, i.e., in 967 B.C.[5] Others, however, have placed it in the reign of Rameses II, the Great, in the early thirteenth century, whom they identify with the pharaoh "who knew not Joseph" (Exod. 1:8) and who oppressed the Hebrews, a date chosen largely because of the statement (Exod. 1:11) that the Israelites built the store-cities of Rameses and Pithom whose ruins show they belonged to his time or to that of his successor Merneptah.[6] The irreconcilability between this and the biblical date has

[3] Sir C. L. Woolley, *Abraham; Recent Discoveries and Hebrew Origins* (New York, 1936). He explains Abraham's 175 years (Gen. 25:7) as a conflate of three to five generations blended in oral tradition (p. 281). T. J. Meek, *Hebrew Origins* (London, 1936).

[4] See Meek, *Amer. Journ. Sem. Lang.*, LVI (1939), 101–31; A. S. Yahuda, *The Accuracy of the Bible; the Stories of Joseph, the Exodus and Genesis confirmed and illustrated by Egyptian Monuments and Language* (New York, 1935), chaps. iii–iv; H. H. Rowley, "Israel's Sojourn in Egypt," *Bull. John Rylands Library*, XXII (1938), 243–90; etc.

[5] This date is found by calculating from the known date of Shalmaneser's victory at Karkar in 845 B.C.; see *C.A.H.*, I, 160. For this view of the Exodus, see John Garstang, *The Foundations of Biblical History: Joshua: Judges* (London, 1931), pp. 54–55, etc.; T. E. Peet, *Egypt and the Old Testament* (Liverpool and London, 1924), and J. W. Jack, *Date of the Exodus in the Light of External Evidence* (Edinburgh, 1925).

[6] He ruled 1301–1234 B.C. according to the new Borchard-Edgerton chronology. W. F. Albright, *From the Stone Age to Christianity: Monotheism and the historical Process* (Baltimore, 1940), p. 113b, gives the date as about 1290 on; in his supplementary *Archaeology and the Religion of Israel* (1941), chap. iv, he places the conquest of Canaan in the latter half of that century.

been variously explained, some even assuming two *exodi* confused by the authors of Exodus.

These early Hebrews (Ibhrim) were related to, but not identical with, the Khapiru or 'Apiru (Habiru), although their names are philologically equivalent [7] and their later fortunes were interwoven. The latter are first mentioned as professional warriors under the ideograms Sa Gaz in Babylonian cuneiform documents of the nineteenth and eighteenth centuries B.C.; then in tablets recently found in the excavations of Assyrian Nuzi near Kirkuk in northern Iraq; and again on the Tell el-Amarna tablets found in 1887 among the buried archives of Amenhotep IV, known as the heretic pharaoh Ikhnaton (*ca.* 1375–1358 B.C.) all of which, with one exception in the Hittite, being written in the Assyro-Babylonian language in the cuneiform character. In some of these, various Egyptian vassal kings in the cities of Palestine and Syria, notably the loyal king Abd-Khipa at Jerusalem, complain of an invasion of Habiru and vainly ask the pharaoh for help. But there is no historical connection between the Israelite invasion of Canaan under Joshua and the Habiru who were associated with the Hittite invasion of Syria and Palestine. While the former entered Canaan from the east via Jericho and spread westward through Gibeon and Aijalon the Habiru came from the north through the coastlands, and the dates of the two invasions were different. If the Hebrews under Joshua entered at the end of the fifteenth century the Habiru revolution occurred some years later, culminating (*ca.* 1380–1365 B.C.) in the reigns of Amenhotep III and IV. Several later passages in the Old Testament also distinguish between Israelites and other Hebrews, e.g. I Samuel 14:21.

The Israelites had been led out of Egypt by the semi-mythical but wholly marvelous national hero Moses (a Hebrew born in Egypt as his name Mosheh indicates [Exod. 2:10]) by way of Kadesh, Midian, and Sinai to the Jordan where he died and where the conquest of Canaan then began under his successor, Joshua. The events which transpired during the forty years of wandering in the wilderness (Num. 14:33) and formed the prelude to the later journeys into Canaan stand at the beginning of Israel's history, for on Sinai she became a nation and received her national religion. The story was later told in parallel columns in Exodus: J (Jehovistic, where in the narrative parts the divine name is called Yahweh), and E (Elohistic, where it is called Elohim). While J was written down by the middle of the ninth century E appeared a century later and the two (JE) were welded together in the seventh. These sources, representing recensions of an original narrative, whose nucleus may antedate the arrival of the Israelites in Canaan, were later amplified by D (Deuteronomic School) in the early sixth when the Bible began to be a connected whole and again, during and after the Exile, supplemented from the viewpoint of the organized priesthood

[7] See C. F. Burney, *Israel's Settlement in Canaan* (2nd ed.; London, 1919), p. 68; S. H. Langdon in *Expository Times*, XXXI (1919–20), 327. On the Habiru also *Jour. Bibl. Lit.*, LVIII (1939), 91–103; Garstang, *op. cit.*, pp. 255–58.

(P), a process completed by the second century B.C. when the Old Testament had reached its almost finished form.[8]

On Sinai Moses gave to his people a simple belief in a personal God later known by the quadriliteral (Tetragrammaton) Y H W H, which formed the "ineffable" name, as St. Jerome called it, of the Supreme Being. This in later times for some reason had the vowels of Adhonai (lord) inserted between the consonants producing the familiar hybrid Jehovah which, though never pronounced by the Jews, appears 5,989 times in the standard Masoretic Hebrew text of the Old Testament and reappears in the Septuagint Greek version as *Kyrios* (lord), as it is retained in English versions. The Talmud says the real name was only pronounced annually ten times on the "Day of Atonement" by the high-priest in prayers and benedictions in the Holy of Holies of the Temple. This was, however, ineffective since, while lost to the Jews, the pronunciation was known in non-Jewish circles until long after the Temple was destroyed. The earliest evidence of its pronunciation comes from the Assyrian pronunciation of Hebrew proper names, e.g. Hizkiyahu (Hezekiah), a name thus compounded with the divine one, Yahu, which was probably the original pronunciation. The name is connected in Exodus 3:14 with the verb "to be" (*hayah*), as its causative or jussive imperfect; there differentiated as a proper name. This is confirmed by late Greek Church Fathers who give the forms Iao and Yaho. Theodoret of Antioch (*ca.* 399–445) says in his time the Samaritans called it Yabe (Yave) and the Jews Aia.[9] Secrecy in pronouncing the divine name may have arisen from a misunderstanding of Leviticus 24:16, by inferring it was an offence thus "to blaspheme" the Lord's name, but more probably from superstitious awe or fear lest it might be profaned by non-Jews in magic. Josephus, of priestly origin through his connection with the Maccabees, says [10] that he is "forbidden to speak the name," and Philo says: [11] "If any one . . . should dare to utter the name unreasonably, let him expect the penalty of death."

Yahweh, then, was the local god of Sinai or Horeb who had been long revered there as a fire-deity of a "smoking mountain" by some clan, though how he was revealed to Israel remains a mystery although Moses may have learned of him during his sojourn with his father-in-law, Jethro (Exod. 1). Yahweh tells Moses (Exod. 6:3) that he had already appeared "unto Abraham, unto Isaac, and unto Jacob as God Almighty, but by my name Jehovah I was not known to them," and had covenanted with them to give them the land of Canaan. The copper mines of Midian and especially of

---

[8] See S. R. Driver, *An Introduction to the Literature of the Old Testament* (Edinburgh, 1891; 9th ed., 1913); J. Wellhausen, *Prolegomena to the History of Israel* (Edinburgh, 1878; 2nd ed., 1885); J. Garstang, *op. cit.,* pp. 4–5.

[9] On the name Yahweh, see S. R. Driver, "Recent Theories of the Tetragrammaton" in *Studia Biblica et Ecclesiastica* (Oxford, 1891–1903), Vol. I; R. Kittel in Schaff-Herzog, *Encycl. of Religious Knowledge,* VII (1912), 470–73; W. F. Albright, *op. cit.,* p. 197 and *Jour. Bibl. Lit.,* XLIII (1924), 370–78, and XLIV, 158–62. Some critics discriminate the tribal god Yahweh of the Hebrews for the Christian Jehovah.

[10] *Antiq.* 2:12, 14 (275).

[11] *Comm. on Lev.* 3:27.

Sinai at Serabit el-Khadem [12] had long been worked by semi-sedentary clans who trafficked with Canaan and Egypt. One such clan, the Kenites, is often mentioned (Gen. 15:19; etc.), a name which means "belonging to copper-smiths," and Yahweh may well have been their local god. Earlier scholars had even assumed that a part of the Israelites had dwelt here before Moses' time, i.e., Leah tribes to whom Moses was related, while the Israelites in Egypt were Rachel tribes.[13] But we know nothing of Yahweh before Moses made him the Hebrew God. The theophany is impressively described in Exodus (19–20) amid

thunder and lightning and a thick cloud upon the mount, and the voice of a trumpet exceeding loud . . . and Mt. Sinai was altogether on smoke because the Lord descended upon it in fire . . . and the whole mount quaked greatly,

which seems reminiscent of the desolation of the rocky waste, especially of its storms, if not of earlier volcanic eruptions which today exist only in adjacent Hauran (ancient Auranitis), despite the notion long popularized by Eduard Meyer and others. It was here, then, that Moses received the tablets of the law, "written with the finger of God" (Exod. 31:18) who from the first disclosed anthropomorphic traits such as love and hate, jealousy and vindictiveness, joy, sorrow and even remorse.[14]

BELIEF IN YAHWEH

Thus Moses, founder of the Hebrew nation, taught the Israelites over three thousand years ago belief in one God, creator and source of justice, human in form though invisible (Exod. 33:23). It was a primitive type of anthropomorphic monotheism rather than what we now understand by the term, for the assigning of cosmic functions to a deity hardly makes men monotheists. Monotheism was not completely achieved by Israel before Amos or Isaiah. The earliest monotheism known seems to have been that of an unknown Egyptian, perhaps a priest, although the honor is usually given to the Pharaoh Ikhnaton, called by Breasted "the first individual in history," in the fourteenth century B.C. The first trace of dividing Amen-Re and replacing Amen with the name of the solar disc "Aten" as the supreme sun-god of Egypt is already found on the walls of the tomb of Amenhotep III (1413–1377), father of Ikhnaton, in an inscription in which Aten is called creator and lord of all lands and peoples. The old name Amen was erased at Karnak from the hymn in which Aten is called "the only God beside which there is no other." But such a cult was too early and too far above the masses to be successful and, after Ikhnaton moved

[12] Its temple with inscriptions of Rameses II was excavated in 1905 by Petrie, *Researches on Sinai* (New York, 1906); and again in 1935 by R. F. S. Starr, *Excavations and Proto-Sinaitic Inscriptions at Serabit* (London, 1936).

[13] See W. Nowack, *Die Entstehung der israelitischen Religion* (Strasburg, 1893).

[14] The traditional "mountain of the law" is Jebel Musa (Mountain of Moses) on Sinai proper which rises to a height of 7,359 feet. Lepsius and Ebers, however, identified it with Jebel Serbal (6,750 feet) to the northeast, and the plain of er-Rahah to the north of it as the place where Israel encamped. Meek, *A.J.S.L.*, XXXVII (1920), 101f., rejects the Kenite view.

his throne from Thebes to Akhetaten (Tell el-Amarna) farther north on the Nile, it caused only reaction and, even if it may have still existed in Lower Egypt in the time of Moses, there is little reason to think it influenced him.

This monotheistic "trend" endured in Israel against polytheistic tendencies of neighboring peoples for centuries after the conquest of Canaan, even though in later centuries alien gods were worshiped, such gods as the Sidonian Baal by Ahab in Samaria (I Kings 16:31–32), the Moabite Chemosh, the Amorite Milcom, and the goddess Ashtoreth, female counterpart of Baal, nature deity of fecundity and war (II Kings 23:13), the latter another name for Phoenician Ashtaroth or Astarte, Egyptian Ashtar, and Babylonian-Assyrian Ishtar.[15]   It was not till the time of Josiah of Judah that the first wholesale destruction of alien idols took place during his religious reforms of 621, when he restored the Temple of Solomon.   During the restoration the high-priest Hilkiah found the "Book of the law," evidently Deuteronomy, which caused the purging of the Temple of all foreign cults and its rededication to Yahweh and the abolition as well of idolatry from all local sanctuaries (II Kings 22:8; 23:20).

The earliest Mosaic ritual, religious, ethical, and hygienic, is found in the Pentateuch, which the Jews of antiquity and the Christians down to the time of the Reformation believed was the work of Moses.[16]   It has been the great problem of biblical criticism for a century past whether these books were the work of one writer or, more certainly, the product of many unknown writers and editors—a position based on the principle that variety in style, diction, and subject-matter shows a variety of sources and authorship with the consequence that Israel's history is not essentially different from that of other people.   Out of this belief has arisen the school of "higher" critics, who now believe the later sections were not composed before the Captivity, while the oldest parts to be written go back before, or to, the time of the Prophets in the ninth and eighth centuries B.C.   Thus the theory of "naturalistic evolution" or development of the Graf (1866)-Wellhausen (1878 and 1896) school still dominates the critical study of the Pentateuch.

After the conquest of Canaan begun by Joshua and after the time of the Judges (individuals selected for their rectitude in adjudicating disputes, shunning Canaanite contamination in religion and in freeing Israel, portions of which were still tributary to the Canaanites)[17] Israel had to fight with the Aegean Philistines who had reached Palestine by the early twelfth century B.C. from Crete and given their name to it,[18] and ruled Israel for

15 See Driver in Hastings' *Dictionary of the Bible* (New York, 1898–1902), I, 167–71; G. A. Barton in *Amer. Journ. of Semitic Languages*, IX (1892), 131f., X (1893), 1f.

16 Philo *Vita Mosis* 3:39; Josephus *Contra Apionem* 1:18 and *Antiq.* 4:8–48 (326). The earlier view of Mosaic authorship has curiously been revived recently by O. T. Allis, *The Five Books of Moses* (Philadelphia, 1943).   He believes (p. 254) that the Pentateuch is "not a late, anonymous, untrustworthy composite," but was composed by Moses.

17 Samson, about 1885–1865 B.C., ends the period.

18 But the extension of the name "Palestine" beyond the original Philistia took place many centuries later in the Byzantine period.   The Philistines originally found an Egyptian garrison on road from Egypt to Syria (Exod. 13:17).

forty years (Judges 13:3). Yahweh now became the lord of hosts, i.e., of Israel, as we see in Exodus 15:3 and 6:

> The Lord is a man of war;
> Thy right hand, O Lord, is glorious in power,
> Thy right hand, O Lord, dasheth in pieces the enemy,

which means he had taken over the character of Baal. Fearful of complete enslavement by the Philistines, whose superiority now lay in their monopoly of iron which was only then coming into use (I Sam. 13:19–22), Israel (ca. 1025 B.C.) changed its earlier commonwealth into a monarchy under Saul. He was regarded as a God-given savior, like the heroes of the book of Judges, since he rescued his people from the Philistines, though he, with his three sons, was later slain by them in battle on Mount Gilboa (I Sam. 31:1f.). He was followed by his armor-bearer David, greatest of Israel's kings and the real founder of the kingdom (ca. 1010–970 B.C.), and he, in turn, by his son Solomon (ca. 970–937 B.C.), reputed to be the wisest of men although his reputation has been much overrated. For a century Israel had been united and prosperous. Solomon built the Temple on Mount Zion after Phoenician models—for there was no temple yet in Israel—and with Phoenician artisans, not as a public place of worship for all Israel, but as a royal chapel to house the Ark of the Covenant, thus placing Yahweh under royal protection. Though invisible, He was enthroned above the cherubim or "winged sphinxes" in its Holy of Holies.

Because of excessive taxes imposed during the golden age of Solomon, taxes which were continued by his feeble son Rehoboam, the kingdom divided soon after the latter's accession, the ten tribes of Israel henceforth forming a northern kingdom with Samaria as its capital, while the two tribes of Judah remained in the more desolate southern kingdom which, however, contained Jerusalem as its capital with the Temple (I Kings 12). Jeroboam, first king of Israel, introduced the worship of the "golden calf" (I Kings 12:28f.) unless this is explained by his using calves not as bull-gods, but as pedestals on which the invisible Yahweh was enthroned.[19] A crisis brought on at this time by the menace of Canaanite worship was turned aside by the Prophetic movement, which was of great importance in the religious story of Israel.

The Hebrew prophet was supposed to be called by Yahweh for a religious mission rather than, like the Greek prophet, to interpret the divine will. The movement originated in sacred dances, which were continued until the dancers swooned and had visions like the later Jewish Hasidim, the Moslem dervishes of the present, and those who, in certain Christian churches today, "get the power." This first or "ecstatic" Prophetic movement culminated in Elijah and the shadowy Elisha in the ninth century B.C. But heathen practices appeared again later in Yahwism, notably the astral practices of the Babylonian-Assyrian Tammuz (Ezek. 8:14) and Ashtoreth, against which the "rhapsodic" prophets contended in the eighth

[19] See Albright, Jour. Bibl. Lit., LVII (1938).

century, notably Amos, Hosea, and Isaiah. Amos was a shepherd in Judah,[20] the "rusticity" of whose book has led some critics since St. Jerome to regard him as a clown, a judgment now happily reversed since his language and diction have given him a secure place in Hebrew literature. Hosea, first of the "minor" prophets, was of high social standing, and Isaiah, a statesman and royal adviser, although he opposed the royal policy of foreign alliances especially with Syria. All three regarded Israel as wicked, her religion paganized and her people oppressed. Amos denounced the wealthy, Hosea the alien contamination of Yahwism, and Isaiah saw Yahweh's judgment ready to descend on his people. Soon that judgment came, first at the hands of the Assyrians and again, over a century later, at those of the Chaldeans.

BABYLONIAN CAPTIVITIES

It was the Assyrian Tiglath-Pileser III (745–727 B.C.) who was originator of the "deportation" policy of subject populations. He took Gilead, Galilee, and Sharon and "carried them captive to Assyria" (II Kings 15:29), and his successor Shalmaneser IV (727–722 B.C.) soon began the siege of Samaria (II Kings 17:3f.) which was completed by Sargon II in 721 B.C. who deported its inhabitants into interior Asia (II Kings 17:5–6). This marks the disappearance of the Ten Tribes doubtless through absorption, despite futile attempts in our day to find their descendants in various parts of the world, among the Chinese, Kashmirs of India, Tartars, Afghans, Tajiks (Iranians of Central Asia), Anglo-Saxons [21] and even the "white" Indians of America supposed by some students to be of Welsh origin. The capital area of Samaria was settled in turn by colonists from the East; thus the North Kingdom ended disastrously under Hoshea, the last of the nineteen rulers who had reigned for 216 years from the beginning of Rehoboam's reign (ca. 937).

The fall of Nineveh over a century later in 612 B.C. meant merely a change of masters for the South Kingdom, Judah, first ruled by Egypt and then by Chaldea whose great king, Nebuchadrezzar, had defeated Pharaoh Necho at Carchemish in Assyria in 605 B.C., which marks Egypt's last attempt at world empire. Jehoiakim, vassal king of Jerusalem, rebelled in 597 B.C. and the capital was besieged by the Chaldean monarch and fell. Under Jehoiakim's successor, the youthful Jehoiachin, eight thousand Jews including Ezekiel the prophet were deported to Babylon where the latter remained a prisoner for nearly forty years. This was the so-called "First Captivity" of the Jews. Zedekiah, one of the exiles, was sent back to govern Jerusalem (Jer. 52:1f.; II Kings 24:17f.), but revolted and Judah in fear became demoralized, with a general corruption of prophets, priests, princes, and people (Ezek. 22:23f.). In 587–586 Nebuchadrezzar besieged the capital again and reduced it by famine. Zedekiah fled, but was taken and

[20] Though clearly an "ecstatic" type, he repudiated the idea that he belonged to the professional prophets of the century before.

[21] A good example of such literature is *Fifty Reasons Why the Anglo-Saxons Are Israelites . . .*, by W. H. Pool, D.D. (London, n. d.).

brought to the Chaldean camp where his sons were slain before his eyes and he himself was blinded and deported (Jer. 39:4–7). Jerusalem was burned, its walls razed, and all the population except the very poor deported. Gedaliah now became governor at a new capital on Mount Mizpah near Jerusalem, called by Renan "the Washington of the old Israelitish federation," where he was soon slain. This was the "Great Captivity," the year 586 marking the end of the kingdom of Judah after its twenty kings had ruled three hundred and fifty-one years (937–586 B.C.). Jeremiah, whose sad life spanned one of the most critical and tragic periods of ancient history, enumerates (52: 28–30) three deportations, the last in 581.

Jewish tradition has the captives remain nearly sixty years in Babylon (596–538 B.C.), though the reality of the "Great Captivity" has recently been needlessly denied. C. C. Torrey has argued that Judah may have been decimated but not destroyed and that some refugees soon returned, thus making Palestine and not Babylon still the center of Jewish life. And if there was no Captivity on a large scale there could have been no restoration and Ezekiel's mission to Babylon becomes apocryphal as well as the narrative in Ezra.[22] But excavations have shown that the Chaldean destruction of Judah was thorough. Ezekiel dwelt in the Jewish community on the river Chebar near the site of Nippur in South Babylonia for a score of years (Ezek. 1:1 and 3, and 3:15) and encouraged the Jews to hope for a restoration through his visions which reached a height of intensity never before known in Israel. His book shows he was psychologically abnormal like many other religious enthusiasts. It displays not only vivid imagination but clairvoyance, that "faculty of perceiving as though visibly some distant scene." Unlike the other great spiritual figure of the Exile, Deutero-Isaiah, whose poems were later added to the work of the older Isaiah (chaps. 40–66),[23] and who likewise encouraged the Jews to expect a speedy restoration, Ezekiel proclaimed an individual rather than collective relationship to God now that Judah was gone. His belief that the Jews formed a sacred nation apart from others helped to preserve their nationality during the Captivity and also their ceremonial practices which culminated in Pharisaic Judaism.

[22] See Torrey's *Ezra Studies* (Chicago, 1910), chap. on "The Exile and Restoration," and his *Pseudo-Ezekiel and the Original Prophecy* (New Haven and London, 1930); also his "The Composition and Historical Value of Ezra-Nehemiah" in *Zeitschrift für die Alttestamentliche Wiss.*, Beiheft II (Giessen, 1896), pp. 1–63 to show that apart from Neh. 1–6 the book is valueless as a source for post-exilic history of the Jews. On the historicity of Ezekiel's mission, see also G. Hölscher, *Hesekiel der Dichter und das Buch* (Giessen, 1921); Fleming Jones, *Personalities of the Old Testament* (New York, 1939), pp. 331–51. The book of Ezekiel was admitted into the Jewish canon tardily and accepted by the Church as the work of Ezekiel, a captive in Babylon (593–570 B.C.). Some students have repudiated it, however, as a late pseudepigraphy composed in Palestine and a compilation. While Hölscher found only about one hundred and seventy verses of it by the poet, recently W. A. Irwin in *The Problem of Ezekiel* (Chicago, 1943) has given him some two hundred and fifty genuine verses and agreed that he prophesied in Jerusalem from about 600 until after the Second Captivity and not in Babylon.

[23] Since Cyrus is mentioned in 45:1, the work was completed nearly two centuries after that of Isaiah.

But release came only after Babylon fell to the Persian Cyrus the Great whose proclamation is given by Ezra (1:2–4). He appointed two influential Jews, Zerubbabel, "begotten in Babylon" to represent royalty and Jeshua (Jesus) to represent the priesthood and others to lead the exiles home to rebuild their city and temple. Between 538 and 522 many returned and Zerubbabel became *pechah* or governor of the Persian province of Judah (Hag. 1:1). It was these returning refugees who were the direct ancestors of the Jews of our time, although as large a portion of the exiles remained behind having become assimilated to their foreign environment, the Babylonian Jews of the Hellenistic Age. For this humane act the grateful Jews called Cyrus "the anointed of Yahweh" (Deutero-Isaiah 45:1), the ancient title of their own kings, and he may rightly be called the first tolerant king of history and worthy the title "Great." The rebuilding of the Temple was delayed seventeen years, "due to the adversaries of Judah and Benjamin," i.e., the Samaritans, the Babylonian religious sect settled by Sargon in Samaria after its fall who, when the Jews refused to let them help, tried to frustrate the plan (Ezra 4:1–10). Aroused by the activity of Haggai and Zechariah, the rebuilding of the Temple began anew in 520 B.C. after authorization by Darius the Great who had confirmed Cyrus' decree, and it was dedicated in 515 B.C. (Ezra 6:14–17). Thus Darius shared with Cyrus the title of patron of the Jews.

Descending to the year 444 B.C., Nehemiah became governor of Judah, rebuilt the walls and restored the worship of Yahweh by making the temple-cult official for Jews in the Persian Empire, as we may deduce from the "Passover Letter" of 419 B.C. found in the ruins of a small synagogue in faraway Elephantine in Upper Egypt. A half-century later, in 397 B.C. (Ezra 7:7–9) the Babylonian Jews asked Artaxerxes Mnemon that Ezra, a priest-scribe and descendant of Zadok, high-priest of Solomon (II Sam. 8:17; Ezra 7:2), might lead more refugees home and reorganize the entire ecclesiastical administration of Judah by restoring the law.[24] Later he named eighty-five Jews who signed a declaration of acceptance of the Pentateuch as divinely revealed, i.e., the canonization of the so-called books of Moses. He published the book of the law (Neh. 8:1f.) brought from Babylon to be the basis of the code. Since, however, the Pentateuch shows little or no post-exilic influence, it may have reached its present form as early as 522 B.C. Later tradition (II Esd. 14) says he restored the law which had been burned. Oral law was abandoned, but the idea of a scion of David again ruling Israel was harbored by the masses, even if without any suggestion of it in the Pentateuch. But many believed that Moses had given other laws not therein, but transmitted orally and so of equal authority with the written ones. It was in such oral law that the idea of a Davidic leader was to be found. Later the Sadducees, because of the canonization of the Pentateuch and encouraged by the Persian edict which gave Ezra the right to appoint judges (Ezra 7:25), long remained in control while the Pharisees, who stood

[24] Artaxerxes' decree is given in Ezra (7:12–26).

for the oral law, no longer had power. Thus, it was Ezra who started the autonomous theocratic state of the Jews within the Persian Empire, ruled by a high-priest representing God. The new state controlled the Temple treasury and had its own coinage. Nehemiah, then, was the physical regenerator as Ezra was the spiritual restorer and second founder of the Jewish religion after Moses.[25]

Judaism, as we call the religion of the Jews after the Captivity—the name "Jews" first occurs in Ezra (4:12)—was now an established religion in Persia in which all Jews shared. It was a religion of faith rather than of belief, one of the few ancient ones founded neither on a revelation nor on the idea of a Savior-god. Its only creed was that Yahweh was God, but with no theological definition of God. In Moses' time Yahweh was, like the Greek Zeus, a glorified human, jealous, dictatorial, capricious, and resentful like an Oriental potentate, a god of love and hate and of war, all on a superhuman scale, i.e., the god of a primitive people. Gradually this concept of a tribal god changed until by Jesus' time it was completely superseded. After the time of the Judges and Samuel earlier Yahwistic cults were united. Amos and his successors already insisted that it was man's conduct rather than Temple sacrifice that was important. By then the Jewish religion had become "a way of life" rather than a theology. In the late eighth century B.C. Micah had already summed up the prophetic message that right conduct and not Temple observance was the center of faith. For to him the Lord was not pleased "with thousands of rams or with ten thousands of rivers of oil," for (6:8)

He hath showed thee, O man, what is good; and what doth the Lord require of thee, but to do justly and to love mercy, and to walk humbly with thy God?

By the time of the Second Isaiah (*ca.* 540 B.C.) Yahweh was not only the Creator but the sole sovereign of the universe. After Ezra's time the written law rivaled Temple worship, since Moses had received it directly from Yahweh. But the Pharisees also stressed the oral law as Yahweh's gift.

THE DIASPORA

The Babylonian Captivity is the outstanding event in ancient Jewish history, for out of it came the Diaspora or dispersion of the Jews among Gentile nations of the Near East and the Mediterranean area. Here we are not concerned with the Babylonian Jews [26] but only with the Western Jews. In Babylon the Jews had had time to attend to the minutiae of their law, the details of which are found in the Talmud, a formalism which, through Pharisaic influence, aroused Jesus' rebellion against the Mosaic

[25] Until recently Ezra was dated before Nehemiah. The shifting of dates is due largely to a Catholic scholar, A. von Hoonacker, and the new dating is now largely accepted. For the older dating, see Albright, *Archaeology and the Bible* (2nd ed.; New York, 1932–33); for the new, Fleming Jones, *op. cit.*, pp. 463f.

[26] Under Arsacid Parthia which had seceded from the Syrian Empire in 249 B.C., they came under Asiatic influences and later, under the Sassanid dynasty and the rehabilitation of Old Persia in A.D. 226, were left to themselves.

religion still taught in the first century (Acts 15:21). Under Ezra according to the Talmud the *Great Synagogue* (Hebrew, *Beth ha-keneseth,* House
of Meeting) was evolved out of the Temple-service with branches everywhere. It was the "child of the Diaspora," and "mother" of the Christian
Church, outlasting the destruction of the Temple in A.D. 70 and, until the
middle of the fifth century, remaining the great Jewish institution for instruction in the law, for prayer, and reading the law on the Sabbath. The
Greek name Synagogue, like that of Church (*Ecclesia*), first meant the congregation and later the visible structure which housed it, such as the magnificent one in Alexandria destroyed during the Jewish persecution there
in 116.

The Diaspora in the West was nurtured not only by deportation but,
during the Hellenistic Age, by the tolerance of Alexander's successors, the
Seleucids of Syria and the Ptolemies of Egypt, both of which dynasties favored voluntary immigration into their lands. Now Jews came into contact with Hellenism which became a unifying principle which strengthened
their bonds and made them a missionary nation. The Diaspora received
further impetus centuries later when Titus destroyed Jerusalem, and still
another after the war with Hadrian, since which time the Jews have had no
national home, but have been scattered everywhere.

In Palestine

In Persian Palestine the Jews enjoyed autonomy in internal affairs under
their priest-kings during the fifth and fourth centuries B.C., when the Near
East reached the height of its political evolution. Palestine was merely a
tiny outpost of the colossal Persian Empire, which stretched from Egypt to
India. When it fell to Alexander, the champion of Hellenism, Greek culture spread over the East in ever-lessening waves as far east as the Punjab
of India. During the following centuries Jews were everywhere exposed
to Greek influence whether ruled by a Seleucid or a Ptolemy, for the basis
of that rule was Greek, the Greek era of Jewish history. But the notion
that Greek influence was unknown earlier beyond the Greek seaboard of
Asia Minor is erroneous. For Syria, Palestine, and Egypt had enjoyed both
cultural and commercial relations with the Greeks since the seventh century B.C. when Greek trading-posts were sown along the coasts as centers
for inland traffic. Greek mercenaries had served in the Egyptian armies of
Psammetichus I (671–617 B.C.) and in those of Chaldean Nebuchadrezzar
(605–562 B.C.). From the sixth century B.C. onward prominent Greeks,
beginning with Solon and Hecataeus and ending with Xenophon of Athens,
visited Egypt and Asia. Greek art flourished and Phoenician kings were
buried in sculptured Greek sarcophagi; Attic coinage had become standard
in Syria and Palestine by the middle of the fifth century B.C. and Greek
coins were imitated in Persia in the fourth, while Ezra struck silver coins
in Palestine on Attic models. Thus, it follows that although Alexander did
not start a revolutionary culture he did accelerate tremendously a movement long in operation. The cities which he and his successors founded in

Asia became oases of Hellenism to which Greeks flocked for centuries thereafter and from which Greek culture radiated.

Alexander's work was continued by his successors after a bitter internecine war, a Greek tragedy in real life culminating at Ipsus in Phrygia, "the battle of the kings," in 301 B.C., when the kingdoms of the Antigonids (Macedonia-Greece), the Seleucids (Asia) and the Ptolemies (Egypt), were definitely outlined. With the last two of these the Jews were vitally concerned, since Palestine lay between them and was coveted by both who fought for its strategic position for over a century. After Alexander, Palestine was first controlled by Egypt but, beginning with Antiochus the Great (in 198 B.C.) by Seleucid Syria.[27] The Syrian capital, Antioch, became a center of Hellenic-Jewish propaganda. The Jewish aristocrats of Palestine, called Antiochenes, spoke Greek and had Greek names, the beginning of "Greek-Jew." "Greek" thereafter became synonymous with "Gentile" (cf. Acts 19:10; Rom. 1:16). Under Antiochus IV Epiphanes (175–164 B.C.) many Jews were willing to become incorporated in the Syrian Empire, though the masses were opposed to it.

It was in this reign that trouble first arose to defeat the pro-Greek trend. Epiphanes, a zealous but misguided Hellenist, made an abortive attempt to destroy Judaism and replace it with Greek polytheism. After he had defeated Ptolemy Philometor at Pelusium on the borders of Egypt the latter rebelled and Epiphanes returned only to be warned by Rome to withdraw (168 B.C.). On hearing that Jerusalem had sympathized with Egypt he turned his vengeance against it and made it an outpost against Egypt. He now desecrated the Temple by placing within it a sanctuary of Zeus Olympius, by introducing the worship of Dionysus and by compelling Jews to sacrifice to the Greek gods and even to eat sacrificed swine contrary to their sacred law. Such cults, however, were in a sense Judaism in Greek dress, since they were at first supported by the party of the high-priest, which thus curried favor with Epiphanes.[28]

It seemed that Judaism was doomed to be replaced by a Syro-Hellenic cult as part of Epiphanes' plan to extinguish minor ethnic religions in order to unify his realm religiously. But the Jews, who had been able to bear annihilation of their political independence under Assyria, Chaldea, Persia, and Syria as necessary evils, became aroused when their religion was menaced. Besides the Jewish Hellenists there was also another hindering party, the pietistic Hasidim who insisted on non-resistance. However, under the aged Mattathias, a minor village priest, and his five sons—collectively known as the Maccabees (from *makeb*, hammer)—a revolt was started in 165 B.C., during which Epiphanes died, a fate attributed by Jews and Greeks alike to his sacrilege (II Macc. 7:36–37). His fate won for his memory the title *Epimanes* (madman) in place of *Epiphanes* (God manifest) and an unenviable place in history as "the little horn" and "wicked prince," as

---

[27] For the period, see E. R. Bevan, *House of Seleucus* (London, 1902), chap. x.

[28] See E. Bickermann, *Der Gott der Makkabaer* (Berlin, 1937); and review by J. A. Montgomery, *Jour. Bibl. Lit.*, LIX (1940), 308f.

we see in the contemporary book of Daniel (7:8; 8:8–9; 9:26; 10:20).[29] Independence did not come until 142 B.C. when the Jews gained a second period of quasi-autonomy under Mattathias' son Simon and his successors as high-priests (I Macc. 14:27–42).[30]

For centuries before, the high-priest, a Sadducee of the house of Zadok, had been head of the state, but now Simon, an ordinary priest, was elevated for his heroism with authority over the Temple. Thus Ezra's theocracy, or rule of God through his priests, became a commonwealth and the Pharisees, who had aided in the revolt, now displaced the Sadducees and began to democratize Jewish life on the basis of Temple-worship, in which the priests shared with the people in its ceremonies, and to liberalize the law by admitting oral tradition.

It has been long assumed that some time after Ezra's time and as the completion of his work there was evolved out of the municipal Council of Elders at Jerusalem,[31] the *Bet Din,* better known to us by the translation of its Greek title *Great Sanhedrin (Synedrion),* the supreme Jewish tribunal of justice with authority over religious, civil, and criminal cases. It met daily except on Sabbaths and festival days in the *Xystos* or chamber "of hewn stone" in the Temple precincts and consisted of seventy-one members (including the president or *nasi,* "prince") all of whom were scholars, i.e., the chief priests, elders, and scribes, mostly Pharisees. It attained great prominence in the Roman period but later, according to the Gemara, its power of condemning to death had to be confirmed by the procurator, which explains the words of John (18:31): "It is not lawful for us to put any man to death" when Pilate told the accusing Jews to try Jesus according to their own law. A branch consisting of twenty-three members, the *Small Sanhedrin,* formed a provincial council in country towns with jurisdiction over minor civil and criminal cases such as profanation of the Sabbath and also with the power to condemn in cases of homicide.

In recent times, however, because the Gospel accounts of Jesus' time are in some ways irreconcilable with Jewish accounts of the legal procedure of the Sanhedrin as seen in the Talmud, it has been contended that there were, co-existent in the Roman period, two such Councils—not only the religious one of later origin, but also a political one continuous with the old Council of Elders mentioned and known from Josephus, of which the high-priest was president, to administer political affairs and the criminal law under the control of the Roman procurators. It sat anywhere and at any time. While it is supposed to have ceased its activities in A.D. 70, the religious one was changed into a civil and religious body under Johanan ben Zaccai, rabbi and disciple of Hillel and the chief instrument in preserving Judaism. He was allowed by the Emperor Titus, since he had opposed

[29] I and II Maccabees, first composed in Hebrew and then translated into Greek, give us the Jewish attitude toward Epiphanes; a more sympathetic appraisal may now be found in Bevan, *op. cit.,* II, 128.

[30] For the revolt, see I and II Macc., and for later fortunes of the family, Cassius Dio, *Roman History,* XXXVII:5, XLI:18 and XLIX:22.

[31] Mentioned by Ezra 5:5, 6:7 and 14; Neh. 9:38.

the Jewish war, to move his Talmudic school from Jerusalem to Jabneh (later Jamnia) between Joppa and Ashdod, which exercised the functions of the Sanhedrin and became the center of the religious and national life of the dispersed Jews, lasting down to the middle of the fifth century. If there was such a political council, Jesus must have been tried by it rather than by the Great Sanhedrin, since his offense was political—treason—because he called himself "King of the Jews." [82]

Simon's son John Hyrcanus (135–105 B.C.) who drove out Hellenism and dissolved the Samaritan sect again turned the commonwealth into a monarchy which continued down to Antigonus II (40–37 B.C.), the last Maccabean prince who was defeated by Herod and slain as a malefactor by Antony at Antioch. But latterly real power was in the hands of Antipater "the Idumaean" who was named procurator of Judaea by Caesar (47–45 B.C.). In the earlier conflict between Hyrcanus II (69f. B.C.) and his brother Aristobulus II, high-priest later slain at Rome in 30 B.C., Pompey had come to Jerusalem (in 63) and his advent marks the beginning of the end of Jewish independence. Antipater's son, Herod, surnamed "the Great," fled to Rome in 40 B.C. and was there named by the Senate as *rex socius* of Judaea and with Roman aid took Jerusalem in 37, for Rome here followed its custom of ruling conquered peoples through native princes, having removed their power of making war, peace, and treaties.

Herod has left the memory of a blood-thirsty tyrant of the Caligula-Nero type, a psychopathic monster given to every form of violence who never conciliated the Jews and was regarded by Rome as a servile vassal. Matthew represents him as massacring the infants of Bethlehem, an act in keeping with his nature, if it were historical. But he restored the Temple [33] and tried to Hellenize the Jews by erecting Greek temples, theaters, and gymnasia, and in 13 B.C. rebuilt Turris Stratonis into a splendid city, to be the Roman capital of Judaea and renamed it Caesarea Sebaste in honor of Augustus. His nightmare reign ended in murder and Josephus (*Antiq.* 17:6, 5) tells of his last order—the massacre of the nobles immediately after his death so that it would cause mourning. He was succeeded by his three sons as tetrarchs, one of whom, Herod Antipas (4 B.C.–A.D. 39) as ruler of Galilee and Peraea, whom Jesus called "that fox" (Luke 13:32), we shall meet in connection with Jesus' trial before Pilate. Another, Archelaus, became ethnarch of Samaria, Idumaea, and Judaea, after whose deposition Judaea was merged in the Roman province Syria and was governed after A.D.6 by Roman procurators stationed at Caesarea, and subordinate to the legates of Syria.[34] Trouble with Rome finally culminated in the great war of 66–70, a struggle between two ideologies, the Jew regarding the State as subordinate to religion, the Roman as above it.

[82] The view of two councils has been worked out by A. Buckler, *Das Synhedrion in Jerusalem* (Wien, 1902); and recently by S. Zeitlin, *Who Crucified Jesus?* (New York, 1942), pp. 68f. It has been criticized by many scholars, notably by Sir George A. Smith, *Jerusalem: The Topography, Economics and History to A.D. 70* (London, 1907), I, 419f.
[33] Josephus *Antiq.* 15:11. Between 20 and 12 B.C.
[34] See Canon Farrar, *The Herods* (New York, 1898).

Thus, during the last century B.C. and the early part of the first Christian century the Jews of Palestine were encircled by Hellenism, Herod making Judaea almost into a Hellenistic kingdom. It was now that Jesus appeared, but we cannot explain his genius by Hellenism. It was Paul rather who interpreted his message in the light of Greek culture in which the Apostle had been bred. Still, some historians have maintained that Jesus was largely influenced by Hellenism, as the following shows:

It is a fact that the appearance of Christ came at the time of the strongest influence of Hellenism on the intellects of the Judaeans [i.e., Jews from the Captivity to Hadrian]; it is a fact that His teaching was a protest against Judaean attachment to the letter of the law, in the spirit of Hellenic liberty, Hellenic humanitarianism, the Hellenic filial relation to a god whom men love.[35]

But when we reflect that Jesus was a Jew of lowly birth and that his activity was wholly within the Synagogue, we should rather call him the "flower" of Judaism than of Hellenism. We cannot explain his personality by the impact of Hellenism on backward Galilee. His genius transcended his environment and defies analysis. A recent writer has said "a man of genius is a biological accident . . . a fortuitous unlikely contradiction." [36] He was a Jew and lost his life through Jews who refused to accept his vision of nobler things in their religion.

During the period between the Maccabean victory and the destruction of Jerusalem there were many conflicting religious and political parties in Judaism. Of these the Sadducees and the Pharisees were the more important. The Sadducees (Zaddokites or descendants of Zadok, II Sam. 8:17) formed a conservative block of officials and merchants who adhered to the written law alone and denounced all doctrines not in the Pentateuch. Throughout the Persian period and down to that of the Maccabees they remained politically strong while their rivals, the Pharisees, only influenced the common man.[37] The Sadducees denied bodily resurrection, rewards and penalties hereafter, angels and spirits (cf. Acts 22:8), since these were unscriptural; rejected the Davidic Messiah and opposed the doctrine of fate, believing rather in the freedom of the will and, like Ben Sira, in man's rather than God's responsibility for sin.[38] After Jerusalem's fall they passed from history, but their influence reappeared in the Medieval Qarites or Karaites who arose in Mesopotamia in the second half of the eighth century and spread over the Near East and parts of Europe. They opposed

[35] Th. Zielinski, *The Religion of Ancient Greece* (Oxford, 1926), p. 217.

[36] F. H. Hankins, *The Racial Basis of Civilization* (New York and London, 1926), p. 375. The word "genius" at first meant a spirit which inspired one, like the "daemon" of Socrates; it is now applied to those rare individuals whose intellects surpass those of ordinary men.

[37] Josephus, who was a member of both groups, tells us about their beliefs: *Jewish War* 2:8, 14 (162–66) and *Antiq.* 18:11–12.

[38] See G. H. Box in *E.R.E.*, XI (1920), 44–45; and G. Hölscher, *Der Saduzaismus* (Leipzig, 1916).

rabbinical Judaism, especially oral law, and claimed that they represented the religion of Moses and the Prophets.

The Pharisees or *Perushim* (Separatists), so-styled contemptuously by the Sadducees for their separation from the Law as a result of their acceptance of a supplementary oral tradition, dominated the Sanhedrin after the Maccabean revolt. They brought all Jewry into personal relation with the Temple-service which had formerly been a priestly monopoly and thus they made Judaism an individual as well as an official religion. Two of their tenets influenced the people: one, that some day God would reunite all Jews under the leadership of a scion of David; two, that there was bodily resurrection and that the soul would receive rewards and penalties hereafter. The Pharisees stressed the study and exact observance of the Law and hence were called "legalists." They founded schools in the belief that anyone might with application become a scholar. Thus they emphasized education, a Greek idea almost unknown to the Orient. Their insistence on extending the Law to cover all conditions of life was likewise Greek. They supplemented the canonical law by new interpretations, e.g. defining what constituted labor in observing the Sabbath.

It was, however, their over-exacting interpretations which later aroused the animosity of Jesus and his disciples.[39] The charge of hypocrisy hurled at them by Jesus was in general unjust since their interpretations were not a heavy burden on the people (Matt. 23:4) but aimed rather to lighten that burden, since they amended the law to conform with changing conditions. There were "false" Pharisees and it is possible that it was such that Jesus was denouncing although his anger at their hostility to himself in Jerusalem seems to be sufficient to explain his attitude toward them. It may also be that Jesus' oft-repeated use of "hypocrite" may be an interpolation.[40] The animosity of the disciples is easily understood since the Pharisees would not accept Jesus as the Messiah and excluded Christians from the law. If they had been really "hypocrites," "whited sepulchres," "serpents," "blind guides," "fools and blind" (Matt. 23:15–17) they would hardly have survived Jerusalem's fall. It was rather the Pharisees who saved Judaism and kept it alive in the Middle Ages and it is their spirit which animates Jews today in their struggle with totalitarian states as it did in their struggle with Epiphanes, Titus, and Hadrian. Present-day Judaism, then, is their heir.[41]

Another small hyper-Pharisaical sect was the Essenes, who originated in Mesopotamia in the second century B.C., and settled in various towns in Judaea but chiefly east of the Dead Sea, where they influenced both Juda-

[39] This ill-feeling is clearly stated in the Synoptics but not in the Fourth Gospel which was written for Gentile Christians who had little interest in Jewish sects.

[40] In Greek it meant an "answerer," i.e., an actor; in the Septuagint (Job 34:30) and in the New Testament, a "dissembler."

[41] It was their doctrines of immortality, etc., which in part made Christianity possible. Cf. Zeitlin, *op. cit.*, pp. 20–22, 137–38; Rabbi L. Finkelstein, *The Pharisees; the Sociological Background of their Faith* (Philadelphia, 1938).

ism and Christianity.[42] They do not appear in the New Testament nor in rabbinical literature and their esoteric literature is lost but we know their tenets largely from Philo, Pliny the Elder, and Josephus, the latter having lived with them as a probationist in his youth.[43] They shared neither in the social, political, nor economic life of the Jews, but lived apart in semi-monastic celibacy, disdaining marriage because of their low opinion of women whom they excluded from their order, and wealth, and regarding temperance as the highest of virtues. They dressed in white as a mark of purity. They preached charity, justice, and truth; opposed oaths—outside their own organization—and above all, war. They observed the Sabbath, the Torah, and the Temple-rites, rejecting only bloody sacrifices, and they took sacramental meals in common like the early Christians. They exorcised evil spirits and were famed for their prophecies. They believed in angels, destiny, and immortality of the soul after the dissolution of the body which latter they regarded as its prison-house, the old Orphic-Pythagorean belief having, perhaps, reached them. They believed in predestination and not in the freedom of the will, thus opposing Sadducees and Pharisees alike. And they practiced a sacramental sort of baptism for admission to their order. Some have imagined Jesus was a member of or greatly influenced by the sect, since he similarly joined asceticism and initiation into the kingdom of God through baptism. John the Baptist may have been one of them, but we know nothing about him beyond his zeal in saving souls from "the wrath to come" (Matt. 3:7) and his baptism of Jesus. We know too little of the Essenes to connect their baptism with the Christian rite.[44] In the second Christian century the Essenes returned to Pharisaic, i.e. orthodox, Judaism or entered the Christian community.

In Alexandria

Outside Palestine the Jews of the Diaspora found their best refuges in Antioch under the successors of Epiphanes, where Josephus says [45] they attracted multitudes of Greeks to their religious ceremonies, and in Alexandria under the beneficent rule of the early Ptolemies. Under Ptolemy Soter, founder of the Graeco-Egyptian monarchy (312 or 306–285 B.C.), Jews enjoyed the same royal protection as Greeks. One of the city's divisions was assigned to them where they had their own civic organization, courts, laws, and customs. They soon forgot their Aramaic and Hebrew tongues and spoke Greek. By the middle of the third century B.C. under

[42] The name seems to have been derived from that of the Hasidim who were similarly noted for sanctity and opposition to war; but Eusebius (*Praeparatio evangelica* 8:11) connects the name with Greek *hosios* (holy).

[43] Philo, *On the Virtuous being Free* 12; Pliny *Hist. nat.* 5:17; Josephus, *Jewish War* 2:8, 2–13 (118–161) and *Antiq.*, 18, 1, 5. Both Philo and Josephus say they numbered only about four thousand souls.

[44] See H. H. Schaeder in *Gnomon*, V (1920), 353–70; G. A. Barton, *Jour. Amer. Orient. Soc.*, LVI (1936), 155–65; Albright, *J.A.O.S.*, XXXIX (1919), 70f. Purificatory washing was a strict Jewish regulation for postulants for admission to Judaism (Lev. 15) but was hardly the origin of Christian baptism. John (4:2) says "Jesus baptized not, but his disciples."

[45] *Jewish War* 7:3, 3 (45).

Ptolemy Philadelphus (285–247 B.C.) the translation of their Bible into Hellenistic Greek was begun, the *Septuagint* usually known by its Latin symbol LXX (Seventy) after the traditional number (72) of translators, whose names are listed by the Pseudo-Aristeas in a work composed about the middle of the second century B.C. As these names are of the period they substantiate the tradition of authorship.[46] The translation was completed in the second century B.C.[47]

Under such favorable conditions there might well have been a Jewish Renascence at Alexandria, but the very tolerance of the Ptolemies made the Jews easily susceptible to Hellenizing. The average Jew thought and spoke Greek, gave his children Greek names and culturally was a Greek, though racially he remained a Jew who kept the Sabbath and practiced circumcision. Here the Jews learned to regard God as the Aristotelian "unmoved mover" or "uncaused cause" of all motion endowed with mind (*nous*) profoundly extended, as the origin and source of all life and motion, the first attempt to found theism on a philosophical basis.[48] Two centuries before they had followed *theocrasia* by identifying Moses with Osiris, and Philo tells us that in somewhat the same way the new Judaism now used the Old Testament to justify the mystic deities of Greece. It was from such Greek-Jews who had laid aside their national prejudices that Christianity largely took its early converts from the synagogues.

An interesting opinion has recently been expressed in this connection by our leading Philonian scholar, E. R. Goodenough, that by the time of Philo (*ca.* 20 B.C.–A.D. 40) and even for two centuries before, a minority of Greek-Jews had transformed Judaism into a mystery-religion. He makes Philo a member of such a brotherhood in which he thinks all his literary labors centered. Jews had long known the mystic philosophies which had turned Oriental mythologies into mystery-cults, and their Pharisaic exclusiveness now yielded to mysticism while certain "liberalistic" Jews remained outside the movement. The Jewish cult aimed at salvation in a mystical sense for God was no longer Yahweh of the Old Testament alone but the "Prime Mover" of Aristotle, connected with the world of phenomena by his "light-stream" or *Logos*. Man's hope was to leave contaminating matter and thus to rise to real life, i.e., immortality. The written Torah became

[46] That some Jews in Alexandria still read Hebrew, however, is shown by the Papyrus Nash which contains the Decalogue in that language. See Albright, *Jour. Bibl. Lit.*, LVI (1937), 145–76. It is the oldest Hebrew papyrus; *ca.* A.D. 50–150.

[47] The *Septuagint* has been in use in the Orthodox Church from its beginning, although other versions have also been used there: viz. the *Hexapla* or six versions in parallel columns collected by Aquila (A.D. 130), Symmachus (end of second century), Theodotion (latter half of second), and the Septuagint. Fragments of other versions also exist.

[48] The modern *Absolute* of the German idealists—Fichte, Schelling, and Hegel—was also in part in Plato, Aristotle, Aquinas, Bruno, and Spinoza. Aristotle, *Metaphysics* XI, 7, 1072A–1074B, called God "incorporeal, immutable, perfect, eternal, good, self-sufficient, and self-contemplative," a definition lacking only the personality of the Christian God. Spinoza defined substance as nature or universe; and God, as "absolutely infinite, self-existent, unconditional, and independent." He called it partly knowable, while Schelling and Kant made it correspond with Plato's self-determined Being or to the relationless Being of Spinoza's pantheism. Kant and Spencer called it the "Unknowable."

the secret teaching of the mystery but, in Platonic phrase, was only a copy or projection of the ideal. This Jewish mystery-cult evolved practices like those already developed by the Near-East mysteries, and achieved a mystic philosophy which embodied the concept God and an aspiration to rejoin him. According to this theory, provocative but not yet well-known, Orphic-Platonic philosophy became the heart of Hellenistic Judaism.[49]

Greek ideas of the hereafter have been traced in Jewish writings well into the third century B.C. and even affected some of the later books of the Old Testament. The vague hereafter appearing in the older parts of the Testament, where it is called "the pit" (Pss. 28:1; 88:4) or "hell" (Job 2:8, though R.V. here is "Sheol"), gradually became more definite after the Captivity but the process was opposed by the Sadducees. While the author of the apocryphal Ecclesiasticus, Jesus son of Sirach (Ben Sira),[50] denies resurrection and makes man's destiny death alone, the almost contemporary Daniel and later Enoch give a different view of the future. In Ecclesiastes, composed about 200 B.C., we even find Epicurean and Stoic ideas of the denial of individual consciousness after death. This goes beyond the Hebrew idea which merely denied activity hereafter for Ecclesiastes makes death a nothingness where (9:5) "the living know that they shall die, but the dead know not anything, neither have they any more reward." Thus it is urged in true Epicurean spirit (2:24; cf. 3:71) that "there is nothing better for a man than that he should eat and drink, and make his soul enjoy good in his labor." But curiously in the same book appears the Stoic doctrine of obligation to duty (12:13) and that man's soul is an offshoot of the world-soul to which it finally returns (12:7): "The dust (shall) return to the earth as it was, and the spirit return unto God who gave it." The reason why Ecclesiastes was received into the canon was the Jewish and the early Christian belief that it was the work of Solomon, a theory rejected by Luther in 1524. Now it is the consensus that Solomon, the Jewish ideal of wisdom, was introduced only as a literary device.

But the Jews, however much Hellenized in Jerusalem, Antioch, Alexandria, or Athens, could not embrace the Hellenic spirit completely because of fundamental differences in nature between Jew and Greek. The former was deeply religious and regimented in his thinking, while the latter was intellectually free and curious, his outlook comprehending all the phenomena of nature and life. It is the spirit of curiosity which we see in all that the Greeks did—always more esthetic than religious or ethical with the exception of the drama which always kept its religious background. Differences between the two races are especially clear in their ideas of the godhead, the Jew regarding his God as unique, while the ordinary Greek paid obeisance to many beautiful celestial forms which ruled all parts of nature, save he might gradually reach monotheism through the ideas of his philosophies. Paul, in his speech before the court of the Areopagus in Athens

[49] See Goodenough, *By Light, Light: The Mystic Gospel of Hellenistic Judaism* (New Haven and London, 1935), chap. ii.

[50] His work was composed about 180 B.C. in Hebrew at Jerusalem and translated into Greek at Alexandria in 132 B.C. by his grandson for the Jews of the Diaspora.

(Acts 17:23) in connection with an altar which he saw dedicated to "the unknown God," i.e., to one added by the Athenians to rectify any possible omission, immediately interpreted it as the Christian God. This is as good an example as any by which to judge the gulf between Greek and Jew.

In Rome

We know little of the beginnings of a Jewish community in Rome except that one existed there as early as 139 B.C., when the praetor Hispalus expelled the Jews together with the Chaldean magicians from Italy for attempting to infect Roman morals with the cult of the Thrako-Phrygian vegetation god, Sabazius.[51] We know that Pompey brought considerable numbers of them to Rome in 63 B.C. after he had taken Jerusalem. From the poet Martial (1:13) and from Philo,[52] we learn that the Jews occupied the poorest parts of Rome, either beyond the Tiber or in the Campus Martius where they carried on their commercial activities—despised as a secret and malevolent group by the ordinary Roman. But these Jews were part of the race whose "skirt," according to the prophecy of Zechariah (8:23), men later "shall even take hold of . . . saying, we will go with you, for we have heard that God is with you."

Suetonius in his *Lives of the Twelve Caesars* also tells us about the early Roman Jews: how at the funeral of Julius Caesar in 44 B.C. they lamented during several nights since he had been the enemy of their hated Pompey who had insolently entered their Holy of Holies; and how in the reign of Tiberius Jewish rites were forbidden and Jews of military age were sent to unhealthy provinces ostensibly to serve in Roman armies while others were exiled on pain of slavery. This expulsion seems to have been due to a scandal recounted by Josephus.[53] A Roman matron, Fulvia, was persuaded by four Jews to send gold and a purple robe to the Temple in Jerusalem only to have them appropriated by the Jews whereupon her husband complained to the Emperor. Suetonius also speaks of a banishment under Claudius, "because of a disturbance at the instigation of Chrestus," a banishment corroborated by Acts (28:2).[54]

The first major difficulty between Jews and Romans, due to the oppression of Gessius Florus, procurator of Judaea, arose under Nero in 66 when rebellious Jews drove Roman officers from Jerusalem, and this precipitated one of the most sanguinary wars in Roman annals. Jerusalem was first besieged by the Roman governor of Syria, and in the next year Vespasian was sent from Antioch to quell the disturbance, but Nero's death interrupted his plans and, after his elevation as emperor, the management of the Jewish war was placed in the hands of his son Titus. After incredible miseries had been inflicted on the Jews, Titus razed the city of Jerusalem in September

[51] Valerius Maximus, *De factis dictisque memorabilibus* 1:3, 2.
[52] *Legatio ad Caium* [Caligula] 23.
[53] *Antiq.* 18:6, 5–6.
[54] See for these occurrences, Suetonius, *Life of Caesar*, chap. 84; *Life of Tiberius*, chap. 36; and *Life of Claudius*, chap. 25.

70, burned the Temple, sold thousands of captives into slavery, and brought many others to Rome or scattered them throughout Italy. After the fall of the capital the survivors were still allowed certain privileges, but the tax which had been imposed on every Jew for permission to practice his religion unmolested was rigorously collected by Domitian.[55]

But out of every evil some good comes and no less in this case, although the good was not for Judaism but for Christianity. If Jerusalem had stood the Jewish Christians there would have kept the "mother" church in that city and its primacy would have had a disastrous effect on the Gentile churches founded by Paul, which had acted as a counterpoise to it, and nascent Christianity would have been endangered if not destroyed. For the separation of Christianity from Judaism would have been impossible and the "mother" church under James, Cleopas, and others of Jesus' family would probably have developed into a dynastic patriarchate like that of the Maccabees. But now that church, with its strict adherence to circumcision, observance of the Sabbath and many other Jewish customs, passed away and the old distinction between Jew and Gentile was ended. The inheritors of the Jerusalem church—the Ebionites—arising in the second century when Hadrian's decree scattered the old church of Jerusalem in 135 soon migrated to Peraea, east of the Jordan, and Christianity's future as a universal Church was untrammeled.

After the fall of the city Titus left the *decima legio* as a permanent garrison in the almost deserted city, where it remained undisturbed for sixty years till 130–131 when Hadrian, then in Antioch, ordered Jerusalem to be restored under a new name, Aelia Capitolina in honor of his family. He erected a temple to Jupiter Optimus Maximus on the site of the former Temple, and one to Venus on Golgotha, thus accomplishing what Epiphanes three centuries before had failed to do even with Jewish help. Now there were no Maccabeans to oppose but his profanation together with his ban on circumcision as an illegal mutilation caused the Jews of all Palestine to rebel again under the leadership of one Simon Bar Cocheba or Kokhba [56] (son of a star), who was remembered by later Jews, however, as a murderous bandit and was renamed after his defeat Bar Chozeba (son of a lie). Still a man who could assemble two hundred thousand Jews—a number doubtless exaggerated—to defend their city must have been one of great power. Against the Jews Hadrian sent his general Julius Severus who, after taking fifty outposts, nine hundred and eighty-five villages, and causing the death of some five hundred and eighty thousand men besides those who perished by famine and disease, reduced the Jews after two years

[55] Suetonius, *Life of Domitian*, chap. 12.

[56] The Roman historians Spartianus and Cassius Dio mention no leader. The name comes from Christian tradition beginning with Justin Martyr (*Apol.* 31) where he mentions Barcochebas, reproduced by Eusebius (*H.E.* 4:8, 4). Eusebius (4:6, 2) says he captivated the ignorant by basing his claim that he was sent by God on his name meaning "Son of a star" and that he was slain 134–135 at his fortress, present Bittir near Jerusalem. Rabbi Akiba, on the basis of Num. (24:17), called him "Son of a star."

of struggle.[57]   Eusebius says that Hadrian then decreed that all Jews should be banned from entering the city and its district on pain of death and that Jerusalem was colonized by foreigners and a new church, under one Bishop Marius, was erected there.   As an added insult, a swine, the insignia of the Tenth legion, was sculptured over the gateway leading to Bethlehem. Thus with her usual ruthlessness Rome put down the last ancient attempt of the Jews to keep their independence.   Five hundred years later the Moslem Caliph Omar (634–644), "commander of the faithful," who organized Islam on a military-religious basis, during his conquest of Persia, Syria, Palestine, and Egypt, again banned Jews from settling in their old home.

The year in which the Jewish revolt ended marks the beginning of the last era of Jewish history, their dispersion over the Western world.   Not again until modern times, when the Nationalist Zionistic movement of Jews "back to Palestine" was launched, did the idea of a Jewish homeland again become active.[58]

For two centuries after Hadrian's destruction, the history of Jerusalem is obscure.   Eusebius [59] recounts how in 325, after the Council of Nicaea, Constantine ordered Bishop Macarius to recover the sites of the Crucifixion and tomb of Jesus.   Two churches were built over the site on which Hadrian had built a temple of Venus, the Holy Sepulchre and a Basilica of the Cross.   While nothing is left of the latter, the former was destroyed by Chosroes II of Persia in 614 and again by the Caliph Hakim in 1010; it was repaired by the Crusaders in 1099, since which time after various reparations it has been the center of a group of ecclesiastical buildings.   Later historians, Socrates, Sozomen, and Theodoret, have Helen, Constantine's mother, play a part in finding the grave and Cross and building a church on the Mount of Olives.[60]

The Theodosian Code tells us of restrictions on the Jews beginning with Constantius (337–361).   One passed in 339 decreed that any Jew who purchased a Gentile slave was liable to have him confiscated if a Christian, and those who purchased Christian slaves would have all their slaves confiscated, and the owner, if he had them circumcised, would be put to death.[61] In the same year another decree proclaimed that any Jew who associated

[57] The revolt is outlined by Cassius Dio, *Roman History*, LXIII, 12–14, and Eusebius *H.E.* 6:6.

[58] The Italian Benedetto Mussolino tried in vain in 1870 to interest the English government in it.   But it was the Hungarian Jew Theodor Herzl who, stirred by Jewish persecutions, renewed it in his day in Russia and Rumania.   Assuming that anti-Semitism was ineradicable, he issued his famous pamphlet *Der Jüden-Staat* (Wien, 1896) which gave a great impetus to Zionism.   While acclaimed by the Jews in England whence thousands emigrated and built cities, schools and industries in Palestine, the movement has now been officially stopped by Britain, protector of Palestine, first because of Arab opposition held in check only by a British army of occupation and later by the opening of the Second World War.   Friends of the movement have hailed it as the solution of the Jewish question, while its opponents have called it the dissolution of Judaism.   See A. Bein, *Th. Herzl, a Biography;* tr. from German by M. Samuel (Philadelphia, 1940).

[59] *Life of Constantine*, 3:25–40.

[60] See Sir Charles W. Wilson, *Golgotha and the Holy Sepulchre* (London, 1906).

[61] *Codex Theodosianus* (cited hereafter as *C.Th.*) XVI:9, 2.

in the rites of Christian women at work in the public textile mills should be put to death.[62]   In 357 a Jew who converted a freeman to Judaism was threatened with confiscation of all his goods.[63]

From Julian to Theodosius the Great (361–395), however, there was no anti-Jewish legislation.   Valentinian I (364–375) even forbade Roman soldiers from being quartered in synagogues and Theodosius, when St. Ambrose urged him to legislate against them (Ep. XXIX), forbade interference with their worship and, sensing that racially and religiously they could not be assimilated, gave them a special status, a policy culminating in a decree of 393 which made Judaism a *religio licita*.[64]   This meant that Jews could own property and hold assemblies unmolested.   However, in 384 a decree had ordained that no Jew could buy a Christian slave and, if he had done so, he must not convert him to Judaism on pain of having all his slaves confiscated; [65] but in 388 intermarriage between Jews and Christians was declared to be a crime of adultery, as it had been under Constantine.[66]

After Theodosius' death persecutions began again.   In 412 Honorius granted a curious concession to the Jews, that courts should not be held on the Sabbath.[67]   In 417 he made the attempt to proselytize Christian slaves a capital crime.[68]   To stop their increase in influence Honorius, in the last year of his reign (423), decreed that no more synagogues should be built.[69]   Already in 404 by a decree (reënacted in 428) Jews were barred from the imperial service, both civil and military, except in municipal affairs.[70]   There were twenty-nine decrees against Jews in *Titulus* VIII of the Code and five in *Titulus* IX.[71]

Theodosius II, grandson of Theodosius the Great, Eastern emperor (408–450), in 425 forbade Jews to act as civil lawyers, and in 439 decreed against the erection of synagogues, against Jewish decisions between themselves and Christians and Jewish possession of Christian slaves.   In his Code, published in 438, Jews were called by such opprobrious titles as *inferiores* and *perversi* (malicious), and Judaism was called *nefaria* (execrable), *ferialis* (dangerous), and a *superstitio,* and its assemblies *sacrilegi coetus,* although it still was a *religio licita*.   Justinian in 537 made Jews ineligible to any public honor—*honore fruantur nullo*—and in 553 banned the Talmud and revised the law against erecting synagogues.   Two centuries later the Caliph Omar II (717–721) similarly ordered his governors

62 *C.Th.* XVI:8, 6.

63 *C.Th.* XVI:8, 7.

64 *C.Th.* XVI:8, 9; reaffirmed in 412 by Honorius; *ibid*. XVI:8, 20.

65 *C.Th.* III:1, 5: cf. *op. cit.* XVI:9, 2 *supra* mitigated by Honorius in 415, when Jews were permitted to have Christian slaves if these were allowed to observe their Christian rites; XVI:9, 3.

66 *C.Th.* III:7, 2; cf. IX:7, 5.

67 *C.Th.* II:8, 26.

68 *C.Th.* XVI:9, 4.

69 *C.Th.* XVI:8, 25.

70 *C.Th.* XVI:7, 6–7; VIII:24, 29; XVI:8, 16 and 24.

71 Boyd, *op. cit.* (see p. 45, n. 92, *supra*), p. 53, n. 1.

to allow no more to be built.   Thus we see that edicts against Jews in our time had their prototypes in the Roman Empire.[72]

ANTI-SEMITISM IN ANTIQUITY

Moreover, such edicts show that the Jews scattered over the Empire were a race apart as they are still today.   Anti-Semitism was not old in the ancient world, seemingly having started in the second century B.C. if we may trust the date of the story of Haman, grand vizier of Ahasuerus (Xerxes) who tried to extirpate all Jews in Persia since they were not law-abiding.[73] By then Jews were "throughout the whole kingdom of Ahasuerus."   Many causes for the ill-feeling toward Jews in antiquity have been given, some of which are still operative, notably by Angus[74] and more recently by H. Valentin.   The former has given four chief causes for it: first, the success of Jews in trade competition, especially at Alexandria; second, their religious scruples which rendered them unsocial and unpatriotic since these kept them (through fear of contamination) from frequenting public banquets, festal occasions, from loyalty to the imperial cult and from supporting such Graeco-Roman social institutions as the gymnasium, theater, and arena; third, the rebellious spirit which characterized them for over three centuries from the Seleucid conquest of Palestine to Hadrian's War of Extermination (198 B.C.–A.D. 132), a spirit which led them to seize every imperial crisis for their own advantage; and, finally, the success of their propaganda in attracting non-Jews into the synagogue.   This latter success was due, according to Emil Schürer,[75] to their presenting only the more attractive features of their religion to pagans, its pure deism without images, its antiquity and divine origin through supernatural revelation, its moral code, and its having profited by the trend toward the promise of blessedness as taught by the mystery-religions, though promising nothing definite, neither rewards nor penalties.   Valentin[76] lists five causes: their refusal to worship alien gods represented by images, which was regarded by their neighbors as godless; their laws about circumcision and prohibition against swine's flesh, regarded with ridicule; their observance of the Sabbath which was unintelligible to the Romans (Seneca saying they thus squandered one-seventh of their lives in idleness); their ceremonial laws regarded as superstition, especially those about clean and unclean foods which were regarded as an attempt at aloofness; their different course of life such as refusing to eat with outsiders, to marry non-Jews, and to share in public worship and sacrifice, and their hatred of other peoples.   Thus Tacitus,

[72] See H. Vogelstein, *Jews in Rome,* tr. by M. Hadas (Philadelphia, 1940), a new ed. of *Geschichte der Jüden in Rom* by H. Vogelstein and P. Kiegen (Berlin, 1895–96). This is an account of Jews in Rome from the second century B.C. to the present.

[73] See the late book of Esther (5:6, 8, 9f.), composed after the Maccabees rather than in the earlier Persian period as it pretends.

[74] *Op. cit. (see* p. 68, n. 78, *supra),* pp. 25f.

[75] *Geschichte des jüdischen Volkes im Zeitalter Jesus Christi* (4th ed.; Leipzig, 1901–11), III, 155f.

[76] *Anti-Semitism Historically and Critically Examined,* tr. from the Swedish by A. S. Chater (New York, 1936), chap. ii.

an anti-Semite, mentions their *odium humanis generis* and their teaching proselytes to despise the country of their origin. Josephus in his *Contra Apionem*, a refutation of charges brought against his fellow-Jews before Caligula in 38, has Apion, who led the deputation of Alexandrians in his defense, say that a law recommended Jews to fatten and kill a Greek each year, eat his entrails and to swear hatred of all Greeks—the origin of the never-ending calumny of ritual murder.

Of all these causes the religious spirit of propaganda was the least important and the ceremonial scruples doubtless the greatest, since their religion has always played the main role in isolating the Jews down to our time. How could the gloomy picture of Sheol attract Gentiles, a picture even gloomier than that of Babylonian Arallu where the dead dwelt in a seven-walled cavern guarded by Nergal and his consort Allatu with a host of daemon servitors, or that of the Greek Hades? Such a hopeless hereafter had no chance beside the joyful millennial future here on earth promised by Jesus or those of the mystery-cults whose votaries were promised beatitude with their gods. It was rather the meticulous observance of physical and dietary restraints of Judaism, the miraculous element in the Old Testament, and even the bad Greek of the Septuagint through which Greeks and Romans first learned about the Jews, which repelled both peoples. Few Greeks knew about the Jewish religion and ethics and fewer Romans. Celsus, the philosopher and anti-Christian writer, has been called the first pagan Roman to have read the Septuagint.

One feature of Judaism which must have helped to render its votaries unpopular was its uncompromising emphasis on the command of Yahweh: "Thou shalt have no other gods before me." The Romans were long accustomed to sharing their polytheistic beliefs with the Oriental religions and so, with their tolerant spirit, regarded the Jew with disfavor and felt he was out of place in their midst. It was this Jewish refusal to endure any other religion that was one of the chief causes in arousing the same hostility to Judaism that it did at first to the Christians when the latter were regarded as a pernicious sect of the former. They were similarly accused of all sorts of crimes—ungodliness, incest, ritual murders. It seems fair to say that the Christians, had they remained a minority sect, would have continued to our time to be equally despised. Intolerance, "the most fatal gift that Christianity received from Judaism," [77] is one from which in later ages Christianity could not free itself. Both religions seemed out of place in tolerant Rome and only after Christianity had become the majority religion was its earlier exclusiveness forgotten. By the end of the fourth century tolerance in religion, which had been the pride of Roman paganism, was destroyed by Gratian and Theodosius, the latter winning his title "Great" from the Christians for his intolerant act of making Christianity the sole religion of the State and banning its rivals. Then the Christians, all outside rivalry removed, turned on themselves in internal dissensions, a characteristic remaining strong to this day.

[77] Th. Zielinski, *op. cit.* (*see* p. 35, n. 92, *supra*), p. 215.

THE OLD TESTAMENT

The Jewish Bible,[78] the Christian Old Testament, is the most important collection of sacred writings (if we except the New Testament) of any of the Near-East religions which became important in the Roman Empire. Its message was for Jews alone, its incorporation into the Christian writings being natural since it was the sacred writ of Jesus, the disciples, Paul and the early converts to Christianity and since it contained prophecies of the Messiah, i.e., Jesus. To the Jew it was the whole truth about God, but to the Christian supplementary truth about God and Christ.

Its tripartite division, each part succeeding in time and importance, corresponds with the stages of its canonization. The nucleus, the Torah or Law, Pentateuch in Greek, the outgrowth of rabbinical thought, was canonized about 400 B.C. at the close of the period when Nehemiah and Ezra were striving to reorganize the reëstablished Jews politically and religiously; the Prophets were completed by scribes about 200 B.C. and the Writings— *Ketubim* in Hebrew, *Hagiology* in Greek—were canonized between about 130 and 100 B.C. Other books were added in the first century B.C. both in Palestine and at Alexandria and the whole process was completed between A.D. 70 and 132 by rabbis headed by Akiba ben Joseph who cut out unacceptable books.[79] Josephus [80] was the first to enumerate a canon of twenty-two books. The "Alexandrian" canon of the Septuagint differed from the Palestinian, the books being grouped more clearly by subjects and new ones added. This was the canon which the Church followed after its separation from Judaism.[81] Fourteen other books were added to the "holy" ones, which St. Jerome in the *Vulgate* called *apocrypha* "hidden away" since they did not appear in regular sacred collections.[82]

[78] The word is derived from the Greek name Byblus (modern Jebeil) above Beirut, the Syrian port famed in antiquity especially as a papyrus mart. In the Septuagint *biblia* is used, from which, through a mistake made in the Middle Ages, the word, a neuter plural, became a feminine singular from which the term Bible appears as a singular in English as in all other European languages. In English versions of the New Testament the Old Testament is called "the scripture" (Acts 8:32), "scriptures" (Matt. 21:44), or "sacred writings" (II Tim. 3:15; A.V. "holy scriptures"), but in the Septuagint it is translated *diatheké*, "covenant," first used in the New Testament by Paul (II Cor. 3:14); "old covenant," while "new testament" appears frequently in Paul's Letters and the Gospels (e.g. I Cor. 11:25; Mark 14:24; R.V. "covenant").

[79] These approximate dates are reached through internal evidence since the Jews never had any historical account of the "canon" or rule by which various books were accepted as "holy" and others rejected.

[80] *Contra Apionem* 1:8.

[81] On the Jewish Canon, see H. E. Ryle, *The Canon of the Old Testament* (2nd ed.; London, 1895); W. Sanday in *E.R.E.*, II (1910), pp. 568–71; G. Wildeboer, *The Origin of the Canon of the Old Testament*; tr. by B. W. Bacon and ed. with preface by G. F. Moore (London, 1895).

[82] In the Septuagint and Vulgate they were scattered among the books by classes— history, poetry, prophecy. Luther in 1534 placed them together at the end of the Old Testament, a plan followed by Coverdale (1535), the first English translation of the entire Bible dedicated to Henry VIII, and by the King James Version of 1611. Since the appearance of the latter, due largely to Puritan disapproval, they are usually published as a separate volume: see E. J. Goodspeed, *The Apocrypha: an American Translation* (Chi-

The Jews of antiquity regarded their Bible as the "Word of God" and believed that the early books, including the Ten Commandments "written by the finger of God" (Exod. 31:18), had been given to Moses by Yahweh. While the Jew Philo said "all that the Scriptures contain is true, and all that is contained in them," the Christian St. Augustine four centuries later affirmed that "the New Testament lies in the Old and the Old Testament is manifest in the New." But the Jews assigned different degrees of authority to the different books, e.g., they regarded the Torah as the most important group of books since the Law covered all requirements of both the community and the individual and, curiously, the Psalms as the least, which Christians have placed among the most beautiful books.

The great merits of the Old Testament—religious, poetic, historical—are self-evident for one needs only to recall such episodes as those of Joseph in Egypt, David's friendship for Jonathan and lament at his death, the graceful idyl of Ruth, the profound meaning of the Prophets the most sincere of reformers, the sensuous Song of Songs, the philosophy of Job, and many of the Psalms whose lyric beauty reaches its height, perhaps, in the Eighteenth and the One Hundred and Fourth. The tribute to the majesty of Yahweh in the latter recalls the spirit of the ritual fragment of Ikhnaton's new cult in Egypt inscribed on the wall of his tomb at Amarna, the earliest vision of a kindly Father who labored for the weal of his creatures so that even the marsh-birds flapped their wings in praise.

But such transcendant merits are accompanied by many equally obvious defects, only natural in so heterogeneous a collection of many hands and of different ages. It is marred by inconsistencies, incoherences, contradictions, repetitions, exaggerations, improbabilities, absurdities, horrors of war, and even obscenities. Violations of natural law perplex the devout Jew and Christian, such as the accounts of a six-day Creation, a global flood with pairs of all beasts and creeping things placed in an ark represented as large as an "Atlantic liner" of our day; the sun and moon stopping the earth's rotation for a day (Josh. 10:12–14), and the turning of the sun's shadow back ten degrees (II Kings 20:9–11); incredible stories of talking serpents (Gen. 3:1–14) and asses (Num. 22:23–30); Jonah alive in the belly of a fish for three days (Jonah 1:17). Wanton cruelty is found in savage war-songs and curses on enemies,[83] for the Old Testament is a veritable arsenal of texts bristling with the cruelties of war. One book alone, Joshua, is saturated with war, its tenth chapter glorifying militarism as a religious duty to a greater degree, perhaps, than any other in literature, with its oft-repeated formulae, "he smote it with the edge of the sword" and "utterly destroyed them and all the souls that were therein."

cago, 1938); *The Story of the Apocrypha* (Chicago, 1939); see also R. H. Charles, *The Apocrypha and Pseudepigrapha of the Old Testament* (Oxford, 1913); G. F. Moore, "Apocrypha" in the *Jewish Encyclopedia* (New York and London, 1902), Vol. II. While Protestants usually omit them they are still used by the Roman (eleven books), Lutheran, and Anglican (fourteen books) churches.

[83] E.g. that against Babylon in Ps. 137:9. "Happy he be that taketh and dasheth thy little ones against the rocks."

Historical inaccuracies in many cases have had to await the modern archaeologist and epigraphist for correction. In Daniel—one of the later books [84]—are various such instances. Nebuchadrezzar is called the father of Belshazzar (5:2, 11, 13, 18) and the latter the last king of Babylon (5:1 and 30; 7:1), a mistake not corrected until 1854 when Sir Henry Rawlinson read a cuneiform inscription found at Ur dating from the first year of Nabonidus which gave the latter—a name not mentioned by Daniel—as the father of Belshazzar, "the first born son," and the last king of Babylon (555–538 B.C.). But Belshazzar never reigned and Nabonidus was unrelated to Nebuchadrezzar but, like the later Persian Darius the Great, was elevated to the throne by a palace revolution.[85] Furthermore, the well-known household story of Belshazzar's feast and "the handwriting on the wall" of his palace and the capture of Babylon by Darius (Dan. 5:1–5) is apocryphal. The latter is an example of a historical "projection" backwards, i.e., an account of a reconquest of the city by Darius in one of its later revolts either in 520 or 519 B.C. when he destroyed its walls. For Cyrus' general Gobryas took the city years before on October 5, 539 B.C. "without fighting" as a contemporary inscription records.[86]

Sometimes, however, critics have assumed inaccuracy where excavations in our time have shown that the Old Testament account is correct, as one example from Joshua (6:10) will show. Here we read: "The wall (of Jericho) fell down flat so that the people went up into the city . . . and they took the city." This was long regarded as a grotesque story until Garstang in his resumption of the excavations of the site in 1930–36 begun by the Germans before the First World War proved that the walls fell outward, probably the result of earthquake, and not inward by attack, the only legendary feature of the account being the belief of the Israelites that the walls fell to the blare of the trumpets of the priests.[87] On the other hand, the account of Joshua's capture of Canaanite Ai in central Palestine (7:3–6, 8:8 and 28–29) when, in fulfillment of the Lord's promise, he took twelve thousand of its inhabitants, burned the city to be a "desolation to this day," hanged its king and buried his body under a heap of stones, is apoc-

---

[84] Modern critics, following the lead of Porphyry in the third century, have placed its composition in the reign of Antiochus Epiphanes (175–164 B.C.) because of the author's predictions centering in the latter's time and his evident familiarity with the period despite his use of older material dating from the Exile. See J. A. Montgomery, *Critical and Exegetical Commentary on the Book of Daniel* (New York, 1927).

[85] See Th. G. Pinches in *Proceed. of Soc. of Biblical Archeology*, V (London, 1884), and H. Winckler in *Zeitschr. für Assyriologie*, II (1887), 2, 3. It should be remembered that before Rawlinson deciphered the cuneiform characters (1835–46) on the basis of Darius' great inscription at Behistun in three languages—Susian, Old Babylonian and Persian—our knowledge of Belshazzar came only from Daniel and the reproduction of his account by Josephus. The native historian Berosus of the third century B.C. had also identified Belshazzar with Nabonidus as "the last king of Babylon," followed by Josephus.

[86] See Pinches, *The Old Testament in the Light of Historical Records of Assyria and Babylonia* (3rd ed.; New York, 1908).

[87] See *The Story of Jericho* by John and J. B. E. Garstang (London, 1940); and Garstang's illustrated article on "Joshua's Storming" in the *London Illustrated News* (Jan. 17, 1931), pp. 94–97.

ryphal since Madame Marquet-Krause in excavating the site in 1933 found that Ai, occupied as early as about 3000 B.C., was destroyed a millennium later, centuries before Joshua's time, and never rebuilt.[88] Without doubt tradition has exaggerated the exploits of Moses' successor who appears to have had less to do with conquering Canaan than his book tells. This has led some mistakenly to regard him as an insignificant local chieftain and to doubt much of the biblical account [89] as not confirmed by later history.

Such historical inaccuracies show the fallacy of maintaining that the Old Testament is equally inspired and true in all its parts as the infallible revelation of God. Its value is not so much theological or historical as it is as a record of the religious, social and moral development of the Hebrews from their earliest days almost to the time when they evolved Christianity and gave the final revelation of their God through Jesus. Jesus understood its imperfections as we see in his oft-repeated formula in the "Sermon on the Mount" (Matt. 5:21–22, etc.): "Ye have heard that it was said by them of old time . . . but I say unto you . . ." Paul often spoke of them in reference to ceremonial law and sacrifice. Thus he says (II Cor. 3:3) that Jesus' law was "written not in ink . . . not in tables of stone, but in tables that are hearts of flesh" and (ibid. 5:6) that "the letter killeth, but the spirit giveth life." The early Church knew nothing of such an idea as the infallibility of the Old Testament, for it first appeared during the Reformation. The Roman Catholics have always opposed the notion since their idea of infallibility is, as has often been said, in the Church rather than in the Bible. They teach that the Bible is true only in the sense intended by the individual writers. The Old Testament is our fullest storehouse of the life of any people of antiquity, in that respect surpassing the sacred writings of Egyptians, Babylonians and Persians. If we are repelled by the barbarity of some of its parts and the revelation of Yahweh in its earlier books as a God of bloodshed and vengeance, we should remember that such beliefs belonged to the childhood of the Hebrew people. For more than anything else the Old Testament is a work of anthropology, its pages replete with survivals of older phases of culture "preserved like fossils" in those of later periods. Such ideas as the sacrifice of the first-born as a burnt-offering (Gen. 22:1–13), the law of the uncleanness of women (Lev. 12:2–5), and the use of the scapegoat on the Day of Atonement (ibid. 16:5), an idea which later played such a role in the thought of Paul, belong to the early days of Israel. We need only read such a work as Sir James Frazer's Folklore in the Old Testament [90] to realize this.

The great spiritual shortcoming of the Old Testament is its imperfect revelation of God, first in beauty so characteristic of Greek polytheism with

[88] As recounted by Albright, op. cit., p. 119, who also dates its destruction about 2100 B.C.

[89] E.g. A. Alt, Der Gott der Väter (Leipzig, 1929); M. Noth in Palestin Jahrbuch, XXXIV (1938), 7–22.

[90] London, 1913; cf. also his earlier essay with the same title in Anthropological Essays Presented to E. B. Tylor (Oxford, 1907), pp. 101–74.

its colorful festivals, beautiful temples and statues and especially its freedom from fear, and then in goodness and truth which occupied the minds of Plato and the Stoics. This imperfect revelation caused Marcion in his second-century church at Rome to reject it for he regarded all its parts equally bad and its God only a demiurge, the subordinate and inferior deity of Plato and the Gnostics, who created the world and thus is distinguished from the later Supreme God revealed in the New Testament.[91]

While the Christians took over the Old Testament, they did not altogether understand its Jewish message which is often out of harmony with Christian teaching. The early stern God of fear pictured by Isaiah (8:13): "The lord of hosts, him shall ye sanctify: and let him be your fear, and let him be your dread," had disappeared from the Jewish concept centuries before Jesus preached his God of love and its teaching has nothing to do with the latter. Yahweh was the outgrowth of that "religious awe" which, in the words of a recent writer, "first began to stir in the feeling of something uncanny, eerie, or weird,"[92] while Jesus' kindly Father aroused feelings not of awe but of affection. The Christians did not abandon the Old Testament even after they had developed their own sacred literature, for they believed that the latter was a supplement to the former, and it still forms three-fourths of our Bible. It has influenced Protestants more than Jews or Roman Catholics since the Jews have always had other spiritual works such as the Talmud and the Catholics have had other guides, what the Church Fathers and theologians recognized as "tradition." Thus at Trent it was decreed that the Church

receives with piety and reverence all the books of the Old and New Testaments, since one God is the author of each, and at the same time it maintains that there is an unwritten word of God over and above Scriptures.

But both Testaments have monopolized the spiritual guidance of Protestants. The Westminster Assembly of Divines, convoked in 1643 by the Long Parliament (1640–53) "to advise for the settling of the liturgy and the government of the Church of England," declared that

the Supreme Judge by which all controversies of religion are to be determined, all decrees of councils, opinions of ancient writers, and private spirits are to be examined and in whose sentence we are to rest, can be no other than the Holy Spirit speaking in the Scriptures.

Thus it is clear that over-emphasis on the sanctity of the Old Testament and its infallibility is due largely to the Protestants. Some, therefore, have maintained that the Reformation "rejudaized" Christianity which the medieval Roman Church tried to avert.

That such reverence has been an impediment to the progress of Christianity by its retention of irrational concepts has long been voiced by many

[91] Cf. Zielinski, *op. cit.*, pp. 212–14.

[92] Rudolph Otto, *The Idea of the Holy*, tr. from the German by J. W. Harvey (London, 1926), pp. 8, 14–15.

sincere Christians.   They point out that it is not strange that the authority
of the Old Testament was reverenced in antiquity, but that it is strange
that it survives in our day of enlightenment in all fields of inquiry at the
hands of the higher critics.   It has been used to settle authoritatively any
practice or belief, such as peace and war, slavery and freedom, monogamy
and polygamy, witch-baiting and torture, capital punishment, woman suf-
frage, child labor, capitalism and communism, temperance and prohibition.[93]

Reverence for the Old Testament, moreover, has furthered the intolerant spirit which has followed Christianity from the first, the spirit which
has defiled it with innumerable wars and persecutions as these words of
an eminent historian show:

It was unfortunate that the early Christians had included in their Scripture the
Jewish writings which reflect the ideas of a low stage of civilization, and are full of
savagery.   It would be difficult to say how much harm has been done in corrupting
the morals of men by the precepts and examples of inhumanity, violence, and bigotry, which the reverent reader of the Old Testament, implicitly believing in its
inspiration, is bound to approve.   It furnished an armoury for the theory of
persecution. . . . Christianity by adopting books of a long past age placed in the
path of human development a particularly nasty stumbling-block.   It may occur to
me to wonder how history might have been altered if the Christians had cut Jehovah out of their program, and, content with the New Testament, had rejected
the inspiration of the Old.[94]

[93] In the First World War William of Germany was called "the Little Horn" of Daniel (7:8) which made war on saints and prevailed against them until "the saints possessed
the kingdom" (7:21–22), and was identified with the beast whose number was 666 (Rev.
13:18).   The number 666 (codex C. 616), typifying Rome as a world power, was first associated with Caligula by the Jews when he tried to place his statue in the Temple.   The
Greek letters of his name KAIOS KAISAR in Hebrew notation added up to 616, and the
letters of NERON KAISAR to 666.

[94] J. B. Bury, *History of Freedom of Thought* (New York, 1913), p. 177.

Chapter IV

CHRISTIANITY: THE PERSONALITY OF JESUS

THE last important religion to reach the early Roman Empire was Christianity which within three and one-half centuries of its origin became the official faith of Rome, the greatest religious influence exerted on the Western mind. Although originating in the Near East Christianity cannot be classified with any of the mystery-religions discussed. In its developed form it contains some of their essential beliefs, especially personal communion with the Deity, communal worship, memorial meal, and immortality; but it also contains many others unknown to them, notably belief in God as the Father and in the brotherhood of the human race. Its method of propagandizing was also different for it had no secret rites of initiation and few external attractions such as pageants. It was preached openly to all, men and women, rich and poor, bond and free, educated and ignorant, if only they would follow the Christian idea of living.

As it reached Rome it was not addressed to the Romans themselves but rather to their Jewish and alien slaves and freedmen expressing doctrines more acceptable to such people than to born Romans. Paul had preached that Jesus was the Messiah, who had died to atone for human sins, had risen from the dead and would return and rule spiritually forever, and that this new religion, like the older Judaism, demanded only faith as the condition of salvation—doctrines strange to Roman ears. By the close of the Antonine period it was preached all over the Empire, a vision of divine fatherhood with its corollary human brotherhood which surpassed the teaching of the Prophets to whom Jesus as completer of their work belonged rather than to the Jewish priests, for Christianity in a sense was their spiritual heir, even if more specifically of the later Jewish apocalyptic writers. Paul's emphasis, like that of Jesus before him, was on the inner spirit rather than on the external law, even if for long the new message was confused with the old in the Roman mind.

Jesus—Yeshua (Joshua) in his native Aramaic [1]—was the son of a village carpenter Joseph and his wife Miriam in Nazareth of Galilee (Mark 6:3–4). In early manhood he preached his message a short time in his native district and finally in the Jewish capital. Here he aroused the hostility of the rabbis who could not accept his identifying himself with the Messiah of Jewish hopes. He was accused of blasphemy and of attempting to subvert civil authority by claiming he was "King of the Jews," was arrested, tried, and condemned to the cross as a rebel in the latter part of Tiberius' reign. It is with this lowly figure, co-founder with Paul of the religion

---

[1] Miscalled Iesous in Greek and Jesus in Latin because of inherent difficulties in transliteration, a common name in Hebrew and Aramaic meaning "Savior."

which is called by his Messianic title, that we are here concerned. Of his advent we quote from a recent book:

With his [Augustus'] regime began not only a new political era for the Roman world, but a new Christian era for all future Western civilization. For when the autocratic Octavian was founding his new Empire, revered as Augustus and *deus*, another king was to be worshipped as divine and to extend his rule over the Roman Empire and far beyond. In contrast to his aristocratic contemporary, he was born in an insignificant village, of obscure peasant parents, from a most hated race, and according to tradition not in a home but in a stable. Yet his Christian Church was destined to enter into the heritage of the Roman Empire itself, and later dominate the Western world, so that it would even reckon its chronology from his birth.[2]

His appearance was opportune since it occurred at

a time of spiritual awakening, of a call to higher destinies which came upon the world, the civilized world which lay around the Mediterranean Sea at the beginning of our era. The calling was concentrated in the life and death of the Founder of Christianity.[3]

Paul, a tent-maker by trade (Acts 18:3) of Tarsus in Cilicia, educated beyond his Jewish contemporaries in Greek culture and possessing the prized title of Roman citizen, after Jesus' death advocated certain phases of the new doctrines, especially sharing with Jesus' immediate followers the belief that Jesus was the Messiah, although the latter had laid claim to supernatural origin only near the close of his ministry. After his miraculous conversion on the road to Damascus, Paul spread these ideas among the Jews of the Diaspora and the Gentiles, preaching in Syria, Asia Minor, Macedonia, Greece, and finally in Italy, visiting a series of early Christian communities from Antioch, where Jesus' followers were first called Christians (Acts 11:26), to Rome where he is believed to have died a martyr's death under Nero during or after the great fire of 64. To Paul, as to Daniel and Enoch before him, Jesus as Messiah was the preëxistent divine person who had voluntarily descended from heaven, where from the beginning he had dwelt with God, to the earth where he had taken on the nature of man to establish "the kingdom of God." Later, in John's Gospel, he became the *Logos* of Jewish and Alexandrian Greek thought which had existed with God before creation, first as the latter's attribute, then as a separate Being, and finally as the Second Person of the Trinity.

Jesus' disciples after his death had continued as a group to await his return in conformity with his promise that he would return during the lifetime of some of his hearers. He had left no written word, but only the memory of his personal presence. There was as yet no vision of a Church, the group being held together only by a common hope. But within a short time it had grown into the "mother church" of Jerusalem

[2] A. A. Trever, *The Roman World* (New York, 1939), p. 353. Quoted by permission of the publishers, Harcourt, Brace & Co.

[3] Percy Gardner, *The Growth of Christianity* (London, 1907), p. 2.

which thus was literally the "child of the waiting." There, as elsewhere, Paul sponsored the novel view that there was no distinction between Jew and Gentile, circumcised and uncircumcised, even though at first such a violent breaking down of barriers caused a serious division within the nascent Church, most Jewish converts believing that the Gospel was for them alone. They at first remained loyal to Temple and Synagogue and followed their Jewish heritage with no idea of a new sect. Thus the first steps toward the universality of the Church were taken by Paul's obliteration of racial distinctions. This, in conjunction with his emphasis on Jesus as "the Christ," makes Paul at least co-founder with Jesus of our religion.

It is difficult nineteen centuries later to extract the essential truth about the primitive faith which was soon colored by varied ideas and interpretations. This can be accomplished only by the subjection of the written sources to ordinary historical methods, by following the results of the so-called "higher critics," divorced from faith. No field of historical research has been so minutely tilled in its every corner as that of the beginnings of our religion in the attempt to understand the faith of the early Christians in one whom they had known as a carpenter's son and had seen die a malefactor's death. Our brief survey will be confined to two problems: the personality of the man Jesus and, in the following chapter, his essential teachings. There will be little effort to say anything new since with the imperfect evidence available everything of importance has already been said, but rather to present Jesus as a historical personage and the Church as a human institution. Jesus will, then, be presented as a man as the Synoptic Gospels present him, apart at least from the birth-stories in Matthew and Luke.[4]

Moreover, the documents which record his life and teaching—Letters of Paul and others and the Gospels—will be presented as being what they appear to be, human and not divine, sacred but not inspired. In reading them we become at once conscious that they do not support many of the tenets now regarded as essential by the Church. Despite indications in John and Jesus' own admissions at his trials as recorded in the Synoptics these do not leave the impression of accepting Jesus as the Messiah or part of the godhead. The Gospels give no hint of a Trinity which, only after a long controversy ending in the first ecumenical council of the Church in 325, became the belief of the Church, nor do they explain the atonement which on the basis of Paul's mystical interpretation of Christ as a scapegoat for human ills is still a cardinal doctrine of Christianity. Nor do they speak of any such veneration of Mary or of her sinlessness as is now believed in both the Orthodox and Roman churches. Nor in the Gospels did Jesus exhort his disciples to observe sacraments, such as baptism, nor

---

[4] These two while appearing to believe in his supernatural birth also speak of him as the carpenter's son (Matt. 3:55–56; Luke 2:48 and 4:22) as does the earlier Mark (6:3). Even John, last of the Gospel writers, while identifying him with the *Logos* also speaks of him as one "whose father and mother we know" (6:42).

of the future "breaking of bread" in his memory.[5] Sacraments came later when the nascent Church, sensing that Jesus would not soon return, needed them for the organization of a continuing group. The sacraments found in John are those of the Church today. They stem not from Jesus, but largely from the unconscious influence of the mystery-religions. By the time of St. Ignatius,[6] martyred in the early years of Trajan's reign, the bread of the Eucharist had become "the medicine of immortality and the antidote that we should not die," the essence still of the Eucharistic sacrament. It is, in short, the absence of such essential sacraments from the New Testament and especially from the Synoptic Gospels which has led some paradoxically to deny Jesus the title of Christian.

SO-CALLED BIOGRAPHIES

While it is not difficult to write biographies of many prominent Greeks and Romans because there is an abundance of material—their writings, contemporary and later biographies such as those by Plutarch, notices by friends and enemies, letters, and in the case of public men, public documents—it is a very different thing to try to write an account of the life of Jesus. Until recent years, however, the task was generally regarded as simple for it seemed that all that was necessary was a chronological outline of events based on Gospel harmony—such as the popular "Lives" by Farrar, Geikie, Edersheim, Andrews, and many others.[7] Such an approach is still followed by those who try to settle Christological questions on the basis alone of the recorded words of Jesus, unmindful that the Gospels, the first three of which were composed over a generation after his death, may have undergone many changes to conform with the changing views of the Church. But critical writers of our time no longer accept them as pure history merely because of Church authority, nor do they accept the narratives as they stand, and most regard the Fourth Gospel as essentially unhistorical. Such scholars have made it clear that Matthew and Luke, instead of showing the general traditional consensus of the early Church, merely revert to the general framework of the basic narrative in Mark, oldest of the Gospels. Thus, critical historians have found the literary tradition about Jesus colored, contradictory, and biased. They have both raised and left unanswered many questions, the possible solutions of which must affect the historical value of the New Testament writings, and have shown how meager our knowledge of Jesus really is.

While Paul, "the apostle of the Gentiles," is the best-known figure from Christian antiquity due to the self-revelation of his Letters and the account

[5] Breaking of bread and drinking of the cup at the "Last Supper" is mentioned by Matthew (26:26–28), Mark (15:22–24) and Luke (22:17–20), but Luke alone adds the words: "This do in remembrance of me," words which seem to refer to the immediate occasion rather than to the future.

[6] In his *Epistle to the Ephesians*, 20.

[7] Canon F. W. Farrar, *Life of Christ* (New York, 1874 and 1903); J. C. Geikie, *Life and Works of Christ* (New York, 1933); A. Edersheim, *The Life and Times of Jesus the Messiah* (New York, 1886); S. J. Andrews, *The Life of our Lord upon Earth* (New York, 1892).

of his missionary journeys and trial in the Acts, Jesus is one of the least known. Of his life, beyond his birth in Nazareth, the fact that he had brothers and sisters, that he followed his father's trade of joinery, and finally that he turned preacher and was slain in Jerusalem, we know almost nothing. There is little basis on which to construct a biography since we have neither dates nor succession of events in his career. It has been calculated that the total number of the days recorded in the Synoptics of his active ministry hardly exceeds fifty. Furthermore, the Gospel writers give us no chronology for each one used common material in an individual way. We know the date of Jesus' birth and death only roughly as occurring in the reigns of Augustus and Tiberius respectively, but almost nothing of the life between beyond his last few days in Jerusalem. The Gospels agree in representing his ministry as beginning after the imprisonment of John the Baptist by Herod (Mark 1:14; Matt. 4:12; Luke 3:20; John 4:43 and 46) and Luke records (3:23) that he was "about thirty years of age" when his itinerant preaching began in Galilee, continued in Peraea (Mark) or Samaria (Luke), and ended in Jerusalem. In the first two of these three divisions events are episodic and become continuous only in the third in connection with his arrest, trials, and death, but even here the Synoptics and John differ so essentially that there can be little trust in any chronology. The only chronological framework possible, though open to different interpretations, is supplied in part by John's record of annual feasts which occurred during Jesus' ministry into which statements in the other Gospels are supposed to fit. While the duration of his ministry is in dispute we can only say that "the probabilities are, upon the whole, in favor of a ministry of more than one year or less than three years." [8]

Recently A. T. Olmstead on the basis of John gives four hundred and seventy-five days, including over a year in Jerusalem, as the duration of his ministry. He dates the beginning of the ministry, December 18, 28 and his death, April 7, 30.[9] Thus only the merest outline based on Jesus' words and acts can be compiled in lieu of a biography. Moreover, until recent years the Church frowned upon applying to the person of Jesus and to the beginnings of our religion the canons of criticism used in other fields. Some churchmen still anathematize the "higher critics" and even common sense and continue to surround the person of Jesus with much that the secular historian would call folklore. Thus a "life" acceptable to any large body of Christians seems impossible and the attempt to write one should be abandoned except within the limits outlined.

Still, despite the meager evidence, there is a vast modern literature on Jesus' "life." An endless number of books continues to appear filled with assumptions and probabilities whose chief value is that they give us an account of Jesus' times and environment. They have been written from many viewpoints—historical, critical, rationalistic, radical, psychological, pathological, pietistic, apocalyptic, impressionistic, as a very few examples

[8] Quoted from E. C. Dargan in *Hasting's Dictionary of Christ and the Gospels* (1901), p. 185; cf. M. S. Enslin, *Christian Beginnings* (New York, 1938), pp. 157–58.
[9] *Jesus in the Light of History* (New York, 1942); see also n. 106, *infra*.

will show.[10] We begin with the epoch-making rational *Leben Jesu* by David Friedrich Strauss for it forms a turning-point in modern theology, all preceding works leading up to it and all subsequent ones starting from it.[11] In it he opposed the earlier rational *Das Leben Jesu* of H. E. G. Paulus,[12] who had distinguished between the purpose and the person of Jesus, the former a transformation of the individual will in the image of God resulting in the possibility of a divine kingdom for all and the latter a miraculous spirit in a human body. Thus, in rejecting the Gospel accounts as fabrications, Strauss dealt a death-blow to Paulus' work by starting the idea that they should be interpreted like any other work of literature and so explained the miracles as mythical embodiments of Christian doctrines unintentionally fabricated. Basing his "mythical" theory on Hegel's philosophy of religion he concluded that the evangelists, on the basis of the messianic prophecies of the Old Testament, ascribed to Jesus words and thoughts which they believed should have been his. In this way the story of Jesus' life beyond the merest outline became the unsubstantial creation of early Christian hopes. This caused Strauss to deny Jesus' divinity.

A year before Strauss published his second edition the romantic *Vie de Jésus* by the Orientalist Ernest Renan appeared, a combination of learning and imagination by a great literary artist. It was written in a Maronite hut in the Lebanon Mountains of Syria with the help only of copies of the New Testament and Josephus,[13] and is redolent of the atmosphere of the East. Renan replaced Strauss' "mythical" theory by a "legendary" one in his attempt to recover Jesus' personality from the social and economic background of Galilee in his day. He pictured him as a gentle and idyllic nature, a favorite of women, full of ambition and vanity, who visioned no other paradise than that of fraternal fellowship here. John the Baptist transformed him from a moral teacher into a revolutionary prophet who assumed the title Messiah, forgetful that such a transformation meant idealization in conflict with reality. In his *Saint Paul* he described Paul,

[10] G. A. Barton has classified ten such groups: "The Person of Christ in Modern Literature Concerning his Life," in *The Anglican Theological Review*, XIII (Jan. 1931), 56f.; cf. also his *Jesus of Nazareth, a Biography* (New York, 1922); and the conclusion of the article by W. D. MacKenzie in *E.R.E.* (1915), pp. 546f.

[11] Issued at Tübingen, 1835–36 (1st English ed. from the 4th German of 1840 by Marian Evans [George Eliot], London, 1846 and New York, 1860, followed by many later translations). Due to attacks on it, Strauss published his *Streitschriften* (Stuttgart, 1836); and in 1864 published a new *Leben Jesu für das deutsche Volk* in which he vainly tried to be constructive, but as in his *Christus des Glaubens und der Jesus der Geschichte* (13th ed.; 1904) he found the data insufficient and concluded "it all still remains in a certain sense a tissue of hypotheses," since he could not close the gap between the Christ of faith and the Jesus of history.

[12] *Das Leben Jesu als Grundlage einer Geschichte des Urchristentums*, 2 vols. (Heidelberg, 1828), a translation of the Synoptics, accompanied by notes; cf. his supplementary work, *Exegetisches Handbuch über die drei ersten Evangelien* (1830–33).

[13] Paris, 1863. The last English edition is in Everyman's Library (New York, 1927). *La Vie de Jésus* forms Vol. I of the author's life-work, *Origines du Christianisme*, completed in 1882.

on the other hand, as "proud, stiff, and abrupt," neither a savant nor a poet but one who believed he was always right, whose writings, though "works of the highest originality, were without charm . . . almost bereft of grace."

Scientific criticism, thus begun by Strauss and Renan, was continued by Karl Th. Keim and his followers [14] who began the great variety of subsequent works on different viewpoints of Jesus. The rational school was continued by W. Wrede in Germany [15] and the late Nathaniel Schmidt in America,[16] the latter contending that Jesus regarded himself as a prophet rather than as the Messiah. An eschatological group of writers was introduced by A. Schweitzer [17] and J. Weiss,[18] the former of whom believed that Jesus' idea of his mission and the announcement of his "kingdom" were similar to views then current among Jewish apocalyptic writers. Recently H. Frank [19] has also explained Jesus' story as the "invention" of Paul who created it by imposing Oriental mystery ideas on the legend of a rural preacher.

An interesting group of "pathological" writers followed Renan in the view that Jesus had delusions like Jeanne d'Arc and only imagined he was the Messiah. Thus Jules Soury [20] believed he suffered from meningoencephalitis or progressive brain paralysis; the Danish Emil Rasmussen [21] that he was an epileptic; the nerve-specialist G. Lomer [22] that he was a paranoiac; the French Jew Charles Binet-Sanglé [23] that he was a megalomaniac. At the basis of such views is the well-known phenomenon, common to many religious mystics of psychological abnormality,[24] since they "hear voices and see visions." Ancient examples may be cited—Moses on Sinai, Isaiah in the Temple, Jeremiah at Anathoth, Ezekiel on the Chebar, Gautama under the Indian bo-tree, Paul near Damascus, St. Augustine at Milan—and many others since. Such cases, however, may rather be called "supernormal" than "abnormal" and are generally explained by material-

[14] *Geschichte Jesus von Nazara* (1867–72), tr. by A. Ransom as *History of Jesus of Nazareth* (2nd ed.; London and Edinburgh, 1876–83); a second vol., tr. by E. M. Geldart.

[15] *Das Messiasgeheimnis in den Evangelien* (Göttingen, 1901).

[16] *The Prophet of Nazareth* (London and New York, 1905 and 1907); and other works.

[17] *The Mystery of the Kingdom of God: the Secret of Jesus' Messiaship and Mission*, tr. by W. Lowrie (New York, 1914 and 1925); also *The Quest of the Historical Jesus; a Critical Study of its Progress from Reimarus to Wrede*, tr. by W. Montgomery (2nd ed.; London, 1922). The latter is the best account of a century and a half's effort to discover the true historical picture of Jesus.

[18] *Die Predigt Jesus vom Reich Gottes* (2nd ed.; Berlin, 1910).

[19] *Jesus, a Modern Story* (New York, 1930).

[20] *Jésus et les évangiles* (Paris, 1878); rev. ed. under the title *Jésus et la religion d'Israel* (1898).

[21] *Jesus; eine vergleichende psychopathologische Studie* (Leipzig, 1905).

[22] *Krankes Christentum: Gedanken eines Arztes über Religion und Kirchenerneuerung* (Leipzig, 1911).

[23] *La folie de Jésus: ses connaissances, ses idées, son delire, ses hallucinations, 1–2* (Paris, 1908–10), Vol. II.

[24] See G. Stanley Hall, *Jesus, the Christ, in the Light of Psychology* (Garden City, 1917).

istic and Freudian writers as the result of suppressed sex impulses.[25]   While
it is impossible to deny that Jesus' nature was mystical and that he had a
supernormal consciousness it is a different matter to regard him as mentally
diseased.

Finally, there is a group of writers who, in emphasizing the comparative-
religious method in treating the Gospels, have tried to show that Jesus
never lived at all.   They explain the Gospel accounts of Jesus as adumbra-
tions of various god-myths in the Near-East mystery-religions, myths which,
as Strauss had maintained, embodied Messianic hopes never realized.
Thus Jesus was merely "the idea" of a savior-god worshiped by some pre-
Christian sect of the pattern of the mystery-cults which contained stories
of incarnate deities who suffered on earth for mankind, died, and rose
again.   In this group are J. M. Robertson, who has written many books
to prove the thesis; [26] A. Drews, a Professor of Philosophy at Karlsruhe; [27]
W. B. Smith, late Professor of Mathematics at Tulane University; [28] the
Danish-Jewish literateur, Georg Brandes; [29] the Assyriologist Hugo Winckler; [30] and, more recently, P. L. Couchoud,[31] and many others.

That these works are the result of misspent labor seems to be shown by
the fact that, even if we cast aside the Gospel accounts, the historicity of the
person of Jesus is established by various notices of pagan writers.   They
have, therefore, called forth many refutations, among others by C. Clemen,[32]
F. C. Conybeare,[33] Joseph Klausner,[34] Maurice Goguel,[35] and S. J. Case,
sometime Dean of the University of Chicago Divinity School.[36]   The last
mentioned has tried to disclose as he says "not the Jesus of the stained glass
window, but the Jesus who lived and walked with men."   Similarly, in a
recent book, Robert Keable [37] has also attempted to distinguish between
the Christ of the Church and the Jesus of history, as Strauss vainly tried to

[25] See J. H. Leuba, *Psychology and Religious Mysticism, a Psychological Survey* (London, 1925; New York, 1929); and others.

[26] Among them are: *Christianity and Mythology* (2nd rev. ed.; London, 1910); *Pagan
Christs* (2nd ed.; London, 1911); *The Jesus Problem; a Restatement of the Myth Theory*
(London, 1917); *The Historical Jesus* (London, 1916); etc.

[27] *Die Christus Mythe* (2nd ed.; Jena, 1911; 3rd ed., 1924), tr. as *The Christ-Myth*
(London, 1910; Chicago, 1911).

[28] *Der vorchristliche Jesus* (Jena, 1906 and 1911); *Ecce Deus* (Jena, 1911), tr. as *Studies of Primitive Christianity* (Chicago, 1913).

[29] *Jesus, a Myth,* tr. by E. Björkmann (New York, 1926).

[30] *Geschichte Israels* (Leipzig, 1895 and 1900).

[31] *Le mystère de Jésus* (Paris, 1924), tr. as *The Enigma of Jesus* (London, 1924).   Cf.
his *The Creation of Christ; an Outline of the Beginnings of Christianity,* tr. by C. B.
Bonner (London, 1939).

[32] *Religionsgeschichtliche Erklärung des Neuen Testaments* (Giessen, 1909), tr. as
Primitive Christianity and its non-Jewish Sources (Edinburg, 1912).

[33] *The Historical Christ: or An Investigation of the Views of J. M. Robertson, A.
Drews, and W. B. Smith* (London, 1914).

[34] *Jesus of Nazareth,* tr. from the Hebrew by H. Danby (New York, 1925).

[35] *Jesus the Nazarene: Myth or History,* tr. by F. Shepherd (New York, 1926); *The Life
of Jesus,* tr. by Olive Wyam (New York, 1933).

[36] *Jesus: a New Biography* (Chicago, 1927); *The Historicity of Jesus* (2nd ed.; Chicago,
1928).

[37] *The Great Galilaean* (Boston, 1929).

do, i.e., between the image of Christ developed throughout the ages by Christian reverence and the real Jesus based on the Gospel accounts. Such works as the latter two show how little similarity exists between the humble carpenter's son and the Christ of the Christian worship, and make it clear that no such person as the latter ever lived except in Christian imagination as the ideal of perfection. But we may be certain that imagination could not have created such a real picture as that of Jesus nor his unique type of preaching.

Another important book, which discloses scepticism of usual views, is the *Jesus* of Charles A. H. Guingebert,[38] a critical study of the problems raised by historical research about Jesus and his teachings. He stresses our ignorance of Jesus' birth and childhood, the notives leading to his baptism, the length of his ministry and its immediate effect, and the obscurity which surrounds his death. He introduces various novel interpretations: of the "Last Supper" as a cult legend;[39] of the Passion as the dramatization of the sordid arrest and death of a Messianic preacher;[40] of the Resurrection as an imaginary misapprehension by Peter of the mist rising from the Sea of Galilee.[41] His conclusion is that Jesus' life is a confused account of early Christian accounts and in no sense biography. H. J. Cadbury[42] has offered a salutary warning that Jesus was a Jew whose thoughts were other than ours, whose apocalyptic vision, theism, obedience to God's will and whose attitude toward exorcism and miracles are all alien to us.

SOURCES OF OUR KNOWLEDGE

For our knowledge of Jesus and the beginnings of Christianity we have two sources only: one the brief objective notices of pagan writers who wrote after his death, most of which are under suspicion; and the New Testament, an esoteric subjective source which, despite bias and contradictions, gives us most of our information. Of pagan notices we are at first surprised that there are so few in the century following Jesus' death until we reflect that the bulk of imperial literature is lost and that what has survived is mostly in the classical tradition of Latin letters. The appearance of a religious teacher in far-away Galilee would interest few beyond his immediate followers, for the later importance of Christianity by Constantine's time must not be confused with its simple beginnings. Before Nero's reign Christianity attracted little attention either in Jewish or Graeco-Roman literature, although by then its followers were scattered through the cities of the Near East, Greece, Egypt, and Italy. The small space devoted to Jesus by Josephus shows the slight impression made on his contemporaries by the Gospels. And Seneca, who was martyred under Nero, makes no mention of Jesus in his many works. Jews were disliked in the West and Christianity

---

38 Paris, 1933, tr. by S. H. Hooke (New York, 1935); cf. also his *The Jewish World in the Time of Jesus*, tr. by Hooke (New York, 1939).
39 *Jesus*, p. 449.
40 *Ibid.*, p. 471.
41 *Ibid.*, p. 512.
42 *The Peril of Modernizing Jesus* (New York, 1937).

was long regarded as an evil form of Judaism of interest only to them. Within a century and a half of Jesus' death, however, one Jewish writer, Josephus,[43] three Roman writers, Pliny the Younger, Tacitus, and Suetonius, and one Greek, the satirist Lucian of Syria, tell us something about the beginnings of Christianity if little about Jesus himself.

The earliest of these notices, if genuine, is in the *Antiquities* of Josephus, who was taken prisoner during the siege of Jerusalem and brought to Rome by Titus where he later became a Roman citizen. He calls Jesus "a wise man if indeed it is lawful to call him a man," since he performed wonders and converted many Jews and Gentiles, "and was the Christ." He adds that Pilate "condemned him to the cross," that he reappeared alive on the third day and that "the tribe of Christians" is "not extinct at this day."[44] There is no mention of Jesus in the original text of the *Jewish War,* but a manuscript of it recently discovered in Russia and composed in Old Slavonic during the Crusades elaborates the passage in the *Antiquities,* although the consensus of critics is that its words: "notwithstanding his works were divine"; "therefore it is impossible for me to call him a man"; "the teachers of the law gave Pilate a bribe of thirty talents"; passages not unlike those in the *Antiquities* are also interpolations since they could have been composed only by a Christian and we know that Josephus was a Pharisaic Jew of priestly origin. Moreover, the manuscripts of his works have all reached us through Christian hands and the Christians would naturally have introduced such glosses to their advantage.[45]

Pliny, when he was governor of Pontus-Bithynia in Asia Minor (*ca.* 105–106),[46] addressed a note to Trajan asking for advice as to how to treat the Christians in his province who refused obeisance to the Emperor's statue. He says that the Christians were everywhere in cities and towns and met on a "fixed day" before dawn when they sang a hymn, i.e., psalm to Christ as "to a god" and bound themselves by solemn oath not to commit any wicked deed such as fraud, theft, perjury, or adultery. He adds that they then separated and later reassembled to partake of food "of an ordinary and in-

[43] *The Jewish War,* first in Aramaic (1:3) and later (A.D. 75–79) translated into Greek (*Contra Apionem* 1, 50), a work composed in his prime under imperial favor, and the *Antiquities of the Jews* (published 93–94), a labored work of his middle life produced under the despotic rule of Domitian; both tr. by H. St. John Thackeray, *L.C.L.* (1926f.), Vol. I, *Against Apion;* Vols. II, III, *The Jewish War* (Bks. 1–7); Vols. IV–VI, *The Antiquities* (Bks. 1–11).

[44] 18:3, 3 (274–75); in 20:9, 1 he again says Jesus was called "Christ."

[45] See A. Berendts and K. Grass, *Flavius Josephus vom jüdischen Kriege* (Dorpat, 1924–26 and 1927); Berendts, *Die Zeugnisse von Christentum im sclavischen "De bello Judaïco" des Josephus* (Leipzig, 1906); R. Eisler, *The Messiah Jesus and John the Baptist according to Flavius Josephus' recently discovered "Capture of Jerusalem,"* tr. by A. H. Krappe (New York, 1931). Here Eisler thinks the Slavic text may be a translation of the Greek in the period between the original Aramaic and the present Greek one; but others believe it may preserve in part the original draft of the *Jewish War;* see J. M. Creed, "The Slavonic Version of Josephus' *History of the Jewish War,*" *Harvard Theol. Rev.,* XXV (1932), 277f.

[46] For the date, of interest in Christian history, see H. Furneaux, *Annals of Tacitus* (Oxford, 1892), II, 570, n. 5.

nocent kind." [47] Trajan in his brief reply, which is also preserved in Pliny's collection (X, 97), advises him not to seek out Christian offenders nor to arrest them on anonymous charges; and, if convicted, to pardon those who recanted. Pliny's letter, written within forty years of Paul's death, makes no mention of the crimes—ritual murder of children, drinking their blood, and impious orgies at their "love-feast" with lights extinguished—which were usually leveled at the Christians by Jews and Gentiles alike. The letter shows how an educated Roman of that day regarded Christianity, merely as one of many Oriental cults then spreading over the Empire.

Suetonius Tranquillus, advocate, historian, and Hadrian's *magister epistolarum* (*ca.* 119–121), an office which gave him access to imperial documents, tells little about Christianity and nothing about Jesus. At some time during the reign of Trajan or Hadrian (98–138) he wrote his *Lives of the Twelve Caesars* from Julius to Domitian, a gossipy and amusing *histoire scandaleuse* which, despite its unreliability, ranks after the works of Tacitus and Cassius Dio (*ca.* 150–235) as a main source for the period. He refers briefly to Christianity twice, in his *Life of Claudius* (chap. 25, 4) and in that of *Nero* (chap. 16, 2). In the former he tells how Claudius banished Jews—doubtless including Christians—from Rome for disturbances "at the instigation of Chrestus." In the latter, in reference to the fire of 64, he says punishment was inflicted on the Christians, "a class of men given to a new and mischievous superstition." [48] The word "mischievous" (*malefica*) implies magic and may refer to Jesus' miraculous powers.

Tacitus in his *Annales,* completed after the close of Trajan's reign in 117 (2:61), is the first classical writer to mention the Crucifixion and the only Roman to refer to Pilate. In writing of the great fire which swept Rome in 64 during his boyhood he says that Nero shifted the blame to the Christians and severely punished them for they were "loathed for their vices" and "hated the human race." He adds that Christ, the founder of the sect, received the death-penalty by sentence of the procurator of Judaea, Pontius Pilate, and that "the pernicious superstition (*exitiabilis superstitio*), thus momentarily checked, broke out again in Judaea" and in Rome "where all things horrible or shameful in the world collect." [49] This passage shows that by the time he wrote the distinction between Jew and Christian had become known as it had not been down to about 70. While most critics have regarded his account and that of the persecution which follows as authentic, others, e.g. A. Drews and especially P. Hochart,[50] have regarded the account as a Christian gloss, the latter also calling the letters of Pliny and Trajan a "pious fraud" and, for good measure, the passage in Suetonius as well.

Lastly, Lucian has left an account of what he thought of the Christians.

[47] Pliny's *Letters*, Bk. X, 96, *L.C.L.*, II, 401–05.
[48] See *Lives of the Twelve Caesars*, tr. by J. C. Rolfe, *L.C.L.* (1914).
[49] *Annales* 15:44, tr. by J. Jackson, *L.C.L.* (1931 and 1937), IV, 283.
[50] The latter in *Études au sujet de la persécution des chrétiens sous Neron* (Paris, 1885).

This "ancient Voltaire" through his fantastic invention, power of paradox and description, has left us an important picture of provincial life in the second century. Although he despised Christianity few pagan writers did more to prepare for its final triumph than he by his ridiculing all sorts of time-honored superstitions. While most of his satires are full of light-hearted flippancy at the expense of Greek and Oriental religious rites, all of which with the exception of those of the *Dea Syria* he regarded as worthless survivals, others, notably his *De morte Peregrini,* seem to be intended as serious. The latter recounts the life and death of the itinerant philosopher Peregrinus Proteus of Parium on the Hellespont who visited Palestine in the Antonine period and there became a Christian although he was soon excommunicated for profaning its sacraments. Later he founded a Cynic school in Athens but, finding his popularity waning, resolved to have a spectacular death by immolating himself on a funeral pyre near Olympia during the celebration of the Games in the two hundred and thirty-sixth Olympiad in 165. Lucian was a spectator of the bizarre event and tells how Proteus had ingratiated himself with the "queer creed" of the Christians:

The Christians, you know, worship a man to this day, the distinguished personage who introduced their novel rites, and was crucified on that account. The activity of these people, in dealing with any matter that affects their community, is something extraordinary; they spare no trouble, no expense. You see, these misguided creatures start with the general conviction that they are immortal for all time, which explains the contempt of death and voluntary self-devotion which are so common among them; and then it was impressed on them by their original lawgiver that they are all brothers, from the moment that they are converted, and they deny the gods of Greece, and worship the crucified sage, and live after his laws. All this they take quite on trust with the result that they despise all worldly goods alike, regarding them merely as common property.[51]

From these pagan notices we get little knowledge of Jesus beyond the fact that he lived. Thus we are left largely dependent on the New Testament for whatever data we have about his life. Within two decades of his death the first specifically "Christian" writings began with the Epistles of Paul which grew out of the needs of his early churches for explanations of the Christian tenets. These were followed by the Gospels and certain Pastoral Letters, but not until the close of the second century did churchmen make an attempt to collect and to select these writings as a "new covenant" to supplement the "old," and to shape a canon of authoritative books.[52]

[51] *The Works of Lucian of Samosata;* tr. by H. W. and F. G. Fowler (Oxford, 1905), IV, 82–83 (selections 11 and 13). This is the most authentic account of Jesus and Christianity by any of the pagan writers.

[52] The Greek word *canon* (rule) was first used in this connection in the "fifty-ninth canon" of the Council of Laodicea in 363 and contemporaneously by Athanasius in his *Epistula festalis;* then by St. Jerome and his associate Rufinus (*ca.* 345–410), after which the name became general.

If we omit the ten Epistles of Paul singled out by the heretic Marcion (*ca.* A.D. 150) who rejected the Gospels and the entire Old Testament for his church in Rome as a first attempt to fix a canon we find the earliest unofficial list of books in the so-called "Muratorian Canon." This is a much damaged fragment of eighty-five lines in barbaric Latin—thus showing it was a translation from Greek—discovered by Lodovico Muratori in the Ambrosian Library at Milan.[53] This merely private list based on certain Christian sentiments of the late second century includes the Four Gospels, the Acts as written by Luke, thirteen Pauline letters (omitting the Epistle to the Hebrews), I and II Peter (their authority already under dispute), John 1–2, Jude, the apocalypses of John (Revelation) and Peter, and the Wisdom of Solomon. Revelation, a composition of Domitian's reign (A.D. 81–96), accepted in the West but rejected in the East down to the time of St. Jerome, is today the sole canonical apocalypse in the New Testament, since that of Peter, composed at Jerusalem sometime between A.D. 100 and 150, is rejected by all Churches. The didactic Shepherd of Hermas whose first four visions seem to have taken place in Rome (*ca.* 100)—"the worst good book ever written," was rejected by Muratori as non-apostolic, for it was long believed to be the composition of the brother of the Roman bishop, Pius (*ca.* 139–154), since it "holds the mirror up to the Roman Church" in his day. Since the "Muratorian Canon" agrees with Tertullian and Irenaeus it may be dated in the reign of Marcus Aurelius or, perhaps, in that of his son Commodus.[54]

Doubts about what should be included continued into the early fourth century as we see from Eusebius [55] who divides the books of the New Testament into "recognized," "disputed," and "rejected." In the first class he places the Gospels, Acts, and Pauline Letters; [56] in the second, James, Jude, II Peter, II–III John, and Hebrews; and in the third, the Acts of Paul, Shepherd, Apocalypse of Peter, Epistle of Barnabas, and the "Didaché" or Teaching of the Apostles (*ca.* 100), rediscovered and published in 1883 by the Greek metropolitan Bryennios. A final Canon was not possible until Constantine had accepted Christianity in 325 and, in reality, not until Theodosius had made Catholicism official in 380–381. Such a canon appears in Athanasius' thirty-ninth Festal Letter of 367 and was accepted at the Synod of Rome convoked in 382 by Pope Damasus and confirmed by Carthage at the Synods of 393, 397, and 419 and ratified by Gelasius (492–496). The East accepted it at the Second "Trullan" [57] or Quinisext-Synod

---

[53] It was published in the third volume of his *Antiquitates Italicae* in 1740.

[54] Edited with notes and facsimile by S. P. Tregelles, *Canon Muratorianus* (Oxford, 1867); Latin text and translation by H. M. Gwatkin in *Selections from Early Writers illustrative of Church History to the Time of Constantine* (2nd ed.; New York and London, 1902); H. Lietzmann, "Das Muratorische Fragment" in *Kleine Texte für theologische Vorlesungen und Uebungen*, No. 1 (Bonn, 1902, 1907).

[55] *The Ecclesiastical History* published in 324–325, 3:25, 1.

[56] In chap. 31:3, 5 he says the fourteen Letters are "obvious and plain," but that some dispute Hebrews. We use the translation of the *H.E.* by K. Lake, *L.C.L.* (1926 and 1932).

[57] So named from the domed hall (*trullus*) of the imperial palace where it was held.

at Constantinople in 692.   The accepted books were called "Sacred," i.e.,
set apart and gradually came to be regarded as "the inspired word of God"
since they formed the New Covenant between God and man, a belief generally held by Christians today.   Irenaeus, who died about 202, first used
the terms "divine" and "perfect," while Clement of Alexandria (ca. 150–
220) first called the books "inspired."

Of all these books I Peter, if it were authentic, would be the earliest
book of the New Testament to give an account of Jesus by one who knew
him, although it actually gives no personal reminiscences of him.   It was
accepted by many of the early Fathers—Tertullian, Clement of Alexandria,
Irenaeus, Origen, Cyprian—and the oldest Syrian version revised by Rabbi
Rabbula, bishop of Edessa in the early fifth century, to standardize the
Syriac text as Jerome had done for the Latin in the Vulgate, and by Basilides
the heretic and Eusebius.   Still the Letter was rejected by the Muratorian
Canon.   Protestant scholars from Baur to Harnack and Jüthner have regarded it as non-Petrine, but the Roman Church accepts its authority as
established.   The authenticity of II Peter, though it is found in the oldest
Sinaitic and Vatican codices, has aroused universal doubt.   Its connection
with Peter rests on his assumed sojourn in Rome after his imprisonment
under Herod Agrippa I (ca. 42).[58]

The Letters of Paul, then, give us our earliest undisputed evidence
about the early Church and Jesus.[59]   They were written for various
churches from Ephesus to Rome between 52 and his death in 64.   While
the "Muratorian Canon" and Eusebius accept thirteen, until a generation
ago only four or five and parts of a sixth were recognized universally as
Pauline—I and II Corinthians, written at Ephesus (16:8) and in Macedonia
(2:13), respectively a year and a half apart after 54; Galatians, composed
in 52 or 53; Romans, in 55 or 56; and by most earlier critics I Thessalonians, earliest of all, and parts of Colossians.   Hebrews is universally
rejected.   Jülicher also says that Philemon "belongs to the least doubtful
part of the Apostle's work."[60]

To-day a longer list is more reasonable and, in addition to those cited,
includes II Thessalonians, Philippians, Colossians and possibly Ephesians,
and parts of Timothy and Titus.[61]   Allusions in the Epistles of Peter, John
and James show that their authors were contemporaries of Paul, while the
latter in Acts is connected with many well-known pagan Romans such as

[58] See Excursus III, infra.
[59] See F. C. Burkitt, The Earliest Sources for the Life of Jesus (2nd ed.; London, 1922).
On the Letters, see R. D. Shaw, The Pauline Epistles: Introductory and Expository Studies
(2nd ed.; Edinburgh, 1907); Sir William M. Ramsay, Pauline and Other Studies in Early
Christian History (London, 1906), St. Paul, the Traveler and the Roman Citizen (New
York, 1896; 7th impression, 1903), and The Teachings of Paul in Terms of the Present
Day (2nd ed.; London, 1902); O. Pfleiderer, Paulinism, tr. by E. Pieters (2nd ed.; London,
1891); A. Schweitzer, Paul and his Interpreters: a Critical History, tr. by W. Montgomery
(London, 1912).
[60] Introduction to the New Testament, tr. by J. P. Ward (London, 1909), p. 127.
[61] B. H. Streeter, C.A.H., II (1936), 257.

Paulus, Gallio, Felix, Festus, and Agrippa.   Such allusions aid in determining the date and provenience of certain Letters, notably of I Thessalonians, which we know was composed during Paul's sojourn in Corinth (Acts 18) when he was arraigned before Gallio, brother of the philosopher Seneca who, as we learn from a Delphic inscription, was proconsul of Achaea in 52–53 under the Emperor Claudius.   He dismissed the Jewish complaint against Paul and his words that "he cared for none of these things" (Acts 18:7) were typical of Roman official indifference to local religions.   Thus in all probability Thessalonians should be the oldest extant Christian document.   Paul's last letters, the disputed Colossians and Ephesians, and Philemon, were written during his imprisonment in Rome.

The Letters constantly refer to Jesus, but give us no biographical data whatever.   However much Paul venerated Jesus' memory he never saw him.   Moreover, he was unfriendly to some of Jesus' disciples, notably to Peter at Antioch, and showed no interest in Jesus the man but only in Christ and "him crucified" (I Cor. 2:2).   He knew Jesus' brother James, long head of the "mother church" in Jerusalem and once visited Peter there for fifteen days (Gal. 1:18–19) and thus had exceptional opportunities to learn about Jesus' life, but apparently made no use of them.   Furthermore, his ideas were his own and were rarely referred to Jesus for authority.   His sole interest in Jesus was his belief that he was God.

The Gospels were also composed with no idea of being "inspired." They were first called such (*evangelia*) by Justin Martyr (*ca.* 150).[62]   It is chiefly in the first three Gospels that we find data about Jesus' life since most critics regard the Fourth Gospel as unhistorical.   There were also many apocryphal versions composed in the second century such as the Gospel according to the Egyptians, to the Hebrews, and to Thomas, which make Jesus a wonder-worker from the beginning.   No historian today would call the four canonical Gospels history or their authors historians, since they all lack objectivity and are given to theological interpretations. All are written in ordinary Hellenistic Greek—the beginning of Luke is classical—and so were intended for ordinary men.   Papias, bishop of Hierapolis in Phrygia in the first quarter of the second century, is quoted by Eusebius as saying that Mark wrote down what he had heard of Peter's memories of Jesus,[63] and so even Mark, earliest of the four, is a secondary source.

In their present form, then, none of the Gospels gives us an autographic record since none of their authors was an eye-witness of the things he chronicles.   All use material differently and at best merely preserve collections of memorable acts and sayings of Jesus in episodic and fragmentary form.   Moreover, they are known to us—apart from older papyrus

---

[62] *Apologia* 1:66.

[63] Eusebius *H.E.* 3:39,16.   Papias' *Exposition of the Lord's Oracles* exists only in excerpts.   It is probably the writing used by Irenaeus in *Adv. haereses* 3:12, in *Ante-Nicene Fathers* (Edinburgh, 1868–69).   See J. B. Lightfoot, *The Apostolic Fathers, Revised Texts from Greek* (London, 1891).

fragments—only from fourth and fifth-century manuscripts at the earliest.[64] Thus the oldest are from a date which would allow ample time for textual changes to conform with changing Church beliefs.

Objections to the credibility of the Gospels were first voiced by the Roman philosopher Celsus of the late second century in his lost *True Discourse,* whose substance, however, has been recovered from Origen's rebuttal *Contra Celsum.*[65] Celsus maintained that much of the Gospel material was fictitious and that it had been rewritten to meet controversial needs.[66] That later textual changes did take place is evidenced by various passages, notably in Matthew 28:19 where we have a late remodelling of the baptismal formula to make it conform with that of the Nicene creed of 325; [67] and Luke 24:44, where Jesus, after his reappearance to his disciples, uses words he is supposed to have uttered earlier, but which fit a later convert better. There is also the conclusion of Mark (16:9–20) where the original text has been replaced by different endings. It is a major problem of biblical criticism to discover what happened to the first-century text, later truncated seemingly in the middle of a sentence "for they were afraid" (16:8).[68] The reasons for the supposed omission—although some scholars maintain there is none—may have been accidental, although it is more likely by design. Conybeare argued that Luke mutilated the first edition of Mark because he disagreed with it and in 1891 he found the name of the supposed author of the present ending, the presbyter Ariston, or Aristion of the second century, in an Armenian MS of the year 986.[69] A shorter conclusion than the one now appearing in the Gospel, published by E. A.

[64] The oldest Greek codices on vellum are *Vaticanus* and *Sinaiticus* of the fourth century; *Alexandrinus* of the fifth and the bilingual *Codex Bezae* of the fifth or fourth; the oldest Syriac are *Curetonianus* of the early fifth and the *Palimpsestus Sinaiticus,* discovered on Sinai in 1892 and published in 1894, of the fourth century, the oldest of all. Six late third-century papyrus fragments were discovered at Oxyrrhynchus in Egypt in 1897; among them *Oxyr. Pap.* Nos. 2 (Matt. 1:1–9, 12, 14, 20); Nos. 208 and 1226 (John 1:15, 16, 20); *Michigan Papyri,* Nos. 1578 (Matt. 26:19–52), 1571 (Acts 18:17–19; 6:15–16). Oldest of all is the Rylands fragment of John, considered below.

[65] In eight books composed at Rome in the reign of Philip the Arab (244–249). See Migne, *P.G.,* XI (1857), 631–1132; and in German, *Celsus Wahres Wort,* reconstructed text and tr. by Th. Keim (1873). Celsus, a bitter opponent of Christianity, wrote *ca.* 176–180.

[66] Origen 2:26–27.

[67] See F. C. Conybeare, "Three Early Doctrinal Modifications of the Texts of the Gospels" in *Hibbert Journal,* I (1902–03), 96–113. The other two modifications are Matt. 1:16 and 19:17.

[68] The argument, however, that the Greek post-positive conjunction *gar* (for) cannot close a sentence has been amply refuted by various scholars, one of whom has collected examples of such usage from Plato onward: M. S. Enslin, "On Mark XVI:8," *Jour. Bibl. Lit.,* XLVI (1927), 62–68.

[69] *Expositor,* 4th Series, VIII (1893), 241; cf. James Moffatt, *Introduction to the Literature of the New Testament* (2nd rev. ed.; Edinburgh, 1912), p. 241; A. J. Edmunds, "The Text of the Resurrection in Mark" in the *Monist* (April 1917), pp. 161–78; and C. R. Bower, *The Resurrection in the New Testament* (New York, 1911). Conybeare suggests that Aristion is the disciple mentioned by Papias, but the date of the MS is too late to settle the matter; see A. J. Maclean, "The Last Twelve Verses" in Hastings, *Dictionary of the Bible,* II (1908), 131–33.

Abbott in 1884, is in the *Twentieth Century New Testament*.[70] Most authors also omit the text of John (7:53–8:11). It must be added, however, that the period between Jesus' death and the composition of the Synoptics, less than forty years, was too short to make many essential changes. The contention, then, that we cannot be certain of the authenticity of a single saying of Jesus or episode in his life is untenable. The common element in the Synoptics, which we shall now briefly discuss, establishes at least the historicity of his person.

The "Synoptic problem"—authorship, dates, sources and aims of the first three Gospels—has exercised the critical mind for over a century, since the German philologist Karl Lachmann first observed in 1835 that Mark underlay Matthew and Luke. So much of Mark appears verbatim in Matthew and Luke [71] that one critic has remarked that "if every copy of it had perished we could still reconstruct large portions of it [Mark] by carefully comparing their narratives." It was further noted that Matthew and Luke included also non-Marcan material—some two hundred verses in common—which required another source than Mark. While the dependence of Matthew and Luke on Mark gives us the "Synoptic" view of Jesus this further lost source called Q (Quelle) by Wellhausen in 1905, either orally transmitted or a written document, complicates the problem. Reconstructions of Q tell us what it contained rather than what it did not. It seems to have included a collection of Jesus' sayings like the "oracles" of Papias and, like Mark, it began with Jesus' baptism with some account of John the Baptist and his warning of "the coming wrath." It contained the story of the centurion's servant at Capernaum (Matt. 8:5–13 and Luke 7:2–20) and possibly that of the Temptation (Matt. 4:1–11; Luke 4:1–13) condensed by Mark into two verses (1:12–13), cure-narratives and, perhaps, the story of the Passion. Accounts in Luke only, such as that of the Prodigal Son (15:11–32), and in Matthew only, such as the laborers in the vineyard (20:1–16), must come from still another source than Q. This dependence, then, of Matthew and Luke on Mark and lost documents is the chief contribution to the Synoptic problem for a century past.[72]

While the dates of none of the Gospels can be established exactly and the names of none of their authors, except possibly Luke, still from internal evidence all four may be arranged chronologically and their aims characterized. We know that Mark as it stands is the oldest, as it is the freest from mysticism and miracle and that it was composed before the fall of Jerusalem in 70, since the "abomination of desolation" (13:14) does not refer to the destruction of the Temple, as usually thought, but rather to a person. Daniel (12:12) concludes with the prophecy that the present world

[70] It is based on the Greek Text of Westcott and Hort (New York, 1899–1901).

[71] A typical example of such copying is Mark 9:1 as found in Matt. 16:28 and Luke 9:27. In modern parlance Matthew and Luke would be called plagiarists.

[72] See F. C. Burkitt, *The Gospel History and its Transmission* (3rd ed.; Edinburgh, 1911); B. H. Streeter, *The Four Gospels, a Study of Origins* (New York, 1925); and *C.A.H.*, II (1936), 259–60.

order will pass thirteen hundred and thirty-five days after the appearance
of "the abomination," i.e., the Antichrist who as "man of sin" and "son of
perdition" "sitteth in the temple of God," as we read in II Thessalonians
(2:1–12), and was supposed to appear again in the Temple before Jesus'
return. This shows that the Temple was still standing when Mark wrote.
As he is called "Mark, my son" in I Peter (5:13) this implies that he followed Peter in composing his Gospel as Eusebius wrote. It is generally believed that he wrote for Jews of the Diaspora who needed his descriptions
of customs and geographical places. Despite his imperfect picture of Jesus,
he is our best source in reconstructing the latter's personality.[73]

As for Luke, Irenaeus [74] says it was written by him whom Paul called
"the beloved physician" (Col. 4:4). It is generally believed that he is identical with the author of Acts, a historical sequel to the Gospel because of
the latter's style, if not of its similar medical terminology,[75] and because
both are addressed to Theophilus. If the author of Acts, Luke would be
the first Christian historian, for the two works present the history of Christianity from the birth of Jesus to the persecution of Nero. That he wrote
his Gospel after Jerusalem's fall seems clear from two prophecies attributed
to Jesus but influenced by their fulfillment later (21:6 and 20). Some have
dated the Acts before the Gospel because of the closing words of the latter
(28:30–33) which record that Paul abode two years at Rome. Thus Harnack, believing the Acts was a sort of brief for the apostle's defence in
Rome, dated it in the early sixties. Others have given a later date on the
possibility that the author used Josephus' *Antiquities* which appeared in
93–94. Recently, however, M. Goguel has dated the Acts 80–90 and believes it was the work not of Luke but of an unknown author.[76]

Since the time of Irenaeus [77] Matthew has been identified with the pub-
lican mentioned in 9:9 and the apostle in 10:3. Eusebius [78] quotes Papias
as saying that he "collected the oracles" of Jesus in Hebrew, i.e., Aramaic.
Such oracles, in relation to the Gospel, must refer to narratives rather than
to sayings such as those found at Oxyrrhynchus dating from the second to
the seventh century.[79] The statement that they were first in Aramaic is

---

[73] See E. P. Gould, *A Critical and Exegetical Commentary on the Gospel according to
St. Mark* (New York, 1896); W. Lowrie, *Jesus according to St. Mark* (London and New
York, 1929) and its simplification in his *The Short Story of Jesus* (New York, 1945) also
based on Mark.

[74] *Adv. haereses* 3:1, 2.

[75] W. K. Hobart, *The Medical Language of St. Luke* (Dublin, 1892), and A. von
Harnack, *Luke the Physician*, tr. by J. R. Wilkinson (2nd ed.; New York, 1909).

[76] *Introduction au Nouveau Testament*, Vol. III, *Le Livre des Actes* (Paris, 1922).
See Harnack, *The Date of the Acts and the Synoptic Gospels*, tr. by J. R. Wilkinson (New
York, 1911); C. C. Torrey, *The Composition and Date of the Acts* (Cambridge, U. S. A.,
1916); H. J. Cadbury, *The Making of Luke-Acts* (New York, 1927); A. Plummer, *A Critical
and Exegetical Commentary on the Gospel according to St. Luke* (5th ed.; New York,
1902).

[77] *Op. cit.*, 6:28, 4.

[78] *H.E.* 3:39, 6.

[79] Eight *logia Iesou* were found in 1897, five in 1903 and others in 1907, and are published in *Oxyrrhynchus Papyri*, ed. by Grenfell and Hunt (London, [Vol. I] 1898, [Vol. IV]
1904, and [Vol. V] 1908).

in doubt except on the recent theory of C. C. Torrey that Mark, Matthew, John, and most of Luke were first composed in Aramaic and then translated into Greek, a theory resting on Greek idiomatic and syntactical peculiarities best explained as translations as well as on errors and misinterpretations.[80] While such a thesis has been sharply criticised [81] many critics have accepted it as natural though it discloses great difficulties in the Aramaic background. The substructure of the Gospels must have been an Aramaic oral tradition which must have existed in the first Christian communities in Palestine even if we cannot trace the development of the written Gospels from such sources. Matthew was a Jew who wrote to prove to his fellow Jews that Jesus was the Messiah of the Prophets for he constantly stresses the fulfillment of Old Testament prophecies. Internal evidence, as in the case of Luke, points to a date 70–80 for his Gospel.[82]

The Fourth Gospel stands apart from the Synoptics, as Origen first noted, for it uses different material, has a different aim and its date is almost certainly later. Although few have taken it as history its view of Jesus as "the word" of God and at the same time as a human being has marked out the *via media* along which Christianity has progressed. It is not a biographical work of Jesus, but rather a mystical interpretation of his teaching. All agree that it was composed for Gentile Christians, the antagonism against the Pharisees so prominent in the Synoptics being absent since Gentiles would have little interest in local Jewish controversies. Its aim is presented in 20:31: "that ye may believe that Jesus is the Christ, the Son of God; and that believing ye may have life in his name." Since it reflects a phase of Jesus too mystical for the ordinary man certain scholars have suggested that it may have been a message held in reserve for an esoteric circle. Its mystic keynote is that Jesus is the *Logos* (1:1f.), wrongly translated as "word" rather than "revelation" or "utterance" of God's will, an idea taken from the Jewish-Alexandrian philosophy of the Greek-Jew Philo, Jesus' contemporary.

Some critics have divided this Gospel into the prologue, for Greek converts to explain the Greek idea of the *Logos,* and the remainder for Jews. But since Strauss compared it with Jesus' "coat without seam" (John 19:23) most have regarded it as a unit. Even if the *Logos* does not appear after the prologue and is not put into the mouth of Jesus, the main message of the Gospel is that Christ is the Son of God. The picture drawn of Jesus, as well as that in the Epistles of John, suggests that the author was an unknown teacher who worked at the end of the first or beginning of the second century. According to Irenaeus the Gospel was published at Ephesus.

[80] See his "Translations Made from the Original Aramaic Gospels" in *Studies in the History of Religions* (New York, 1912), pp. 269–317; and *Our Translated Gospels; Some of the Evidence* (New York and London, 1936).

[81] See D. W. Riddle, *Jour. Bibl. Lit.,* LIV (1935), 127–38.

[82] See M. S. Enslin, *Christian Beginnings* (New York and London, 1938), p. 400; A. Plummer, *An Exegetical Commentary on the Gospel according to St. Matthew* (London, 1910).

Loisy [83] calls its author a Christian of "Judaeo-Alexandrian" extraction, "a theologian far removed from every historical preoccupation" and "a seer who lived the Gospel which he propounds." [84] Older dates have ranged from 160–170 (Baur) to 80–110 (Harnack), the earlier dating because Irenaeus says the author lived into Trajan's reign (98–117). Professor Olmstead [85] brings the date *prior* to the year 40 and furthermore argues that the narrative parts reconstruct Jesus' life better than the Synoptics do. This is in marked contrast with the view expressed by Eduard Meyer twenty years before: *"Im allgemeinen wird sie den zahlreichen Apokryphen Evangelien gleichartig gewesen sein; doch enthielt sie vereinzelte noch wertvolle Nachrichten. . . ."* [86] The publication of the Rylands papyrus fragment of John, a tiny bit only a few square inches in extent found in 1935 in a collection of fragments in the John Rylands Museum in Manchester and dating from the early second century and so the earliest fragment of the New Testament,[87] throws little light on the date of John.

After this survey of the New Testament writings we find that we are indebted almost entirely to the Synoptic Gospels for what little we know of Jesus' life and teachings. To begin with his birth, we find that they offer us only confused and contradictory accounts of his birthplace, whether Nazareth or Bethlehem.[88] Mark, following the universal custom of antiquity of identifying a man by the place of his birth, repeatedly calls Jesus a Nazarene and makes no allusion to Bethlehem. Luke has him conceived in Nazareth but has his parents go to Bethlehem to be enrolled in the census of Quirinius "because he [Joseph] was of the house and family of David" (2:4) and adds (2:39) that Joseph and Mary after Jesus' birth in Bethlehem returned "to their own city Nazareth." He also has them take the child to Jerusalem for circumcision (2:21–24) and presentation to the Lord. Only Matthew, who wrote to show the Jews that Jesus was the Messiah, has the parents flee into Egypt, an episode evidently clumsily inserted into the text to fulfill a prophesy of Hosea (11:1): "I called my son out of Egypt." He had little idea of the difficulties of such a journey for two peasants. Josephus, though he narrates with the utmost exactness the horrors of Herod's last years, makes no mention of any "massacre" of infants under two years

[83] *Le quatrième évangile* (2nd ed.; Paris, 1921), p. 291.

[84] Since the author of John's Epistles 2–3 calls himself the "Elder" the latter may be John the Presbyter of Eusebius (*H.E.* 3:39) and identical with John of the Gospel.

[85] In his book cited *supra*, p. 113, n. 9, see p. 291.

[86] *Ursprung und Anfänge des Christentums* (4th and 5th eds.; Stüttgart and Berlin, 1924), I, 340; cf. the similar view of Canon Streeter in *C.A.H.*, XI, 261. For a statement of the Johannine problem, see J. A. Montgomery, *The Origin of the Gospel according to St. John* (Philadelphia, 1923), and cf. W. F. Albright in *Harvard Theological Review*, XVII (1924), 193f.

[87] It contains five Greek verses, 18:31–33 and 37–38, seven lines on the obverse and six on the reverse. See *Cat. of Gk. and Lat. Papyri in the John Rylands Library*, ed. by C. H. Roberts (Manchester, 1935), No. 456.

[88] For a critical study of the latter, see Guingebert, *op. cit.*, pp. 90–96; and Sir William M. Ramsay, *Was Christ Born at Bethlehem? A Study on the Credibility of St. Luke* (2nd ed.; London, 1898).

of age in Bethlehem, so that its historicity is nil. At the time Bethlehem could have contained hardly a thousand inhabitants who would have yielded only perhaps a dozen such infants while "all the borders thereof" would have added only a few more. The Church, however, still celebrates the "Feast of the Holy Innocents" on December 29, in commemoration of the supposed "massacre."

Thus it seems clear that the Bethlehem story, beautiful and reverenced as it is with all its Christmas associations, was a later addition made to connect Jesus as Messiah with David, Israel's greatest king, and in consequence of a prophecy in Micah (5:2): "But thou, Bethlehem . . . out of thee shall one come forth unto me that is the ruler of Israel," i.e., a descendant of David who would restore the kingdom destroyed six centuries before. For Bethlehem was the traditional birthplace of David. It was an ancient town, its original name Ephrath or Ephrata (Ruth 4:11; Ps. 132:6), where Jacob buried his wife Rachel. But it is no less than incredible that the Roman government should have required its people to go to the towns of their ancestors for enrollment. In that case perhaps a hundred thousand Jews of the Diaspora would have to return annually to Palestine. And it is even incredible that two peasants should have been compelled to travel the eighty miles from Nazareth to Bethlehem. Moreover, we do not know Mary's lineage, although there is no reason to connect her with David's house.[89] From a variety of sources we know that Rome required enrollment for purposes of taxation only in the towns where people lived.

Moreover, little weight can be placed on the enrollment of Qurinius in connection with Jesus' birth. Quirinius was consul in 12 B.C. and *legatus Augusti,* i.e., governor of Syria A.D. 6–9 (and perhaps to 11). Eusebius [90] wrongly assumed that the census referred to by Luke (2:1; cf. Acts 5:37) was the same as that mentioned by Josephus,[91] when Quirinius was governor and when Judas of Galilee rebelled against the tax. If this were so there could be no reconciliation with the account of Matthew and Luke since that census took place A.D. 7 or long after Herod's death in 4 B.C., unless we follow Ramsay's unsupported suggestion that there was an earlier census in Herod's time during an earlier governorship of Quirinius.[92] Long ago J. Marquardt [93] showed that Luke's account of the census was wrong on three points: that the census he names was not in the time of Herod, but A.D. 6 or 7; that it was not "for all the world"; and that his words "in those days" are vague and may even refer to Augustus' census of the Em-

[89] See Luke 1:27 and 2:5.

[90] *H.E.* 1:5, 2–3.

[91] *Jewish War* 2:8, 1; *Antiq.* 17:12, 5 and 18:1, 6.

[92] *Op. cit.,* p. 201 (6 B.C.); in *Jour. Rom. Stud.,* VII (1917), 274, Ramsay gives 8 B.C. While an earlier governorship is possible, although his predecessor is named as Quintilius Varus, no census under Herod was possible.

[93] *Römische Staatsverwaltung* (2nd ed.; Leipzig, 1881–85), II, 211–14 and p. 211, n. 4; cf. also his *L'organization financière chez les Romains* (1888), pp. 366–67; A. von Premerstein, *Die fünf neugefundenen Edikte des Augustus aus Cyrene,* pp. 450–51, who gives A.D. 6–7 for Syria. On the date, see also T. Rice Holmes, *The Architect of the Roman Empire* (Oxford, 1928 and 1931), II, 90.

pire begun in Gaul in 27 B.C. It was, then, rather the census mentioned by Josephus the year after Judaea became a Roman province, A.D. 6.

The lack of connection of Jesus with David's house is not only shown by the unhistorical Bethlehem birth-story but also by the two genealogies of Jesus, or rather of his father; one in Matthew (1:1–17) from Abraham downward through David and his son Solomon in three periods of fourteen generations each ending with Joseph; the other in Luke (3:23–38) from Jesus upward through Nathan, another son of David, to Adam "the son of God." Curiously, since Jesus is represented as being conceived of Mary by the Holy Ghost (Matt. 1:18f.; Luke 1:26), both genealogies trace the descent only to Joseph. The Annunciation, or declaration of the angel Gabriel to the Virgin Mary that she is to become the mother of Our Lord, is commemorated in some of the Western churches as "Lady's Day" on March 25. The real condition of affairs, however, is hinted at by Luke (3:23), who says that Jesus was "the son (as was supposed) of Joseph."

The "Annunciation" has led to doctrines hardly hinted at in the Gospels, to Mary's deification as "Mother of God" already discussed in connection with Isis, and to two others: her "perpetual virginity" and consequent "absolute sinlessness." Jesus makes no reference to the matter of his birth and Paul's statement (Rom. 1:3) that he was of the seed of David is irreconcilable with the "virgin birth." Nor was such a doctrine as "perpetual virginity" taught in the Church during its first three centuries. It is not hinted at until the time of Justin Martyr in the early second century. It had a non-Catholic origin in the apocryphal *Protevangelium Jacobi* composed at the end of the second or beginning of the third century which was proscribed in the earliest *Index librorum prohibitorum* of Pope Gelasius (492–496).[94] But there was no "cult" of the Virgin before the close of the fourth century. Then St. Jerome defended the doctrine in his *Adversus Helvidium* (before 387), in which he attempted to refute Helvidius' argument that Mary bore other children to Joseph, even as Tertullian two centuries before had said in his *Contra Marcionum* (4:29). In his *De viris illustribus* (2) Jerome maintained that these children were cousins of Jesus by an older sister of Mary of the same name, wife of Clopas, who with other women viewed the Crucifixion afar off (Mark 16:40; John 19:25) and that this Mary had two daughters and four sons, two of the latter of whom became disciples. This notion was refuted in 1865 by J. B. Lightfoot, bishop of Durham.[95] Others, following an ancient tradition, made these children half-brothers and half-sisters of Jesus by an assumed earlier wife of Joseph of which nothing is known. This idea was known as *epiphanium* from its zealous advocate Epiphanius, bishop of Constantia on Cyprus (367–403),

[94] Text in Tischendorf's *Evangelia apocrypha* (2nd ed.; Leipzig, 1876); tr. by A. Walker in *Ante-Nicene Fathers*, VIII, 361–67.

[95] In "Brothers of the Lord" in his *Commentary on St. Paul's Epistle to the Galatians* (London, 1865), pp. 252f. See also W. Patrick, *James, the Brother of the Lord* (Edinburgh, 1906), pp. 5f.

who in his treatise on heresies, the *Panarion* already mentioned, called all who opposed his view "heretics." Still others, notably Helvidius, in harmony with the Synoptic account (Matt. 13:55–56; Mark 6:3), believed that they were brothers and sisters of Jesus born to Joseph and Mary after Jesus' birth. In any case at the Council of Chalcedon in 451 Mary received her official title "perpetual virgin" and since has enjoyed great eminence in both the Orthodox, as *Panaghia* (All Holy), and Roman churches. The doctrine of her "absolute sinlessness," i.e., that as predestined mother of God she was preserved from all stain, both original or racial and actual or personal, was also unknown to the early Church. St. Augustine said she was born in original sin,[96] and seven centuries later St. Anselm, archbishop of Canterbury, made the same assertion. But the doctrine of the Immaculate Conception was finally made an article of Catholic faith by a bull of Pius IX, December 8, 1854, *Ineffabilis Deus,* which declared that

the doctrine which holds that the Blessed Virgin Mary from the instant of her conception was by a most singular grace and privilege of Almighty God . . . preserved from all stain of original sin, is a doctrine reverenced by God and therefore to be firmly and steadfastly believed by all the faithful.[97]

Not all early Christians believed in the Virgin birth. Thus the Ebionites—Ebionim (poor men) sect,[98] often confounded with the Nazarenes—accepted Jesus as Messiah, but denied his divinity, and believed that he was the son of Joseph and Mary according to the ordinary course of nature. In this connection a different reading of Matthew, 1:16, should be noted in the oldest manuscript of the New Testament (the Syriac *Palimpsestus Sinaiticus*) which must have emanated from some Jewish-Christian sect similar to that of the Ebionites.[99] The upper text of the palimpsest contains "Lives of the Saints" composed in 788 by John the Anchorite while the recovered text beneath gives the Gospels with *lacunae.* In the *textus receptus* Matthew, at the close of Joseph's genealogy, reads (1:16):

And Jacob begat Joseph, the husband of Mary, of whom [*ex hes* and not *ex hou,* i.e. Mary, not Joseph] was born Jesus, who is called the Christ.

[96] *De genesi ad litteram* 10:18, ed. Zyche (Vindobonae et Lipsiae, 1894).

[97] This singular doctrine was accepted twenty-four years after the appearance of Sir Charles Lyell's *Principles of Geology* (1830–33), which opposed catastrophism in geology, and five years before Darwin's *On the Origin of Species* (1859), both of which accustomed men to think about the vast changes in nature wrought over inconceivable periods of time and so, following Lamarck and others, began the reign of evolution at the base of all modern scientific thinking. In the Roman Church Mary is the most exalted of created beings, but infinitely below God and Christ in the latter's human nature; while angels and saints enjoy *dulia* (i.e., worship), she enjoys *hyperdulia* and her intercession is invoked above that of all others.

[98] On the name, see Eusebius *H.E.* 3:27, 6; and for their tenets Irenaeus *Adv. haereses* 1:26, 2.

[99] It is in the monastery of St. Catharine on Sinai founded by Justinian in honor of the Transfiguration, but later changing its name in honor of receiving the relics of the Egyptian St. Catharine traditionally beheaded by Maximian in 307. Here it was found by Mrs. Agnes Smith Lewis and her sister Mrs. M. D. Gibson in 1892. See M. D. Gibson, *How the Codex Was Found; a Narrative of Two Visits to Sinai* (Cambridge, U. S. A., 1892). The text was published by R. Harris, B. L. Bensley, and F. C. Burkitt, in 1894.

But in the Syriac version it reads:

Joseph, to whom the maiden Mariam was betrothed, begat Jesus, the so-called Christ.[100]

It was difficult enough to harmonize such views of Mary as her "virginity" and "sinlessness" with Jesus' negligent treatment of his mother (John 2:4) and with her evident ignorance of his mission.[101]   These doctrines have left two great ideals—"motherhood" and "feminine purity"—so blended in Mary that the Jewish poet Heine called her "the first flower of poesy."

If we know nothing definite about Jesus' birth we are in no better case in regard to his childhood and youth.   The only event recorded of the former is Luke's apocryphal account of his disputing with the Jewish doctors in the Temple when he was twelve (2:42–50), for Matthew and Mark begin their accounts with his ministry.   If we wish stories of his childish powers we must turn to the Apocryphal Gospels, especially to that of Thomas.   We know he practiced his father's trade of village joiner (Mark 6:3) and wore the physical sign of circumcision which differentiated Jews from Gentiles (Luke 21:2).   Doubtless he attended the Synagogue school in Nazareth where he was taught the Law and sacred books of his people in the customary uncritical fashion.   He quotes from many Old Testament books in his discourses, but omits others such as Proverbs, Job, Canticles, Ruth, Lamentations, Ecclesiastes, Esther, Ezra, Nehemiah, and Chronicles.   Our New Testament quotations from him come from the Septuagint, but there is no indication that Jesus knew Greek, even if his native Galilee was bilingual.   We know he could read his native Aramaic from his first sermon at Nazareth when he read from Isaiah (Luke 4:16–19). John's statement (8:6) that he wrote on the ground with his finger has no significance, though there is no reason to doubt his ability to write.   John says (7:15) that the Jews who heard him speak in the Temple were astonished and asked "How knoweth this man letters, having never learned?" Origen tells us that Celsus found his language "poor and clownish" which does not harmonize with Luke's statement (4:22) that "all wondered at the words of grace which proceeded out of his mouth."   And we still wonder at his sayings even in translation.[102]

Jesus' faith, like that of the ordinary Jew of his day and of the ordinary Christian of ours, was simple and naïve as a few examples will show.   He believed in the Jewish version (Gen. 6–9) of a universal flood (Matt. 24: 37–39; Luke 17:26–27) as many Christians still do.   Sir Leonard Woolley

---

[100] See footnote in E. Nestle, *Novum Testamentum Graece* (Stüttgart, 1906).   It does not appear in Westcott and Hort's *Novum Testamentum,* nor in any English or American edition.

[101] If we admit, following most authorities, that the canticle of praise, "the Magnificat," assigned to her by Luke (1:46–55) is really that to her cousin Elizabeth, the name "Mary" (v. 46) inserted by a later scribe.   See Harnack, "Das Magnificat der Elizabeth nebst Bemerkungen zu Luc. 1f.," *Sitz. ber. d. Berl. Akad. der Wiss.* (1900), pp. 538–56, and F. C. Burkitt, "Who Spoke the Magnificat?," *Jour. Theol. Stud.* (Jan. 1906).

[102] On Jesus' education, see Sir William M. Ramsay, *The Education of Christ; Hillside Reveries* (2nd ed.; London, 1902).

thought he had demonstrated by his excavations at Ur in 1929 the reality of its origin in the proof of an unprecedented local flood of the Tigris and Euphrates accompanied, perhaps, by a tidal wave up the Persian Gulf sometime in the latter part of the fourth millennium B.C. It was great enough to have been exaggerated into global dimensions by the Hebrews who may have learned of it through Babylon or the Canaanites who were under Babylonian influence.[103] However, his finding a stratum of loam eight feet thick which contained no artifacts, though these exist above and below it, is not entirely conclusive since similar deposits, both earlier and later, have been found elsewhere in Babylonia. Jesus also believed in the story of Jonah swallowed by the fish and his deliverance after three days and three nights unharmed (Matt. 12:39–41; Jonah 1:17) though the story was more likely intended merely as a moral romance, as it is common elsewhere in the folklore of primitive peoples.[104] He believed also in the prophecy of the apocalyptic Daniel about "the abomination of desolation" (Matt. 24:15; Mark 13:4) and frequently spoke of hell-fire as many Christians do now, e.g. of going "into hell into the unquenchable fire" (Mark 9:43; cf. Matt. 5:22, 29, 30).[105] He also believed in a personal Satan and his angels (Matt. 25:41). He shared with the Pharisees belief in bodily resurrection but, like them, had no idea of its physical difficulties. He has left a vivid picture of the Last Judgment (Matt. 25:31–46) when he will return and judge the good and evil, a description which has inspired many Renaissance paintings, including Fra Angelico's fresco in Florence and Michelangelo's in the Sistine Chapel in Rome, the latter the world's most famous single painting.

His parables show that he must have meditated deeply on religion, morality, and the mystery of life, for whatever real education he had came from observation of nature and association with poverty. Like Amos centuries before him Jesus developed an insight which comes only from lonely communion with nature. The parables reflect country scenes—ploughing, sowing, reaping, viticulture, bee-keeping, lost sheep, feeding of swine, cock-

---

[103] See his *Excavations at Ur and the Hebrew Records* (London, 1929) and (with others) *The Royal Cemetery: Report of Excavations at Ur* (Oxford, 1934). The biblical account is a composite of two traditions, Yahwistic (J) and Elohistic or Priestly (P). Similarly, two traditions are merged in the account of the Flood in the *Deluge Tablet* published by George Smith in 1872 and in the oldest account in the Gilgamesh Epic (Bk. XI) and its Sumerian analogs. A. T. Clay, *A Hebrew Deluge Story in Cuneiform* (New Haven, 1922), pointed out that the Flood stories do not exactly fit conditions in the alluvial plain of southern Babylonia. E. Suess, followed by Sir J. G. Frazer in *Folklore in the Old Testament* (I, 104–361), believes that since the average rainfall there is not excessive the real cause of the flood was water driven up the Gulf by a typhoon, since Ur, now one hundred and sixty miles from its head, then lay on or near the coast, though this fact does not appear in the traditions.

[104] One such is that of Saktideva in Sanskrit literature. He embarked for the isle of Utshala, was shipwrecked and swallowed by a great fish which, when caught, gave him up unharmed; in the *Kathasarit sagara* (LIV) or collection of stories by Somadevabhatta of Kashmir, composed 1063–1081, but taken from the first- or second-century *Brihatkathe* or *Great Narration* by Gundadhya.

[105] But cf. J. Kroll, *Gott und die Hölle: der Mythos vom Descensuskampf*, chap. i (Studien der Bibliotek Warburg, xx, Leipzig, 1932).

crowing; they disclose as well his fondness for flowers, especially the lily, for some of his disciples, his understanding of erring women and, above all, his love for little children.

Jesus knew little of the great world beyond Judaea and peopled all nature with daemons. Of astronomy he knew nothing nor of the laws of nature since he explained all that happened by the capricious will of a personal God so near to men that he numbered the hairs on their heads (Luke 12:7). Like Gautama before and Mohammed after him he knew nothing of history, his mind, like theirs, being confined within the frame of his class and environment. Of the literatures of Greece and Rome he, in strong contrast with Paul, was ignorant. In art it seems certain he never saw a painting nor a statue—except that of Caesar. Of philosophy he knew nothing and of politics only obedience to the things that were Caesar's, which later as obedience to authority became a cardinal virtue of Christianity. He had no notion of loyalty to a state and little respect for domestic ties, rejecting even his own mother and brothers (Matt. 12:48 and 50; Mark 3:33 and 35); in one passage (Luke 14:26) telling his followers to hate their fathers, mothers, wives, children, brothers, and sisters in order to become his disciples. He continually evinced a desire to be recognized and threatened all sorts of penalties even including hell on those who did not believe in him. Some of his "dark" sayings can hardly be explained, e.g., the passage (Matt. 10:34–36) in which he said he brought not peace but a sword, and came to set men at variance with their fathers, and daughters with their mothers, so that a man's enemies were of his own household.

Like Socrates he was no ascetic and possessed most human frailties for he hungered and thirsted (the latter on the Cross, the former on his reappearances), became angry (at the Pharisees) and even senselessly so when he blasted the fig-tree for not producing fruit although out of season, an act as irrational as Xerxes' scourging the Hellespont. He sought solitude (as in his agony at Gethsemane) and wept; but he was generally sociable, even preserving the memory of once being convivial, if there be truth in the jibes of his enemies who said (Matt. 11:19) that "he came eating and drinking" and even called him a glutton and a wine-bibber. His first miracle was performed at a marriage-feast where he turned water into wine (John 2:1–11). Unlike Socrates, Gautama and Mohammed, he never married though his death came too early in life for us to say whether he believed in celibacy, a custom which Papal policy has followed seeing the advantage to the Church of an unmarried priesthood without family ties.

When fully matured, stirred to enthusiasm by reports of John the Baptist which had reached Nazareth, Jesus sought him out, was baptized and entered on his ministry, chiefly as an exorcist "casting out devils" and as a faith-curist, believing that he had been summoned to carry on God's work among the poor and unfortunate and he thus gathered a few devoted companions around him. In his first sermon at Nazareth [106] he preached de-

---

[106] Olmstead, *op. cit.*, n. 8, dates it Dec. 18, 28, basing the date on a triennial cycle of scriptural readings used in the synagogues, i.e., on the sixty-second Sabbath of the cycle beginning on the first Sabbath at the end of the Feast of Tabernacles, Oct. 13, 27. But it is doubtful if the complete cycle of readings was known in his day.

liverance from sin and finally after varied adventures he came to Jerusalem where his efforts were crowned with death. The rumor had spread among rabbis and rabble that he was trying to overthrow not only the Synagogue but the State as well despite his frequent denial that his "kingdom" had anything to do with this world. Nor were such rumors idle since Judaea, almost alone among the provinces of Rome, was at the time full of discontent and hatred of the Roman yoke, the Jewish leaders being especially incensed at the presence of Roman soldiers within the city, a discontent that had smouldered ever since the time of Judas of Galilee and would continue yet a generation after Jesus' passing until it culminated in the rebellion which destroyed the capital and tens of thousands of Jews. The masses were looking for a Messiah who would lead them to victory and restore the kingdom of a thousand years before.

THE PASSION

While we know little of Jesus' early years we have full accounts of his last days in Jerusalem during the climax of his brief career—the so-called Passion—his arrest, trials, condemnation and death, a story full of human interest even if certain critics have found in it merely the rehearsal of rites belonging to preceding religious festivals. His death on the Cross as recounted in the Gospels has become one of the great events of Western history since it has not only aroused the affection of myriads of worshipers but has influenced various aspects of our culture by inspiring painters, sculptors, composers, and poets, and by leaving its impress on philosophy and social and political life. In brief, it has been largely responsible for the success of our religion. Paul, followed by the early Church Fathers, asserted that through the blood of Jesus a covenant was made with his followers, and the Church has recognized in him the Paschal Lamb sacrificed to redeem the world from sin. The final scenes in the tragedy, indelibly fixed in the mind of every Christian, are, as narrated in the Gospels, obscure and inconsistent, since Matthew and Luke differ from each other in detail and both differ from Mark, while in the Fourth Gospel a very different picture is presented. Despite such variations all agree on the essential events, Mark's account being the earliest and simplest and John's the latest and most complex.

Jesus reached Jerusalem via Peraea, then the vague territory beyond the Jordan, just prior to the annual Feast of Unleavened Bread as the Synoptics call it or the Passover as John does, a name referring to the Paschal Lamb killed on the fourteenth Nisan as it had been in the Captivity (Ezek. 6:19) and for centuries before in commemoration of the escape of the Hebrews from Egypt. The "Passover" progressively displaced the older "Unleavened Bread" after Jerusalem's fall and finally superseded it altogether as we see in John (1:13 and *passim*). Jesus entered Jerusalem on an ass, believed to be in fulfillment of a prophecy in Zechariah (9:9; cf. Matt. 11:7), and deliberately cast aside all secrecy and allowed the rabble to hail him as their deliverer. His first acts—driving the money-changers from the Temple precincts, proclaiming that he was the representative of God, foretelling the destruction of the Temple, the preservation of his followers, coming calamities, and the manner of his own death—aroused not only hostility but fear in the High-Priest whose authority over the Temple precincts was unbounded and sealed Jesus' fate.

During the Paschal meal, the "Last Supper" with his disciples in secret on the evening of the first day of the Feast according to the Synoptics but on the night before it began according to John, he foretold his betrayal by one of them and that they would all forsake him and let him meet his fate alone and gave them bread and wine in his memory. Then they all repaired to the Mount of Olives and Jesus entered the Garden of Gethsemane where the horror of his impending fate drew from him a prayer so agonizing that "his sweat became as it were great drops of blood" (Luke 22:44). Soon he became reconciled to that fate and with his awakened companions went forward to meet Judas who was leading a band of armed men to arrest him, the betrayer kissing Jesus as a signal that he was the one they sought. This was a curious incident since Jesus was well known in the city nor do we know why Judas was his enemy. John merely says that he led the guards to the place where he knew Jesus was accustomed to resort with his disciples (18:2). All fled except Peter who followed at a safe distance.

Then came the trials.[107] The first was at the house of the High-Priest, Caiaphas or his father-in-law Annas, then the political representative of the Jews before the Roman authorities, in whose presence Jesus confessed he was "the Christ" and predicted that they would see Daniel's vision fulfilled with him "sitting at the right hand of power" and coming "with the clouds of heaven" (Mark 14:62), which was stark blasphemy to the ears of his judges. Then, when no agreement was reached, Jesus was led at dawn before the procurator Pilate and was here arraigned no longer as a religious but as a political offender, his crime one against the Roman State since he called himself "King of the Jews." Pilate advised the Jews to try him by their own law as he was willing to consider his crime a religious one in which, as a Roman official, he had no interest. If this had been done and with Pilate's concurrence Jesus would have been put to death not on a cross, a Roman instrument of death, but in Jewish fashion either by stoning, strangling, beheading, or even hanging.

Pilate, finding no fault in Jesus, first turned him over to Herod Antipas who happened to be in the city and who, as Tetrarch of Galilee, had jurisdiction over him only to have him revile Jesus and clothe him in gorgeous raiment in mockery of his royal claims. Then the unwilling Pilate, taking advantage of the Jewish custom of delivering to the people a prisoner during the Passover, gave them their choice between Jesus and a rebel agitator Barabbas, who was then in prison. They chose the latter but still clamored for the death of Jesus. To satisfy them Pilate finally yielded, apparently terrified by the fanatical tumult. He had Jesus scourged, the usual

107 See H. Lietzmann, *Der Prozess Jesu* (Berlin, 1931); R. W. Husband, *The Prosecution of Jesus; its Date, History, and Legality* (Princeton, 1916).

preliminary to crucifixion, and, after the guards had placed a crown of thorns on his head, ordered the sentence of death. John says (19:19f.) that he wrote, and this was in accordance with a Roman custom noted by Suetonius in his *Life of Caligula* (32), on a placard or *titulus* the reason for his judgment and placed it on the Cross above Jesus' head [108] with the words "Jesus of Nazareth, the King of the Jews," in Hebrew, Greek, and Latin, and adds that the chief priests urged him "Write not, the King of the Jews; but that he said, I am the King of the Jews," to which Pilate answered "What I have written, I have written."

Thus, according to the Gospels, Pilate, a contemptuous but not contemptible Roman official, through fear was compelled to yield to the clamor of the Jews, though he found Jesus guiltless, and to deliver him to the Cross. But for nineteen centuries Christians have followed the Gospel narratives which largely exonerate Pilate from intent and inculpate rather the Jews for the crime of putting Jesus to death. Critics, e.g., Salomon Reinach, have pointed out the difference between the weak official Pilate swayed by the mob who gave to the Jews a choice between Jesus and Barabbas and washed his hands of the blood he was about to shed and the Pilate described by Philo, Josephus, and Eusebius, all of whom laid against him charges of cruelty and other crimes.[109] In his favor is the fact that he kept peace in turbulent Judaea, Idumaea, and Samaria for a decade (26–36) as Eusebius (1:9, 2) tells us. Josephus relates [110] that he was finally removed from office because of setting Roman troops on the Samaritans gathered on their sacred Mt. Gerizim, that he was then banished to Vienna in Gaul where he committed suicide. He has become the subject of many legends. Tertullian calls him a Christian and the Coptic Church celebrates his martyrdom while the Abyssinian Church celebrates him as a saint on June twenty-fifth and the Orthodox Church honors both him and his wife, Procula, on October twenty-seventh.

A recent writer has ineffectively tried to exonerate the Jews from the crime and to place the blame altogether on Pilate by relieving the latter of the Gospel bias in his favor.[111] He does this on the ground that the religious Sanhedrin had nothing to do with the trial but only the political one and that the High Priest merely surrendered Jesus to the Procurator and so finds the Jews only morally at fault. He supports his argument by Paul's statement (I Cor. 2:8) that Jesus was crucified "by the rulers of this world," i.e., the Romans; that the Apostolic Fathers did not accuse the High Priest; and that Tacitus said [112] that Jesus died "by the sentence of

---

[108] This incidentally shows that it was the *crux immissa* or Latin Church cross of four arms, and not the *crux commissa* or T cross but the New Testament says nothing of the form of the cross and it was not mentioned until the time of Justin Martyr.

[109] Philo *De legatione ad Gaium*, written in his old age about A.D. 40 when he went to Rome to persuade Caligula not to compel the Jews to adore the Emperor's statue; Josephus, *Jewish War* 2:9, 2–4 (169–177); Eusebius *H.E.* 2:6, 6 and 2:5, 7.

[110] *Antiq.* 18:41, 2; cf. Eusebius *H.E.* 2:7, 1.

[111] Zeitlin, *op. cit.* (cited on p. 91, n. 32, *supra*), chap. x, pp. 144f.

[112] *Annales* 15:44.

the procurator, Pontius Pilate," which, so far as the judicial aspect of the case is concerned, none can deny. But the Gospel accounts, unless we admit their bias, show that it is improbable that Pilate would have given his verdict had he not been constrained by the Jews. After washing his hands before the multitude he said: "I am innocent of the blood of this righteous man; see ye to it," and "all the people answered and said, His blood be on us, and on our children" (Matt. 27:24–25). Better testimony of their guilt comes from the Acts (4:27) where four individuals or groups are named as "against the holy servant Jesus"—Herod, Pontius Pilate, the Gentiles, and "the people of Israel."

Crucifixion was a barbarous form of torture of which Cicero said [113] "There is no fitting word that can possibly describe so horrible a deed." During the Second Punic War the Romans seem to have taken this infamous instrument of death from the Carthaginians who had used it long before, an inheritance from their Phoenician homeland; it was used by Egyptians, Persians, and other Orientals and was known but not used by Greeks. Thus Plato mentions it (*Gorgias* 473 C) and Alexander in Asia at the death of Hephaestion crucified his Persian physician.[114] But the Greeks generally were repelled by so horrible a type of penalty as is shown by King Pausanias after Plataea who refused the suggestion of a fellow-Greek to impale the corpse of Mardonius in requital for the latter's similar treatment of that of Leonidas.[115] It was not in the old Jewish law which, however, in Israelitish days countenanced the similar "hanging from a tree," [116] whose victims were "accursed of God," but was introduced into Palestine by the Romans to replace in part the usual Jewish custom of stoning to death. Josephus tells us [117] that Titus during the siege of Jerusalem forty years after Jesus' death crucified so many Jews "that space could not be found for the crosses, nor crosses for the bodies," thus hoping to frighten the survivors into submission. It was abolished in the Empire by Constantine after he saw the Cross in the heavens in 312 and after his mother Helena is said to have discovered the true Cross in Jerusalem in 326 together with Pilate's superscription and even the nails by which Jesus had been fastened, relics which her son sent to Rome where they are believed to rest still in the church of Sta. Croce in Gerusalemme. The discovery has been commemorated in the Roman Church by the festival of the "Invention of the Holy Cross" on May third.

The cross, for over five centuries, was the usual punishment of slaves (*servile supplicium*) and rebels and was regularly preceded by scourging, but was rarely used for the punishment of Roman citizens.[118] The ig-

[113] *In Verrem* 2:5, 66 (170). Josephus *Antiq.* 13:4, 2, speaks of its cruelty and illegality in Palestine. Seneca later calls the cross *infelix lignum; Epist.* 101, 14: *acuta crux, ibid.,* 11–12.

[114] Plutarch, *Alexander,* 7:2.

[115] Herodotus 7:138 and 9:78.

[116] Deut. 21:22–23 (quoted by Paul, Gal. 3:13), and Josh. 8:29, 10:26.

[117] *Jewish War* 5:11, 1 (451).

[118] Cicero tells with utter indignation of the crucifixion of Publius Gavius by Verres at Messina: *In Verrem* 2:5, 61f. (158f.).

nominy of such a punishment for Jesus, the Messiah, is evidenced by Paul's speaking of "the stumbling-block of the Cross" (Gal. 5:11) and saying that "Christ became a curse for us" (*ibid.* 3:1). But the cross, once the instrument of shame (Heb. 12:2), has become the most hallowed of Christian symbols whether displayed in the churches or worn as a crucifix. The custom of making the sign of the cross was in full use at the end of the second century for Tertullian [119] says that on all occasions—going in or out, dressing, putting on the shoes, at the bath, at bed-time, "we mark the forehead with the sign of the Cross." Jewish customs and laws, recognized by the Romans, helped to mitigate the horrors of crucifixion. Thus, on reaching Golgotha, Jesus was given wine intended to stupefy the victim, though Matthew says (27:3) that he tasted "wine mixed with gall" but "would not drink." Instead of lingering for days on the Cross until exhaustion or starvation brought release, death was accelerated, and the body was removed and buried the same day in accord with Deuteronomy (21:23). This was especially the case with Jesus whose body was removed on Friday evening before the beginning of the Paschal Sabbath of great sanctity.

Jesus was crucified outside the city-walls on Golgotha between two robbers, one of whom reviled him—Mark (15:32) and Matthew (27:44) say both robbers did—while the other repented and Jesus promised him "To-day shalt thou be with me in Paradise" (Luke 23:43), an example of late repentance diligently urged by the Church ever since. John alone of the disciples was present and it was into his care that Jesus in the Johannine account (19:26–27) placed his mother who had followed him from Galilee and was not spared from seeing her son slain as a malefactor. While the ordinary *cruciatus* shrieked and cursed in his agony Jesus is represented by Luke (23:34) as uttering a prayer in answer to the jeers of the multitude: "Father, forgive them; for they know not what they do," words which, even if interpolated, form a real part of tradition. His last words are recorded variously: Mark (15:34) and Matthew (27:46) saying that he repeated the words found in Psalms (22:1): *"Eloi, Eloi, lama sabachthani"* ("My God, my God, why hast thou forsaken me?"), the only Aramaic words known to every Christian, while Luke (23:46) records the words as "Father, into thy hands I commend my spirit," and John (19:30) more simply "It is finished" (*tetelestai*) when "he gave up his spirit." Just before or after these words one of the soldiers filled a sponge with vinegar (Matt. 27:49; Mark 15:36) and lifted it on a reed—John (19:29) on a hyssop branch [120]—to his lips to slack his thirst. Other incidents recorded at the end both by Matthew (27:45 and 51–54) and Luke (23:44–45)—darkness over the earth from the sixth to the ninth hour, rending of the Temple curtain, earthquake with the rending of rocks, the dead rising from their graves and later seen by many

---

[119] *De corona militis* 3.

[120] Hebrew *'ezobh* of the O.T. (Exod. 12:22; etc.) and Greek *hyssopos* of the N.T. have been referred to eighteen different plants. It was probably related to Arabic sa 'atar—as Maimonides suggested—a species of Satureia (thymus) or, perhaps, was the caper-plant (*capparis spinosa*) which grows as a garden plant in Syria and Palestine. See G. E. Post in Hastings, *Dict. of the Bible*, II, 442. Vinegar mixed with water, Greek *oxus* and Latin *posca*, was the ordinary acidulated drink of Roman soldiers on duty.

in Jerusalem—are merely embellishments taken from the Jewish Messianic eschatology. The evangelists mercifully draw a curtain over the final ghastly scene contenting themselves with the words "they crucified him" (John 19:18, etc.). The Jewish rulers asked Pilate that Jesus' death might be accelerated by the usual *crucifragium* or breaking of the legs by a mallet, which was granted. This was done to the two thieves but Jesus was already dead which caused Pilate to wonder (Matt. 15:44), and a soldier merely drove his spear into his side to make sure (John 19:34). Then the body was given to Joseph of Arimathea, a follower of Jesus, and placed in his rock-cut tomb.

Thus Jesus died as a political offender and his garments, as usual in such cases rather than in alleged fulfillment of the prophecy found in Psalms (22:18) and repeated by John (19:24), were divided among four guards, while his seamless coat (23–24) was raffled by lot, instead of, as in the case of religious offenders, returned to his family. Luke leaves no doubt of the accusations brought against Jesus (23:22): "perverting our nation, and forbidding to give tribute to Caesar, and saying that he himself is Christ, a King." Such charges recall the not wholly dissimilar ones brought against Socrates in Athens over four centuries before.[121]

The date of the crucifixion is uncertain because of discrepancies between the accounts of the Synoptics and that of John. While the former identify the "Last Supper" with the Paschal meal on the eve of Passover after which Jesus was arrested and crucified on the following day, i.e., on Friday the fifteenth Nisan (Mark 14:12; Matt. 26:2; Luke 22:7), John has him arrested the night before the Passover, when the Last Supper was eaten, and crucified the next day, i.e., on the fourteenth Nisan (13:1, 18:28 and cf. 19:31). Either day, on the eve of a holiday or "high" day (John 19:31) such as the Sabbath or the Passover, was impossible in Jewish law which forbade executions on such occasions, and the Gospel accounts may, therefore, be explained on the ground that Jesus' crucifixion was a Roman affair. Most critics have found the two accounts irreconcilable.[122] Those who, like Olmstead,[123] accept John's account as historical, regard the Synoptic date as mistaken, and vice versa. He places the crucifixion April 7, 30, while v. Harnack long ago placed it roughly in 30 or 29.[124] It seems curious that Mark who wrote down Peter's memorials of Jesus should have been mistaken in so solemn a date, especially since Peter was at the Last Supper

---

[121] On details of the crucifixion, see also A. M. Fairbairn, *Studies in the Life of Christ*, "Crucifixion" (New York, 1882 and 1900); David Smith in *Dict. of Christ and the Gospels*, I, 397–99. E. L. Stapfer, *The Death and Resurrection of Jesus Christ*, tr. from the French by L. S. Houghton (New York, 1898). Dr. F. O. Walker, "The Physical Sufferings of Our Lord," *Catholic News*, 1905. For the charges against Socrates, see Plato, *Apology* 24B and cf. 26B; Xenophon's *Memorabilia* 1, 1:1; and Diogenes Laertius' *Lives of Eminent Philosophers*, II, 40 and cf. II, 32.

[122] C. C. Torrey, "The Date of the Crucifixion according to the Fourth Gospel," *Jour. Bibl. Lit.*, L (1931), 227–41; cf. J. K. Fotheringham, *Jour. Theol. Stud.*, XXXV (1934), 146f.

[123] "The Chronology of Jesus' Life," *Anglican Theol. Rev.*, XXIV (1942), 237f., and in his book cited, p. 280.

[124] *Gesch. d. altchristlichen Litteratur* already cited; II (Chronologie), 236–37.

and presumably at the second trial. Olmstead, relying on John, further-more has Jesus enter Jerusalem not once, as in the Synoptics, but three times: first, when he went up secretly and taught in the Temple (7:10); again at the winter "Feast of Dedication," the festival inaugurated by Ju-das Maccabaeus, when he fled beyond the Jordan (10:22 and 40); and finally six days before the Passover, i.e. a second Passover, when he came to Beth-any, supped with Martha and Lazarus, and on the following day entered Jerusalem on an ass (12:1, 14)—this being the entrance described in the Synoptics. Such a program seems to mean that the Synoptic writers tele-scoped three visits comprising over a year into a few days. There are indeed indications of such telescoping in both Mark and Luke, the former (11:19) saying Jesus left the city "every evening for Bethany" and the latter (20:1) speaking of "one of the days" on which Jesus preached in the Temple.

Thus passed Jesus, the man of mystery, whose words and acts perplex his followers still.

THE RESURRECTION

But was this, then, the end of Jesus' earthly career and did he die on the Cross to which he was certainly bound as the evangelists [125] and Paul be-lieved, or did he return to his disciples as he had promised and as his later apparitions seem to indicate? If not, what happened to the body which the Gospel accounts agree disappeared from the tomb?

Although Jesus' resurrection forms the central doctrine of Christianity—without which the entire fabric of Christian apologetics falls and with it the Christian hope of immortality—doubts of its reality have been raised since the beginning and have been renewed by biblical scholars of our time who have sincerely tried to explain the phenomenon on naturalistic grounds. Matthew records (28:11f.) the rumor that the Jewish leaders bribed the guards set over the tomb by Pilate to say that the disciples stole the body by night while the guards slept—a naïve feature of the account!—a rumor which spread among the Jews and continued "until this day." The Evangelists record that the disciples received the risen Christ either with incredulity (Matt. 28:17; Luke 29:11; John 16:11; Mark Appendix 16:14) or with terror supposing that "they beheld a spirit" (Luke 24:37). Paul mentions (I Cor. 18:12) that some in the church at Corinth said "there was no resurrection of the dead," referring doubtless to Sadducees or Hel-lenes, to which denial he answered: "and if Christ hath not been raised,

---

[125] They enumerate many witnesses of the event: Matt. 27:36–41; Mark 15:23–41; Luke 23:33–49; John 19:18–29. An Associated Press dispatch dated October 2, 1945, an-nounced the discovery of a funerary urn in a cave-tomb on the Bethlehem Road south of Jerusalem with Greek and Hebrew inscriptions. One in Greek expresses lamentation over Jesus' death—perhaps by an eye-witness—which Prof. Sukenik at the Hebrew Univer-sity in Jerusalem dates "immediately preceding the destruction of the Second Temple," i.e., in A.D. 70, and believes is the oldest archaeological record of Christianity, confirming the Crucifixion. Its authenticity is proved by other symbols on the urn and by pottery, lamps, and bottles found with it.

then is our preaching vain, and your faith also is vain." This is still the essence of the Christian position. Celsus,[126] while accepting the Crucifixion as an undisputed fact, found the accounts of the Resurrection self-contradictory and a corruption of the doctrine of transmigration. His contemporary Lucian, as we have already shown, likewise ridiculed it.

Paul asserts that both he and others had seen the risen Christ and summarizes, in chronological order, a portion of the Gospel evidence—omitting that of the holy women at the tomb—saying (I Cor. 15:5-8) that

he appeared to Cephas; then to the twelve; then he appeared to above five-hundred brethren at once . . . ; then he appeared to James; then to all the apostles; and last of all, as unto one born out of due time, he appeared to me also,

words which form the oldest written testimony to the Resurrection, being composed in the year 53, twenty-three years after the supposed event and long after his own conversion on the road to Damascus. Thus, the apparitions are based on the collective evidence of the Gospels, those in Judaea mostly in Luke and those, with one exception, in Galilee in Matthew, and Paul who adds three more, those to James, the brother of Jesus, to more than five hundred brethren and to himself, a total of twelve, with general confirmation notes in I Peter, Hebrews, and the Apocalypse of John. The apparitions are omitted in our truncated text of Mark, appearing only in the later Appendix there (16:9f.). It was, therefore, a matter of belief before the Gospels were written—as shown by Paul—and an important factor in the founding of the early Church.

Such, then, is the evidence that Jesus was seen, that he spoke, ate, walked, and acted as he had done before his burial. The apparitions were regarded as the sequel to his oft-repeated prophecy that he would return within the lifetime of some of his hearers, a prophecy repeated three times by Matthew and Mark and twice by Luke as proof that his message to men came straight from God. Thus, the Resurrection is one of the best attested incidents recorded in the New Testament although its details are among the least satisfactory since they abound in contradictions, myth, and the telescoping of events. A good example of the latter is furnished by Luke who (24:13-51) condenses the apparitions, which seem to have spread over many weeks in John, as all happening on "that very day," i.e., Easter Sunday on which Jesus arose. This would include the legendary journey with two disciples to Emmaus, a village seven miles from Jerusalem, and return to the capital whence at midnight "he led them out until they were over against Bethany," i.e., on the Mount of Olives "where he blessed them and was carried up into heaven" (50-51).

Some of the apparitions are recorded in a thoroughly materialistic manner. Thus, on the night of the Resurrection he appeared to the disciples assembled at Jerusalem, saying (Luke 24:39): "See my hands and my feet, that it is I myself; handle me, and see; for a spirit hath not flesh and bones, as ye behold me having," and asked for food (41-43), "and they gave him a piece of broiled fish, and he took it and did eat before them." Eight days

[126] Origen *Contra Celsum* 2:55.

later, according to John (20:27), Thomas who had not been present on that occasion and doubted the report unless he could see the print of the nails in Jesus' hands and put his hand into his side, was with the other disciples when Jesus reappeared in their midst and said to him: "Reach hither thy finger, and see my hands; and reach hither thy hand, and put it into my side, and be not faithless, but believing," and Thomas was convinced.

On the basis of such circumstantial evidence, which is no better than that for the miracles at Lourdes in our time, there is little wonder that many critical minds have refused to accept the Christian Resurrection and tried to explain belief in it on naturalistic grounds. They regard the "fact" of the Resurrection as of little importance compared with the spirit of Jesus still active in the world. While, then, denying both the Resurrection and the Ascension, they have sought other explanations of the disappearance of Jesus' body. Some have doubted if he actually died on the Cross, but believe he was resuscitated and finally gave up the attempt to reveal himself to his disciples as a rehabilitated man, as this was fraught with danger, and so passed from history, dying in some obscure retreat. We mention briefly five of the more important naturalistic explanations of the phenomenon, all of which are under attack.[127]

The crudest and most repellent explanation is the "theft" theory, alluded to by Matthew and nearly two centuries ago sponsored by Reimarus who denied all miracles and mysteries.[128] According to this theory, now universally discredited, some interested persons stole the body from the tomb—either the apostles to propagate the idea that Jesus had risen, Pilate and the Sanhedrists through remorse for their acts, Joseph of Arimathea, Mary Magdalene or even the gardener of the sepulchre area, as Tertullian thought, to avoid having his vegetables trampled by visitors to the tomb! If Jesus' enemies stole the body they certainly would have produced it without fear, and if his own followers, Christianity would rest on a fraud.

The "swoon" theory, once popular and sponsored by the older rationalists, e.g. Paulus and Schleiermacher, and having advocates still, has Jesus' body removed from the Cross and revived in the rock-tomb of Joseph by healing ointments and medicaments administered, perhaps, by Essenes, and all this despite the unanimous evidence of the Evangelists that he had died, John even recording (19:34), as we have seen, that his side was pierced by the centurion's spear. Such a theory, like the foregoing, contains an element of fraud, that Jesus pretended he had died. To be sure there are ex-

---

[127] The fullest discussions of these are in the already mentioned work of Keim, *The History of Jesus of Nazara*, Vol. VI, 274f. (The Resurrection), 323-65 (Explanations of the Facts); and in that of A. B. Bruce, *Apologetics; or Christianity Defensively Stated* (Edinburgh, 1897), chap. iv (Jesus Risen), pp. 383-98. See also W. J. Sparrow Simpson, *Our Lord's Resurrection* (London and New York, 1905), *The Resurrection and Modern Thought* (1911), and *Dict. of Christ and the Gospels*, II, 505-14; T. W. Crafer in *E.R.E.*, I, 617; Kirsopp Lake, *The Historical Evidence for the Resurrection of Jesus Christ* (New York, 1907). Cf. Olmstead, *op. cit.*, chap. xiii, "The Risen Messiah."

[128] In his posthumous work *Apologie . . . für die vernünftigen Verehrer des Gottes* (1756), brought out by Lessing (Leipzig, 1772-78). Cf. T. H. Huxley, *Collected Essays*, V (1902), "Science and Lore."

amples from antiquity of men taken from a cross who lived.[129]   Strauss denounced the theory as inconsistent with Jesus' character and as physiologi-
cally difficult since it involved such points as the healing of Jesus' hands
pierced by nails.[130]   It has been attacked more recently at length by Albert
Réville who says it *"a le malheur d'être un tissu d'invraisemblances maté-
rielles et morales,"* adding that *"la crucifixion et ses effets physiologiques s'y
opposent absolument."* [131]   He, as have many others, points out the im-
probability of a man who had been scourged and fastened to a cross for six
hours, being sufficiently resuscitated thirty-six hours later to be able to walk
to Emmaus and back.   It must be remembered that Jesus had been too
weak to carry his Cross beyond the city-gate where the soldiers had to impress Simon of Cyrene, a by-stander, to carry it farther, and that they "carry
him" (Mark 15:22, *pherousin auton*) to Golgotha (rather than "bring" him
as the English translations say).   The theory has furnished the plot of a
modern novel in which Jesus is represented as dwelling for years after the
crucifixion in an Essene retreat where Paul visited him and aroused his remorse when he was told of the furor he had caused in the world.[132]

Most recent critics have switched their attack from external circumstances to psychological ones, to the feelings and thoughts which became
so firmly impressed upon the minds of the disciples that they saw what
their hearts wished them to see.   From this has risen the "vision" theory,
sponsored by Spinoza, Strauss, Renan—based on their belief that "heroes
do not die"—Réville, Scholten, Holsten, and many others, the most favored
anti-Christian explanation of all.   To them the Resurrection was a subjective phenomenon, a hallucination due to the excitement of the apostles
after the Crucifixion, when they longed to see their master again and believed that they did see him.   Celsus long ago believed that Mary Magdalene had such a vision.[133]   Strauss believed that the Resurrection was such
a phenomenon, similar to that experienced by Paul who tells us he was
predestined to ecstatic conditions and visions (II Cor. 12:1f.) which critics
have referred to epileptic attacks, or to some form of neurasthenia, since
he was temporarily blinded and unable to eat or drink for three days after
Jesus appeared to him (Acts 9:9).

A compromise "vision" explanation is the "telegram" theory of Keim
who believes that the visions had an objective cause, that not the body of
Jesus but his glorified spirit was seen and this produced the visions by

[129] E.g. Josephus *Vita* 420–21, thus saved an acquaintance at Tekoah, twelve miles
south of Jerusalem; Herodotus 7:194 (a Persian); Cicero *In Verrem* 2:5, 6 (Roman slaves
at Messina); etc.

[130] It seems certain from John 20:20, 25, 27, that his feet were tied and not nailed;
only Luke (24:39) says "see my hands and feet."

[131] *Jésus de Nazareth* (Paris, 1897), II, 455.

[132] *Brook Kerith; a Syrian Tale* by George Moore (Collected Works, Vol. XVII, New
York, 1922–24).

[133] She was an excitable woman from whom seven devils had been cast (Luke 8:2;
Mark App. 16:9), Jesus' most devoted woman follower, who first visited the empty tomb
on Easter morning (John 20:1) and first saw the risen Christ (John 20:11–18; Mark 16:
9–11).

which, through "telegrams" from heaven as it were, Jesus comforted the disciples that he was not dead but still lived in spirit. Even here Keim has not explained away the supernatural nor freed the apostles from hallucinations since they believed that they saw Jesus in the flesh and not in heaven in the spirit. He concludes that the problem is beyond the range of history and science and can be explained only by the help of faith.

A less important "mythical" theory has been advanced by Weizsäcker and Martineau that there were really no historical apparitions at all, but that the supposed ones grew out of the apostles' way of speaking about Jesus' continued life which gave rise to misunderstanding in the primitive Church, a misunderstanding embodied in the Gospel Christophanies.

Whatever explanation one may choose—whether supernatural or one of the many naturalistic ones within the limits of physical and psychological science—it will only add one more mystery to those which surround the figure of Jesus.

Chapter V

CHRISTIANITY: THE TEACHING OF JESUS

WHILE traditional beliefs in supernatural Christianity have been shaken in the minds of many by the advance of science and historical criticism as applied to the Gospels, spiritual Christianity lives on and, unless science some day shall reign alone, will continue to do so. While the outgrown creeds rested on the belief in an atonement and the latter, in turn, on that of the "fall of man," science has disproved the latter and shown rather that man has risen through evolutionary processes from lower forms. But as Goldwin Smith has said: "If we have lost the Jesus of Bethlehem, we have not lost the Jesus of Nazareth." [1] For, if we can explain away many of the miracles attributed to Jesus, one, the greatest of all remains: the transformation of the Western world by his life and teaching. If we find little in the Gospels with which to reconstruct the story of his life, these do disclose a personality of the highest order. While some of the Hebrew prophets and psalmists were "men of unequalled spiritual genius" and while analogies exist between their utterances and those of Jesus, none of them exhibits such a personality as the Gospels disclose in their ideal portrait of the carpenter's son. None speaks so simply and directly of a personal God, the Father of men, and the relationship between them. Jesus is still the best manifestation of the spiritual life known to the West, "the genius," as he has been called in the Roman sense of the word, of nineteen centuries past. The critic of the Roman Church, Alfred Loisy, has said: "The spirit of the Gospels is the highest manifestation of the human conscience seeking happiness in justice." [2]

The Gospels also disclose a great teacher as well as personality. The main features of his message are too well known to need more than the briefest recapitulation here. At the outset it should be remembered, however, that Jesus was neither a philosopher nor a theologian and that he displayed no capacity for metaphysical speculations or for abstract thinking about any of the principles which he enunciated. That had its beginning with Paul who tried to build a system out of Jesus' words consisting largely of his own reactions to them which have perplexed the Church ever since. And Jesus' thought soon became complicated by Christianity's contact with Greek thought which confused his simple ideas still more. But Jesus was a man of the people, his language ordinary, and his thought direct and unencumbered. The presentation of his thought was so simple and obvious that it is amazing that it could have formed the basis of a system so complex as historical Christianity.

[1] In his lecture *The Founder of Christendom* (Boston, 1903), p. vi.
[2] *Quelques Lettres* (1908), p. 17.

In a brief survey his teaching cannot be presented systematically nor can his position in the history of religion be properly appraised. The subject is too large, its literature of interpretation too vast, and the views of trained critics too varied and often irreconcilable. It was, however, just this lack of a system which has made Christianity the religion of many peoples and ages. If it had been a formal, ritualistic system such as that of Roman religion it might never have made any progress toward universalism. The first and yet the last feature of its doctrines to be emphasized is that it was not new for Jesus' ideas were already known to Judaism and other religions even to those of the Far East, but most of these lacked a dynamic personality, such as Jesus', to drive them home. It is this that makes his ideas seem to us new.

JESUS' MESSAGE

The central doctrine of Jesus' message, in which his ethics and historical Christianity are rooted, was the Fatherhood of God who "lives and forgives his creatures." This was an elementary concept expressed for the early Greeks a millennium before by Homer in the *Iliad* where Zeus is called "father of gods and men" and invoked as "Father Zeus" in prayers which have hardly been equalled since. Later, after Socrates and especially in the writings of Plato and the Stoics, this idea of fatherhood was embodied in the concept of God as creator and director of the universe. In Palestine Yahweh had been father to the Jews alone and his fatherhood had been expressed by the finest spirits of Judaism as we may see from expressions in many of the Psalms: e.g. "The Lord is my shepherd, I shall not want" (23:1); "For thou, Lord, art good and ready to forgive; and plenteous in mercy unto all them that call upon thee" (86:5; cf. *ibid.* 15); "Blessed are all they that put their faith in him" (2:12)—such thoughts are replete with the concept of God the Father. But Jesus changed it by replacing Yahweh with a God of love (II Cor. 13:11; Rom. 8:39f.). To this simple all-embracing idea Jesus added nothing but simply taught a personal Father, a "God of love," a "Holy Spirit," accentuating different aspects of his goodness. This simple idea that God is a Father to whom men may pray and from whom they may receive help in trouble has been one of the chief attractions in furthering Christianity.

The accompanying doctrine of the brotherhood of man was another of his great revelations. It had been inadequately expressed long before by Greek thinkers who down to the time of Alexander had regarded all non-Greeks as barbarians or "unintelligible folk" fitted by nature to be slaves, since Aristotle himself believed slavery was a part of nature's law. But Jesus revealed the Father as delighting in showering blessings on all men, good and evil, just and unjust, and emphasized forgiveness of injury at the hands of our fellow-men not "until seven times; but until seventy times seven" (Matt. 18:22). Marcion of Pontus whose church at Rome tried to remove the Jewish element from the Catholic Church found forgiveness the real distinction between Christianity and Judaism. To him the Old

Testament, while literally true, was merely the product of matter and law, and Yahweh while righteous was vengeful and the Law just but brutal, inflexible, and incapable of forgiveness, but the God of the New Testament revealed by Jesus was one of mercy and grace.[3] A similar idea is hinted at in the Fourth Gospel (1:17): "for the law was given by Moses; grace and truth came of Jesus Christ."   Jesus spoke often of our service to our brother and so doing the Father's will, as we see from such stories as that of the Good Samaritan, and the rich young man whom he asked to give up his wealth and follow him.

There is nothing new in Jesus' ethical message beyond that of his predecessors, since he followed Hillel and contemporary schoolmen as a comparison of his sayings with rabbinical ones in the Talmud and elsewhere amply shows.[4]   The cornerstone of his ethics, the so-called "Golden Rule" (Luke 6:31), has parallels which reach back at least to a seventh-century Assyrian command: "As for him who doeth evil to thee, requite him with good." [5]   It appears in various Far-Eastern religions and, closer to Jesus, in the words of Hillel: "What is hateful to thyself do not to thy fellow: This is the whole Torah, and the rest is commentary; go, study." [6]   But Jesus freed the sayings of the rabbis from scholasticism and ritualistic detail and boldly simplified their code.   Nowhere else do we find such an accumulation of high precepts of conduct as in Jesus' sayings—even if many of them are too exacting for normal human beings to follow.   He made it clear that conduct was the real purpose of religion and to this day Christian sermons dwell almost exclusively on ethics while paying little attention to Jesus' other ideas, since right living is believed to be the preparation for the world hereafter.   Hence Harnack found Jesus' ethical teachings more important than all else in Christianity.   Its mysticism, theology, organization, and sacraments were secondary, since he believed Christianity was a religious life rather than a system of theology.   While Jesus accepted in truncated form (Matt. 5:21f.; 19:18–19) the Decalogue (Exod. 20:3–17) he went far beyond its spirit in interpreting its several parts, notably the *lex talionis* by tempering its Mosaic spirit with that of humanity.

He thus instituted a new idea of conduct, the reversal of natural interest which had been the basis of morality in the Mediterranean world summarized in the thought: "Outdo your friends in acts of kindness, your enemies in deeds of evil."   Thus Xenophon [7] records the prayer of Cyrus the

[3] See A. Harnack, *History of Dogma*, tr. from the 3rd German ed. of 1893 by N. Buchanan (Boston, 1894–99), I, 266–86; *Marcion* (Leipzig, 1921), and *Neue Studien zu Marcion* (Leipzig, 1928), n. 2; J. Knox, *Marcion and the New Testament* (Chicago, 1942); M. S. Enslin, "The Pontic Mouse," *Anglican Theological Review*, XXVII (1945), 1–16.

[4] Parallels collected by H. L. Strack and P. Billerbeck, *Kommentar zum Neuen Testament aus Talmud und Midrash* (München, 1922–28).

[5] S. H. Langdon, *Babylonian Wisdom* (London, 1923), p. 90.

[6] See C. Taylor, *Sayings of the Jewish Fathers* (Cambridge, 1897), pp. 20f. and notes 26, 29, and especially 33.   On Hillel, a casuist rather than a deep thinker and spiritually far below Jesus, see Franz Delitzsch, *Jesus und Hillel* (3rd ed.; Erlangen, 1879), and E. L. Stapfer, *Les idées religieuses en Palestine à l'époque de Jésus-Christ* (Paris, 1876).

[7] *Anabasis* 1:9, 1.

Younger, a Persian prince with a Greek background, who in 401 B.C. made war on his elder brother Artaxerxes Mnemon in the attempt to replace him on the throne, that he "might live so long until he outdid both those who did him well and those who did him ill, by requital." Three centuries later Sulla, the most murderous of Roman dictators, had a similar sentiment composed by himself carved on his monument in the Campus Martius that "no friend ever surpassed him in kindness and no enemy in mischief." [8] Such pagan sentiments show the immense advance made by Jesus in ethical outlook.

He warred on what the Gospels and the Letters of Paul call "sin" as the great obstacle to happiness, by that term meaning envy, hypocrisy, vituperation, violence, blasphemy, and moral insensibility, all of which should be forgiven except only "blasphemy against the Spirit (A.V., Holy Ghost) shall not be forgiven" (Matt. 12:31; cf. Mark 3:29; Luke 12:10).[9] He taught that the remission of sin could be effected through moral regeneration alone. This differed completely from the Mosaic ideal of ritual purification where sin defiled a man and made him ceremonially unclean and so unfit for worship. It also differed from sacraments of the Near-East mystery-religions. The idea of Jesus as mediator through his sufferings and death came from Paul, for it is hardly found in the Gospels.

That Jesus taught the value of pacifism both individually and collectively (war) is shown by the general spirit of his ethics and by many individual sayings and acts. Thus, at the time of his arrest, when one of his companions in anger cut off the ear of the High Priest's servant Jesus said (Matt. 26:52): "Put up again thy sword in its place; for all they that take the sword shall perish by the sword." There are, however, cryptic passages ascribed to Jesus which apparently deny this injunction, notably the one in Matthew (10:34) already quoted. The Church during the first three centuries lived up to the pacific ideal insofar as its relation to the Roman State allowed since Christians were opposed to serving as professional killers in the Roman armies. This early spirit, however, gradually changed, markedly after Constantine's supposed vision of the Cross in the heavens at noonday, sometime before his battle with Maxentius at the Milvian Bridge on the Tiber in 312.[10] Without doubt war is Christianity's greatest failure, although it is not altogether to blame, since religion in modern states is everywhere under political control and the State can easily convince its citizens that every war it undertakes is a holy one.

[8] Plutarch, *Life of Sulla*, p. 38.

[9] Mark 7:21–22 enumerates thirteen types of sin. A recent writer, J. F. Walvoord, has collected thirty-five different words for "sin" in the New Testament: *Bibliotheca Sacra*, C (1943), Nos. I (Jan.–March); II (April–June); III (July–Sept.).

[10] Eusebius, *Life of Constantine*, 1:28–31; *Nicene and Post-Nicene Fathers*, 2nd Ser., I (1890), 481–559 (especially 490–91), tr. by E. C. Richardson. For the battles of Saxa Rubra and the Milvian Bridge, important in Church history, see Lactantius *De mortibus persecutorum* 44. The story of the Cross has been doubted from the beginning and regarded by many as a political manoeuver only.

While such prophets as Amos denounced the wealthy for oppressing the poor, Jesus defended poverty as the best condition for receiving his Gospel, teaching that wealth is an obstacle to the spiritual life. He acknowledged nevertheless the right to property and intended no social revolution to right human wrongs, since he had no idea of a civic state, often reiterating that his kingdom was not of this world. No civilized state can exist without individual and corporate wealth and so the Church has never taken Jesus' idea of social levelling literally any more than it has his denial of private redress. If the latter were vigorously carried out all law and order would vanish and the evil would overwhelm the good. His reflection "how hardly shall they that have riches enter into the kingdom of God" (Mark 10:23), after he had counselled the rich young man to sell all and accumulate treasure in heaven, and his further remark that it was "easier for a camel to go through a needle's eye than for a rich man to enter into the kingdom of God" (Mark 10:25; Matt. 19:24) have never been and can never be carried out. Already in the second century Clement of Alexandria [11] laid down the principle to be followed by the Church that it was not the possession of wealth but its misuse that should be condemned.

Another essential teaching of Jesus was his announcement of the approaching "kingdom of heaven" (Matt. 4:17) or "kingdom of God" (Luke 17:20–21) shortened by John (18:36) and Paul (I Cor. 15:2) to "kingdom" alone. This also was no new idea since the Prophets had spoken of the theocratic god-king who would become "king over all the earth" (Zech. 14:9; Isaiah 9:6–7; Obad. 21; and cf. Dan. 2:44; 7:14, 27). While Jesus often spoke of the kingdom as within us, a spiritual kingdom in the conscience of man ruled by God and attainable only through "being born anew" (John 3:3), in many other passages he connects it with the future, a kingdom to be set up on this earth, its beginning heralded by a final judgment when the good and evil will be separated. While the idea of a hereafter had been vague in the Old Testament many Jews of Jesus' time, especially the Pharisees, influenced by the apocalyptic books of Daniel and Enoch, had reached a fairly uniform idea of it, namely that it would follow the present world order and be ushered in by a demonstration of God's cosmic power, the heavens to open and reveal God in person. Such a demonstration, as we see from Jesus' eschatological discourse in Matthew (24: 5f.; cf. Mark 13:14f.), when the "abomination of desolation" or antichrist will sit in the temple, is expressive of the tribulation to come at the end of the world.[12]

[11] In his tract *Who is the Rich Man that shall be Saved?* (based on the Marcan passage cited), *L.C.L.* (1919), pp. 270f., especially chap. xvi.

[12] The name "antichrist" has been given by Christians to heretics and enemies of religion ever since. The idea first appears in Judaism in the second century B.C. in Daniel, but has been traced to the Babylonian Creation Epic as the outgrowth of the struggle between the winged dragon Tiamat, personification of original chaos, and Marduk, lord of law and order; see S. Reinach, *A Short History of Christianity;* tr. (from his larger work *Orpheus*) by F. Simmons (London, 1922). For the Epic, see G. W. Gilmore in *The New Schaff-Herzog Encycl. of Relig. Knowl.*, III (1909), 296–99; W. Bousset, art. "Antichrist" in

But Jesus' presentation of the "kingdom" is certainly not systematic. Sometimes, as in the passage cited from Matthew, its beginning is connected with the destruction of Jerusalem and the present world-order; again as in Matthew 13 it is described in various parables as a gradual realization; and again (Matt. 24:36f.) he connects it with his own return, the time of which no man knows, but only the Father. In John (5:24–29) it is either an individual rebirth or a universal physical resurrection when the dead shall rise and hear the voice of the Son of man and be judged, the good "unto the resurrection of life," the evil "unto the resurrection of judgment." Paul says little of the hereafter or of future rewards and punishments, but seems to accept Jesus' idea of the annihilation of the wicked rather than their relegation to a place of torment. Thus the New Testament offers no consistent presentation of the hereafter beyond the general spirit of Jesus' message which makes it clear that "the kingdom of heaven" or the hereafter was to be here on this earth. To quote F. C. Conybeare:

From a religion which claims to be a final revelation we surely expect some teaching that we can lay hold of about the soul, about spirit, about immortality. But its founder had none. He looked forward to a miraculous epoch of material prosperity on this earth, in a land where the lost sheep of the house of Israel were to pasture once more under the immediate protection and guidance of Jehovah. This blessed era was to dawn at once, and the just among the dead were to rise from their graves and participate in the flesh with those who should be still alive when it opened. The Church has tried, lamely enough, to interpret these millennial beliefs of the first age with reference to a life which awaits us all beyond the grave; but any such idea was foreign to the mind of Jesus. He was probably incapable of conceiving a purely spiritual existence in detachment from the body. . . .[13]

So long as Christians expected the early return of Jesus and the beginning of the millennial kingdom on earth the idea of individual destiny, whether for weal or woe, cannot have been important.

Whence then came the prevalent Christian belief in a definite life after death, a blissful heaven above for the good and a hell of torment below for the evil if it cannot be traced to either Jesus or Paul with their simple notion of the happiness of the former and the annihilation of the latter? Such ideas entered Christianity only after the close of the Apostolic Age. The sufferings of the wicked in hell appear first in great detail in a fragment of the apocryphal *Apocalypse of Peter*,[14] a document composed before 150. It describes visions in which Christ shows Peter the righteous in heaven and the wicked in hell and various types of sinners enduring torments appropriate to their crimes. Thus blasphemers are hung by their

---

E.R.E., pp. 578–81, and *Der Antichrist in der Überlieferung des Jüdentums, des Neuen Testaments, u. der alten Kirche* (Göttingen, 1893), tr. by A. H. Keane as *The Antichrist Legend, a Chapter in Christian and Jewish Folklore* (London, 1896); *Religion des Jüdentums im neu-testamentlichen Zeitalter* (2nd ed.; Berlin, 1906), pp. 291f. (3rd ed.; by H. Gressmann, Berlin, 1926). See also the older work of E. Renan, *L'antechrist* (3rd ed.; Paris, 1873).

[13] *Myth, Magic and Morals* (1st ed.; London, 1910), p. 359.

[14] It was discovered in Egypt in 1892; the complete text in 1913.

tongues, perjurers have their mouths filled with fire, the rich roll in rags over burning stones, adulterers hang by their feet with their heads in burning mud, and murderers are placed in serpents' caves. A. Dietrich [15] has derived this repulsive picture from the Orphics even if there is little evidence that the genuine Orphics of the sixth century B.C. formulated a penal code for Pluto's realm so opposed to Homer's pallid picture of Hades. We find nothing like it in the unimaginative religion of the Romans and little in that of the Etruscans who peopled their hell with horrendous monsters.   We find an echo in the description of Hades in Aristophanes' *Frogs,* probably of Orphic origin, as a chamber of horrors full of evil monsters where sinners "lie in the mud" amid awful pains.[16]   Franz Cumont,[17] on the other hand, has derived the infernal picture of the *Apocalypse* from the Near-East.   He compares it with descriptions of pains endured by those who have disregarded the commands of Osiris as shown in the Egyptian *Book of the Dead* and those described in the Mazdaean book *Arta Viraf,* and above all from the contrast between the delights of heaven and the sufferings of hell taught by the Near-East mystery-religions which thus influenced the Christian idea of the hereafter.   But, whether Greek, Oriental or both, the *Apocalypse of Peter* shows a background other than Christian. However wrongly understood by the early Christians this picture in later ages, deepened by artists and poets—especially by Dante and Milton—has both frightened and comforted the Christian world since.[18]

THE MESSIAH

Jesus' chief self-designation was Son of Man which has given rise to many interpretations from that simply of "man" in Job (25:6), Ezekiel (ninety times), and often in the Psalms, e.g. 8:4 and 80:17, to that of the supernatural "Son of man" who in Daniel's vision (7:13–14) "came with the clouds of heaven," to whom was given "dominion and glory, and a kingdom . . . which shall not pass away and . . . which shall not be destroyed."   A similar idea is found in the Similitudes of Enoch, a composition of fragments crystallized around the name of the patriarch who (Gen. 5:24) "walked with God; and he was not: for God took him," written in the last two centuries B.C., the oldest parts before the Maccabees (167 B.C.) and its Messianic sections (37–71) after 38 B.C.   It formed the apocalyptic "Bible" of Judaism in the time of Jesus.[19]   The title occurs eighty-one times

[15] *Nekyia: Beiträge zur Erklärung der neu-entdeckten Petrus-Apokalypse* (Leipzig, 1893; 2nd ed. after the recovery of the entire text).

[16] Especially lines 185; 273–79; 288–95; 470–77.

[17] *After Life in Roman Paganism* (New Haven, 1922), chap. vii, pp. 171f.

[18] See also R. H. Charles, *Critical History of the Doctrine of a Future Life in Israel, in Judaism, and in Christianity* (London, 1899 and 1913); and Kroll's work mentioned *supra,* p. 133, n. 5, "Der Descensus im Christlichen Altertum"; R. Otto, *Reich Gottes u. Menschensohn* (München, 1934), tr. by F. V. Filson and B. L. Woolf, *The Kingdom of God and Son of Man* (Grand Rapids).

[19] It was reverenced in the Western Church to the time of St. Jerome and even later in the Alexandrian Church.   It disappeared from 800 to 1773 when three Ethiopic manuscripts, based on Greek, were recovered in Abyssinia by the Scotch African explorer James Bruce. See R. H. Charles, *The Book of Enoch* (Oxford, 1893), pp. 312–17.

in the Gospels, all of which, except the passage in John to be noted, are spoken by Jesus himself. It does not appear in the Pauline Letters, I and II Peter, James or Jude, and the only other New Testament character to use it is Stephen who, at his trial (Acts 7:56), looked up to heaven and said: "Behold, I see the heavens opened and the Son of man standing on the right hand of God," echoes of Daniel which also appear in Revelation (1:13 and 14:14).[20]

In the Gospels the title is largely associated with the earthly life of Jesus (Mark 2:10; Luke 19:10) especially with his sufferings (Mark 8:31) and second advent "in glory" (Matt. 25:31 and 26:64). Earlier New Testament critics maintained that Jesus used the title without consciousness of its Messianic import or that he reached the belief that he was the Messiah only late in his career. In either case they regarded the Messianic coloring of the Gospels as of little importance on the ground that it reached the Church in the Apostolic Age or later. To-day, however, the recognized antiquity and the Messianic meaning of "Son of man" have supported the belief that the Messiahship was the chief feature of Jesus' later ministry when Jesus came to believe himself to be, as Peter said, "the Christ, the Son of the living God" (Matt. 16:16) who was to die as a vicarious sacrifice for the Jews, the idea extended by Paul to include the Gentiles. Thus it is pretty generally accepted that Jesus used the title merely to express his Messiahship which was first acknowledged secretly to his disciples at Caesarea-Philippi and later publicly avowed at his trials before the High Priest [21] and Pilate.[22]

The word "Messiah" (A.V., Messias) is a transliteration of Greek "Messias" whose final letter was changed to "h" due to the spelling of the Hebrew *hamashiah* (Aramaic *mashiha*), "the anointed one." In the early books of the Old Testament it is used as an adjective of priests "anointed" into office with consecrated oil (Lev. 4:3, 5 and 16), but as a noun of the "anointed" kings, especially those of Israel from Saul on (I Sam. 2:35), since "the Lord's anointed" were believed to rule by divine right granted them by Yahweh (I Sam. 24:6 and 10). Samuel here follows the Oriental custom of "anointed" rulers which dates back in Egypt and Babylonia at least to the fourteenth century B.C. as we see from the Tell el-Amarna tablets. The title was later given to Cyrus the Great (Deutero-Isaiah 45:1), and in the Psalms (105:15) "mine anointed" refers to Israel as Yahweh's priest-people. In the New Testament Messiah refers to Jesus alone of the Prophets as it does later in the Koran to Mohammed, "the Masiah." Elsewhere in the Gospels it is replaced by its Greek equivalent, Christ, i.e., the "Anointed."

After the fall of the monarchy the great Prophets of Israel were convinced that a king of the house of David would one day with the help of Yahweh restore the Israelites to their ancient glory. This hope became the

---

[20] All such passages are collected by J. Stalker, *The Christology of Jesus* (2nd ed.; New York, 1900), pp. 86f. See the interpretation of the term by N. Schmidt, *Encycl. Biblica*, IV (1903), 4705–40.

[21] Mark 14:61–62; Matt. 26:63–64; Luke 22:70.

[22] Mark 15:2; Matt. 27:11; Luke 27:31; John 15:33.

main feature in the belief in Israel's salvation from evil and reconciliation with Yahweh; but the word "Messiah" was narrowed only to one part of that hope. Such a belief in the political restoration of power is common among peoples who have lost such power.[23]

The Hebrew belief first appears in Amos (9:11–15) who in general terms speaks of the restoration of David's dynasty rather than of a personal king; and in Hosea who (1:11) speaks of "one head" who will gather together again the children of Judah and Israel and (3:5) more individually of "David their king," though these passages in the opinion of most critics are regarded as post-exilic interpolations. The first certain expression of the Messianic hope in the strict sense of a future savior-king is found in Isaiah (7:14, cf. 8:8), who foretells that "a virgin shall conceive, and bear a son . . . Immanuel," and (9:6–7) adds that "a child is born, unto us a son is given; and the government shall be upon his shoulder, and his name shall be called 'Wonderful, Counsellor, Mighty God, Everlasting Father, The Prince of Peace,' " and of "peace there shall be no end, upon the throne of David . . . from henceforth even for ever." These latter passages have little connection with a scion of David, but others (11:1 and 10–11) refer directly to him: "and there shall come forth a shoot out of the stock of Jesse, and a branch out of his roots shall bear fruit . . . and the root of Jesse . . . shall the nations seek . . . and the Lord shall set his hand again the second time to recover the remnant of his people."

Isaiah's contemporary Micah speaks even more definitely of a ruler in peace from David's city of Bethlehem (5:2): "But thou, Bethlehem Ephrathah . . . out of thee shall one come forth unto me that is to be ruler in Israel." Both Jeremiah (23:5–6, cf. 33:15) and Ezekiel (34:24–25 and 37:24–26) speak individually of the Messiah of national hope born of David's seed; the former having Yahweh say "I will raise unto David a righteous Branch and he shall reign as king . . ." and the latter during the Exile speaks of "my servant David" who "shall be king over them . . . and shall be their prince for ever." [24] Some writers, however, looked for deliverance through the collective sufferings of the people rather than through a personal deliverer, e.g. Deutero-Isaiah (53).

Apart from the vague hope of a national hero of the seed of David who would redeem Israel there is also a different expectation of a "heavenly Messiah" in Jewish apocalyptic literature in the books of Daniel and Enoch and in the later apocalypses of Baruch and IV Esdras.[25] Both Dan-

---

[23] E.g. the belief in German and French folklore that Charlemagne is not dead but sleeping and one day will awake and restore his people; or that of the German peasantry that Fritz "the Redbeard" (Friedrich Barbarossa) will one day emerge from his tomb in the Kyffhäuser hills in Thuringia and inaugurate a Golden Age of peace.

[24] After the Exile, Haggai (2:23) names Zerubbabel, governor of Judah, thus for the first time identifying the Messiah with a contemporary historical person; and Zechariah (3:8 and 6:12–13) speaks of Yahweh's bringing forth "my servant the Branch" and "the man whose name is the Branch . . . shall sit and rule upon his (David's) throne."

[25] See M. Buttenwieser, *Outline of the Neo-Hebraic Apocalyptic Literature* (Cincinnati, 1901), and his article under the same title in the *Jewish Encyclopedia*, I (1901), 675–85.

iel (7:13–14) and Enoch (45:1f.) describe a "heavenly" type of "son of Man" in which Jesus found the best expression of the Messiahship which he assumed (John 4:25–26). The only addition he made to the belief was that the Messiah must die, doubtless because of the hostility his claims had aroused. After his death Paul called him the preëxistent king who had descended from heaven to earth, his death a mystical blood-sacrifice for the sins of men. But this heavenly "Son of man" was not commonly understood in the Messianic sense by the Jews of Jesus' day for John (12:34) has the multitude ask "who is this Son of man?"

At what time in his career Jesus came to the belief that he was the Messiah cannot be determined. While Mark and Q assume it began with his ministry it is more probable that it came later when Jesus told his disciples of his surmise and charged them "to tell no man that he was the Christ" (Matt. 16:20). It may have come to him because of his success in healing and the enthusiasm of his disciples. The idea, in embryo in the Synoptics, is formulated by John (6:53–58) who reproduces Jesus' words spoken in the synagogue at Capernaum.[26] The question whether Jesus *was* the Messiah as he thought himself to be, is a matter of faith rather than of historical fact, since it was then, as now, supported by hope alone. Although most of his contemporary Jews rejected Jesus' pretensions, the belief in a coming liberator continued long after his death both in Palestine and elsewhere and various "false Christs" assumed the title and for a time gathered followers. Suetonius[27] recounts how "an old and established belief" had spread over the Orient that it was fated "for men coming from Judaea to rule the world"; and Josephus[28] says that belief in the imminent advent of the Messiah was the chief impulse to the rebellion which caused the great war with Rome, 66–70, and that the hope continued to the close of that war among the party of the Zealots. Josephus identified the Messiah with Vespasian since the latter had been proclaimed emperor by his soldiers on Jewish soil. Vespasian, who entertained secret hopes of becoming Nero's successor, had them confirmed on consulting the oracle of Yahweh and Baal on Mt. Carmel in Judaea.[29] Josephus when taken prisoner told him privately that he had been sent by God to predict that Vespasian and his son Titus would become Caesars and "masters of the whole human race."[30]

During the war with Hadrian (132f.) Simon bar Kokhba who, as already recounted, defied the might of Rome for over two years, was regarded

---

[26] Those words led Loisy to say: "It is only in the Gospel of John that the sayings and acts of Jesus tend to prove His supernatural mission, His celestial origin and His divinity. This peculiarity indicates the theological and non-historical character of the Fourth Gospel." *Simples reflexions* (1907) whose aim is discussed in the Epilogue *infra*.

[27] *Life of Vespasian*, 4:5.

[28] *Jewish War*, 6:5,4 (312); cf. also Tacitus, *Histories* 5:13. For the connection between the statements of the two historians, see E. Norden, "Josephus und Tacitus über Jesus Christus" in *Neue-Jahrb. des klass. Altertums*, XXXI (1913), 637–66; and P. Corssen, "Die Zeugnisse des Tacitus und Pseudo-Josephus über Christus" in *Ztschr. für die Neutestamentliche Wiss. und die Kunde des Urchristentums*, XV (1914), 114–40.

[29] Suetonius, *Life of Vespasian* 5:6.

[30] *Jewish War*, 3:8, 9 (401–02).

by the masses as the Messiah. But with the destruction of the city, both his memory and the belief in a Messiah fell into disfavor. Nevertheless for centuries thereafter, some Jews kept their faith in the latter. Thus the second article of the Jewish creed of Maimonides, who died in 1204, reads: "I believe with perfect faith in the coming of the Messiah, and though he tarry I will wait for his coming." But today while some Orthodox Jews still look for a great king, liberal Jews no longer look for a political personal Messiah but have spiritualized the idea by making it personify a system of ideas and beliefs.[31] Many other Jews are still unwilling to yield their belief that they are "the chosen of God" and believe that at the Messiah's advent their ideas and religion will become universal. But to most Jews the political deliverer who failed so often to restore the Jews to power "lies buried in the ruins of the sacred city" even if all Jews of the Diaspora are expected to include him in their daily prayers.

Some scholars [32] have seen Graeco-Roman ideas touching the "periphery" of the Jewish Messianic hope, especially in Vergil's so-called *Messianic Eclogue* which has been called "a vision of the new Golden Age of Augustus." [33] Whether the child to be born, at whose maturity the Golden Age will be introduced,[34] was to be Octavian's and Scribonia's or that of Asinius Pollio, consul in 40 B.C., to whom the poem is addressed in gratitude for his having saved the poet's farm from confiscation in 43 B.C. is in doubt. The poem contains Old Testament parallels (Isaiah 7:14–15) especially in its description of the era of Paradise in the Golden Age.

This inadequate survey of Jesus' teaching shows that it was not its novelty but the personality behind which attracted converts. In the words of Arthur Weigall:

The things He taught had been preached in one part or another by great thinkers of widely separated portions and areas: but never have they been put so clearly or forcibly as by Him, never have they been so knit together to constitute a ready guide to ordinary men, never have they been backed up by so fine an example of how one gallant individual can live for the good of others, never have they been so free of the teacher's own peculiar theology and eschatology.[35]

JESUS' REBELLION

It is well known that Jesus discarded many beliefs and customs of his mother religion, Judaism, and was especially rebellious against the formalism conserved by the Pharisees since the Exile. Curiously, he makes no mention of the Jewish custom of circumcision, nor did he share with many Jews the idea of identifying Synagogue and State, since he had no

[31] See C. J. Montefiori, *Outlines of Liberal Judaism* (London, 1903), pp. 280, 314.

[32] E.g. W. Bousset, *Religion des Judentums im neutestamentlichen Zeitalter* (2nd ed.; Berlin, 1906), p. 258.

[33] See J. B. Mayor, W. W. Fowler, and R. S. Conway, *Virgil's Messianic Eclogue* (London, 1907).

[34] See W. W. Fowler, *Roman Ideas of Deity*, Lecture IV.

[35] *The Paganism in our Christianity* (New York and London, 1928), pp. 267–68. Similarly, W. E. H. Lecky, *History of European Morals* (3rd ed. rev.; New York, 1890), II, 3.

concept of any civil or political institution. He regarded sacraments, dogmas, and rituals as trivial in comparison with his vision of the kingdom of heaven. He opposed his fellow-Jews who held to the letter of the Law and had forgotten Hosea's sentiment about God (6:6): "For I desire mercy, and not sacrifice, and the knowledge of God more than burnt offerings." His rebellion against illiberalism was real and he lost his life trying to remove the shackles which he believed were stifling the true spirit of Judaism. Similarly Paul, who interpreted circumcision "as that of the heart, in the spirit and not in the letter" (Rom. 2:29), said that "we serve in newness of the spirit, and not in oldness of the letter" (Rom. 7:6).

We get various phases of Jesus' opposition to the teaching of the Synagogue from his controversies with the Pharisees in the Synoptics and especially from the so-called "Sermon on the Mount," that collection of various sayings supposed to have been delivered in Galilee and brought together by Matthew into one discourse (5–7:27). It is the spiritual message at the basis of Christianity and goes beyond rather than against the Pentateuchal teaching whose validity as an ethical guide some have mistakenly thought Jesus undermined. While the Pharisees insisted on carrying out the law strictly in the belief that no state could exist without law, Jesus with his lack of interest in a state appealed to the Jewish conscience in interpreting it. He refused, as he said (Matt. 9:17), to cramp his teaching in old wineskins, i.e., Judaism.

He opposed various old Jewish customs such as public almsgiving (Matt. 6:2–4); public prayers in synagogue or on the street rather than in secret to the Father "which is in secret" (Matt. 6:6); and public fastings, a custom as old as the time of David (II Sam. 12:21–23) and long regarded as efficacious in calamities (Matt. 6:16–18). The Pharisees accused him and the disciples of disregarding the national fast-days such as those commemorating the first destruction of the Temple and its restoration, a custom which had been carefully kept since the Exile (9:14f.). He opposed public funeral rites, on one occasion (8:22) saying "Follow me: and leave the dead to bury their own dead." Both Mark (7:1–13) and Matthew (15:1–6) say that the Pharisees complained that his disciples did not follow the usual Jewish custom of hand-washing at meat—since in the East then (as now) people ate with their fingers, dipping them into a common dish—and of not keeping the *Corban*, "a gift of God" (i.e., vow rather than "gift," A.V., in reference to a vow not to maintain one's parents).[36] All three Synoptists accused him of sitting at table with publicans and sinners (Mark 2:15–17; Matt. 9:10–13; Luke 5:30–32). This the Pharisees refused to do, not, perhaps, because of pride but rather because they regarded the table as not

[36] The Talmudic treatise on Vows (*Nedarim*) shows that the Jews were addicted to rash vows and that *Corban* had become a mere formula of interdiction without reference to making the thing interdicted a "gift" to God. While Deuteronomy (23:21–23) forbade any retraction of a vow, Jesus opposed this literal interpretation and denounced a system which, as in this case, allowed a son by pronouncing the word *Corban* to relieve himself from the duty of caring for his parents, and taught that duty to parents transcended the fulfillment of any rash vow. See J. T. Marshall in *Hastings Dict. of the Bible*, I, 479.

only for food but for the exchange of ideas about which sinners, at least, were supposed to be ignorant. As for publicans all patriotic Jews despised them as thieves because they collected taxes for the Roman oppressors. Jesus, too, hated the Roman yoke, but associated with publicans and sinners in the hope of recalling them from their evil ways since he was wont to draw converts from all classes, even the robber on the cross. Similarly, the Jewish Hasidim of the eighteenth century associated with sinners and thieves and were similarly despised by the rabbis of their day.

Jesus rebelled against the meticulous observance of the Sabbath, which went back to the Decalog and earlier. He knew that no work was allowed on that day except what concerned the Temple service, priestly duties and the saving of life. When he and his disciples plucked the ears of corn he claimed dispensation from the law on the ground of being a rabbi and because he believed he was of David's house and the Messiah, lord of the Sabbath, claims which the Pharisees would not accept. As for his healing on the Sabbath they refused to admit that he had medical training and that, if he healed, it was through "the prince of the devils, Beelzebub" (Mark 3: 24; Matt. 12:22–24). He maintained that the Sabbath was for man.[37]

His attitude toward the chief Pentateuchal law, that of retaliation,[38] has been used to show that he was opposed to Mosaic law in general. But we have his definite denial since he said (Matt. 5:18;cf. Luke 16:17): "Till heaven and earth pass away, one jot or one tittle shall in no wise pass away from the law, till all things be accomplished," and adds that whosoever "shall break one of the least commandments, and shall teach men so, shall be called least in the kingdom of heaven." Moreover, in his censure of the Pharisees as "blind guides," he says that they and the scribes sit on Moses' seat and adds (Matt. 23:3): "all things whatsoever they bid you, these do and observe." How, then, can such apparently divergent sayings as these be reconciled with the Golden Rule?

The *lex talionis* is as old as the race, its spirit ingrained in human nature for all time and underlies every legal code from that of the Babylonian Hammurabi to those of our day. Jesus knew how impossible it was to rid human nature of it and so his attitude in interpreting it became one of leniency. The Pharisees had largely renounced it by various subterfuges to make it fit individual cases but Jesus went farther with a general appeal to the Jewish conscience, teaching that men should soften its interpretation. Thus, while accepting the law as a general statement of justice he appealed to the people not to use their right on every occasion as it was laid down in the Mosaic Code. He relied on ethical exhortation while the Pharisees relied on literal interpretation. It is Jesus' softening spirit, as well as that of Stoicism in Roman law, which has animated all civilized courts to our time. Josephus[39] says that Moses during his final exhortation to Israel

---

[37] See Excursus II, *infra*.
[38] Lev. 24:19–20; Matt. 5:38–42; cf. Exod. 21:24–25, and Deut. 19:21.
[39] *Antiq.* 4:8, 35 (280).

on the banks of the Jordan where he died interpreted the *lex talionis* as a private rather than public enactment to be used only where satisfaction between litigants could not be reached through payment of a fine. Mark reveals Jesus' meaning in following its spirit rather than its letter when he reports Jesus as saying (4:24; cf. Matt. 7:2 and Luke 6:38): "with what measure ye mete it shall be measured unto you." He was out of sympathy with Pharisaic views here as in the case of the *Corban* cited, for the Pharisees were legalists and casuists. It may be that had he literally accepted the Pentateuchal law and could have visioned the future, Jesus would have denounced Christianity which has renounced its spirit. Curiously, he said (Matt. 5:43–44): "Ye have heard that it was said, Thou shalt love thy neighbor and hate thine enemy . . . ," a statement which refers to Leviticus (19:18), but there we read only "but thou shalt love thy neighbor as thyself," with nothing about hating one's enemy.

He opposed the law of divorce on all grounds except fornication. He said (Matt. 5:31–32; cf. 19:3–9, Mark 10:2–12, and Luke 16:18) that whoever married a divorced woman committed adultery, but the Law (Deut. 24:1) allowed a bill of divorcement on other grounds such as "if she find no favor in his [the husband's] eyes" which Jesus regarded as sinful. While the law of adultery was explicit (Exod. 20:14) as to the actual occurrence, he went further and said the mere intent in one's heart constituted a crime as much as the act itself (Matt. 5:28). In respect of oaths, while Moses had said they must be kept (Deut. 23:21), he said simply: "Swear not at all . . . but let your speech be yea, yea; nay, nay: and whatsoever is more than these is of the evil one" (Matt. 5:34–37). In reference to the law of murder he widened the liability (Exod. 20:13) even to harboring a feeling of violence (Matt. 5:22), another example of ethics extended to established law.

JESUS AND PAUL

In studying early Christianity it is difficult to pierce the mist which envelopes some of Jesus' teachings as interpreted by his followers and notably by Paul whose ideas were largely alien to those ascribed to Jesus in the Gospels. The first step to overcome is to separate the teaching of these two. In so doing we find that Jesus was not the founder of Christianity as we know it for some of the most essential doctrines were formulated rather by Paul. Two of these we shall note—one evil and the other good. The former is the Pauline idea of man's redemption from evil as necessary because of an assumed prehistoric sin which had caused a spiritual gulf between God and man, the so-called "fall of man" described in Genesis (2–3), a gulf to be closed only by the voluntary vicarious sacrifice of Jesus who offered himself as the heaven-sent scapegoat for human sins. Thus we read in Romans (5:10–11):

For if, while we were enemies, we were reconciled to God through the death of his Son, much more, being reconciled, shall we be saved by his life; and not only so, but we also rejoice in God through our Lord Jesus Christ, through whom we have now received the reconciliation (A.V. "atonement").

This notion of original sin, redemption, and grace was added to Jesus' simple ethics by Paul.   It rested on the early Greek and Jewish ideas of expia-
tion, that a guilty man must suffer to make amends for his fault and that an
innocent man may suffer for one who is guilty.   Thus Aeschylus (525–456
B.C.) in his dramas had taught that an innocent man might suffer for a
crime committed by someone far back in his line, for until that crime was
expiated the moral equilibrium disturbed by it could not be restored.   But
both ideas, personal suffering and vicarious atonement, had been condemned by the Athenian Greeks in the century after that of the founder of
Greek tragedy.   Plato said that punishment should be remedial and not
revengeful.[40]   Athenian law also pronounced that punishment should be
personal like the fault.   Thus Paul started Christian theology with a false
belief, the truth having been discovered centuries before.   His error finds
no echo in the scientific thought of sociology and criminology in our day,
though still accepted by the Church.   Such an error began eighteen centuries of barren dispute.

Another Pauline doctrine, however, bore good fruit, the belief that Jesus was not only the Messiah of the Jews but the Savior of the Gentile
world, the motive force of Christianity through the ages.   Jesus, whatever
he thought of himself as the Messiah, was a Jew who lived and died within
the Synagogue.   Throughout his ministry he disclosed little or no interest
in non-Jews, not even for the Judaized Samaritans, the descendants of the
Babylonians and Assyrians who replaced Israelites deported by Sargon from
Samaria in 722–721 B.C.   For he warned his disciples against them, saying (Matt. 10:5–6): "Go not into any way of the Gentiles, and enter not into
any city of the Samaritans: but go rather to the lost sheep of the house of
Israel."   On another occasion when turning aside the petition of a Canaanite woman who had followed him to the coast of Tyre and Sidon to beseech
him to free her little daughter from an unclean spirit he said to his disciples
who stood about (Matt. 15:24–28): "I was not sent but unto the lost sheep
of the house of Israel."   And to the woman: "It is not meet to take the children's bread and cast it to the dogs."   But finally because of her faith he
granted her request.

Thus Jesus' sole aim was to guide his own people into a deeper appreciation of the value of their religion.   He had no vision of a world-wide
new religion, only of a reformed Judaism, even if it is impossible to say how
far he sensed the gulf his teaching opened.[41]

Paul's interest after his conversion was to identify Jesus with a universal
Messiah.   In so doing he helped to separate Jesus' followers from the Syna-

[40] This is the teaching of present-day schools of criminologists such as that of the
Italian Jew, Cesare Lombroso.   See his *Crime, its Causes and Remedies,* tr. by H. P. Hor-
ton (Boston, 1911); *Criminal Man,* summarized in English by his daughter, Gina Lom-
broso-Ferrero (New York and London, 1911); *The Female Offender* (New York, 1895).

[41] This is also the contention of the recent book of J. Klausner, *From Jesus to Paul,*
tr. from Hebrew by W. F. Stinespring (New York, 1943), a corollary to his earlier interpretation of Jesus' work.   He limits the outlook of both Jesus and Paul on the future.
See M. S. Enslin's unfavorable review of this "dangerous book" in *The Crozer Quarterly,*
XXI (1944), 160–63.

gogue, i.e., Christianity from Judaism, presenting the former as a universal faith to Jews, Syrians, Greeks, and Romans. It was Paul, therefore, rather than Jesus, who was the real founder of Christianity [42] whose name is derived from "Christ" rather than from "Jesus." A fundamentalist of our time should, therefore, go back to Jesus, i.e. to Judaism, rather than to Paul or to the doctrine which led to the Trinity, the logical consequence of Paul's God-man. At base Christianity is a mixture of the ideas of these two, the words of Jesus interpreted by Paul, but the initial dualism still exists. This brings us to the question, who then founded the Church?

The word "church," in Greek *ecclesia* (assembly), occurs only three times in the Gospels, all three in Matthew (16:18 and twice 18:17), though often enough elsewhere in the New Testament. In these passages it seems out of place, although the first, the most famous in the New Testament if judged by its consequences, has been the chief support of the claim of the Papacy to the foundation of the Roman Church and its primacy. Jesus elsewhere does not speak of a Church, but of the kingdom of God only. It was at Caesarea Philippi or Paneas [43] that in answer to Jesus asking his disciples who they thought he was, Peter called him "the Christ" (Matt. 16: 16). Matthew in the following verses (17–19) adds Jesus' further words:

And I also say unto thee, that thou art Peter, and upon this rock [Petros in Greek and Cephas in Aramaic mean "rock"] I will build my church; and the gates of Hades shall not prevail against it. I will give unto thee the keys of the kingdom of heaven; and whatsoever thou shalt bind on earth shall be bound in heaven; and whatsoever thou shalt loose on earth shall be loosed in heaven.

These words were taken probably from the prophecy about "the key of the house of David" given to Eliakim in Isaiah (22:22): "and he shall open, and none shall shut, and he shall shut, and none shall open," although in Jesus' time the words "binding" and "loosing" were technical terms used by the scribes in legal documents. However, the parallel passages about the charge to Peter found in Mark (8:29–30) and Luke (9:20–21)—almost identical one with the other—say nothing of this, nor give any hint of the primacy of Peter among the disciples. The question may well arise why Mark, who is believed to have taken the matter of his Gospel from Peter, should have omitted the words had Jesus actually spoken them.

While Protestants have disputed its meaning, the Roman Church has based on this passage Peter's primacy in the long line of pontiffs down to our time. Protestants believe that such an interpretation is nullified, *inter alia,* by the fact that whatever authority Jesus may have given to Peter must have been shared by the other disciples. They point out that according to Paul (Eph. 2:20) Jesus' followers "are fellow-citizens with the saints, and of the household of God, being built upon the foundation of the apostles and

[42] The contention of W. Wrede's *Paul,* tr. from the 2nd German ed. by E. Lummis (London, 1907). J. Weiss has opposed this view in his *Paul and Jesus,* tr. by H. J. Chaytor (London and New York, 1909).

[43] The first name came from its founder, *Philip,* tetrarch of Galilee, who founded it in 3 B.C.; the second from the local deity, Pan, to whom a nearby grotto, the source of the Jordan, was dedicated.

prophets, Christ Jesus himself being the chief corner stone." Moreover, in Revelation (21:14), the wall of the "holy city of Jerusalem coming down out of heaven," i.e., the Church, "had twelve foundations, and on them twelve names of the twelve apostles of the Lamb." St. Cyprian,[44] bishop of Carthage (248–258), although arguing that Peter founded the Roman Church, admits that the same power was extended to the other apostles, as on the occasion recounted by Matthew (18:18), just before which (v. 17) the word "church" is mentioned twice.

Why Mark, Luke, and John do not say anything about granting the keys of heaven to Peter is a difficult question to answer if the passage in Matthew is genuine and not an interpolation. There is no reason to argue that Jesus set a chief over the Church if he had no idea of one. He said of his followers only this (Matt. 18:20): "For where two or three are gathered together in my name, there am I in the midst of them." The idea of a bishop, *episcopus* (overseer), could also not have been in Jesus' mind since it took form long after his death. Even if it were possible to argue that Jesus conceived of a Church and a bishop it is certain that he would not have visioned them in faraway Rome. And if he had reference to some synagogue it was an unknown one.[45] Consequently many Protestant critics have rejected the Matthew passage as an interpolation made some time after the Roman Church had begun its existence. What evidence there is has been interpreted authoritatively by the Roman Church and thus is to be believed by Catholic Christians only, who continue to affirm that Jesus named Peter "rock" and head of their Church and the founder of the Papacy.[46]

In estimating the figure of Jesus on the basis of what little we know of his life and teaching one cannot question his greatness, for he has had no superior and hardly a peer in captivating the imagination of humanity. But to make one of the best of men, "an incomparable man" as Renan called him, into God of the universe on the basis of our meager and disputed records has been regarded by many to be the outstanding misapprehension of Western history. If it be such, it should be added immediately that it has proved a glorious one, since it has brought and will continue to bring solace to countless mortals. In the words of Loisy the story of Jesus is hardly that of God,

but rather of a village carpenter turned prophet and, failing in his prophecies, condemned as an agitator of the proletariate.

It is a long cry from so simple a characterization to the acceptance of Jesus as "very God" by the Christian Church of today.

Jesus' success, although ending in his death as a criminal, was neither adventitious nor dependent on his environment, but is rather to be found

---

[44] *De unitate catholicae ecclesiae,* called forth in 251 by a schism in Carthage and the Novatian one in Rome.

[45] Cf. F. J. A. Hort, *The Christian Ecclesia* (London, 1914), p. 9.

[46] See Excursus III, *infra.*

in his personality which reached the deeper roots of human nature with his simple revelation of a personal God and his simple idea of the purpose of life. He made his hearers feel their truth. He worked alone without the help of any party, without any revolution beyond that of the inner life, and without any formal program. Thus in many ways he differed from other founders of religions. Like Gautama and Socrates before him, he left no written record, for in all three leaders we have only the spoken word committed to writing by others. Later, his words were written down in the Gospels which, after changes were made to meet the trend of early Church doctrines, have finally reached us.

While Jewish, Greek, and Roman worship became encrusted with the minutiae of ceremony and ritual, the product of centuries of pious accretions, Jesus revealed that the essence of religion was not in these things. What he taught he abundantly illustrated by his own life. The tragedy of his life-work was that his simple teaching has gradually developed into an organized, conventional system, the fate of every religion which has attacked empty, outworn beliefs and replaced them with new. Today the Church, since the developed formalism and crystallization achieved already by the fourth century, remains a conventionalized institution, which continues to teach as cardinal beliefs much that would have been unintelligible to Jesus, if not to Paul. It has been said that should Jesus return he would be a stranger in the Church which arose to await his advent and that he might be astonished that men had made him out to be God.

It was Lessing who somewhere said: "Christianity has been tried for eighteen centuries, but the religion of Christ remains yet to be tried."

Chapter VI

PROGRESS OF CHRISTIANITY

AFTER presenting the personality and essential teachings of Jesus it remains to outline the major events in the progress of Christianity in the Roman Empire: in the present chapter, to the time of Constantine the Great who stopped all further persecution by making it the favored religion of his court; and in the following, the events of the later fourth century, which culminated in the victory of Catholicism over all its rivals when Theodosius the Great made it the sole official faith of the Roman State; and, finally, the fortunes of Christianity in the fifth and final century of the Empire.

THE FIRST CENTURY

After Jesus' death he was soon forgotten by the Jewish mob but not by his immediate circle of followers. Leaderless, they started back to Galilee where, or on the road thither, they underwent a remarkable experience, seemingly corroborated by eye-witnesses. For they were convinced that they saw the risen Jesus, perhaps, like his other apparitions to be explained as a group hallucination such as are well known to psychologists. On returning to Jerusalem some one hundred and twenty met for prayer (Acts 1:15), their only bond the memory of their master and the belief that he would return in glory and inaugurate his promised kingdom of heaven on earth. As Jews they were still loyal to Synagogue and Temple, the only cleavage between them and other Jews being their belief that Jesus was the Messiah. But the rift between them and Judaism had begun, whether we regard Jesus as merely a reformer who hoped that the Jews would accept his teaching or believe that his recasting of Jewish ethics in terms of humanity, figuratively putting new wine into fresh wineskins (Luke 5:37–38), made this impossible since the sequel showed that the Jews generally preferred the old wine of Judaism.

Nor is it hard to understand the position which confronted the Jews who were now asked to choose between the old dispensation and its new spiritualization by Jesus. The Jews had had a glorious past, one, in some respect, unparalleled among the peoples of antiquity. Consequently they had long believed that they were the chosen of Yahweh under a covenant made by him with Israel. If the new dispensation were true their past with its Messianic hopes and glories was gone. Justin Martyr [1] describes such a typical Jew of a later period, one Trypho, who said that they had been brought up to expect the "Son of man," but that it was "incredible and almost impossible" to accept the idea that "God endured being begot-

---

[1] In his polemic against the Jews, *Dialogus cum Tryphone,* a dialogue said by Eusebius (*H.E.* 4:15) to have been held at Ephesus between 132 and 134.

ten and becoming a man," that the lowly Jesus could not be the Son of man and that it was too much to demand that they give up their God for a pagan one.

Many Jews among Jesus' followers, whose numbers at Pentecost seven weeks after his death had increased to about three thousand souls (Acts 2: 41), found that they were no longer welcome in the Synagogue and so evolved the "Mother Church" of Christendom thus "born of the waiting" for Jesus' return. Jesus' brother James, called "the Just" because of his prestige and whom Paul numbered (Gal. 2:9) among "the pillars" of the Church, became its head being given, as Eusebius says,[2] "the throne of the bishopric in Jerusalem" which he held till his death. James had remained unmolested during the persecution of Herod Agrippa I in 44 (Acts 12:1f.), but Eusebius recounts [3] his death some years later when during a celebration of the Passover he was appealed to by Pharisees and scribes because of his influence to persuade the people publicly, from the battlements of the Temple, not to be led astray by faith in Christ, only to confess his own faith in the Messiahship of Jesus, and in consequence was thrown down, stoned, and clubbed to death. Josephus adds [4] that this crime was ordered by the High-Priest Ananus, the violent Sadducee who held office for three months in 62, and Eusebius says [5] that the wise men of the Jews believed it was the cause of the later Roman siege of Jerusalem.

Now came the most momentous rift in the early Church, one not closed till the end of the Roman war in 70.[6] While Peter, John, and James believed that Jesus had been sent to the Jews alone Paul, a Greek-Jew, confessed (Gal. 1:16) that he had been called by God "to reveal his Son in me, that I might preach him among the Gentiles." Thus his conversion proved epochal in the fortunes of Christianity for it raised the question, hardly faced by Jesus, of the right of Gentiles to a place in the Christian community without being subjected to the Mosaic Law. Paul was convinced that the new preaching could not be reconciled with that of the Synagogue and so took Jesus' followers far afield in denying the strict observance of the Law and in inaugurating a new policy. He believed that the Old Testament had been completed with the advent of Christ and that there was now little further use for the older Judaism since the new faith alone pointed the way to salvation. After he had meditated in Arabia he returned to Damascus and finally three years later went to Jerusalem where he tarried fifteen days with Peter seeing only James among the other apostles. He then visited Syria and Cilicia, for he was still unknown to the churches of Judaea (Gal. 1:17–22).

At Antioch after Paul and Barnabas returned from their missionary journey they found that certain Jewish Christians were teaching that salva-

---

2 *Ibid.* 2:25, 1; cf. Acts 15:13 and 21:18.

3 *Ibid.* 2:23, 6f.

4 *Antiq.* 20:91 (197, 199–203), quoted by Eusebius *H.E.* 2:23, 21–22.

5 *H.E.* 2:23, 19.

6 And continued by the Ebionites thereafter.

tion could come only through circumcision (Acts 15:1) which was causing great disturbance among the Gentile believers. The two men were sent to Jerusalem where Luke (Acts 15) tells of the discussion at the so-called "Apostolic Council" held by the churches of Jerusalem and Antioch to settle disputes between Jewish and Gentile apostles and their respective fields of labor and to define the relationship, on the basis of circumcision, between Jewish and Gentile converts.[7] While some demanded the observance of the custom of circumcision, Peter declared that salvation was through faith alone. After Paul and Barnabas had told of the success of their mission to the Gentiles James gave his verdict (Acts 15:19–20): "that we trouble not them, which from among the Gentiles turn to God," and sent a letter to the Syrians and Cilicians which enjoined four prohibitions: those from the pollution of idols, i.e., the eating of sacrificial animals; from fornication since looseness of morals was tolerated in Gentile lands; "from what is strangled, and from blood," i.e. disapproval of certain Gentile food habits. They were allowed to preach the Gospel to Gentiles unbound by the Law except for these restrictions while the "Mother Church" in Jerusalem was to continue to demand circumcision of its converts (cf. Gal. 2:9).

Thus the Church, having faced the choice of remaining a Jewish institution under the leadership of Jesus' kin or becoming universal, had chosen the latter. When he went to Antioch later, Peter was rebuked by Paul for his change of heart about the Gentiles, a change which had won over even Barnabas (Gal. 2:12–13). The accuracy of the notion, however, that Peter first championed a liberal policy toward the Gentiles and later changed his mind at Antioch has been questioned. For, if the meeting at Antioch occurred after the so-called Council of Jerusalem, Peter's change of heart is difficult to explain. Ramsay has solved the difficulty on the assumption that Peter took his liberal stand at an "informal" conference with Paul and others at Jerusalem, vacillated at Antioch and spoke his real conviction at a later "Council" in Jerusalem. Others find no reconciliation between the accounts in Acts (15) and Galatians (2).

After the Council Paul and Silas started their missionary journey from Antioch, visiting groups in Asia Minor and, in consequence of a vision, passing over to Macedonia and Greece (Acts 16:6–18:2), and then returned to Antioch. Thus, due to Paul's zeal churches were founded in communities largely composed of Gentiles whom old-fashioned Jews regarded as

[7] But it is questionable whether a real council then took place or any official decree about the matter was passed. The account in Acts may represent some telescoping of Paul's two visits at Jerusalem as outlined in Galatians (1:18 and 2:1f.), for Paul says the Council took place fourteen years after his vision, though his account is not so clear as the one in Acts (15:68). The question is discussed by Lake, "The Apostolic Council of Jerusalem" in Foakes-Jackson and K. Lake's *Beginnings of Christianity* (London, 1933), Pt. 1, pp. 195–212. Olmstead places the meeting in 43, which is out of harmony with the account in Galatians, i.e., before the so-called "Famine" visit mentioned in Acts (11:28) which took place 46–47. The Council has been generally placed in 51 or 52, though some go back to 47 or 49, i.e., between the missionary journey of Paul and Barnabas and that of Paul alone.

outcasts. It was from Antioch, whose church was then second only to that of Jerusalem, that Christianity was propagated among Gentiles as well as Jews and became universal. Here also the followers of Jesus had early been called "Christians" (Acts 11:26), a name chosen more for convenience than reproach since it designated the converts more exactly than any of the colorless names which preceded it such as: "brethren" (Acts 13:9), their standing name among themselves; "saints" (Rom. 8:27) a name taken from Judaism; "believers" (Acts 5:14); "elect" (Matt. 13:20); "poor" (Luke 6:20); "sons of God" (Rom. 8:15); and collectively the "Church" (Acts 19:39). The Jews had called them "Nazarenes" (Acts 24:5) or "Galileans," the latter name appearing explicitly only in Luke (13:1; 22:59).[8] The name "Christians" occurs only twice again in the New Testament: in Acts (26:28) —where Agrippa answers Paul, perhaps contemptuously, "with but little persuasion thou wouldst fain make me a Christian"—and in I Peter (4:16). The tenth-century lexicographer Suidas says the name was first used in Claudius' reign when Peter designated Evodius as his successor in the bishopric of Antioch, i.e., in 43.

Paul's extension of the faith to include Gentiles largely freed it from its Jewish shackles since he said (Gal. 3:28): "there can be neither Jew nor Greek" (i.e., Gentile). Great events followed this pronouncement for this was the real beginning of the infant Church universal and its formal introduction to the Roman world, the chief event in the first century of its existence. Paul defined its universality for all time in these words (Eph. 4: 4–6): "There is one body, and one spirit . . . one Lord, one faith, one baptism, one God and Father of all, who is over all, and through all, and in all." Thus early all Christians, despite local differences, felt themselves united as in Tertullian's phrase [9] *"tertia gens dicimur."* Paul continued to form churches after the pattern of that in Antioch and soon the Christian community included "all of the way" (Acts 9:2), both Gentiles and Jews of the Diaspora. But the connection with the Synagogue was not completely broken since he told the Ephesian elders (Acts 20:28): "Take heed . . . to feed the church of God which he purchased with his own blood," an adaptation of Psalm 74:2. The Church took over the Jewish scriptures, preaching their fulfillment in the life of Jesus. Paul extended the new faith over the Greek half of the Empire—Syria, Asia Minor, Macedonia, Greece—its introduction into Europe being at Philippi in Macedonia. Later he addressed an Epistle to the Philippians, written probably from Rome before his acquittal in 63, long contested for genuineness but now almost universally accepted. The new faith entered Rome perhaps in the closing years of Tiberius' reign or, more probably, in the early part of that of Claudius (41–54).[10] Years later Paul sent his famous Epistle to the Romans [11] whose faith he says was already "proclaimed throughout the

[8] On these names, see R. Mackintosh in *E.R.E.*, III (1910), 573–76.

[9] *Ad Nationes* 1:8.

[10] Cf. G. P. Fisher, *The Beginnings of Christianity* (New York, 1877), pp. 520–33.

[11] It was written probably at Corinth where he spent eighteen months, 51–53 (Acts 18: 1–2).

whole world" (1:8). He alludes to Gentiles in the church there although the Romans at the time still confused Jews and Christians.

The year of Nero's fire and the subsequent persecution of the Christians introduced Christianity to world notice although for long thereafter it remained a secret society under police surveillance. The disastrous fire began at the southeastern corner of the Circus Maximus, an area filled with inflammable wooden shops, on July 18, 64 and, accelerated by wind, burned for six days and nights and again, later, raged for two days, completely destroying three of the fourteen *regiones* of the city. But the damage recorded by Tacitus in his description [12] must be exaggerated since the historian remembered the disaster only as a boy of about ten years and completed the *Annales* a half century later at the close of Trajan's reign.[13] He recounts [14] how Nero, when he learned at Antium that the fire was nearing his palace—the *domus transitoria* (so-named from its passage-way)—returned to the city and aided the distressed by opening to them the Campus Martius, the house and gardens of Agrippa, the Pantheon, and his own gardens across the Tiber, and by lowering the price of grain. Still, because of his well-known crimes, the rumor spread that he had instigated the fire either to get space for his proposed "Golden House" or, his imagination being fired by the sublimity of the terrible scene, to give him an opportunity to watch it from his private theater or the Tower of Maecenas where he might sing his aria on the subject of the Destruction of Troy. But his *Troica,* unfortunately for this story, was first read in public a year later. To kill the rumor he placed the blame on the unpopular Christians.

While Tacitus is cautious about blaming Nero he says none dared to check the fire, since those who threw firebrands declared that "they had one who authorized them" (38–39). But Suetonius, Cassius Dio, and Pliny the Elder [15] all blame him outright. In any case the mob, enraged not only by the loss of their homes but by the destruction of temples, statues, and other treasures of the Roman past, found a convenient scapegoat in the Christians, now distinguished from Jews,[16] while the Empress Poppaea Sabina, a convert to Judaism, protected the latter. The Christians were particularly unpopular because of their prophesy of a final world conflagration on Christ's return. Tacitus says "vast numbers were convicted not so much on the count of arson as for their hatred of the human race" [17]—since Jewish misanthropy was proverbial.

The ensuing persecution—Tacitus alone connects it immediately with the fire though it must have been later—has received undue attention be-

---

[12] *Annales* 15:38–41.

[13] On the date of completion ?115 or 116, see H. Furneaux, *The Annals of Tacitus* (Oxford, 1891), II, 4.

[14] Cf. Suetonius, *Life of Nero,* chap. 31.

[15] Suetonius, *Life of Nero,* chap. 38; Dio, *History,* LXII:17; Pliny *Hist. nat.* 17:5.

[16] Not only Tacitus, but Sulpicius Severus in a passage in his *Chronicon* apparently transcribed from the last part of Bk. V of the former's *Histories,* make it clear that the distinction between Jew and Christian was now known.

[17] *Annales* 15:44; *L.C.L.* (1937).

cause of the tradition that Paul was among its victims and the fact that Tacitus is the earliest Latin writer to mention in this connection the Crucifixion. The tradition about Paul, however, seems improbable on chronological grounds since the persecution probably did not begin, at the earliest, before the autumn of 64 which makes the interval from the close of his two-year stay in Rome (Acts 28:30) until 64 too long. Furthermore tradition [18] has him beheaded, while Nero's victims were crucified. Tacitus tells realistically how "they were covered with wild beasts' skins and torn to death by dogs or were fastened on crosses and, when daylight failed, were burned to serve as lamps at night." This was in connection with Nero's "spectacle" in his Circus where he appeared in the habit of a charioteer or mounted on his car.[19] Tacitus adds that, despite their deserved punishment, a sentiment of pity arose because of the belief that they were being sacrificed not for the State's welfare but because of one man's ferocity.

The site of this first Christian persecution was, as Tacitus tells us, in Nero's gardens beyond the Tiber. Here in an area at the foot of the Vatican Hill [20] Nero held his chariot races. To the north lay the temple areas of Cybele and Mithra while on the *spina* of the Circus itself stood the red granite obelisk transported by Caligula from Heliopolis in Egypt, which today stands in the center of St. Peter's Piazza.

Juvenal, Tacitus' contemporary (*ca.* 60–140), alludes to the persecution twice. In Satire 1 (155–57) he speaks of burning live bodies and dragging them across the arena, while in 8 (235) he mentions the *tunica molesta* (shirt of evil), in which, lined with pitch, the victims were burned—the ordinary punishment at Rome for incendiaries.[21] The earliest Christian writer to refer to the persecution was Melito, bishop of Sardis (*ca.* 170), a fragment of whose letter to Antoninus preserved by Eusebius [22] couples Nero and Domitian as the only emperors who had slandered Christianity. Eusebius also says Nero was "the first of the emperors to be pointed out as a foe of divine religion." [23] Thus to Christians, Nero was a diabolical monster, identified with the mystic antichrist. At his early death at thirty, not, however, because of his persecution of Christians, his statues were broken, his name erased from public monuments, and his Golden House dismantled. Curiously, however, his memory was secretly revered since flowers were long renewed on his grave and down to Trajan's reign it was even believed that he was not dead but was somewhere in the East and

---

[18] As in Tertullian *De praescriptione haereticorum* 36.

[19] The "spectacle" was evidently the *ludus matutinus*, or "morning-hunt of beasts," usually exhibited in the Circus Maximus, in which Christian women and girls were now dressed to play mythological parts, such as Danaids and Dirce, ending in their death.

[20] The present Borgo, containing the Piazza and Basilica of St. Peter's and, centuries before Nero's time, the farmlands of the legendary Cincinnatus (dictator in 458 B.C.), and more recently the gardens of Agrippina (Suetonius, *Life of Claudius*, chap. 21); Caligula had begun a Circus here which Claudius completed and hence it was called by both names in common (Pliny *H.N.* 36:74).

[21] Martial in Epigram 10:25, and Seneca in *Epist.* XIV, 5 also mention the shirt.

[22] *H.E.* 4:26, 9.

[23] *Ibid.* 2:25, 30.

would return.[24]   During the Middle Ages, down to the eleventh century, he remained the incarnation of evil, his spirit, it was believed, haunting the Pincian Hill on which he was buried.   His persecution, however, was confined to Rome with only slight repercussions elsewhere (?cf. Rev. 2:13).   It was political and personal rather than religious like those which followed. Still his mock-festival—perhaps on August 1, 64—is one of the most solemn dates in Christian history.   It proved to be a blood baptism for Christianity which made it possible for it to live on.[25]

Domitian, at the close of the first century (81–96), is credited by Christian writers with persecuting the followers of their religion.   He championed the imperial cult to the exclusion of all others except that of Isis-Serapis to whom he erected a temple.   For a century men had voluntarily taken an oath by the "Genius" of the Emperor but Domitian was the first to make it a real test of "personal" loyalty by compelling men to swear by it in all public documents.   This caused trouble for both Jews and Christians since they alone refused to sanction his divinity.   Suetonius [26] tells us that he levied a poll tax on the Jews, both "on those who lived after the manner of the Jews in the city, without publicly professing themselves to be such"—perhaps Gentile converts to Judaism—"and on those who, by concealing their origin, avoided the tribute imposed upon that people." He adds that in his youth he saw an old man of ninety years have his person exposed in a crowded court that the Procurator might determine if he were circumcised.   The Emperor's cousin, Flavius Clemens, consul of the year 95, and his wife Domitilla were condemned because they favored either Christianity or, perhaps, Judaism.   One was executed and the other banished, though Domitian had named their sons his heirs.[27]   He condemned others also though he instituted no general persecution.   Eusebius [28] says he ordered the execution of the surviving family of Joseph and Mary and had the two grandsons of Judas (Jude), brother of Jesus, brought before him, but on finding that they were simple-minded let them go.   Dante's mention in the *Purgatorio* (22:89–91) of the secret conversion to Christianity of the poet Statius,[29] Vergil's imitator, who had profited by Domitian's patronage because of his fulsome adoration, rests on no ancient authority.

[24] Tacitus, *Histories* 2:18; Suetonius, *Life of Nero*, chap. 57.

[25] For problems concerning the persecution, see H. Furneaux, *op. cit.*, II (App.), 570–78, "The Neronian Persecution of the Christians"; J. B. Bury's ed. of Gibbon, II, 570ff. (App.), "Persecution in the First and Second Centuries"; E. G. Hardy, *Christianity and the Roman Government* (London and New York, 1894).   C. Pascal, in *L'Incendio di Roma e i primi Cristiani* (Milano, 1900), accuses the Christians as did Tacitus, but A. Profumo, *Le Fonti ed i tempi dello incendio Neroniano* (1905), defends them.   See P. Allard, *Histoire des persécutions* (2nd ed.; Paris, 1892), I, 35–80; and his *Histoire des persécutions pendant les deux premiers siècles* (3rd ed.; Paris, 1903).

[26] *Life of Domitian*, chap. 12.

[27] Vogelstein believes that they were Jewish converts and that Domitilla was not identical with the Christian of the same name which appears on the walls of the Catacombs; see Pauly-Wissowo, *Real-Encycl.* (cited hereafter as *R.E.*), VI, cols. 2536–39 (Stein) and 2732–35.

[28] *H.E.* 3:19–20.

[29] See his *Silvae* 4:2; cf. Allard, *op. cit.*, I, 96–124.

THE SECOND CENTURY

Reference has been made to Pliny's correspondence with Trajan about recalcitrant Christians in Bithynia. That correspondence indicates how Rome handled such matters in the humane era of Trajan who wrote that any other course than leniency was "not in accordance with the spirit of our time." His statement that proof of guilt must be established was of advantage to Christians and in no sense a persecution.[30] Trajan's advice marks the first act friendly to Christianity by the head of the Empire. The martyrdom of Ignatius, bishop of Antioch, supposed to have died under Trajan between 104 and 117 is unhistorical being supported only by the *Martyrium Ignatii*. But such martyrologies, once followed by Church historians, are no longer accepted as evidence.

Trajan's policy of clemency lasted until the reign of Marcus Aurelius (161–180) and with that exception until the middle of the third century and the formidable persecution of Decius. An isolated incident in the reign of Marcus' predecessor, Antoninus Pius (138–161), may, however, be mentioned, the martyrdom of the aged Polycarp, bishop of Smyrna who was publicly burned in 155.[31] Polycarp's answer to his enemies is preserved by Eusebius (*H.E.* 4:15, 20) and should not be forgotten: "For eighty-six years have I been his servant, and he has done me no wrong, and how can I blaspheme my King who saved me." The mob then demanded that a lion should be loosed on him, but instead he was publicly burned, his courage closing a noble life with a noble death.

In the reign of Marcus Aurelius, the Stoic emperor, the Christian Church emerges again into the clear light of history, since it then suffered persecution in various parts of the Empire. This has caused many to denounce Marcus although his hostility to the Christians was merely the logical result of his training, since from boyhood he had been taught to regard the imperial cult and the imperial ideal as identical and to feel that Christianity opposed them. He seems to have ordered various governors to punish "sacrilege" which he regarded as the great crime of the Christians. In reference to the persecution in Gaul in 177 Eusebius says [32] that the governor there had written for advice and the emperor's reply was that "they should be tortured to death, but that if any should recant they should be let go." Consequently, refractory citizens were to be beheaded and

---

[30] The early fifth-century Christian historian Orosius says (7:12) that Pliny's request for advice led Trajan to mitigate a ruling that already existed. His *Historiae adversus paganos* was dedicated to his friend St. Augustine, an abridged translation of which by Alfred the Great is still extant in Anglo-Saxon. See C. Bigg, *The Origin of Christianity*, ed. T. B. Strong (Oxford, 1909), chap. ix.

[31] Eusebius, *Chronicon*, gives 166, i.e., in the reign of Marcus Aurelius, a date accepted until 1867 when W. H. Waddington's *Mémoire sur la chronologie de la vie du rheteur Aristide* appeared. This showed that Statius Quadratus (cf. the *Martyrium* or the *Epistle* of the Smyrna church to that of Philomelium) who was present was proconsul of Asia, 155–156, so that the martyrdom fell Feb. 23, 155.

[32] *H.E.* 5:1, 44, 47.

others sent to the beasts, i.e., the traditional methods of punishing citizens and non-citizens respectively. Marcus knew little about the Christians as he spent most of his reign engrossed in the war with the Quadi and Marcomanni on the Danube and was seldom in the capital.[33] In his *Meditations* he mentions the Christians only once in reference to their "obstinacy" (XI:3). While some have explained that harsh indictment as an interpolation it was rather in harmony with the usual reaction of the better classes of the day. For the Christians by then were dangerous since they taught a corporate unity above that of the State. This seems sufficient reason why the best of emperors instituted a grave persecution. His biographer Julius Capitolinus calls him "a man so great and good, and an associate of the gods in life and death, so that at his funeral all were sure he had been lent to men by the gods and now returned to them." [34]

Eusebius [35] says Justin Martyr met his death at Rome in his reign and there were also martyrdoms in Pergamum, Africa and, above all, in Gaul where in 177 forty-eight Christians were killed, the only large-scale persecution of the second century. Eusebius,[36] on the basis of a letter sent by the Gallic churches of Lugdunum (Lyon) and Vienna (Vienne) to the churches of Asia and Phrygia, details the tortures, imprisonments, and deaths at Lyon. Such martyrs were first excluded from houses, baths, markets, and all public places; then tortured and imprisoned and finally led into the Forum to be publicly interrogated by the tribune in the absence of the governor and, when the latter returned, brought before him where they were called parricides and cannibals and were again tortured with fiendish ingenuity. One of them, Blandina (17–19; 40–42; 55–56), was tortured by relays night and day till her body was torn apart but still breathed. Then she was bound to a stake in the arena and exposed to the wild beasts. When these refused to touch her she was again imprisoned and, finally, after scourging and again being offered to the beasts, she, still breathing, was roasted and thrown into a net to be tossed by bulls, and finally died. Some of the dead were kept for days from burial, but at last the bodies had to be burned and the ashes thrown into the Rhone.

There is also an official narrative of the trials of Christians from Scillium in Numidian Africa before a Roman proconsul at Carthage in documents which can be dated 180, i.e., the last year of the reign of Marcus.[37] Here the proconsul Saturninus asked the accused "to return to a right mind," i.e., swear by the Emperor's "genius," when one of them answered: "I do not recognize the empire of this world, but rather I serve that God

---

[33] He died in camp probably of the plague either in Vindobona (Aurelius Victor *De Caesaribus* 16:12 and *Epit.* 16:2) or Sirmium in Pannonia (Tertullian *Apoligeticus* written in favor of the Christians, 25).

[34] See *Scriptores Historiae Augustae*, L.C.L. (1922–32), I, 177 (Capitolinus 18:4).

[35] *H.E.* 4:16, 7–8.

[36] *Ibid.* 5:1.

[37] The *Acta* of these Scillian martyrs form the earliest documents of the African Church and the first Christian Latin ones. The translations are by C. E. Owen, *Some Authentic Acts of the Early Martyrs* (Oxford, 1927), pp. 71–77, from a ninth-century Latin MS discovered in the British Museum by Dean J. Armitage Robinson, *Texts and Studies in Biblical Literature*, I–II (1891), 106f.

whom no man has seen nor can see"; and another: "We have none other to fear save the Lord our God who is in heaven." Refusing a thirty-day reprieve they all, twelve in number, were sentenced "to suffer by the sword." With such treasonable answers, there could be no other solution possible.

Just before this, in 174, occurred what is known in Christian tradition as the miracle of the "Thundering Legion" during the war with the Quadi as told by Eusebius and Cassius Dio.[38] On one occasion the Roman army was oppressed with thirst and the Christian soldiers in one legion bent on their knees and prayed for relief. Suddenly a shower arose which refreshed the Romans and the lightning put the enemy to flight. While Dio ascribed the miracle to an Egyptian magician in the army the Christians naturally ascribed it to the prayers of their soldiers. The Emperor is said to have given the name "Thundering" (XII *Fulminata*) to the legion, but unfortunately for the story this name came more likely from the representation of a thunderbolt on the soldiers' shields since the title goes back to the time of Nero or even Augustus as Dio says.[39] The miracle is, however, commemorated on the sculptured reliefs depicting scenes in the war with the Marcomanni on the so-called Column of Antoninus in the Piazza Colonna, Rome, erected to glorify Marcus' victories by his son Commodus,[40] and restored by Sixtus V in 1589.

We cannot leave Marcus without mentioning his famous book of *Meditations,* a private work of devotion composed in Greek during his Danubian campaigns. It displays neither system nor originality but is rather a collection of brief, disconnected thoughts of the last great Stoic, often called "philosopher on the throne." Its benevolent spirit, so out of harmony with the persecutions discussed, is transparent, so that the sentiments expressed seem to have been lived rather than merely written. He believed in a religion of reason, i.e., Stoicism, which made all men fellow-citizens and which Renan called "independent of race or country." [41] It contains many examples of the emperor's humanitarian spirit such as the manumission of slaves, relief for the poor, equity in legislation, foundations of charity, e.g. establishing a trust-fund in honor of his disloyal wife to support five thousand poor girls. The work has influenced many great men and has been one of the factors in keeping Stoicism alive to our day.[42]

THE THIRD CENTURY

Soon after the death of Commodus, the unworthy son of Marcus, who was assassinated on New Year's Eve 192, the "Carthagino-Syrian Dynasty" of the Severi was founded by Septimius Severus who was dominantly Car-

[38] Eusebius *H.E.* 5:51–52; Dio, *History* Bk. LXXII, 8–10.

[39] *History* Bk. LV, 23.

[40] Capitolinus in his *Life of Marcus Aurelius* attributes the rain to a prayer offered by the Emperor himself; Eusebius (*H.E.* 20:4, 4f.) quotes confirmation of the story by Tertullian and says letters of Marcus were extant in his day in which the Emperor said that Christian prayers saved the army.

[41] *Marc-Aurèle et la fin du monde antique* (3rd ed.; Paris, 1882), XVI, 272.

[42] See H. D. Sedgwick, *Marcus Aurelius* (Oxford, 1921).

thaginian in blood and had learned Latin as a foreign language. The dynasty lasted nearly a half-century (193–235) and under it the imperial government began to be radically changed in the direction of despotism. Septimius was the first emperor to assume the title *dominus* and the first to rely on the army for support.[43] Although he personally favored the Christians (at least until 202), there were persecutions by provincial officials during his reign in Egypt—Alexandria and the Thebaid—and in the province of Africa in 197–198 and again in 211. The former called forth Tertullian's defense of Christianity, the *Apologeticus,* in 197 and perhaps his *Ad Martyres.* Severus' son, Caracalla, remembered for his *Constitutio Antoniniana* (212) which gave citizenship to all mature males of the Empire, was soon followed by the "Amazing Emperor Heliogabalus," [44] his real name being Varius Avitus. He was grandson of Septimius' Syrian wife Julia Domna and a high-priest of the Syrian solar Baal of Emesa (Homs). This depraved and profligate boy-emperor is remembered for having ensconced on the Palatine the black-stone fetish of the Sun-god—*sol invictus Elagabal*—where for a season it superseded the State-cult and over which the emasculated priest-emperor presided. It was his wild dream to institute an all-absorbing monotheism in heaven like his own autocracy on earth. But his dream died quickly for when he was scarcely eighteen he and his intriguing mother Soaemias were slain in a pretorian mutiny and his body was dragged through the streets and cast into the Tiber and the hated fetish was returned to Syria.

His folly was redeemed by his cousin, Alexander, who succeeded him (222–235)—called Severus by his soldiers because of his rigorous discipline. His biographer Lampridius [45] pictures him as an unusually broad-minded ruler who evinced favorable feeling for Christianity. In his private chapel he placed busts, not only of deified emperors, but those of various religious teachers including Apollonius of Tyana, Abraham, Orpheus, Christ, and "others of the same character" (29:2), and planned a temple to Christ and a place for him in the Roman pantheon but was dissuaded by his *augur* who warned that if he did so "all men would become Christians" and all other temples would be abandoned (43:6–7). He had engraved on the walls of his palace and public buildings the "Golden Rule" in the negative form: "What you do not wish that a man should do to you, do not do to him." He reversed Septimius' decree forbidding conversion to Judaism and Christianity (17:1) and extended the privileges of both (22:4). But, while trying to restore the glories of the Antonine Age, he suffered the fate of all others of his line, assassination.

The middle years of the third century are remembered for the great crisis of the Empire, the prelude to the long agony of its decline which

---

[43] For an unfavorable view of his administration, see M. I. Rostovtzeff, *Social and Economic History of the Roman Empire* (Oxford, 1926); for a more favorable one, W. Platnauer, *Life and Reign of Septimius Severus* (Oxford, 1918).

[44] So John S. Hay entitled his biography of him (London, 1911).

[45] In *Scriptores historiae Augustae* II:179–313.

lasted for two centuries more. It was a period of anarchy and economic and social distress aggravated by famines, plagues, and military collapse, the worst in Roman history until its close surpassing in violence the crisis at the end of the Republic when the government was the tool of ambitious aristocrats. Still the State survived the disaster but only by yielding to revolutionary political changes by which the older classical type of government was turned into an Oriental despotism. The severity of the crisis may be judged by the fact that from the death of Commodus to the accession of Diocletian (193–284) the throne was the sport of the armies. Out of thirty-three emperors—some reigning simultaneously—twenty-five were murdered, three died in battle, one in exile, one by a lightning-stroke, one by suicide, and only two in their beds. During the height of the crisis from Maximin to Diocletian (235–284) [46] there were twenty-six emperors of whom nineteen were murdered, three fell in battle, one died in exile, one by lightning, one by suicide and one by the plague. This was the long period of the "barrack emperors" as Thomas Hodgkin called them. Exclusive of the Thirty Tyrants,[47] the emperors reigned an average of about two years each. Several were fine soldiers and sincerely tried to restore the State from anarchy within and invasion without but could not control the armies, the real masters of Rome. Rome was no longer the capital but the army camps on the frontiers, the government being personified in the general then chosen.

St. Cyprian, bishop of Carthage (248–258), has left a realistic account of internal affairs at the time in a letter to Donatus in which he speaks of "roads closed by brigands, the sea blocked by pirates, the bloodshed and horror of universal strife. The world drips with mutual slaughter, and homicide, considered a crime when perpetrated by individuals, is regarded as virtuous when committed publicly." [48] Beyond the northern frontier the Germans were now trained in the Roman fashion and grouped in confederacies eager to seize the fertile lands across the Rhine and Danube. Saxon pirates harassed the Atlantic coast; the Franks menaced the Rhone valley; the Alemanni, other parts of Gaul; the Marcomanni, Rhaetia and Noricum, while Goths and Sarmatians threatened the lower Danubian provinces of Moesia and Thrace, and other Goths above the Black Sea (Ukraine) menaced the Roman provinces in Asia. The Parthians or reorganized Persians (since Ardashir founded the Sassanid dynasty in 226) ruled from Ctesiphon on the Tigris with the title of "King of kings." They boasted that they were the equals of the Caesars and were ready again to continue the almost ceaseless struggle with Rome begun by Crassus three centuries before.

[46] A. Alföldi, *C.A.H.*, VII (1939), 165–231, dates the actual crisis 249–270 only, i.e., from Decius to Aurelian. It will be remembered that Gibbon started the "Decline" of Rome in the reign of Marcus Aurelius. See M. I. Rostovtzeff, "La crise social et politique de l'Empire romain au III siècle ap. J.-C." in *Musée Belge*, XXVII (1923), 233–42.

[47] Lives by Trebellius Pollio, *Scriptores historiae Augustae*, III, 65–151. Out of thirty-two names from Decius to Claudius II only nine were authentic pretenders and these only during the reign of Gallienus; l. c., p. 64, n. 1.

[48] *Ep.* I, chap. vi; tr. by Cochrane, *op. cit.* (*supra*, p. 33, n. 49), p. 154.

During the reign of Valerian and his son Gallienus (253–268) Rome reached the nadir of her collapse, for the former was taken prisoner by the Parthians and the latter could not rescue him and the Empire lost large sections of its territory. Postumus in the West set up an independent Gaul (258–59) and Zenobia, self-styled "Queen of the East," claimed the vast area from the Taurus Mountains to the Arabian and Persian gulfs and Egypt as her own. She, like Postumus, believed that in consequence of Valerian's misfortunes Rome could not defy her and broke with the imperial government in 266. Recovery of the lost areas was slow. Begun by Claudius the Goth, it was completed by Aurelian. The latter conquered Tetricus, last of the Gallic pretenders, near Châlons in 274, and the year before took Zenobia's oasis-capital, Palmyra, but chivalrously gave the queen her freedom. On his way back to Europe, learning that she had revolted he returned, destroyed her city and brought her captive to Rome where, shackled with golden chains and weighted with gems, and accompanied by her two sons and the captured Tetricus, she was led in his triumphal procession, but was allowed to live thereafter as a Roman matron at Tibur.[49] Thus passed one of the small group of women to attain world renown. Of her capital in the Syrian Desert, Harold Mattingly has said: "It flamed like a meteor across the political firmament and like a meteor it passed in the night."[50]

The "barrack" emperors ended with Diocletian, who brought cessation of decay by means of an Oriental despotism—the so-called *Dominate*—which continued in the West until the latter's dissolution in the late fifth century and in the East until the end of the Byzantine Empire in the fifteenth. It was this recovery which made possible during the Middle Ages in the West the assimilation of much of ancient culture.

During the crisis the Church underwent one of its worst persecutions— the clemency of Trajan being forgotten. The mildness of Alexander Severus had its reaction in a slight persecution under the Thracian peasant emperor Maximin (235–238).[51] Tradition has the Roman Bishop Pontianus (230–235) and Hippolytus, bishop of Portus Romanus (Porto opposite Ostia)[52] and disciple of Irenaeus, exiled to the *insula nocina* of Sardinia. Maximin, self-styled "friend and advocate of the military order," never entered Rome but governed it through a prefect and was slain by his soldiers under the walls of Aquileia during a revolt begun by Gordian in Africa.[53]

---

[49] See *Life of Aurelian* by Flavius Vopiscus in *Scriptores historiae Augustae* III, 193f.

[50] *C.A.H.*, XII (1939), 305.

[51] Elevated by his soldiers because of his great size and strength as Eusebius tells us (*H.E.* 6:28). In his reign Origen composed his treatise *Exhortation to Martyrdom* (*The Protrepticon*).

[52] Hippolytus was the last churchman of the West to use Greek in the Roman Church. Little was known of him until 1851 when the *Philosophumina*, written in Greek, and supposedly by him, was published. It was a polemic against heretics. It was discovered in part on Mt. Athos in 1842.

[53] Capitolinus compresses the accounts of two Maximins, father and son, into one; *Scriptores historiae Augustae* II, 315–79.

After the three Gordians (238–244) came Philip, son of an Arab sheik, who ruled 244–249. Eusebius calls him a Christian [54] which, if true, would make him, rather than Constantine, the first Christian emperor of Rome. He was followed by Decius (249–251), a man of the old Roman type but who tarnished his name by carrying out the worst persecution of the century. A year before his proclamation he tried to compel Christians to sacrifice to the Roman gods. The persecution following was not motivated so much by his personal hostility to the Church as by his program of restoring the ancient institutions and religion of Rome which he felt was impossible if Christianity, an *imperium in imperio* as it really was, continued.[55] By Decius' time the Church contained nobles, the wealthy and educated classes. The emperor's claim to divinity was hateful to the Christians. Thus Decius made his persecution a test of loyalty and began it against the Church leaders. On January 20, 250, he imprisoned the Roman bishop, Fabianus, and for fifteen months there was a break in the "apostolic succession" until, during a lull in the persecution, Cornelius succeeded (251–253) only to be expelled by Decius' successor, Trebonianus Gallus (251–253).

By June 250 the persecution had become more severe; decrees were then sent out to the provinces that all, even priests of the pagan cults and children, must appear before committees of five and demonstrate their loyalty to the religion of Rome and receive a certificate—*libellus*—or suffer death. Many such *libelli*, dating from June twelfth to July fifteenth, have been found on papyrus in the Fayûm in Egypt, in which Christians swore that they had made offerings to the Roman gods. A typical one, found in 1893, was issued to one Aurelius Diogenes of Alexander Island, a man of seventy-two, who swore: "I have always sacrificed to the gods; and now, in your presence, and according to the terms of the edict, I have sacrificed, and [poured libations] and [tasted] the sacrificial victims, and I ask you to append your signature." [56] Eusebius tells [57] how Origen was imprisoned and tortured but was finally set free although he soon died of his sufferings. Porphyry, the Neo-Platonist and enemy of Christianity who died about 304, says thousands were slain. At the close of this eventful year the war against the Goths started again and Decius was slain in the following year, his death probably forestalling further persecution. It did not injure the Church greatly even though his successor Gallus continued it but his short reign made it ineffective. He did not renew Decius' decree which had imposed "universal sacrifices."

Valerian, formerly Decius' censor, on his accession was at first friendly to Christianity, but later was influenced against it by Macrianus, ruler of the Egyptian Synagogue.[58] He was delayed in renewing Decius' persecu-

[54] *H.E.* 6:34.

[55] Origen in his *Contra Celsum* (3:15) had said that Christ was stronger than the emperor and his ministers, than the princes of Rome.

[56] J. A. F. Gregg, *The Decian Persecution* (London and Edinburgh, 1897), pp. 155f. Cf. H. B. Workman, *Persecutions in the Early Church* (4th ed.; London, 1923), pp. 340f.

[57] *H.E.* 6:39, 5.

[58] *Ibid.* 7:10, 3–4.

tion by the military crisis, but later, to cover up his defeats at the hands of the Goths, he followed Nero's example of shifting the blame and popular ill-feeling against himself to the Christians. He began his persecutions with the higher clergy and on pain of death forbade Christian meetings and especially the entrance into cemeteries, around which since the days of the catacombs it had been customary to group workshops and Church administrative buildings. Later, many of the higher clergy and laity were executed and their property confiscated, among the former the Roman bishop Xystus (Sixtus) II (257–258).

The persecution seems to have lasted during parts of three years, but was ended around 259–260 with Valerian's capture by the Parthian king Sapor I.[59] Christian tradition has Valerian suffer unspeakable indignities in Ctesiphon, the Persian capital. But again, as after Decius' persecution, the Church was not seriously imperilled. St. Dionysius the Great, bishop of Alexandria from 247, and St. Cyprian, bishop of Carthage, were both exiled. The latter had sought safety in exile under Decius but had returned to Carthage under Gallus and there had readmitted the *lapsi*, i.e., those who, though once baptized, had fallen away and sacrificed to the idols through fear of persecution. On the other hand, Novatian who had had himself named bishop of Rome in place of Cornelius in 251 advocated permanent excommunication of the *lapsi*. St. Cyprian was banished and recalled by the Roman bishop Stephen I (254–257), but finally was beheaded by his successor, Sixtus II in 258—the first African bishop to achieve martyrdom.[60]

During the half-century between the beginning of Gallienus' reign and the final persecution under Diocletian and Galerius (260–303), the Christians were largely unmolested. Gallienus reversed his father's policy because of his ineffective efforts to withstand barbarian onslaughts. This military weakness resulted in the successive rebellions of the provincial generals of the West beginning with Tetricus. But Gallienus has received less than his due at the hands of Pollio, Eutropius, and Aurelius Victor, all of whom picture him as a debauché, in order, perhaps, to enhance the merits of his successor Claudius. Zosimus[61] and the later Byzantine historian Zonaras[62] in their histories are more favorable to him and are followed by some moderns, e.g. Leon P. Homo[63] who makes him out to be an able man.

[59] On the contested chronology of the time, see A. Stein, "Zur Chronologie der römischen Kaiser von Decius bis Diocletian," *Archiv für Papyrusforschung*, VII (1923), 30–51 and VIII (1926), 11–13; and *id.*, "Zeitbestimmungen von Gallienus bis Aurelian," *Klio*, XXI (1926–27), 78–82.

[60] See P. Allard, *Histoire des persécutions pendant la première moitié du troisième siècle* which includes Decius (3rd ed.; 1905, Paris); and his *Les dernières persécutions du troisième siècle* which includes Gallus, Valerian, and Aurelian (2nd ed.; Paris, 1898). Socrates (*H.E.* 4:28) says that Novatian was martyred under Valerian and that his views were long kept alive by his followers, the Novatians.

[61] *History of the Roman Empire*, 1:30–40.

[62] *Annales* 12:24–25.

[63] *Rev. histor.*, CXIII (1913), 1–22 and 225–67 (especially 263–67); cf. also his *Les empereurs romains et le Christianisme* (Paris, 1931).

Claudius was surnamed "Gothicus" because of his great victory over the Goths at Naissus (Nisch in Jugoslavia) in 269 in memory of which his great monument still stands in Constantinople. His successor was the Illyrian Aurelian (270–275), rightly called *restitutor orbis* because of his victories in the West and East by which the imperial unity was restored. He followed Septimius in calling himself *dominus,* to which title he was the first to add *deus* as we see from his medals. In 274 he erected a splendid temple in Rome to the Palmyrene Baal called *Sol dominus imperii romani* whose images he brought from Zenobia's capital. He established a college of *pontifices Solis* and instituted quadrennial games for the new cult. Thus again, as in the time of Heliogabalus, a Sun-god became head of the Roman religion; but, unlike his predecessor, he tried to Romanize the Oriental cult to make it acceptable. At the close of his life he showed hostility to the Christians, but his reign was too brief to reveal his intentions.[64]

THE FOURTH CENTURY

The fourth century was ushered in by the last persecution of Christianity in the Empire, that under Diocletian and his colleague Galerius (303–311). The former ended the third century crisis at the expense of completing the changing of the Empire into the despotic Dominate of Oriental pattern. The excessive taxes needed for its upkeep led the contemporary Lactantius Firmianus (*ca.* 260–*ca.* 340) to declare it was "equally expensive to live or die." [65] Diocletian kept *Sol invictus* on his coins as well as images of Jupiter, the "Genius" of the Roman people, and the title Jovius, the latter to show his relationship to Jupiter. He ruled as god-emperor by grace of Mithra whom he called protector,[66] as was shown in the account of Mithraism above. He rebuilt Nicomedia (Ismid) into a splendid capital where in his *sacrum palatium* seated on his *sella sacra* he held his court approached by Oriental *proscynesis* (prostration), his person clothed in Parthian trappings of royalty, a purple toga embroidered with gold and studded with gems, with a rayless diadem on his head, and holding a scepter in his hand mounted with the ancient Assyrian eagle.

Such a regime had been foreshadowed by previous emperors and was the child of the third-century crisis which, instead of marking the defeat of civilization by "superstition and barbarism," brought about a complete reversal of Graeco-Roman ideas of government, the new type inherited by Constantine who again infused new life into the ancient fabric, not by restoring its religion as Augustus had done three centuries before, but by the creation of a new order, the union of Church and State, and thus the beginning of centuries of controversy.

[64] See L. Homo, *Essai sur le règne de l'empereur Aurelian* (Paris, 1904); and Groag in *R.E.,* V, col. 1347f.

[65] *De mortibus persecutorum* 23. He taught rhetoric at the new capital, Nicomedia in Bithynia, from 290.

[66] *C.I.L.,* III, No. 4413. See *supra,* pp. 45 and 62 and n. 56.

We need not rehearse Diocletian's political, social, and economic reforms—his partnership emperors or tetrarchy with four rulers and capitals, his *sacrum collegium* which administered affairs without Senate approval, his well-intended but futile edict *De pretiis rerum venalium* of 302,[67] nor his elaborate organization like that of a great modern state but with this difference that the Roman state was treated as a vast armed camp, the civilian population as camp-followers.[68] For here we are concerned only with his anti-Christian policy. He, like Decius and Aurelius before him, felt that Christianity was a menace and that the State must either destroy or yield to it, and in consequence instituted the most ruthless persecution which lasted long after his abdication in 305, i.e. from 303 to 311. By his time Christianity was the strongest organized group in the State numbering, perhaps, a tenth of the population and as much as one-half of that in Asia Minor. For, as Harnack has said, it was "a religion of towns and cities." Its numbers, therefore, even if in a minority, exerted a disproportionate influence. The new despot, albeit naturally tolerant and, in addition, married to a Christian wife and having a Christian daughter, was aroused against the Christians by his brutal Caesar Galerius (292–305) who had advanced through the army and was instigated by the Neo-Platonists. He succeeded Diocletian after the latter's abdication. To him Diocletian, unfortunately, left the management of the persecution. It is on his shoulders, therefore, that the chief blame rests.

There is no contemporary history of the persecution and no official text of the three decrees issued in the years 303–304 but we can follow the main events in the summary of Eusebius written two decades after it began [69] and in the *De mortibus persecutorum* (314–315).[70] The first edict, followed in rapid sequence by the others, was issued on February 23, 303 and ordered all Christian churches and places of assembly closed, the Scriptures and liturgical books publicly burned, Church officials expelled from office and deprived of immunity from torture and all Christians placed outside the law, i.e., without recourse to the courts. For it was decided to crush Christianity at one blow at the annual festival of the *Terminalia* on that date, a festival believed to have been instituted by Numa.[71] At the time when imperial agents had begun the destruction of the cathedral at Nicomedia two mysterious fires occurred in the palace. These, Lactantius says, were instigated by Galerius while the latter said it was the work of the Christians. A reign of terror ensued. In the words of Eusebius "whole families and in heaps, were in some cases butchered with the sword; while

[67] *C.I.L.*, III, 801–41; late additions in *Hermes*, XXIII (1890), 17f.; Dessau, *op. cit.*, I, No. 642, pp. 144–47.

[68] So Cochrane, *op. cit.* (*supra*, p. 33, n. 49), p. 175.

[69] *H.E.* 8:2, 4f.

[70] See P. Allard, *La Persécution de Dioclétien et le triomphe de l'église* (2nd ed.; Paris, 1900); and the old work of A. J. Mason, *The Persecution of Diocletian* (Cambridge, 1876). For a short account of the persecution and the dates of the edicts and their contents, see H. M. D. Parker, *A History of the Roman World from A.D. 138 to 337* (London, 1935), Pt. 5, chap. i, pp. 236f. and notes 64–69.

[71] Plutarch, *Life of Numa*, p. 16.

others were perfected by fire, when it is recorded that men and women leaped upon the pyre with a divine eagerness. . . ." [72] By a second edict issued when it was rumored that the Christians were trying to overthrow the government in the district of Melitene in Armenia Secunda and in Syria it was ordered that bishops, priests, and deacons be imprisoned. As a result the prisons were so crowded that no space was left for ordinary criminals. It was at this time (304) that Diocletian went to Rome to celebrate his *vicennalia*, an occasion on which it was customary for an emperor to release criminals by general amnesty. Liberty therefore was then promised to those who would sacrifice to the Roman gods, otherwise they would be mutilated. Diocletian became ill in Rome and was so broken in health on his return to Nicomedia that it was rumored he had died. Galerius took the opportunity to issue the third edict in 304 which ordered all to sacrifice on pain of death.

Eusebius grows eloquent in describing the tortures inflicted on Christians in Tyre, Palestine, and especially in the Egyptian Thebaid [73]—where bodies were torn with sharp shards, women completely nude were fastened by one foot and swung aloft with heads downward, and men were tied by their legs to the bent branches of trees in Persian fashion which when released tore them asunder. In Egypt as many as one hundred victims perished in a day and the slaughter was kept up intermittently for years. But it is doubtful if the persecution was carried out on the scale reported by the Church historian for its ruthlessness depended largely on the feelings of the rulers of the tetrarchy, two of whom, Maxentius (306–312) and Constantine in the West, seem to have ordered no deaths. The fact that the populace was somewhat friendly toward the Christians also mitigated its severity even in the East. Diocletian's abdication in 305 was in part the sequel of Galerius' victory.

When the latter became Augustus the Eastern Caesar, his nephew, Maximinus Daia (305–308), subsequently the emperor Galerius Valerius Maximinus (308–313), decreed in 306 that all provincial governors should enforce sacrifice on all and the persecution in the East began anew with greater ferocity. In 309 Daia as co-emperor again promulgated an edict that pagan temples be rebuilt and that all must share in the rites of sacrifice. Finally, the elder Galerius fell ill [74] at Serdica (Sofia) and, whether conscience-stricken at the approach of death as the pious Eusebius thought or because of the persuasions of his colleagues Licinius and Constantine, issued his palinode on April 30, 311—the famous Edict of Toleration. The persecution, apart from sporadic outbreaks kept up in the East by Daia, ceased.

[72] *H.E.* 8:6, 6. Sections 6–16 describe various tortures inflicted in the capital where many of the victims were imperial servants theretofore trusted and beloved, especially the superhuman courage in face of torture and death of a certain Peter, "truly worthy of his name" (*ibid.* 8:6, 2–4).

[73] *Ibid.* 8:7.

[74] Eusebius, quoting Luke's words (17:1) "woe unto him through whom they [occasions of stumbling] come," says he died of a loathsome disease divinely sent, accompanied by an abscess and ulcer, brought on by gluttony, from which worms and stench issued.

The edict was published in the name of Galerius, Licinius, and Constantine,[75] the original Latin text being preserved in Lactantinus' treatise mentioned. A translation of this famous document so important in the history of Christianity follows:

It has been our aim in an especial manner, that the Christians also, who had abandoned the religion of their forefathers, should return to right opinions. For such wilfulness and folly had, we know not how, taken possession of them, that instead of observing those ancient institutions, which possibly their own forefathers had established, they, through caprice, made laws to themselves, and drew together into different societies many men of widely different persuasions.

After the publication of our edict, ordaining the Christians to betake themselves to the observance of the ancient institutions, many of them were subdued through the fear of danger, and moreover many of them were exposed to jeopardy; nevertheless, because great numbers still persist in their opinions, and because we have perceived that at present they neither pay reverence and due adoration to the gods, nor yet worship their own God, therefore we, from our wonted clemency in bestowing pardon on all, have judged it fit to extend our indulgence to those men, and to permit them again to be Christians, and to establish the places of their religious assemblies; yet so as that they offend not against good order. . . .

Wherefore it will be the duty of the Christians, in consequence of this our toleration, to pray to their God for our welfare and for that of the public, and for their own, that the commonweal may continue safe in every quarter, and that they themselves may live securely in their habitations.[76]

Two years later another edict signed by Licinius and Constantine is supposed to have been issued at Milan, known as the "Edict of Milan," its purpose being to reëmphasize and amplify the earlier one. But it is doubtful if such an "edict" was ever issued since nothing has survived except a letter addressed by Licinius in that year to a governor ordering that it be made known to his province. This may have been written at Milan referring to the Edict already discussed. It should, therefore, be called only a rescript of the former, which was intended for the East. Some historians therefore following the lead of Otto Seeck [77] have denied its existence, except as a repetition of the Edict of 311, while others have argued that the text of the edict found in Lactantius' work, together with a slightly differ-

[75] Lactantius includes Maximinus Daia and some MSS omit Licinius. Because of differences in style, grammar, and tone from other works of Lactantius, his authorship has been questioned, though ascribed to him in 393 by St. Jerome (De viribus illustr. 80). It is defended by Ebert, "Über den Verfasser des Buches de mortibus persecutorum" (Ber. der Saechs. Gesellsch. der Wiss., phil.-histor. Classe, 1870), and denied by S. Brandt, "Über die Entstehungsverhältnisse der Prosaschrift des Lact. und des Buches de mort. persec." (Sitzber. der Wiener Akad., Abhandl. VI, CXXV, 1892). The whole question is discussed by Bury in his ed. of Gibbon's Rome, I, App. I, pp. 482–84. The text of the treatise was first published by the French historian, Étienne Baluze.

[76] Tr. by W. Fletcher, Ante-Nicene Fathers of the Christian Church (New York, 1896), VIII, 315.

[77] "Das sogennante Edikt von Mailand," Ztschr. für Kirchengeschichte, XII (1891), 381–86. The text is translated by Fletcher, op. cit., p. 320, and also in the University of Pennsylvania Reprints, I (1907), 20–30.

ent Greek translation preserved by Eusebius,[78] does form an edict because its text is too formal and explicit to admit of doubt. But it seems more probable that Constantine and Licinius on meeting at Milan in 313 agreed on the future policy of toleration for both the West and East and that later Licinius drew up a rescript of instructions for governors, which amounted to the republication of the edict of 311. But N. H. Baynes rightly concludes: "The Edict of Milan may have been a fiction, but the fact for which the term stood remains untouched." [79]

The "Edict of Toleration" of 311 (with the rescript of 313) forms the chief document thus far in the history of Christianity, for it proclaimed liberty of conscience in religion and presaged the final victory of the Church to which it thus gave official recognition, even though the old Roman paganism and the Oriental cults were to last for nearly another century. Thus, despite the horrors of the last persecution Christianity emerged victorious for it was now no longer suspect and illegal but a *religio licita*. Men could now openly profess the Christian faith since all legal disabilities were removed and the Church as a corporation could hold property legally. Adherents to all other religions were treated similarly, as the further words of the Edict show: *"Ut daremus et Christianis et omnibus liberam potestatem sequendi religionem quam quisque voluisset."* This edict closing the first period of Christianity, therefore, marks a turning-point in the destinies not only of Christianity but of humanity. For the Dominate, religious toleration outranked the shifting of gravity of the State from West to East as symbolized a few years later by Constantine's transferring the capital from old Rome to New Rome on the Bosphorus.[80] For Constantine's favor of Christianity was the beginning of the deepest cleavage in the history of Europe. Emperor-worship and polytheism now yielded to that of the Christian God and belief in immortality and the ethics of Jesus replaced Graeco-Roman ideas. It was left for Theodosius seventy years later (in 381) to make Christianity the official faith of the State. With this action the principle of toleration, long one of the reasons for Roman greatness, was ended since the institution of a State Church meant the banning of all other religions. Before Constantine the connection between religion and government had been no more than political, the State-cult a moral support to politics. After him the old alliance was gradually dissolved with the union of Christianity and the State coming ever closer, the transition being retarded only by the fact that the old pagan cult was intimately interwoven with popular tradition.

Two questions remain: why did Christianity arouse such hostility in Rome especially among the commons, a hostility which took the official

[78] *H.E.* 10:5, 2–14.

[79] In his essay, "Constantine the Great and the Christian Church," *Proceed. Brit. Acad.*, XV (London, 1929), 341–442, 349.

[80] For an account of the inauguration ceremonies by Christian ecclesiastics May 11, 330, see Sozomen, *Eccles. Hist.* II, chap. iii. It was then called Nova Roma and dedicated to the Blessed Virgin.

form of persecution; and why, in spite of this hostility, did Christianity triumph? The chief cause of hostility in an Empire which allowed all forms of religion if only their devotees also supported the State-cult and Roman institutions may be laid to the intolerance of the Christians themselves. This intolerance surpassed that of Judaism and all the pagan cults of Rome in refusing to compromise with the imperial and polytheistic religion of the State, since Christianity regarded such worship as idolatry and the Oriental religions as devil-made and their believers lost. The masses easily believed that such Christian obstinacy invited the enmity of the gods toward the State while the educated classes for long had regarded it as veiled treason.

Such intolerance was opposed to the spirit of the age—and there never has been a more tolerant one—which was itself the result of a long evolution beginning with the spread of Hellenism under Alexander and his successors, the break-up of the narrow city-state idea in Greece and the general cosmopolitan spirit in so extended an empire as that of Rome. Polytheism is naturally tolerant and hospitable to alien faiths and this had grown in the later period of religious syncretism. Rome placed no barriers to any religion which was willing to compromise with that of the State. Its citizens were willing to try any religion or philosophy in seeking salvation. Christianity, on the other hand, increased the intolerance which it inherited from Judaism bringing the same odium on its members as had once been visited on the Jews. It declared its doctrines to be the only righteous ones, remained exclusive, and demanded of every candidate for admission the unconditional surrender of his past. It aroused not only hostility, but, when attacked, fanatical devotion.

The greatest ill-feeling against the Christians was aroused by their refusal to place incense in the incense-burner on the emperor's statue, the symbol of the imperial cult and of loyalty to the emperor—an act no more difficult to observe than the modern custom of saluting a national flag. Like the Jews they refused to share in the official festivals, especially in the triumphs of returning generals and, until Saxa Rubra in 312, to join willingly the Roman armies, a refusal regarded as treasonable since the ultimate duty of citizenship was the defense of the State. Further, they, like the Jews, held aloof from public amusements of circus and arena and refused to illuminate their houses and to hang garlands over their doors on festal occasions. Consequently, they were regarded as a group which refused to bear the full responsibility of citizenship. Their secret meetings were illegal, but the Church had become the largest secret society in the Empire where secret religious assemblies, *hetaeriae,* as Trajan called them in his letter to Pliny (X:43, 1), were banned on political grounds. Pliny said "their worst crime was their meeting at stated times for religious service," merely because such meetings were secret. Curiously, the Roman Church has inherited this characteristic from the Empire, for it still frowns on all secret societies. The Christian doctrine of brotherly love and social equality, coupled with the expectation that Jesus would return to change the present world-order into the "kingdom of heaven" aroused not only resentment but fear of revolution in a State which had suffered so greatly from revolutions at the end of the Republic.

One of the worst of Christian crimes was interference with vested economic interests—always dangerous. Jesus established the pattern of such interference when he drove "those who sold and those who bought" from the Temple (Mark 11:15). The reaction to this attitude was typified by Demetrius, the silversmith of Ephesus, whole sale of metal shrines of Diana being threatened by Paul's preaching that there were no gods "made with hands," roused his fellow craftsmen. Pliny said that the temples of Bithynia were deserted and that there were no purchasers of sacrificial animals.

It is, therefore, no wonder that the masses were motivated in their hostility, religiously, socially, economically; and the government, politically. It is, rather, surprising that the Christians did not rouse greater hostility. From the official point of view, the failure of the persecution was lamentable; for unquestionably persecution, rather than injuring Christianity, had engendered strength through the examples of heroic martyrdoms. This the Christians understood for Tertullian, bred a pagan but early converted, said (near the close of the second century): "We multiply whenever we are thrown down by you; the blood of Christians is seed. Many among you preach the endurance of pain and death . . . and their words never find so many disciples as the Christians win, who teach by deeds." [81]

CAUSES OF GROWTH

Why then, despite its un-Roman intolerance, did Christianity grow ever stronger? Of one thing we are certain: that Christianity would not have transcended the boundaries of Palestine for long, even with the zeal of a Paul behind it, had it not been for the imperial organization and the unity of the Empire. Early Christian writers liked to regard the Empire as a *praeparatio evangelica*. The spread of a humane spirit through the Empire, largely as a result of Stoicism, is clearly reflected by the time of Trajan, Hadrian, and the Antonines. The Spanish Christian poet Prudentius in the second half of the fourth century said:

God willed peoples of discord and tongues, kingdoms of conflicting laws, to be brought together under one empire, because concord alone knows God. Hence He taught all nations to bow their necks under the same laws and to become Romans. Common rights made all men equal and bound the vanquished with the bonds of fraternity. The City is the fatherland of all humanity, our very blood is mingled, and one stock is woven out of many races. This is the fruit of the triumphs of Rome; they opened the doors for Christ to enter.[82]

This was true and certain phases of Roman civilization also helped to extend the new religion. The Mediterranean, for centuries the highway

[81] *Apologeticus* 50:13–14, tr. by T. R. Glover, *L.C.L.* (1931), p. 227.
[82] Tr. by Charles Bigg, *Wayside Sketches in Ecclesiastical History* (London and Bombay, 1906), p. 24. For Prudentius, see T. R. Glover, *Life and Letters in the Fourth Century*, chap. xi.

of civilization and the clearing-house of ideas, was free from pirates; the great military roads radiating in trunk-lines from the *miliarium aureum* in the Forum to the uttermost parts of the Empire with branch-networks in every province made communication easy and safe. It has been said that private travel in the Antonine Age was not equaled for safety, rapidity and comfort down to the advent of railways and steamships. There were only two principal languages, Latin and Greek, understood by the educated and mercantile classes everywhere. Rome had rid herself of local prejudices, political, social, and especially religious, and the union of many peoples with common sentiments laid the sure basis for a progressive religion. As Ernest Renan wrote:

Think of the apostles in the face of an Asia Minor, a Greece, and Italy divided into a hundred little republics; of a Gaul, a Spain, an Africa, in possession of old national institutions—and it is no longer possible to conceive of their success, or even to understand how their project would have had its birth. The unity of the Empire was the condition precedent to any great religious proselytism which should set itself above nationalities.[83]

After Constantine's time Christianity easily penetrated to the Germans beyond the Danube and Rhine whose tribes, except the Saxons and Franks, became converted to its Arian form largely through fugitives from the great controversy at Nicaea. This conversion took place before the Germans overran the Western Empire in the late fifth century. It has often been said that had they not then been converted they might never have become Christians for as conquerors they would hardly have accepted the religion of the conquered.

But the imperial organization also facilitated the progress of the Oriental mystery-religions and the old civic religion of Rome and yet these failed but Christianity survived. Consequently one must look deeper for the secret of Christianity's hold on the people and finally on the State. For over a century and a half historians have been occupied with the subject.[84] Merivale[85] gave four reasons for Christianity's success: external evidence of the fulfillment of prophecy and the miracles; the internal evidence as satisfying the spiritual needs of the Empire; the purity of the lives and the heroic deaths of the early Christians; and the temporal success with which Christianity was crowned by Constantine. Ernest Renan[86] found the secret in "the new discipline of hope which it introduced into the world"; Alfred Loisy[87] in the emphasis on monotheism and the doctrine of the Incarnation; W. E. H. Lecky[88] in "the conformity of its teaching with the spiritual nature of mankind"; Salomon Reinach[89] in its "sim-

[83] *Lectures on the Influence of the Institutions, Thought, and Culture of Rome on Christianity*, tr. by Charles Beard (4th ed.; London, 1898), pp. 18–19.

[84] See S. Angus' collection of such causes, *op. cit.* (see *supra*, p. 62, n. 56), 273f.

[85] *Conversion of the Roman Empire* (2nd ed.; London, 1865), pp. viiif.

[86] *Marc-Aurèle* (8th ed.; Paris, 1899), chaps. xxxi–xxxiv, 561f.

[87] *Les mystères païens et le mystère chrétien* (Paris, 1914).

[88] *History of European Morals* (New York, 1873), I, 388–89.

[89] *Orpheus*, tr. by F. Simmonds (New York and London, 1909), p. 108.

plicity and purity"; Franz Cumont [90] in "the culmination of a long evolution of beliefs"; A. C. McGiffert,[91] "because it had far more of the elements of power and permanence, combined with a greater number of attractive features, and satisfied a greater variety of views than any other system." In the collective work *History of Christianity in the Light of Modern Knowledge*,[92] five reasons for Christianity's success are given: its promise of salvation, its enthusiasm for a lofty moral ideal, its fellowship based on charity, i.e., *agape* (love), the appeal of the Church as a quasi-political institution, and its philosophy, based on reason and authority which absorbed all that was vital in ancient thought.

In J. Klausner's *From Jesus to Paul* (1943), three "fundamental causes of the rise of Christianity" are given: the foundation formed by the ruins of the uprooted Judaism of the Diaspora, the Jews forming economically insecure and emotionally unstable communities with a half-assimilated fringe of proselytes and God-fearers; the spiritual conditions of the Gentile world, i.e., the unity of the Empire, the lofty ideas of the Stoics, the spiritual hunger for mystical and sacramental salvation cultivated by the mystery-religions—all of which helped to make the new religion a "half-Jewish, half-pagan faith" and furthered Paul's success; and, lastly, the bridge of ideas and methods of persuasion used by aggressive disciples which differed from those of Judaism and Hellenism. The great work of Edward Gibbon [93] contains one of the best analyses of Christianity's success under five main heads, although it is to be criticized for its omissions since there were other contributory causes such as have been enumerated, e.g. by v. Harnack [94] and others since. These were, in brief, the zeal of the early Church converts; the belief in immortality with the promise of future rewards; claims of the early Church to miraculous powers; the ethical standard of its early professors; and the organization of the Church on the imperial pattern. Of these we have already discussed immortality and ethics and now will briefly examine Gibbon's other grounds.

The zeal of the early Christians transcended that of the Jews during the latter's period of propaganda. During persecution this zeal rose to un-

[90] *The Oriental Religions in Roman Paganism*, tr. by G. Showerman (Chicago, 1911), p. xxiv.

[91] "The Influence of Christianity upon the Roman Empire," *Harvard Theol. Rev.*, II (1909), 43.

[92] Ed. by H. Dodd (Edinburgh and Glasgow, 1929), pp. 431–33. It is based on Harnack's *The Mission and Expansion of Christianity in the First Three Centuries*, tr. and ed. by J. Moffatt (2nd ed.; New York and London, 1908), I, Bk. 2, "The Mission-Preaching in Word and Deed."

[93] *The Decline and Fall of the Roman Empire* appeared in 1776–88. Dean Milman's edition appeared in 1839 (and 1845) and was reissued with further critical notes by Wm. Smith in 1854 (and 1872). The latter remained standard until the edition of J. B. Bury (London, 1897–1900, 10th ed. 1928–1938). Gibbon's vindication of his religious views appeared in 1779, for thus early the famous chapters xv–xvi had provoked "a library of controversy." These chapters appeared separately as *The History of Christianity* (New York, 1891). Cf. also *Gibbon's Antagonism to Christianity* by S. T. McCloy (Chapel Hill, 1933).

[94] See n. 92, *supra*.

heard of heights much of which was fanatical and irrational—the result of delusion and over-confidence in the reality of Jesus' promises but which gave his followers the fortitude to suffer incredible tortures—even to death. This spirit is latent in our day of quiescent tolerance when political partisanship has largely taken the place of religious controversy. The practice of Christian virtues many of which were already known to the Jews and to the Graeco-Roman world—forgiveness, brotherly love, pacifism, chastity and keeping the marital vow as a sacrament, condemnation of luxury and sensual pleasures, exhortation to charity and placing emphasis not on existing government and the "now" but regarding life here as a preparation for the one to come—all these were stressed by the Christians but were relatively weak in their rivals and so set the latter apart.

The belief in Jesus' miraculous powers caught the imagination of his immediate followers who looked for "signs and wonders" when extraordinary guarantees of Jesus' divinity were needed in the face of hostility.[95] It may be said that Christianity would hardly have survived in backward Palestine without faith in the greatest miracle, the Resurrection. We, however, no longer live in the first century when Jesus' followers saw thaumaturgy in all he did but in the twentieth when the age of miracles has yielded to that of the reign of natural law. While earlier apologists relied on the truth of the miracles recorded in the Gospels the modern attitude both in and out of the Church is that even if Einstein, Eddington, and other physicists have broken down the idea of fixity in the physical world, any deviation from the known laws of nature in the past if exposed to historical evidence should not be accepted.

The belief of the Pharisee Nicodemus who said to Jesus, "Rabbi, we know that thou art a teacher come from God, for no man can do these signs that thou doest, except God be with him" (John 3:2), was long accepted by the Church which taught that the miracles, i.e., supernatural occurrences beyond human experience, meant the interference of natural law by divine intervention and thus were credentials of Jesus' revelation. St. Augustine defined a miracle as "not something contrary to nature, but to what we know of nature," and thus not so much a violation of law as the interposition of higher over lower law as our human experience widens. In that sense, which is still acceptable, such phenomena as wireless telegraphy, Roentgen rays, radio activity, television, and many others are still miracles to the layman. The later Schoolmen, however, disagreed with St. Augustine, Thomas Aquinas defining a miracle as "something out of the order of nature." Luther accepted the "physical" miracles of Jesus, although he placed the "spiritual" miracle of "grace" above them. Grotius, in his defence of Christianity,[96] maintained that his argument rested

---

[95] Cf. A. B. Bruce, *The Marvellous Element in the Gospels* (New York, 1906); and A. C. Headlam, *The Miracles of the New Testament* (London, 1914). Cf. Ivor Ll. Tuckett, *The Evidence for the Supernatural* (London, 1911), especially chap. vi on Jesus and Christianity, pp. 167ff.

[96] *De veritate religionis Christianae* (Amstelaedami, 1627; 2nd ed., by J. Clericus, 1709, and London, 1772).

on miracles; Leibnitz accepted them as "events inexplicable by natural causes," and Kant did not deny their possibility.

But Jesus' miraculous powers have been denied by many since Francis Bacon (1561–1626) said: "Miracles have been wrought to convert idolaters and the superstitious, because no light of nature extendeth to declare the will and true worship of God." Later in the seventeenth century Spinoza (1632–77), who identified God with nature, said: "Nothing happens in nature which is in contradiction with its universal laws." David Hume (1711–76) also said no amount of evidence can establish the occurrence of a miracle which he defined as "a variation of the Law of Nature." [97] In the early nineteenth century H. E. G. Paullus called miracles "exaggerations or misunderstandings of ordinary events"; and in the present century A. Harnack has said: "We are of the unalterable conviction that what happens in time or space is subject to the universal laws of movement, that accordingly there cannot be any miracle in this sense, i.e., interruptions of the continuity of nature." [98] Then there are those who can neither accept nor deny the miracles of the New Testament—the "suprahistorians," to borrow a term first employed by Karl Barth. While accepting the desupernaturalizing process applied to the miracles they try to keep the "supernatural facts" which most evolutionists would reject. This seems to be the viewpoint of Professor Albright in his *From the Stone Man to Christianity*. While calling himself an evolutionist, whose interpretation is "rational empiricism in dealing with historical problems," [99] in reference to the miracles he says: "Here the historian has no right to deny what he cannot disprove . . . in the presence of authentic mysteries his duty is to stop and not to attempt to cross the threshold into a world where he has no right of citizenship," [100] and adds in reference to the Virgin Birth and Resurrection that (p. 307) "the historian cannot control the details and thus has no right to pass judgment on them historically." To him, then, the supernatural events of the New Testament are not on the plane of history and so the historian must remain agnostic in regard to them, unable to deny or to accept them.

While liberal theologians of our day largely deny their reality, conservative churchmen regard the miracles of Jesus as an essential part of his activity, just as the Gospel writers and Paul had done, and have tried to find some natural law to explain them, at least the healing ones. Matthew Arnold [101] was among the first to ascribe the latter to moral therapeutics on the ground that Jesus understood the moral root of certain diseases, though the connection between moral fault and disease is still little understood by medical science. Modern psycho-therapy might give some support to such a theory but it could at best only explain some of the healing miracles

[97] In his famous "Essay on Miracles," in *Philosophical Essays*, 1749; essay reprinted, London, 1940. See A. E. Taylor, *David Hume and the Miraculous* (Cambridge, 1927).

[98] *What Is Christianity?* tr. from the German by T. Bailey Saunders (New York, 1903), p. 17. See also remarks of Th. Huxley, *Coll. Essays*, IV, Essay 3, "Evolution," p. 47.

[99] P. 319, n. 210.

[100] P. 300.

[101] *Literature and Dogma* (London, 1875), pp. 143–44.

though many of the diseases which Jesus is said to have healed would not on any bacteriological basis yield to such methods. Nor would they explain the "nature" miracles, such as stilling the storm, withering the fig-tree and raising the dead, and yet these are as well attested in the Gospels as the others. The most circumstantial of the latter was the raising of Lazarus from the dead as recounted by John (11:1–44 and 12:1–17). He had lain in the tomb four days and decomposition of his body had already begun but at Jesus' command he came forth "bound hand and foot with grave clothes, and his face was bound about with a napkin." Still he walked out and later Jesus sat at table with him and his sisters, Mary and Martha, in Bethany. Renan explained this particular miracle as "a pious fraud" concocted by family enthusiasm. Others have been explained by self-deception on the part of credulous witnesses, by legends, and even by natural causes. Some certainly arose from wrong translations of oral Aramaic, e.g., Jesus' "walking on the sea" which reads in the Peshito "along the sea."

Still, when all is said, in respect to the healing miracles Jesus must have possessed some personal magnetic power, however exaggerated in the accounts, such as has been exercised by various individuals in our time. It was believed that he could even use this power at a distance, as in the case of healing the centurion's servant of palsy (Matt. 8:5–13); or that it went from him unconsciously, as in the case of the woman with an issue of blood who came behind him and touched the border of his garment, when Jesus said to his disciples (Luke 8:46): "Some one did touch me; for I perceived that power had gone forth from me." Many churchmen, however, have found it better to stress the spiritual and ethical message of Jesus rather than to make him out, on contested evidence, a wonder-worker. It was this that made Schleiermacher eliminate miracles from his Christian system because he believed it was lowered by this supernatural element.[102] Jesus himself rebuked the scribes and Pharisees who asked for a sign, saying (Matt. 12:39): "an evil and adulterous generation seeketh after a sign."

The supposedly miraculous gift of the apostles was conferred only by "laying on of hands" although the dead were believed to be resurrected as late as the time of Papias [103] and Irenaeus still later said the miraculous power was universal in the Church of his day. The supposed words ascribed to Jesus on his reappearance (Mark 16:17–18):

And these signs shall follow them that believe: in my name shall they cast out devils; they shall speak with new tongues; they shall take up serpents; and if they drink any deadly thing, it shall in no wise hurt them; they shall lay hands on the sick, and they shall recover,

have been taken to mean the residence of miraculous powers in the Church for all time. In any case, since they appear among the suspected verses which replaced the original text of Mark, they cannot be used as evidence.

---

[102] *On Religion: Speeches to its Cultivated Despisers,* tr. from the 3rd German ed. 1821, by J. Oman (London, 1893).

[103] Eusebius *H.E.* 3:39, 9.

Even if accepted they would refer only to the immediate converts of the apostles as verse 20 shows. Lecky long ago somewhere pointed out that the farther we are removed from Jesus' time the rarer miracles become, a blanket argument against them, to replace the refutation of each miracle on its individual merits. Still in the Roman Church, both in the Middle Ages and in modern times, the ability to work miracles is ascribed to saints, but the character of most of them makes them improbable and such records of miracles as exist in the later Church are only imitative—what Jesus and the Apostles did can yet be done. The idea has been emphasized anew by the latest of the important Protestant Churches to evolve in America in which astonishing miracles, even those of the "nature" sort, are believed to be performed daily.

Finally, a word about the organization of the Church, which was necessary for its unity and the standardization of its doctrine. Such organization was very simple in the synagogues in which Paul and other apostles preached, but as the Jewish influence in the Church waned it grew complicated and eventually followed the pattern of the Empire—in the West becoming ever more monarchical and with similar gradations of rank. The Oriental mystery-religions remained local organizations independent of one another and with little in common except their inherited mythology and theology while Christianity everywhere had the same organization, a factor which greatly helped its success over its rivals and one that aided Constantine to favor it since he rightly believed that loyalty to the Church could be transformed into loyalty to the State. We learn of the early Church government first from the Acts and Letters, then from the Didaché or *Teaching of the Twelve Apostles* composed in the early second century, and lastly from scattered notices in the works of the early Fathers.

Almost from the beginning there were three types of Church officials, all with Greek names, all at first interchangeable: bishops (*episcopi* or overseers), elders (*presbyters* or priests), and deacons (*diakoni,* servants or ministers).[104] If at first the traveling apostles or "prophets" were the more important, as the prophetic gift or custom waned the work of the Church fell altogether on the local officials who by the time of Ignatius, Bishop of Antioch in the early second century, were well established. In Apostolic times the deacons had vague duties but later became servants of the elders and managed Church property and finances, cared for the sick and distributed alms among the indigent, like the seven men mentioned in Acts (6: 1–6) appointed to look after the neglected widows of the Greek-Jews. Ignatius preached that all should be subject to the "bishop" and to one another since Christ was Father of all and that all Christians should regard him as they would the Lord himself. The presbyters, midway between bishops and deacons, were patterned after similar officials in the synagogues —the *Zekenim* (elders).

[104] Paul speaks of "bishops and deacons" (Phil. 1:1) and of "deacons" (I Tim. 3:8 and 13).

By the early second century bishops and priests were sharply differentiated, the former being in control of several churches with authority over the priests who were in charge of one or more small churches. By the close of the second century the bishops of large towns were reverenced above those of smaller centers; especially was this true of towns with apostolic connections—such as Antioch, Corinth, Ephesus, Alexandria (the latter then the intellectual center of the Empire), and Rome, the capital, where Paul and Peter were believed to have labored. By the time of Marcus Aurelius these officials formed compact groups with a hierarchy of rank. The hostility of the State and the theological dissensions within the Church kept the organization a close one. The Church soon assumed the right to excommunicate and punish troublesome members apart from the civil courts. Episcopal control over priests and deacons was almost absolute.

In the third century the exalting of one "metropolitan" bishop over others took place despite the protests of such bishops as Cyprian of Carthage who opposed the growing ascendancy of the bishop of Rome and claimed that all bishops should be equal. Finally there were five chief bishops or patriarchs—the name survives in the Orthodox Eastern Church—four in the East, at Antioch and Alexandria, and from 381 at Constantinople, and from 451 at Jerusalem, the home of the "mother" church, accepted only at the Council of Chalcedon, and one in the West, at Rome.

In the fourth century Constantine fitted the expanded Church into Diocletian's political divisions of the Dominate—four great prefectures, fourteen dioceses (these to form the units of administration), one hundred and twenty provinces, and countless municipalities. A "metropolitan" was in charge of each prefecture and lesser bishops of the dioceses, the latter under the control of the former. The lesser bishops could be convoked at any time by the metropolitan of the area to settle theological and other disputes. To effect a real monarchy in the Church leadership, however, one of the five patriarchs had to be raised above the others. Rome gradually achieved primacy because of the belief already widespread by the time of the Antonines that the Apostles Peter and Paul had founded the Church at the capital and there had sealed their work by martyrdoms under Nero.[105] By the time of Constantine's death in 337 the machinery of centralized monarchical government of the bishopric of Rome had progressed far. But the consummation of such primacy was not accomplished during the Dominate, but only by the eighth century when Roman pretensions were aided by the political power of the Carolingian dynasty and the Church had begun its division into East and West, a cleavage made irreconcilable in the twelfth century. In spirit, at least, this primacy was finally completed in 1870 when the Roman Pope proclaimed his "Infallibility." [106]

[105] Thus the ecclesiastical future of Rome was determined, as was recognized by Tertullian (*De praescriptione* 21:36), Irenaeus (*Adv. haereses* 3:3, 2) and Cyprian of Carthage (*Ep.* 52:55).

[106] See Epilogue, *infra*. The title *Papa* had been restricted by custom to the bishop of Rome to the sixth century and by decree of Gregory VII in 1073 to him alone.

Chapter VII

THE TRIUMPH OF CHRISTIANITY

CONSTANTINE the Great is generally recognized as the first of a series of Christian emperors who, for the century and a half left to the Western Empire and for many more in the Eastern, favored Christianity. His favor, it should be noted, was of greater help to Eastern than to Western Christianity since the invasions and cataclysms which befell the Empire in the fifth century spared the new capital on the Bosphorus but so impaired that on the Tiber that Roman primacy developing in the second and third centuries was relatively unimportant in the Church as a whole. In this sense Constantine began the separation of the Church, East and West. But, for a season, the Roman West was recompensed by the Church organization and her conversion of the barbarians; and in the end her alliance with the Carolingian dynasty caused her rebirth as a temporal power after three centuries of relative quiescence. Thereafter for eight centuries until the time of the Reformation the Roman Church remained the center of all Western life.

Constantine's favor was three-fold: the extension of privileges to the Christian clergy that had long been enjoyed by the priests of the civil cult, i.e., exemptions from economic and military burdens; legalization of ecclesiastical courts as part of Roman law, i.e., giving them equal validity with the imperial ones so that litigants might be tried in either; and corporate rights to the Church, i.e., permission to receive and to hold property, which gradually made it a wealthy institution. Similar corporate rights had been granted for short periods by his immediate predecessors; thus Maxentius, just before his death in 312, had authorized Pope Melchiades (310–314) to reclaim the property which had been confiscated during the Galerian persecution and Licinius (307–324) had granted similar privileges to the "corporation" of the Church in the East. Even in the third century such rights had been granted by Valerian and Aurelian before which time the Church had enjoyed only the rights of *collegia* (societies). But Constantine's legal rights proved permanent.

Since Constantine did not withdraw support from the old State-cult his policy toward Christianity has ever since been a matter of controversy and a vast literature has accumulated around it.[1] Historians still debate whether his favor came from a political motive: the balancing of Christians and pagans to unify the State;[2] or whether he was a sincere Christian

[1] Bibliography to 1890 collected in the Introduction to the translation of Eusebius' *Church History* by A. C. McGiffert in Schaff's *Select Library of Nicene and Post-Nicene Fathers of the Christian Church*, Series 2 (New York, 1890), I, 455–65.

[2] This is the general view since Jakob Burckhardt's *Die Zeit Konstantins des Grossen* (1st ed. Basel, 1853; 4th, Leipzig, 1924). For a similar view, see also T. Brieger, "Konstantin der Grosse als Religionspolitiker," *Ztsch. für Kirchengeschichte*, IV (1881), 163–203.

constrained by political conditions and the exigencies of his position from openly destroying paganism. For nearly three hundred and fifty years it had been the duty of Roman emperors to support the idea that the favor of the gods had caused the greatness of Rome, a fact which makes it understandable why Constantine and his successors down to Gratian kept the ancient title *Pontifex maximus* as heads of the State-cult, and also why Constantine, until the middle of his life, kept emblems of the pagan gods on his coinage.

To help solve this question there is a mass of evidence—opinions of contemporaries, inscriptions, legislation, and Constantine's own acts—all of which has been interpreted variously. Contemporary and succeeding Christian writers naturally believed in his Christian sincerity and even the pagan writers did not accuse him of hypocrisy. Among the latter, however, was the biased fifth-century anti-Christian Zosimus,[3] still the main support of those who doubt the sincerity of Constantine's Christianity. Zosimus repeats the aspersions of Julian and accuses Constantine of having no religious convictions. His credibility, however, has been doubted because of his frequent variance from other writers. Thus his statement that Constantine first erected pagan temples in Constantinople is contrary to that of Eusebius who has all such temples antedate the refounding of the capital. Zosimus rehearses his many moral blemishes.[4] Thus he put many to death for political reasons; caused the suicide of his father-in-law Maximian in 310 after he had been driven from Rome by the latter's son, Maxentius, and had taken refuge with Constantine in Arles, because he was implicated in a plot against the Emperor; had his colleague in the East, Licinius, husband of his half-sister Constantia, and his young grandson slain at Thessalonica, after the former's defeat at Chrysopolis in 323, for alleged treasonable correspondence with Rome's enemies, although he had promised him immunity; and worst of all had his own son Crispus slain in 326 for treason although the story that made the youth a victim of intrigue fostered by his step-mother, Fausta, seems apocryphal.[5] It is more probable that Licinius' army demanded his death as often happened with defeated troops in late Roman history, and V. Schultze has tried to show that Fausta whom Constantine is said to have slain because of her adultery outlived her husband by three years.[6] Over against Zosimus is the Christian picture of the Emperor drawn by Eusebius. This, to be sure, is rather a eulogy than sober history, since Eusebius was a favorite who lived on terms of intimacy with Constantine, knew his policies, wrote his biography, received him at Nicaea with a panegyric and helped frame the creed there adopted. He says all the Emperor's enterprises were accompanied by good fortune—good fortune which Constantine himself believed was due to Christianity as may be inferred from the concluding words of the Edict of Milan in which the Em-

---

[3] *Historia romana* (from Augustus to 410), Bks. 1–6.

[4] *Ibid.* 2:7–28.

[5] See Görres und Seeck, "Die Verwandtenmörder Constantins des Grossen," *Zeitschr. für wiss. Theol.*, XXX (1887), 343f. and XXXIII (1890), 63f.

[6] *Ztschr. für Kirchengeschichte*, VIII (1887), 534.

peror states his hope that "the divine favor which he had experienced at this critical juncture of his life should continue forever the same benefits upon his successors."

Inscriptions adduced to show his pagan attachment are inconclusive as one example will show. The Umbrian town of Hispellum (Spello) petitioned to be allowed to erect a temple and to institute games in Constantine's honor but he ordered that "no building dedicated to our name shall be polluted by the contagion of any superstition" and he did not follow the imperial cult.[7] The cult ended with him as being out of harmony with Christianity—one of the principal reasons for believing in the sincerity of Constantine's belief in Christianity. His baptism, delayed until the night of his death, has been used to show his vacillation. It was and always has been a Christian tenet that this sacrament, however late administered, cleanses the baptized of all earthly guilt. His friendship for pagan officials was like that of the later Theodosius who, though a bigoted Christian, patronized pagans such as the rhetorician Libanius and the orator-statesman Symmachus, the latter of whom he made consul in 391 despite his pagan zeal.

Nor was his legislation, at least down to his break with Licinius in 323, an attack on paganism in favor of Christianity. Licinius had aroused the pagan prejudices of his Eastern subjects and Constantine merely tried to forestall this in the West. In 319 he banned secret divination but allowed it in public; private consultation with a *haruspex* was penalized by the death of the diviner and the confiscation of the property and the exile of the patron.[8] He banned black magic, i.e., against life, on penalty of death and ordered that all interpretations of State calamities by augurs should first be submitted to him and decreed against compelling Christians to observe the rites of the State religion.[9] He introduced the Mithraic Sunday, "the day of the Lord," in 321,[10] and in the same year removed public burdens from the clergy lest these might call them from their sacred duties through someone's malice.[11]

Long after Licinius had signed the Edict of Toleration with Constantine and Galerius and its rescript with Constantine in 313 Licinius remained a pagan and regarded Constantine as a Christian, as we gather from his address to his troops at Chrysopolis near Chalcedon (modern Scutari) September 8, 324. That speech shows that the war between the two Augusti

[7] V. Schultze, *ibid.*, VII (1886), 343, 360.

[8] *Codex Theodosianus* IX:16, 12. (Cited hereafter as *C.Th.*) This *Codex* presents imperial constitutions from Constantine down to 438 when it was published in the East and to Valentinian III in the West (425–455). The latest edition is by T. Mommsen and R. M. Meyer, *Theodosiani Libri XVI* (Berolini, 1904), revised by E. Kiegel (1926). But here we quote from W. K. Boyd's *Ecclesiastical Edicts of the Code* (1905), and refer also to Maude A. Huttmann's *The Establishment of Christianity and the Proscription of Paganism* (New York, 1914).

[9] *C.Th.* II:16, 3; XVI:10, 1 (an injury to the Colosseum struck by lightning in 321).

[10] See Excursus II, below.

[11] *C.Th.* XVI:7, 2. Cf. the decree of 326 (XVI:2, 6) reënacted by Gratian in 377 (XVI:2, 24).

was in part religious. For Licinius accused Constantine of being false to the ancestral worship and of adopting "atheistical sentiments" in his infatuation for "some strange and unheard of deity, with whose despicable standard he now disgraces the army" and declared that the impending battle would decide, as the sequel showed, "between our gods and those which Constantine honors." [12]

After Licinius' defeat Constantine's legislation became more favorable to Christianity.[13] In an edict confirming that of 311 for the provinces he said:

Let those, therefore, who still delight in error be made welcome to the same degree of peace and tranquility which they have who believe . . . let them have, if they please, their temples of lies; we have the glorious edifice of Thy truth, which Thou hast given us as our native home.[14]

If this quotation is authentic, as Seeck [15] believes, it is the first declaration for Christianity by Contantine alone. It was preceded by his naming Christian governors for the East and the renewal of earlier edicts against divination and sacrifice which Eusebius [16] says had not been enforced. Later edicts banned pagan sacrifice, mystic rites, gladiatorial fights, and ordered temple restorations.[17] Thus about all he left to paganism was its legal status which it now shared with Christianity, and this chiefly because of its connection with festivals, games, and the like, a connection which could not be easily overthrown especially since many public officials were pagans.

His conversion, assuming that he experienced one, was gradual rather than the result of any single event such as his seeing the Cross in the heavens in 312 or his baptism in 337. Perhaps a fair statement of the problem of Constantine's religion is that his interest in Christianity was first aroused by political motives since he saw in the Church a heretofore unused means to unify the State and on it to found a dynasty and that only gradually did he lean toward it as a religion. We know that he built churches in Constantinople and Rome, in the former city one dedicated to the Trinity, later called the "Twelve Apostles," in which he was buried, and that he treated his mother Helena, a devout Christian, with marked distinction.[18] She had been repudiated by his father, Constantius Chlorus, on the latter's becoming Caesar of the West in 292 when Chlorus was compelled by Diocletian to marry Theodora, a daughter of Maximian. At an

---

[12] Eusebius *Vita Constantini* 2:5, tr. in Schaff, *op. cit.* (p. 193, n. 1, *supra*), I.

[13] Thus an edict recalled Christians from exile and restored their property: Eusebius *ibid.* 2:35–42.

[14] Eusebius *ibid.* 2:56.

[15] *Op. cit.*, XVIII (1903); as the first declaration, *ibid.*, XII (1897), 381; cf. Schultze, *ibid.*, XIV (1899), who doubts it.

[16] *Ibid.* 2:44–45.

[17] *C.Th.* XVI:10, 2 and 1, 3 (Eusebius *Vita Constantini* 4:25, in part).

[18] She was the daughter of an innkeeper at Drepanum, a village in Bithynia, as St. Ambrose tells us, renamed Helenopolis, by her son in her honor. See Ambrose *De obitu Theodosii* 42. But Eusebius *Vita Const.* 3:46, has her born at Naïssus (Nisch) on the Margus (Morava) in Upper Moesia (Serbia) where Constantine was also born.

advanced age tradition, but quite unsupported contemporaneously, has her make a pilgrimage to Palestine (*ca.* 325–326) where with her son's aid she is said to have built the Church of the Nativity in Bethlehem, and that of the Holy Sepulchre in Jerusalem. Her name is connected, as has been noted, with the finding of the true cross, a tradition of the fourth century originating in the West but not mentioned by either Eusebius or Cyril, the latter bishop of Jerusalem (350–386). She and her son are revered in the Orthodox Church on May twenty-first, and she alone, as saint, in the Roman on August eighteenth.

On the evidence, then, one may agree with N. H. Baynes [19] that Constantine was neither a deliberate hypocrite nor a political saint, if not entirely with Baynes' further conclusion that "he identified himself definitely with Christianity, with the Christian church and the Christian creed." Inconsistencies in his religious attitude were due, then, not so much to perversity as to the difficulty he had in breaking with the past. We quote this judgment from a recent writer:

He is, perhaps, unique as the one human being to have enjoyed the distinction of being deified as a pagan god while, at the same time, he was popularly venerated as a Christian saint.[20]

Although the Church has ever regarded Constantine as its benefactor and has given him the title "Great" his favors were not altogether to its advantage for their price was deterioration. By aligning itself with the imperial trend the Church caused essential changes in its inner life. As soon as a mere profession of Christianity was enough to lead to political and social preferment, the pristine virtues of simplicity and sincerity yielded to hypocrisy. Many professed Christians were pagans at heart. The court, by becoming nominally Christian, had not bettered itself morally. Both St. Chrysostom (347–407) and St. Jerome (340–420) acknowledged that imperial favor had made the Church less virtuous, the latter saying, "*divitiis major, virtutibus minor,*" a condemnation still made by modern historians.[21]

To the time of Constantine Christians had displayed a moral purity seldom, if ever, surpassed. They had held themselves aloof from affairs

[19] "Constantine and the Christian Church," *Proceed. of the Brit. Acad.,* XV (1927), 367. But E. Schwartz, *Constantin und die Christliche Kirche* (Leipzig, 1913), p. 155, speaks of the "diabolical cleverness" of the Emperor.

[20] C. N. Cochrane, *op. cit.* (*supra,* p. 33, n. 49), p. 212. See also Burckhardt for his attempt to unify Christianity and heliolatry; Loeschke, "Das Syntagma des Gelasius," in *Rhein. Museum,* LXI (1906), 44f.; Cumont, *The Oriental Religions,* p. 288, n. 30; Huttmann, *op. cit.,* chap. xxi, "Constantine's Personal Religion"; *Cambridge Medieval History* (cited hereafter as *C.M.H.*), I (1911), chap. i; V. Schultze, *Gesch. des Untergangs des gr.-röm. Heidentums* (Jena, 1887–92), Vol. I.

[21] E.g. Dean Farrar of Canterbury (1895–1903) has said: "The apparent triumph of Christianity was in some sense and for a time a real defeat, the corruption of its simplicity, the defacement of its purest and loftiest beauty"; and his contemporary, the historian Lecky, that "the triumph of the Church, by introducing numerous nominal Christians into its pale, by exposing it to the temptations of wealth and prosperity, and by forcing it into connection with secular politics, must have dampened its zeal and impaired its purity" (*Hist. of European Morals,* I, 12).

of the Empire, showed little interest in politics and, in short, had been uncontaminated by their surroundings.   The spirit of intolerance which has
marked Christianity ever since was now accelerated.   Tertullian in the
first years of the third century had said it was "a fundamental human
right, a privilege of nature, that every man should worship according to
his own convictions; it is assuredly no part of religion forcibly to impose
religion, to which free will and not force should lead us." [22]   A century
later Lactantius, then tutor of Crispus in Gaul (ca. 313), expressed a similar thought: "Religion cannot be imposed by force; if you wish to defend
religion by bloodshed and by torture and by guilt, it will no longer be
defended, but will be polluted and profaned." [23]   But this excellent spirit
now largely disappeared.   St. Chrysostom, who was contemporary with the
intolerant Gratian and Theodosius, while approving the denial of the right
of assembly to heretics still recommended that Christian love be shown
them.[24]   But, after Theodosius had made Christianity the sole faith of the
State, St. Augustine became reconciled to forced conformity with Catholicism though saying it was "better that men should be brought to serve
God by instruction than by fear of punishment," adding, however, that
the latter method must not be neglected.[25]   Pope Leo the Great (440–461),
according to Bishop Creighton, "accepted as a duty the suppression of
heresy and raised no objection to legislation which treated heresy as a crime
against civil society, and declared it punishable with death." [26]

The deterioration is especially visible in the treatment of classical literature and science.   The Church had always been hostile to the classics
and now being in power exploited that antagonism, though producing, in
their place, little beyond dry and controversial theological literature.
Christians to Constantine's time were generally ignorant, being opposed
to sending their children to pagan schools over which they had no control.
Their fear of contamination by pagan poetry which, since the time of
Homer, had been replete with immoral stories of the gods is understandable but not their condemnation of prose, the vehicle of history and science.   During the crisis of the third century and throughout most of the
fourth all pagan literature and science were banned.   We quote a passage
from the *Apostolic Constitutions* (composed ca. 254) which reflects ante-
Nicene thought but has not been sanctioned by any Church Council:

Refrain from all the writings of the heathen; for what hast thou to do with strange
discourses, laws, or false prophets, which in truth turn aside from the faith those
who are weak in understanding?   For if thou wilt explore history, thou hast the
Books of the Kings; or seekest thou for words of wisdom and eloquence, thou hast
the Prophets, Job, and the Book of Proverbs, wherein thou shalt find a more perfect knowledge of all eloquence and wisdom, for they are the voice of the Lord, the

---

[22] *Ad scapulum* 2, composed about 212 as a warning to the then persecuting proconsul of Africa, tr. by Boyd, *op. cit.*, p. 59.
[23] *Divinae institutiones* 1–7; 5, 2, tr. by Boyd, *op. cit.*, p. 60; cf. P. Schaff, *Progress of
Religious Freedom, as shown in the History of Toleration Acts* (New York, 1889), pp. 5–6.
[24] *Homilies* XXIX, XLVI (latter, *In Matthaeum*).
[25] *Epist.* 185.
[26] Mandel Creighton, *Persecution and Tolerance* (London, 1895), pp. 76–77.

only wise God.   Or dost thou long for tuneful strains, thou hast the Psalms; or to explore the origin of things, thou hast the Book of Genesis; or for customs and observances, thou hast the excellent law of the Lord God.   Wherefore, abstain scrupulously from all strange and devilish books.[27]

When St. Augustine, called by Harnack "the greatest man between Paul the Apostle and Luther the Reformer the Christian Church has possessed," said: "Nothing is to be accepted except on the authority of Scripture, since greater is that authority than all powers of the human mind," [28] ignorance was sure to become a matter of piety and inquiry, a sacrilege.   At the Fourth Council of Carthage (398) the reading of all secular books was stopped by the bishops.   St. Jerome, a most learned man, rejoiced in the neglect of Plato and warned his fellow-Christians against all pagan letters. Many Church Fathers had been learned men until their conversion.

We see the tendency best in the Church attitude toward science which grew out of Paul's statement that the wisdom of the world is foolishness with God.   The sphericity of the earth had been known to the school of Pythagoras and later to Aristotle, some of whose proofs of it, such as lunar eclipses, still appear in our text-books of astronomy.[29]   Aristarchus of Samos (fl. 284–264 B.C.) had even proclaimed the heliocentric system of our solar system [30] although his successors, Hipparchus and the later Ptolemy, reverted to the older geocentric system.   It had to wait eighteen centuries to be demonstrated by Nicolas Copernicus in 1543.[31]   Aristotle, followed by Strabo and others, had asserted that voyagers could reach Asia by sailing west from Spain as Columbus set out to do in 1492.   Notwithstanding all this St. Augustine could say it was impossible that man should exist on the other side of the earth "since no such race is recorded in Scripture among the descendants of Adam."   Still another Christian writer said: "if the earth were round, how could all men see Christ at his coming?"   Lactantius somewhere makes a statement, however, which unconsciously adumbrated the Newtonian theory of gravitation:

Is it possible men can believe that the crops and trees on the other side of the earth hang downward, and that men can have their feet higher than their heads?   If you ask them how they defend these monstrosities, how things do not fall away from the earth on that side, they reply that the nature of things is such that heavy bodies tend toward the center, while light bodies, as clouds, fire, and smoke, tend from the

[27] Quoted from J. B. Mullinger, *Schools of Charles the Great and Restoration of Education in the Ninth Century* (London, 1877), p. 8.   Similarly, the English Puritans of the seventeenth century condemned Shakespeare and his Elizabethan contemporaries.

[28] *Monasticism, its Ideals and History, and the Confessions of Augustine,* tr. by E. E. Kellett and F. H. Marseille (London, 1901), p. 123.

[29] *De coelo* 2:14, 297b.

[30] Not known from his only extant book *On the Magnitudes and Distances of the Sun and Moon* (probably an earlier work), but from a notice in Archimedes' *Sand-reckoner*.

[31] *De revolutionibus orbium coelestium* (Nürnberg, 1543).   He mentions his indebtedness not in this work, but in the original MS recovered in the last century in Prague; cf. footnote in the reëdition of Copernicus' work published at Thorn in 1873, 34; and A. Armitage, *Copernicus* (London, 1938); and W. W. Hyde, "Copernicus: 1473–1943," *Crozer Quarterly*, XX, No. 4 (Oct. 1943), 314–30.

center to the heavens on all sides. Now I am really at a loss what to say of those who, when they have gone wrong, steadily persist in their folly, and defend one absurd position by another.

The destruction of pagan books began under Theodosius. Theophilus had the Serapeum, which is supposed to have then contained the lesser Alexandrian library as well as astronomical instruments, destroyed in 391— a story doubted, however, by many moderns,[32] since nearly three centuries later (ca. 640) Amr, the Arabian conqueror of Egypt, having taken the city after a fourteen months' siege, was accused of burning the same library because it contained no truth not in the Koran. The tale of how he used it for a half-year to supply the furnaces of the public baths is apocryphal as well as the rest of the account.

Despite shortcomings of emperors and churchmen, however, Christianity was a boon to Rome; it taught many things to which theretofore little heed had been paid by pagan Rome: the sanctity of life, protection of infants, mitigation of slavery, banishment for the crime of attempted suicide (which had been allowed by Stoics and Epicureans), organization of charity and, finally, the ending of gladiatorial fights which St. Augustine had called "the most brutal and yet the most fascinating of the arena sports." [33]

One of the worst evils to grow out of Constantine's protection of the Church remains to be mentioned: the persecution of paganism. In the process Christians quite forgot Jesus' admonition and used violence, destroying temples and statues, closing pagan schools, trampling on pagan sensibilities and even killing adherents of opposing faiths. Indeed Roman history from Constantine's death to the close of the fourth century and even later is filled with the story of Christian reprisals. And when a half-century later it was officially over and all rivals were banished the struggle proved to have been only a forerunner of worse persecutions within the ranks of the Church itself—persecutions which dwarfed those of Rome. These later ones were not political as the earlier ones from Nero to Diocletian had been in the main but theological, each persecuting sect justifying the torture of men's bodies on the ground that its brand of faith alone could save their souls. During the fourth century, with which we are here mostly concerned, the mystery-religions, the old civic polytheistic cult, and Neo-Platonic philosophy felt themselves arrayed in a common fight against Christianity. Roman polytheism was especially marked out by the Christians for destruction.

EARLY CHURCH COUNCILS

Before outlining that story of persecution known mostly from decrees in the Theodosian code attention must be drawn to Constantine's intervention in the internal affairs of the Church, especially in the two disputes which culminated at Arles in 314 and Nicaea in 325. These emphasize the change wrought in the Church by the Edict of Toleration: it could now

[32] Latterly by Bury in his edition of Gibbon, III, 210–13, and App. 10, p. 524.
[33] *Confessions* 6:8.

dictate spiritually and in so doing disclose its power preparatory to its final political role in the Empire—the destruction of paganism. Constantine regarded religious dissension as a menace to State unity and felt that it should be suppressed with the aid of secular authority, and this he did. During these three centuries of its life little need had arisen to define general Church doctrine for the diocesan bishops settled disputes alone or at provincial synods. Christianity had taken into its membership men trained in Greek speculation for even in its decadent period the Greek mind retained its characteristic love of speculation and controversy. Thus many variant interpretations of doctrine had already arisen; the original simplicity of Jesus' teaching had begun to develop into a dogmatic system. From Constantine's day to ours there have been universal Church councils, "the pitched battles of Church history," invoked by emperors or the bishops of Rome to settle disputes. At such councils the majority vote meant orthodoxy; the minority, heresy. For a heretic, as defined by Bossuet, the seventeenth-century bishop of Meaux in France, is merely "a man with an opinion" where, it should be added, none is wanted.

Before Constantine there had been various heresies—Gnostics, Docetists, Ebionites, Marcionites, Montanists, Sabellians, and many others. Some of these had merely shown the curious vagaries of the religious mind such as the Docetists, a Gnostic sect which denied the human nature of Christ as an illusion and the Crucifixion as only apparent, since Christ's body was merely a phantasm,[34] an idea already exploited centuries before by the Greek tragedian Euripides in his phantom Helen. But none of these, so far as the West was concerned, though they continued in the East,[35] had needed a general Council to end it, nothing, indeed, beyond excommunication by a bishop. Thus Montanus—who had founded a heretic Church of "true Christians" in Phrygia and Africa (in which province Tertullian was its best disciple) which taught in opposition to the secularism of Christianity a new standard of moral obligations characterized by asceticism, severe discipline and various millennarian beliefs—had been excommunicated in 175, and Sabellius because of his differing views of the Trinity which he conceived as only temporal had been similarly excommunicated by Pope Calistus (218–222). But by Constantine's time the Church in the West had become well established and such heresies were regarded as menacing. While theoretically the Church was a unit, if serious disputes arose the only way to settle them was by convoking an ecumenical council of bishops from all churches.

The first such dispute to come under the Emperor's notice was the "Donatist" schism, not so much a heresy as a disciplinary problem caused by a double election of bishops to the see of Carthage. It arose from dis-

[34] Already combated in the Johannine Letters (I, 1:1–2; 2:22; 4:1–3; 5:5–6; II, v. 7), in a passage in the Fourth Gospel (20:24f.), and in various letters of Ignatius.
[35] The historian Socrates (H.E. 2:40) cites the first instance of an Eastern appeal against the decree of a Synod to a higher council as that of Cyril of Jerusalem at Seleucia in 359, which led to his reinstatement as bishop in 361.

sension over readmitting to Church fellowship the *lapsi traditores,* those who, to escape persecution under Diocletian, had surrendered the sacred books. When one of these, Caecilianus, was named bishop in 311 seventy Numidian bishops led by Secundus,[36] the primate of Numidia, demanded that no priest so consecrated should administer baptism and in consequence set up a rival bishop Majorinus. The faction of the "rigorists" was aided by a wealthy woman who was resentful of Caecilian's reproof for her too great zeal, so that the history of the schism—*De schismate Donatistarum*—said it throve on the wrath of a woman while ambition fostered and avarice strengthened it. Caecilian was excommunicated and Majorinus became bishop. Pope Melchiades condemned the schism in 313 and the Council convoked by the Emperor at Arelate (Arles) in Gaul the next year confirmed the decision. But the schism continued through five tribunals. It was revived under Julian (361–363) but in 393 St. Augustine moved against it and in 405 and 411 Honorius confiscated its property and ordered the sectarians to return to the Church.[37] In 411 St. Augustine, then bishop of the neighboring Hippo, practically ended it in Africa although it was broken into minor parties which still continued. In all it had lasted for a period of over three centuries down to the Moslem invasion in the seventh—the most stupid of all controversies of the early Church.

Arles was a provincial western council where thirty-three bishops only—including three from Britain—attended and their decision proved futile. Eleven years later Constantine, now sole emperor rather than ruler of the West alone, with the sanction of Pope Sylvester (314–335) called the first ecumenical council of bishops, i.e. from both the West and the East, at Nicaea in Bithynia, near the royal residence at Nicomedia, to settle a far more serious dispute which had penetrated the entire Christian world, i.e., to reconcile Christ's deity with monotheism. The Trinitarian formula there adopted has endured for good or evil to our time, the sole bond that unites the main branches of the Church—Greek, Roman, and Protestant. The dispute was carried on by able men trained in Greek speculation who tried to fit Christianity into the framework of reasoned philosophy. Since "deity" to the Greek mind was an indivisible unit, "absolute mind," it was questioned whether Christ was wholly divine or partly human. Christian teaching in the East was based on Aristotelian logic and Aristotle's concept of God as "causeless cause." In the Fourth Gospel the solution of Christ's nature had been reached by identifying him with the *Logos,* i.e., the spirit emanating from God, his "utterance" or the verbal transmission of his thought which had created and ruled the world—an idea emanating from the Alexandrian Philo and Greek thought and identified by John with Jesus Christ.

In the second and third centuries, before the doctrine of the *Logos* was definitely settled at Nicaea, there were many Christologies in the Church. Prominent among these were the "humanitarians" or "monarchians"—the

---

[36] The sect gets its name, however, from Donatus "the Great," of Casae Nigrae, who was elected in 315 as Majorinus' successor by the "rigorists" under whom the sect became established.

[37] *C.Th.* XVI:5, 58.

latter name coined by Tertullian (*ca.* 200) to include all dissentients from Trinitarianism—whose common beliefs were that God was a single being and Christ his incarnation and so in opposition to the doctrine of personal subsistence of the *Logos*. Such "unitarian" doctrines developed into two schools of thought: the "dynamistic" humanitarians who regarded Jesus as a man, son of God by adoption, and the "modalistic" humanitarians who regarded Christ and the Holy Spirit as divine but indistinguishable from God, merely the manifestations or "modes" of the latter. The leader of the former school at first was Theodotus, the tanner of Byzantium who went to Rome near the close of the second century and taught a small circle of converts—only to be excommunicated by Pope Victor I (between ?192 and 202). To him Jesus was a man, born miraculously of a virgin through the operation of the Holy Spirit but without divine essence until the latter descended on him at his baptism when he became Christ, but not God. In the early third century the heretic Artemas or Artemon, excommunicated by Pope Zephyrinus (?202–217), revived the doctrine at Rome agreeing with Theodotus in denying the epithet God to Christ. Still later his doctrines were developed by Paul of Samosata, Bishop of Antioch, the then chief Eastern See, who also was condemned by an Asiatic synod in 268. He denied Christ's essential divinity and regarded the Father, Son, and Holy Spirit as one and the same Being, the Son (*Logos*) and Spirit (Wisdom) qualities of God, but not personalities.

The "modalistic" monarchians, on the other hand, first led by Praxeas at Carthage (*ca.* 190) whose heresy was controverted by Tertullian in his *Contra Praxean,* played a minor rôle in Rome and the West in the face of Catholic opposition there. Their adherents were called "Patripassians" since, in identifying Father and Son as manifestations of one Being, they argued that if there were only one God and Jesus was his incarnation the Father logically must have suffered and died on the Cross. In the East under the leadership of Sabellius (*fl.* 230) who had also taught at Rome they were important. The Sabellians became a collective term for "unitarian" adherents who still accepted the divine nature of Christ. Sabellius differed from other "modalists" in asserting that the Father, Son, and Holy Ghost were not merely three names or "modes" attached to the same person God, but in affirming that these manifestations were not simultaneous but successive in their activity—the Father as Creator, the Son as Redeemer, and the Holy Spirit as Life-giver—a view which prepared the way later for something quite different, the trinitarianism of St. Augustine.[38]

Thus, there were two concepts of God, one Jewish taught by Jesus and understood by the ordinary man, the other Greek based on Aristotle and understood only by the educated. From the one came God the Father, from the other the theological creeds. Both concepts were preserved in

[38] See Harnack in Schaff-Herzog, *Encyclopedia of Religious Knowledge* (New York, 1910), "Monarchianism," VII, 454f., and his *History of Dogma,* tr. from the 3rd German ed. and ed. by N. Buchanan and others (London, 1896–99), Vol. III. We may add that the "Monarchian" doctrine with modifications reappeared among the Socinians of the sixteenth century in Italy, prototypes of modern Unitarians.

the East, while in the West there was opposition to the idea that Christ emanated from an "incomprehensible absolute." In Rome he was God—with little attention paid to the deity of Greek speculation, the *Logos* being sufficient.[39]

The issue of Christ's nature came to the fore again when Arius, a priest of Alexandria, argued that if Christ were the *Logos* of God he was secondary to him, i.e., his "radiation" rather than God himself. Alexander, bishop of Alexandria, led the opposition to this view, to be succeeded by a greater man, Athanasius, who has been called "Father of Orthodoxy" and who has given his name to the Athanasian party while Arius has given his to its "Arian" opponents. The Arians, following Aristotle's idea that self-existence is characteristic of deity alone, argued that the Son, created by the Father, was inferior, his nature divine, but of "like substance" (*homoiousios*) with him, while Athanasius maintained that Christ was of the "same substance" (*homoousios*) with God, coëternal and consubstantial with him. In the ironical words of Gibbon:

The Greek word which was chosen to express the mysterious resemblance bears so close an affinity to the orthodox symbol that the profane of every age have derided the furious contests which the differences of a single diphthong excited between the Homoousians and Homoiousians. Metaphysical opinions of Athanasius and Arius could not influence their moral character; and they were alike actuated by the intolerant spirit which has been extracted from the pure and simple maxims of the Gospel.[40]

The argument was not unlike the earlier one between the Stoa and the Lyceum about the nature of the Greek gods but with this difference: for out of Nicaea came deeds rather than mere arguments, i.e., persecutions, one side maintaining that it was on the side of God, the other that its opponents were on the side of the devil. But here there was no Aristotle nor Zeno but men of far lesser mold.

The debate spread over the East and threatened the West. Constantine, with little understanding of it, but convinced that disunion in the Church meant disunity in the State and that the schism was "more evil and dangerous than any kind of war," sent a letter by Hosius of Corduba to Alexander and Arius advising them to compose "these small and very insignificant questions . . . characteristic of childish ignorance rather than consistent with the wisdom of priests and men of sense." [41] Finding this futile he called the Council which lasted nearly ten weeks—May 20–July 25, 325. Some three hundred and eighteen bishops came, only six of whom were from the West including two legates from the Roman bishop Sylvester (314–335). The Emperor appeared in person and opened the initial session with an address in which he counselled all to compose their differences [42] and regularly attended throughout the hearing. Debates contin-

---

[39] See among others E. H. Goodenough, *Religious Tradition and Myth* (New Haven, 1937), chap. iii.
[40] *Decline and Fall*, chap. xxi.
[41] Eusebius *Vita Const.* 2:6.
[42] Eusebius *ibid.* 3:12.

ued as to whether, in a word, Christianity should continue as theretofore a mystery-religion with a God-man the center of worship and so based on faith, or should become a philosophical-ethical system with little religious significance as the Athanasians claimed the Arians wished.

Athanasius through his eloquence and the favor of the Emperor won, the Arians were banished as heretics, and the Nicene creed, based on the baptismal one of Caesarea in Palestine, was presented by Eusebius and signed by all present except five bishops who objected to the word *homoousios*. The creed adopted ran:

We believe in one God, the Father Almighty, maker of all things visible and invisible:—and in one Lord Jesus Christ, the Son of God, the only-begotten of the Father, that is of the substance of the Father; God of God and Light of Light: true God of true God; begotten, not made, consubstantial [*homoousios*] with the Father; by whom all things were made, both which are in heaven and on earth; who for the sake of us men, and on account of our salvation, descended, became incarnate, and was made man; suffered, arose again the third day, and ascended into the heavens; and will come again to judge the living and the dead. [We] also [believe] in the Holy Spirit. . . .[43]

Constantine confirmed the action and all who refused to accept it were anathematized.[44] It became law, with the Church thus becoming a division of government. But the Arians were not convinced. While the creed of "the great and holy Council" was accepted in the West, in the East, ten years later at the Council of Tyre, Athanasius was deposed by the Arian bishops there assembled. During the forty-five years in which he held office as bishop and patriarch (328–373) he was deposed five times. Constantine later came under Arian influence and tried to neutralize the Nicene formula in the direction of Arianism by condoning Arian attacks on Athanasius at Tyre. A year thereafter he had Arius recalled and in 337 was baptized by the Arian bishop then installed in Nicomedia and died an Arian Christian. The struggle continued until 381 when the Nicene creed was reaffirmed.[45]

Constantine reigned thirty-one years (306–337), longer than any of his predecessors except Augustus, and his dynasty survived his death for twenty-six years until 363. He willed the throne like a private domain to his three sons as emperors and to two nephews—one of the latter as Caesar, the other with the title *nobilissimus*. Soon a palace revolution, almost certainly instigated by his second son Constantius, resulted in the death of all of Constantine's male relatives except two cousins. After a short interregnum the three brothers divided the Empire, Constantine II taking the West, Constantius, the East, and Constans, Italy, Western Illyricum and part of Roman Africa, an area lying between the domains of the other two.

[43] Socrates *H.E.* I, chap. viii, tr. by A. C. Zenos, in Schaff, *Nicene and Post-Nicene Fathers* (2nd Ser., 1890), II, 11.

[44] Eusebius *ibid.* 3:17, 19–20; Rufinus *Hist. Eccles.*, Latin free translation and continuation of Eusebius' *Church History* (324–395) 1:5; Socrates *op. cit.* 1:9.

[45] For accounts of the Council, see Eusebius *op. cit.* 3:6f.; Rufinus *op. cit.* 1:5; Socrates *op. cit.* 1:8f.

In 340 Constantine fell in a fratricidal war with Constans and the latter took over the entire West until his death ten years later at the hands of the emissaries of the usurper Magnentius, who reigned 350–353. After the latter's defeat at Mursa (Essek on the Drave) in 351 and in Gaul in 353 Constantius reigned alone till his death in 361.

Here should be mentioned several Church councils, called between 340 and 344 to adjust doctrinal and disciplinary difficulties resulting from the Arian controversy, which strained relations between Rome and the Eastern churches and thus laid the basis for the Great Schism consummated centuries later. The first was convoked at Rome by Pope Julius I in 340 to reinstate Athanasius then in exile and to allow his Arian accusers to plead their cause anew. The invited Eastern bishops replied by letter from Antioch that they stood for the equality of all churches and so disclaimed the right of the Pope to rejudge a condemned bishop, but Athanasius was acquitted. In 341 the Oriental bishops held their own council at Antioch and reaffirmed the principles of Arianism in a milder form than at Nicaea. At the close of 342 or the beginning of 343 Constans, with the approval of Constantius, called a third council at Serdica (Sofia) on the confines of their territories to reaffirm the Nicene creed and the supremacy of Rome. The Eastern bishops came but opposed the reopening of the cases of Arian bishops deposed in 340 and 341 and the reconsideration of the Nicene doctrine. Seventy-six of them withdrew to Philippopolis, capital of Thrace, where in 344 they again protested against the pretensions of Rome to reverse sentences passed by an Oriental council, and ended by excommunicating the reinstated Athanasian bishops including Pope Julius and deposed those of the East who sympathized with the West. The orthodox bishops, East and West, addressed letters to the excommunicated ones in which they reaffirmed their deference to Rome to which see they gave the right to decide all appeals from condemnations pronounced by other bishops, thus declaring that Rome was the center of orthodox Christianity; but the bishops at Philippopolis replied that they refused to accept Roman supremacy, but only that of individual councils in such matters. Thus started the "schismatic" churches of the East and the preëminence of Rome in the West. Later events increased the tension until the final rupture in 1054.[46]

It was under Constans that Roman paganism suffered its first blows, the beginning of its outlawry a half-century later. In 344 he decreed that pagan sacrifice be banned and that all temples be closed,[47] thus reversing the policy by which paganism had persecuted the Church through the three preceding centuries. As the spirit of Lactantius' Divinae Institutiones had

[46] For these councils, see L. Duchesne, Histoire ancienne de l'église (5th ed.; Paris, 1910), II, chap. vi; also tr. of the 4th edition as Early History of the Christian Church from its Foundation to the End of the Fifth Century (New York, 1909–24).

[47] C.Th. XVI:10, 2, 3, 4 (2 exempted those connected with amusements and those "without the walls"); Sozomen, H.E., III, 17.

characterized the Age of Constantine the *De errore profanarum religionum* of one Firmicus Maternus, published in 347, did that of Constantius. His regime was one of intolerance, persecution, and bigotry which at his death made Julian's reaction inevitable. In 346 he ordered the temples transformed into museums, all access to altars banned, confiscation and death for those who continued sacrifices, and fines for the magistrates who hesitated to prosecute.[48] Again in 353 he forbade "nightly sacrifices" which Magnentius had allowed. Although affirming that "heathen superstition must be ended" his edict was not carried out since pagan festivals reappeared on the religious calendar the following year. He reaffirmed the legal status of the Vestals.[49] In 357 he made it a crime to consult a *haruspex, hariolus,* or *mathematicus* since they worked with magic arts.[50] During his *vicennalia* celebrated in Rome in 357, as described by Ammianus,[51] he removed from the *Curia* at Rome—then the seat of a provincial board—the altar and statue of Victory placed there four centuries before by Augustus in memory of his defeat of Antony and Cleopatra at Actium. This monument had been one of the focal points of Augustus' religious revival and latterly had helped the revolt of Magnentius (350–353), since the usurper, though a Christian, needed pagan support. He thought he could easily end Roman paganism, but he had little idea of its latent strength among the aristocrats of the old capital. Ammianus[52] gives us a photographic picture of this curious man on that occasion—cruel, calm, narrow, bigoted—under the influence of his wife and officials as was usual in the Oriental type of monarchy where the monarch was almost entirely removed from public contact. His final edict, promulgated in 361, exempted monks from all public obligations.[53] The enforcement of all these decrees depended, of course, on public sentiment as Sozomen[54] says and so several were ineffective.

JULIAN THE APOSTATE

Reaction to the intolerant rule of Constantius came with the nineteen-months rule of Julian (361–363), Caesar of the West since 355 and the last of the Constantinians. Julian will always be remembered for his abortive attempt to withdraw the imperial favor from Christianity by replacing it with a form of paganism accompanied by a philosophical and cultural pro-

[48] *C.Th.* XVI:10, 3, 4, 6.

[49] *C.Th.* IX:17, 2; XVI:10, 6.

[50] *C.Th.* IX:16, 4–6; cf. XVI:10, 5–6 (for the years 357 and 358).

[51] *History* (from A.D. 96–378, a continuation of Tacitus in thirty-one books), 16:10, 11–15. On the removal of the altar and statue, see St. Ambrose *Epist.* 18:32; and cf. *R.E.,* IV, 2, col. 1081.

[52] *Op. cit.* 14:5, 2, 21; 16:1–7, 10 (character and appearance). His portrait-bust in Palazzo dei Conservatori in Rome is reproduced as the frontispiece to Vol. II of J. Rolfe's translation, *L.C.L.* (1939).

[53] *C.Th.* XVI:2, 16. He died in Cilicia November 3, 361, being baptized like his father by an Arian bishop; Ammianus 21:15. For an account of his life, see *R.E.,* IV, 2, cols. 1044–94.

[54] *Hist.* 3:17.

gram known as "Hellenism." He was the last Roman emperor to oppose Christianity, and the last ruler of any Christian country until the time of Lenin and Hitler to try to suppress it. Consequently, whatever may be thought of his motives, we must regard Julian as a crucial figure in the story of religion.[55]

It has been argued that Julian's reign was one of the few times when Christianity was in actual danger since he proposed to fight it, not with force but with ideas. Throughout the third century the question of what religion should be added to moribund Roman paganism had been a matter of imperial policy. Thus the Syrian boy-emperor Elagabal (218–222) had placed a Syro-Phoenician *Sol invictus* at the head of Roman religion and a half century later Aurelian (270–275) had placed a Palmyrane *Sol invictus* in that position. At the beginning of the fourth century Diocletian and Galerius had made the Persian Mithra protector of the State and now Julian tried to restore a form of Greek polytheism together with the traditional culture of classical antiquity—an effort to be effected chiefly through education by transferring the schools from Christian hands to those of pagans. Such a program was in line with the Graeco-Roman past as Christianity was not, and had not a Parthian arrow during his ill-fated Mesopotamian expedition cut short his life at thirty-two Julian might possibly have succeeded in destroying Christianity. It has been further argued that if he had lived longer the West, freed from later reactionary influence of Christianity, might have emerged earlier from the so-called Dark Ages even if it be a futile pastime to speculate on what might have been. Such writers point to the success he did achieve and to the manifest relief of his Christian contemporaries at his death, as shown in the diatribes of St. Chrysostom and the two invectives of St. Gregory of Nazianzus.[56] But we should not overlook the possibility, if not probability, that Julian's effort in time might have proved equally as intolerant as Christianity did under Gratian and Theodosius. In any case fate ruled otherwise, for Julian was slain, the Church overcame the supposed danger and in revenge coupled his name with the opprobrious title of "Apostate."

Although he failed in his attempt Julian's character and genius are evident from his military prowess against the Germans in Gaul as Caesar (356–358) and his statesmanlike qualities displayed as emperor, especially in his tolerance as shown in his initial decree which promised liberty of conscience to all faiths in the Empire. Although his friend, the historian Ammianus despised his superstition, as did Socrates, Sozomen, Zosimus, and others; and despite Gibbon's sneers; Auguste Comte's proposal to have one day each year set aside to execrate his memory; and Strauss' verdict that

[55] On Julian, see G. H. Randall, *The Emperor Julian* (Cambridge, 1879); T. R. Glover, *Life and Letters in the Fourth Century* (Cambridge, 1901), chap. iii; G. Negri, *Julian the Apostate*, tr. from 2nd Italian ed. by the Duchess Litta-Visconti-Arese (London, 1905); J. Geffcken, *Der Kaiser Julianus* (Leipzig, 1908, 1914); F. A. Ridley, *Julian the Apostate and the Rise of Christianity* (London, 1937); Cochrane, *op. cit.*, pp. 261–91.

[56] Especially the *Contra Julianum et Gentiles* of the former and the *Orations* IV and V of the latter.

he was only a vain dreamer, later biographers, nevertheless, from Randall (1879) to Ridley (1937) agree that he was one of the best of the emperors. Although his religious passion came from his intellect and not from his heart, since he knew nothing of the Christian doctrine of love and grace, many have found his character worthy to stand beside that of Marcus Aurelius who, two centuries before, had similarly tried to unite philosophy with the imperial purple. His death was the harbinger of the passing of Roman paganism, as the prophetic words, apocryphally ascribed to him at his passing, attest—words poetically phrased by Swinburne, "Thou hast conquered, O pale Galilaean." When, further, we consider that his proposed substitute for Christianity aroused small enthusiasm among the older adherents of paganism and none among the Christians and that it was supported only by a small group of intellectuals, we may safely conclude that it was no real rival to Christianity which after his death continued its interrupted career of success. In Gibbon's words: "it was destitute of theological principles, of moral precepts and of intellectual discipline." And we may agree with his further conclusion that, considering the then strength of the Church, before Julian could have destroyed it he would have involved Rome in civil war.

Reared as a boy by Christian teachers, his formal education was completed in the pagan schools of Athens where, disillusioned by the bigotry and ill-treatment of his cousin Constantius, he learned to regard Christianity as a travesty on philosophy and a political tool. He hated the despotism inaugurated by Diocletian and completed by Constantine and refused the title *dominus,* merely accepting that of *consul.* The text of his lost indictment of Christianity, *In Galilaeos,* we can recover in part from its later refutation by Cyril the bishop of Alexandria whose zeal culminated in instigating the monks to slay Hypatia (*ca.* 415) in the city streets. Julian regarded Christianity not as the beginning of a new world, but rather as the latest phase in the struggle between civilization and barbarism and a local Galilaean superstition (43A; 253B; 280D).[57] He affirmed that history witnessed that the Jews, far from being God's favorites, were a God-forsaken race (209DE; 213A) and that the divinity of Jesus was a fable for he was only an illiterate peasant whose preaching was impracticable (39AB; 191D) and whose revelation was blasphemous (49A; 94A). Only through reason can we learn the divine essence (52B) and evil, instead of being an imperfection of the cosmos, is merely a human perversion (49A; 75B; 86A). He based his theology on Neo-Platonism, thus putting Plato's theories into practice. Starting with Platonic solar monotheism he placed Helios, identified with Zeus, Mithra and Horus, at the head of the pantheon as creator and ruler and below a hierarchy of lesser gods. He restored temples and statues and the ritual of sacrifice and inaugurated a new priesthood. From a letter which he wrote in 362 to Arsacius, High Priest of Galatia, we learn that he warned his priests to emulate the examples and methods of those of Christianity for he was not pleased with the results of his Hellenism so

[57] The numbers are taken from the translation of Cyril by W. C. Wright, *L.C.L.* (1913–23): *The Works of the Emperor Julian.*

far achieved and laid the blame on its priesthood.[58]   He was a tragic figure like Cato Uticensis of an earlier age.   The latter spent the last night before his suicide reading Plato's arguments for immortality in the *Phaedo* and Julian spent his last hours with his companions discussing the same problem.   Both threw away their opportunities in pursuit of lost causes.

We get a different estimate of the Christian priests from that of Julian in a letter addressed to Julian by Libanius (?314–393), the teacher of Sts. Basil and Chryostom and best-known rhetorician of the fourth century.[59] Here Libanius speaks of the "black-robed throng" who "eat more gluttonously than elephants" and whose each "potion is accompanied by a chant" and who, contrary to law, "go through the land like mountain-torrents" laying waste the countryside, destroying temples, altars, and homes "under pretext of attacking the temples."

Julian's successors, Jovian called "Christianissimus imperator" because of his restoration of Christian privileges,[60] Valentinian I (364–375) and his brother Valens (364–378) who at first ruled West and East respectively, called in an inscription *fratres concordissimi,* were all tolerant men. Valentinian restored Christian teachers to the schools [61] and while tolerating paganism and confirming its legal status [62] he made (364) magical rites, apart from those of Hellenic mysteries and astrology, a capital offense.[63] Ammianus says he troubled no one religiously and left religion as he found it,[64] though Arianism was now strong.   Sozomen also records [65] that he left religious matters to the priests.   Indeed, he may be said to be Rome's last emperor to represent religious freedom in the sense that Julian and Constantine had understood it.

Valentinian's son Gratian—Emperor of the West (375–383) and after Valens' death in 378, of the East as well—reversed the general rule of tolerance which had existed since 311 for he determined to destroy paganism. Ammianus [66] tells us that while in his youth he displayed a character rivaling that of the most distinguished emperors, later his natural instincts, urged on by his intimates, turned him into a Commodus.   He became a zealous Catholic, and on his accession he was the first of the emperors to

---

[58] Letter in Sozomen's *H.E.* 5:16; and No. XLIX in Wright's translation, *op. cit.,* III, 67–71.   For Church affairs during his reign, see W. Bright, *The Age of the Fathers* (London and New York, 1903), I, 325–36.

[59] *Ep.* 2, 164, tr. by J. W. H. Walden, *Universities of Ancient Greece* (New York, 1909), pp. 117–18.

[60] See Sozomen, *op. cit.* 6:4; Theodoret, bishop of Cyrrhus, in his continuation of Eusebius' *Church History* 4:4; tr. by B. Jackson, *Nicene and Post-Nicene Fathers* (Ser. 2:3).

[61] This edict of 371 is lost, but is referred to by Sozomen *op. cit.* 6:7 and in *C.Th.* IX:16, 9.   In 365 he had already confirmed Christian immunities and exemptions: *ibid.* XVI:1, 1.

[62] *C.Th.* XII:1, 60.

[63] *C.Th.* IX:16, 17 (364); IX:16, 8 (370); and IX:16, 9 (371).

[64] *Op. cit.* 30:9, 5.

[65] *Op. cit.* 6:7.

[66] *Op. cit.* 31:18, 180.

refuse the title and robes of *pontifex maximus* since, as Zosimus tells us,[67] he said "it did not become a Christian prince." In one of his earliest edicts, of 375 or 376 reënacted in 378,[68] he showed his hostility to the pagans by forbidding their "heretical" meetings and by confiscating their places of assembly. But curiously, after Valens' death at Adrianople in the great battle with the Goths—at least he was never seen again—Gratian decreed toleration toward most cults and removed personal taxes from the clergy and Church officials [69] thus following Constantine's decrees of 319 and 326.[70] On January 19, 379, he named Theodosius, son of the Spanish-Roman general of the same name, as his colleague in the East, who has been called "the ablest ecclesiastical politician of the West." The two met at Milan with St. Ambrose to confer about "the entrance of divine light." Since then both emperors have been known in Church history for their "rigid orthodoxy" and submissiveness to the prejudiced Bishop who helped to turn them against paganism. For soon they rescinded all edicts which had guaranteed tolerance. One signed by Gratian, Theodosius, and their boy-colleague Valentinian II (375–392) ordered that "all heresies opposed to divine or imperial laws, should end." [71]

THEODOSIUS THE GREAT

After Theodosius recovered from a severe illness at Thessalonica in 380 he was baptized by an Athanasian bishop [72] and on February twenty-seventh of that year the three Augusti issued the famous edict which imposed Catholicism on the basis of the Nicene creed on all subjects of the Empire. This edict marks the end of Roman official tolerance by making Christianity the sole religion. It ran:

It is our will that all the peoples whom the government of our clemency rules shall follow that religion which a pious belief from Peter to the present declares the holy Peter delivered to the Romans . . . that is, according to the apostolic discipline and evangelical doctrine, we believe in the deity of the Father and the Son and the Holy Ghost of equal majesty in a holy trinity. Those who follow this law we command shall be comprised under the name of Catholic Christians; but others, indeed, we require, as insane and raving, to bear the infamy of heretical teaching; their gatherings shall not receive the name of churches, they are to be smitten first with the divine punishment and after that by the vengeance of our indignation, which has the divine approval.[73]

In January 381, further edicts forbade all assemblies of heretics and ordered that the name of the Christian God alone should be used and the

---

[67] *Op. cit.* 4:36.
[68] The edict is lost but is referred to in *C.Th.* XVI:5, 4.
[69] *C.Th.* XVI:5, 4 and XVI:2, 24, respectively.
[70] *C.Th.* XVI:2, 2, 6.
[71] *C.Th.* XVI:5, 5.
[72] Sozomen *op. cit.* 7:4.
[73] *C.Th.* XVI:1, 2; tr. by J. C. Ayer, *A Source Book for Ancient History* (New York, 1913), pp. 367–68.

Nicene creed be maintained. In May of that year Theodosius summoned the so-called Second Ecumenical Council at Constantinople under the presidency of Meletius, bishop of Antioch, who died during the deliberations. Since, however, there was no delegate from the West among the one hundred and fifty Oriental and thirty-six Macedonian bishops present it was merely an Eastern Council. Tradition since the sixth century has the creed known as the *Niceno-Constantinopolitanum* drawn up by this Council as a reaffirmation of the older Nicene creed of 325, "an amended definition of Orthodoxy" as Gwatkin has called it. But the tradition is no longer tenable since Harnack and others have shown that there is no existing record of such a creed between 381 and 451, not even at the Ecumenical Council of Ephesus in 431 nor at the so-called "Robber Council" held there in 449, but that it was first mentioned at the Council of Chalcedon in 451 together with the Nicene creed and was then ascribed to Theodosius' Council which was only then officially called "ecumenical." There is no further evidence of it until the sixth century when it began to be mentioned frequently. Moreover, it was hardly a reaffirmation of the Nicene creed but contained only certain Nicene insertions and was based on an older baptismal creed, probably that of Jerusalem framed by Cyril, bishop of Jerusalem. It was accepted in the East some time between 450 and 500, and is older than the Nicene in its sources but later in its reception.[74] It certainly antedates 381 and may go back to 362, but we have no idea how it got its long name.

Whatever its origin it was accepted as "the perfect expression of orthodoxy" by the Greek, Roman, and heretical churches of the East—Syrian Jacobite, Chaldean Nestorian, Egyptian Coptic, and others. Its essential paragraph runs:

I believe in one God, the Father Almighty, maker of heaven and earth, and of all things visible and invisible. And in one Lord Jesus Christ, the only begotten Son of God, begotten of his Father before all worlds [God of God,], Light of Light, very God of very God, begotten, not made, being of one substance with the Father, by whom all things were made. . . . And I believe in the Holy Ghost, the Lord and giver of life, who proceedeth from the Father [and the Son;]; who with the Father and the Son together is worshiped and glorified . . . and I believe in one holy Catholic and Apostolic Church. . . .[75]

While the Nicene creed said of the Holy Spirit:

We believe in the deity of the Father and the Son and the Holy Ghost of equal majesty,

finally in this creed the Holy Spirit, which some maintain was foreshadowed in the Old Testament [76] as the spirit of Yahweh and the active divine prin-

---

[74] See Harnack in Herzog-Hauck, *Realencyclopädie für protestantische Theologie und Kirche* (3rd ed. 1896–1909), VII, 212–30; and in Schaff-Herzog, *op. cit.*, III, 256–60; cf. also his *History of Dogma*, IV, 97f.; I, 98.

[75] *C.Th.* XVI:5, 6; Sozomen *op. cit.* 7:9:P. Schaff, *Creeds of Christendom* (4th ed.; New York, 1896), II, 58–59; cf. *Encycl. Brit.* (ed. 1937), *s.v.* "Creeds," pp. 656f.

[76] Gen. 1:2; I Sam. 16:13; Ps. 104:30.

ciple in nature, but based on the New,[77] now at the close of the fourth century and only after the deity of Jesus had received full ecclesiastical sanction became a personality as real as God, the third person in the Trinity, and has remained so ever since. As to the value of the idea of the Trinity to the Church, opinions will always vary. While a recent writer calls

One divine nature representing itself simultaneously in three persons . . . each fully God, and yet . . . not three natures, not three Gods, but one nature and one God, a perfect meaningless paradox,[78]

a still later one has said that

the trinitarian idea of God has immeasurably enriched the concept of monotheism, without in the least detracting from its unified character.[79]

Neither the Nicene nor the later Niceno-Constantinopolitan creed has ousted two other ancient creeds, the Apostolic and Athanasian, which have continued concurrently in the Church. The oldest creed known in the West is the Roman Church confession which we have, in Greek, in a letter of Bishop Marcellus of Ancyra written around 340, and in various Latin translations. The fact that it was written in Greek indicates for the original a date anterior to 250 when Greek ceased to be the language of the Roman Church, but the Latin translations were also early.[80] All Latin creeds of the West are derived from it, and notably the Apostles' Creed still used in Western Christendom both in the Roman and Protestant Churches. It was long ascribed to the apostles since it contains a summary of faith in twelve articles which reflect apostolic teaching. Harnack believes it represents in its present form the baptismal confession of the Church of southern Gaul in the second half of the fifth or beginning of the sixth century and that it developed out of a simpler earlier form, the "Old Roman Symbol," a summary of Apostolic teaching known at Rome by the middle of the second century or even earlier.[81] The two forms vary but little in beliefs about the Trinity, supernatural birth, death, resurrection and ascension of Jesus. While the text of Marcellus reads: "I believe in God [the] Father Almighty; And in Jesus Christ, His only begotten Son, our Lord; Who was born of the Holy Ghost and the Virgin Mary . . . And in the Holy Ghost, the holy Church . . . ," the present official *Apostolicum* reads: "I believe in God the Father, the Almighty, creator of heaven and earth;

[77] John 14:26 as "the comforter, even the Holy Spirit"; Rom. 8:10–11, as the principle of divine life in the community; Gal. 5:2, as the source of the spiritual graces.

[78] E. R. Goodenough, *The Church in the Roman Empire* (New York, 1931), p. 63.

[79] W. F. Albright, *From the Stone Age to Christianity*, p. 304.

[80] E.g., in Tertullian's *De praescriptione haereticorum* 13, 36.

[81] See his "*Apostolisches Symbolon*" in Herzog-Hauck, *op. cit.*, I, 741–55. F. Kattenbusch, *Das apostolische Symbol* (Leipzig, 1894, 1900), who dates the Roman symbol about 100; A. C. McGiffert, *The Apostles' Creed, its Origin, its Purpose and its Historical Interpretation* (New York, 1902); J. K. Blunt, *The Annotated Book of Common Prayer* (London, 1907), pp. 195f.; C. P. Caspari, *Alte und neue Quellen zur Geschichte des Tauf Symbols . . .* (Christiania, 1879).

And in Jesus Christ, his only Son, our Lord; Who was conceived by the Holy Ghost, born of the Virgin Mary . . . I believe in the Holy Ghost, a holy Catholic Christian Church. . . ." The later so-called "Athanasian" creed (called *Symbol quicunque vult* from its opening words)—a compendium of forty theses about the Trinity and the Incarnation—is used in the Greek, Roman, and Anglican churches but is not found in the American *Book of Common Prayer*. It was wrongly ascribed to St. Athanasius (*ca.* 278–373) but is of earlier origin. It attained great importance during the Carolingian period.[82] It, also, makes the three persons of the Trinity coequal.

At the Council of Constantinople, Arian bishops were exiled as they had been at Nicaea which now meant the "official" death but not the extinction of Arianism in the Empire. Most of the Germanic tribes above the Lower Danube, already converted by Ulfilas (Gothic Wulfila, "Little Wolf") bishop of the Visigoths (341–383),[83] remained Arian Christians for another century and a half. Ulfilas' translation of the Bible into Gothic for which he supplemented the Greek letters by Gothic runes when necessary is known as the oldest literary work of the Germans, preserved only in fragments mostly of the Gospels and Epistles and parts of the Old Testament.[84]

At the Council of 381 St. Gregory of Nazianzus was named patriarch of Constantinople and the latter was given second ecclesiastical rank after Rome. In the same year Gratian convened a Council at Aquileia where it was proclaimed that the clergy should pray for the Emperor, a custom extended later to all Christian rulers down to our time. It had already been enjoined as "a Christian duty" by Galerius and his colleagues in 311. After Constantinople there were only three more recognized ecumenical councils in antiquity: the Third at Ephesus in 431, the Fourth at Chalcedon in 451, and the Fifth again at Constantinople in 553. The twenty-eighth canon passed at Chalcedon, which confirmed the action of 381 in making Constantinople a patriarchate second to Rome, was not confirmed by the Roman bishop and this became a further step in the later schism in the Christian Church into West and East. During and since the Middle Ages fifteen more ecumenical councils have been recognized by the Roman Church but only the first seven by the Orthodox.[85]

[82] See "Authorship of the Quicumque vult," *Jour. Theol. Stud.*, XXVII (1926), 19–28. The Jesuit, H. Brewer, ascribed it to St. Ambrose (333–397) in *Das sogennante athanasianische Glaubensbekenntniss* (1909).

[83] C. A. Scott, *Ulfilas; Apostle of the Goths* (London, 1885); E. Bernhardt, *Ulfila oder die Gotische Bibel* (Halle, 1875).

[84] The chief manuscript—a facsimile of the original—is now at Uppsala, the *Codex Argenteus*, in which the characters are in silver against a purple background.

[85] Official Roman list by Mgr. C. J. v. Hefele, *Conciliengeschichte*. The first edition carried the list to Trent, 1545f. (Freiburg, 1855); the second edition, through the Vatican Council, 1869–70 (1873–90). Vols. V–VII were revised by A. Knöpfler; vols. VIII–IX, by Cardinal Hergenröther. English translation to 737 is from first edition; from 326 to 1869–70 is from second (Edinburgh, 1871f.).

In the same eventful year of 381 Theodosius and his colleague began the systematic abolition of polytheism. Such legislation was continued by Theodosius' sons Honorius in the West and Arcadius in the East and by the latter's son Theodosius II. Gibbon says of the destruction of paganism by these princes that "it is perhaps the only example of the total extirpation of any ancient and popular superstition, and may therefore deserve to be considered as a singular event in the history of the human mind." [86] A first edict forbade pagan rites by day or night and the use of shrines for divination.[87] Another of 382 turned all temples with their treasures into public museums and forbade access to altars.[88] Another withdrew support from the colleges of pontiffs and Vestals, turned their endowments over to the State and rescinded all exemptions still enjoyed by pagan priests.[89]

In 382 Gratian under the influence of St. Ambrose removed for the last time the altar and statue of Victory from the Roman Senate-house. The successive removals and restorations of this venerable monument are an index to the changes in the struggle between the government and the polytheistic Roman aristocracy.[90] The Senate sent a petition to Gratian through their spokesman, the orator Q. Aurelius Symmachus, the zealous representative of dying paganism in Rome, to protest against the removal and against other anti-pagan decrees. But he accomplished nothing since St. Ambrose sent a counter-letter [91] and he was ordered to remove one hundred miles from Rome. Later, in 384, when Symmachus was prefect over Rome and Gratian had been defeated and slain in Gaul by the Spanish usurper Magnus Maximus, Emperor of Britain, Gaul and Spain, Symmachus addressed a sacred protest to Valentinian II, urging the restoration of the pagan deities, but again was unsuccessful. His plea, the famous *Relatio de ara Victoriae,* was a masterpiece of eloquence admired by both pagans and Christians despite the falsity of some of its arguments. The answer of St. Ambrose was a far less capable work since it was replete with sophistry, abuse, and threats, saying among other things that the restoration of the altar would mean "a persecution of Christianity, and the emperor merely would become an apostate." He even threatened that the clergy "would no longer perform their services, if the altar went back." [92]

Symmachus' speech has been called "the last formal and public protest of Roman paganism," since it was the last time that classicism and Christianity stood opposed in court. In the following passage Rome, personified, speaks:

Permit me to continue to hold to my ancestral belief, for I take my delight in it. Permit me to live after my own fashion, for I am a free man. This religion has

[86] *Decline and Fall,* chap. xxviii, *init.*
[87] *C.Th.* XVI:10, 7.
[88] *C.Th.* XVI:10, 8; cf. similar decrees by Constantius in 346, repeated in 356; XVI: 10, 3, 4, 6.
[89] *C.Th.* XVI:10, 20.
[90] G. Boissier *La fin du paganisme* (Paris, 1903), II, 6, chap. i. The last restoration had been under Julian.
[91] *Ep.* 17:9, 10.
[92] *Ep.* 1:18, 2.

laid the circle of the earth at my feet, has beaten back Hannibal from my walls, and the Gauls from the Capitol. Was I kept alive only to be attacked in my old age?

We ask for peace and for our native, indigenous gods. We cultivate the same soil, we are one in thought, we behold the same stars, the same heaven, and the same world surroundings. Why should not each, according to his own purpose, seek the truth? The Great Mystery cannot be approached by one road. The divine mind distributed various cults and guardians in the cities; as various spirits in youth, so the fatal genii are divided among nations.[93]

In 387, because of sympathy with Maximus, Symmachus was arrested for treason but later Theodosius received him back and made him Consul for 391. When Valentinian II was murdered in 392 and Arbogastes placed his puppet Eugenius on the throne (392–394) Symmachus was again exiled but Eugenius restored the famous altar, by then a meaningless act.

Back in 385 Roman auspices had been prohibited [94] and in 391 two edicts forbade pollution from the sacrifice of an innocent victim and entrance into a temple to revere idols "made by human toil." [95] It was in that year, as we have already noted, that the Serapeum in Alexandria was destroyed, a shrine ranking in magnificence after that of the Capitoline Jupiter in Rome and that of the Olympian Zeus in Athens. In 392 a final—as was believed—enactment against the pagans forbade the worship even of the household gods. It was never repealed and may be said to mark the end of legal protection of the ancient Roman religion.[96] In 393 the Olympic Games were closed in the two hundred and ninety-third Olympiad, having been celebrated over a period of eleven hundred and sixty-nine years since their reputed foundation in 776 B.C.[97] In 394 the chryselephantine statue of Zeus by Phidias, one of the wonders of the ancient world, was removed from his temple at Olympia to Constantinople where Cedrenus of the eleventh century records its destruction during the burning of the palace of Lausus in 476. The temple itself was demolished either by Goths or Christian zeal under Theodosius II and later reduced by earthquakes to its present ruins.

In 391 Theodosius had placed the young Valentinian II in the care of his Frankish general Arbogast and allowed the latter to name his civil and military officials which he did in favor of pagans and Germans. Valentinian met his death at Vienna in Gaul the next year probably through

[93] *Relationes* 3:19. Cf. O. Seeck, *Mon. Germaniae histor. auctores antiquissimi* (Berolini, 1883), p. 282. On Symmachus, see Bury's ed. of Gibbon, III, App. I, p. 511; and Glover *Life and Letters in the Fourth Century*, chap. vii, and *Quintus Aurelius Symmachus and the Senatorial Aristocracy of the West* by John A. McGeachie, Jr. (Chicago, 1942), especially chap. v.

[94] *C.Th.* XVI:10, 9.

[95] *C.Th.* XVI:10, 10 and 11.

[96] *C.Th.* XVI:10, 12. For translation, see Huttmann, *op. cit.* (p. 195, n. 8, *supra*), p. 216.

[97] For their history, see E. N. Gardiner, *Greek Athletic Sports and Festivals* (London, 1910); and W. W. Hyde, *Olympic Victor Monuments and Greek Athletic Art* (Washington, 1921), chap. i.

the instrumentality of Arbogast,[98] who named Eugenius in his place. Eugenius had been a Gallic teacher of rhetoric and later a secretary in the imperial service at Rome. He was nominally a Christian but friendly to the pagan aristocrats. He tried to be tolerant as he needed pagan support as had Magnentius before him. He restored temples, pagan cemeteries, and public processions in Rome, replaced the Cross on military standards with images of Hercules, proclaimed a three-months' cessation of business to purify Rome and other cities of Italy and allowed all religions to post their festivals on the religious calendar. This was the last pagan revival in the Empire.

Theodosius at the news of the elevation of Eugenius started west in May 394 with an army with which he defeated Arbogast and Eugenius in battle near the Frigidus River (Wipbach or Hubel in Carniola) in the Julian Alps. Eugenius fled but was caught and executed while Arbogast escaped to the mountains where three days later, September 8, 394, he committed suicide—one of the best soldiers and statesmen of the later Empire.[99] Now for a brief four months Theodosius was sole emperor, the last time but one in the story of the Empire that one man ruled East and West.[100] In Rome he asked the Senators "to relinquish their former errors and to embrace the Christian faith which promises absolution for all sins and impurities," but "no one individual could be persuaded," and then he "abolished the sacred rites and ceremonies" revived by Eugenius.[101] He died in the prime of life in Milan, January 17, 395, leaving the Empire, as had Constantine, as a private domain to his sons: the West to Honorius (395–423), then a boy of eleven under the care of the Vandal Stilicho as *magister utriusque militiae,* the real power, and the East to Arcadius (395–408) then twelve years old under the same protection and that of the treacherous Rufinus, his chief minister. Both, in the words of Gibbon, "slumbered on their thrones."

Theodosius in his zeal for Catholicism, a zeal in suppressing paganism likened by St. Ambrose [102] to that of Josiah king of Judah in destroying all forms of idolatrous worship, despite some redeeming qualities such as mercy and clemency to defeated enemies, had shown himself a bigoted Christian. He never questioned his religious beliefs, but regarded divergences from them as wicked. To be sure he lived at a time when the-

---

[98] Ambrose in a sermon preached at the time denounced him as the murderer: *Ep.* 1: 5, 7.

[99] See T. Hodgkin, *Italy and her Invaders* (2nd ed.; Oxford, 1892–1916), I, chap. xi.

[100] If we omit his naming his elder son, Arcadius, "Augustus" in 383 when five years old and his younger son, Honorius, in 394, then ten years old. Theodosius II, on the death of his uncle, Honorius, in 423, ruled alone till 425 when he named his cousin, Valentinian III, then six years old, Caesar of the West, under the regency of his mother Galla Placidia.

[101] Zosimus *op. cit.* 4:59 and 5:30. This Roman visit, however, has been doubted by some who believe it is confused with a visit after the rebellion of Maximus in 389; see Bury's Gibbon, III, App. 9, p. 524.

[102] *De obitu Theodosii* 4:35–38.

ology was largely reduced to quibblings as we may see in these words of his contemporary Gregory, Metropolitan of Cappadocia (372–375 and 378–396) at Nyssa:

If you desire a man to change a piece of silver, he informs you wherein the Son differs from the Father; and if you ask the price of a loaf, you are told by way of reply that the Son was created out of nothing.[103]

That he prized earthly honors is amply shown by his increasing the Oriental forms which had surrounded the emperor since Diocletian for under him everything became sacred: *sacrum palatium, urbs sanctissima, divinae epulae* (State banquets), *caelestia statuta* (edicts), and he allowed only a few "to touch the purple" and "adore his serenity." [104]

Naturally merciful, he was, nevertheless, subject to fits of terrible rage and vengefulness. Thus after a riot at Thessalonica in 390 during which an officer and some soldiers were killed he had seven thousand citizens slain in the Circus. For this act St. Ambrose refused him admission to the church in Milan until his next birthday at which time he publicly asked God's forgiveness, threw himself on the ground, tore his hair, struck his forehead and wept. Not even then was he allowed within the altar rail, a deacon warning him that only priests were permitted there and that "a purple robe makes emperors, not priests." [105]

Much of the blame for his intolerant spirit should be laid on St. Ambrose, the master-mind behind his policies, whose narrow but strong personality dominated both Theodosius and Gratian. He was the scourge of both Arians and pagans, opposing both Valentinian II's mother, Justina, and the German troops in Milan by denying to them the use of any church in the city although Justina demanded the use of two churches. Ambrose defied her and was ready to die rather than submit.[106] But when Maximus took Milan in 387 and Justina and her son had fled he remained to aid the population even melting the consecrated vessels of the church on their behalf.

THE SUCCESSORS OF THEODOSIUS THE GREAT

Theodosius had declared all forms of paganism legally dead but polytheism still showed signs of life as the decrees of his sons and grandson against it attest. While Constantine and Theodosius had laid the foundation of a new order which was to rise to its supreme height of power in the church of the Middle Ages, the immediate result of their activities was the destruction of the foundations of the old order. The period after the latter's death was one of "twilight government by twilight men," [107] unable to ward off the coming doom. For a period of twenty years preceding and following Theodosius' death the East suffered the destruction of cities and

---

[103] *Oratio de Filio et Spiritu Sancto;* Migne, *Patrol. Graeca* (*P.G.*), XLVI, 357.
[104] Cf. *C.Th.* VI:24, 4 (387).
[105] Theodoret *H.E.* V, 17–18; cf. *C.A.H.*, I (1924), 244f.
[106] *Ep.* 1:20.
[107] Cochrane, *op. cit.*, p. 351.

country-side and the interruption of communications as graphically described by St. Jerome.[108] He speaks of its being overrun by German hordes, of Christian bishops being imprisoned, churches plundered, horses stabled "at the altars of Christ," and the bones of martyrs thrown from their graves. In the year of Theodosius' death Alaric left the Roman service to become King of the Visigoths and then (396–397) invaded Greece but was stopped by Stilicho. During this long period of two decades the Eastern Empire was the victim not only of war, but of poverty and depopulation.

With the year 401 a similar period of terror began in the West when the Germans began to invade the Western provinces of Rome. In that year Alaric invaded Italy where, in 402, he fought an indecisive battle against Stilicho at Pollentia (Pollenza in Piedmont).[109]

In consequence of the battle the imperial residence was moved from Milan to Ravenna, the tenth legion was recalled from Britain and the invasion of the savage Radagaisus was made possible. The latter with a mixed army of Ostrogoths, Vandals, Quadi, and Alani in 405 crossed the Alps, the Po, and the Apennines as far as Faesulae (Fiesole) where he was defeated and treacherously slain by Stilicho. At the close of 406 an army of Vandals, Alani, Suevi and Burgundians, apparently connected with Radagaisus, invaded Gaul and three years later Spain, and this marked "the fall of the Empire beyond the Alps." The invasion was further complicated in 407 by the appearance of another usurper, Constantine, named emperor by the legions of Britain, who crossed to Gaul and Spain. He was recognized by Honorius who, however, had him slain in 411. In 408 Alaric returned and besieged Rome but was bought off by a heavy ransom. In 409 he came again and set up the puppet Attalus in place of Honorius now deposed and a third time returned and sacked the Eternal City for six days in August 410. This was an eventful date in Roman history, since it was the eight hundredth anniversary of the only previous sack of Rome, that under Brennus the Gaul. It shook the Empire to its foundations, St. Jerome briefly saying that "the city which captured the whole world is herself taken captive." [110] It marked a grave convulsion in the Western Empire and the beginning of Teutonic states in the West.

While these events were transpiring the adherents of polytheism were again active. While the law of 392 which had proscribed it was still in force Honorius curiously decreed that temples should be preserved and festivals allowed although he forbade "sacrifices and profane rites." [111] But Arcadius in the East abolished all priestly privileges and sanctioned the

---

108 In *Ep.* 60, 16.

109 Both Cassiodorus, historian-statesman under Theodoric the Great (493–526), in his *Chronica* (published in 519), and the Gothic historian, Jordanes, in his *De origine Getarum* (published in 551), and based on an abridgment of Cassiodorus' lost *Historia Gothorum,* say the Romans were defeated. Alaric continued his way to Rome but, after being raised to the rank of *magister militum,* left Italy.

110 *Ep.* 122, 12. On the effect of the sack on the world of the time, see Sir S. Dill, *Roman Society in the Last Century of the Western Empire* (2nd ed.; London, 1899), p. 305.

111 *C.Th.* XVI:10, 15, 17, 18.

destruction of temples.[112] As early as 395 the pagan religious calendar, which for a millennium past had recorded Roman festivals and anniversaries, had been replaced by the Christian one. Sunday games were abolished in 409 [113] although Constantine had made Sunday a legal holiday in 321 by an edict reaffirmed by Theodosius in 386 with penalties for its desecration.[114] The prohibition of pagan festivals ended one of the chief bonds with Rome's past.

One good act of Honorius should be remembered, his banning of gladiatorial fights in 404. They had been instituted in the Forum in 264 B.C. by Marcus and Decimus Brutus at the funeral of their father.[115] Women had begun to fight under Domitian [116] but such fighting was banned in 200 by an edict of Severus.[117] Constantine had abolished gladiatorial fights by edict in 325 [118] and they had been denounced by Lactantius [119] and later by Prudentius, but they had never ceased. In 404 a Syrian monk, one Telemachus, eager to sacrifice his life for a good cause, leaped into the arena and was stoned to death by the enraged spectators when he tried to separate the fighters. Honorius then proclaimed him a martyr and abolished "human sacrifice" in the arena. Telemachus is, as Gibbon remarks, the only monk to die a martyr for humanity but "no church or altar has ever been erected to him."

After the assassination of Stilicho in August 408 at the order of the jealous Honorius the latter's religious moderation yielded to intolerance. He and Arcadius now passed the famous decree which, unlike the ineffective one of Theodosius in 392, really outlawed paganism for it ordered all surviving temple images to be destroyed, all temples to be appropriated to public purposes, the closing of all altars and services in honor of pagan gods, and Christian bishops to enforce the decree.[120]

The pagans of the West centered their hopes on the Greek Flavius Attalus who had been prefect of Rome in 409 when Alaric first besieged the city and had been proclaimed emperor by the latter. He reigned for less than a year (409–410) as the puppet of Alaric and, as *Pontifex maximus*, gave the high State-offices to pagans, but he soon fell out with Alaric and was deposed. After Alaric's death the latter's brother-in-law Ataulph again put Attalus forward in 414 but he was soon imprisoned by Honorius

---

[112] *C.Th.* XVII:10, 13–14, 16.
[113] *C.Th.* II (*De feriis*): 8, 22.
[114] *C.Th.* II:8, 1; reaffirmed II:8, 15.
[115] Valerius Maximus 2:4, 17.
[116] Suetonius, *Life of Domitian*, chap. iv.
[117] Dio, *History*, LXXV, 16.
[118] *C.Th.* 1:15, 1.

[119] *Instit. div.* 1:6. See L. Friedländer, *Roman Life and Manners in the Early Empire*, tr. by J. H. Freese and L. C. Magnus from the 7th German edition of 1901 (London and New York, n. d.), II, 41–62 and App. XXXV (*Abolition of Gladiatorial Games*), IV, 192f.

[120] *C.Th.* XVI:10, 19. Cf. Orosius *Adversus paganos* 7:38.

and in 416 was banished to the island of Lipara and the last hope of paganism as a political power vanished. In 415 Honorius and Theodosius II—son of Arcadius—decreed that all pagan corporations in the Empire be dissolved and that all moneys of "this wretched superstition" be surrendered to the government.[121]

In the East, Theodosius II (408–450) followed his father's and grandfather's religious policies and decreed the destruction of all remaining temples and the abolition of all privileges left to the pagan priests. The historian Socrates has left a curious picture of this weak but amiable prince who, only seven at his succession, ruled first through his prefect and after 414 through his sister Pulcheria. He "surpassed all in clemency and humanity" and "observed with accuracy all the prescribed forms of Christianity." His palace was like a monastery where he and his sisters assembled early in the morning to recite hymns responsively in God's praise. He knew much of the Bible by heart and discussed religion with his bishops with the learning of a priest.[122] He also made an effort to revive Roman culture—minus its religion—by founding a Christian university in Constantinople to compete with the pagan schools of Athens. Here he founded chairs of jurisprudence whose incumbents aided in producing the "Theodosian Code." In 423 he said in an edict that "We believe that they [the pagans] are no more." [123]

But pagans lived on for the government did not compel them to become Christians. A law of 423 even forbade their molestation if they made no trouble.[124] Thus "there were pagans still, although there was no longer paganism." [125] Members of various pagan religions lingered on through the fifth century and later. As a philosophy pagan cults were taught in the schools of Athens and Alexandria until they were closed in 529 by Justinian under whom the final Roman legal code was consolidated from its predecessors, the famous *Corpus iuris civilis*,[126] still the legal basis of Latin countries of Western Europe and of the American state of Louisiana.

The final retreat for the remnants of Roman paganism—the ancient civic cult and the mystery-religions—was largely in remote country districts where Christianity progressed slowly and ancient customs endured longest. For this reason the ecclesiastical word *paganus*, to designate all except Jews and Christians, has been thought mistakenly to refer to a "countryman" as it did in early Roman times. Its direct meaning appears in an edict of Valentinian I for the first time in 371 where it is applied to all whose "minds

[121] *C.Th.* XVI:10, 20.

[122] Socrates *H.E.* VII, chap. xxii, tr. by A. C. Zenos in *Nicene and Post-Nicene Fathers,* 2nd Ser., II (1890), 164.

[123] *C.Th.* XVI:10, 22.

[124] *C.Th.* XVI:10, 25.

[125] P. Allard, *Le christianisme et l'empire romain de Néron à Theodose* (4th ed.; Paris, 1898), p. 277.

[126] In two collections: *Codex constitutionum* (529) and *Digesta vel Pandectae* (533). To these were added the *Institutiones* (533), and the entire work was reissued as *Codex repetitae praelectionis* (534), the Code which we have. Still later (533–565) the *Novellae constitutiones* were added.

have been excited against the most sacred law by certain perversions," obviously referring to Julian.[127]   But the word in that sense antedates Valentinian, for we find it in the *De corona militis* of Tertullian (composed *ca.* 200): *apud hunc* [*Christum*] *tam miles est paganus fidelis quam paganus est miles infidelis* (line 11), where *paganus* is in opposition to *miles,* i.e., a civilian.   Out of this developed the difference between *ius militum* and *ius paganorum,* the latter meaning "private" law.   Kurtz [128] believes the distinction arose out of the soldiers' viewpoint since they called those living outside their *castra, pagani.*   By the fourth century, then, in both juristic and ecclesiastical Latin, the meaning had changed and *pagani* and *gentiles* were interchangeable referring to "foreigners," "outsiders," or "heathen," [129] without any reference to "countrymen."

CAUSES OF ROME'S DECLINE

While the Christians gave to Theodosius his title "Great," his efforts in the political field, though he brought the East for a season out of chaos into order, hardly deserve it.   Following Diocletian and Constantine he was the third to try to reorganize the Roman State, and was the least of the three.[130]   The ancient world had been dying since the crisis of the third century, for its illness was mortal.   Historians have long been busy in diagnosing that illness and in appraising the causes which led to Rome's downfall, which Gibbon, viewing it from the close of the Eastern Empire in 1453 (or 1461) called it—and the description is equally true of the disappearance of the West at the close of the fifth century in 476 (or 480)—"the greatest, perhaps, and most awful scene in the history of mankind." [131]   By Honorius' death in 323 the West was still intact except for the voluntary loss of Britain (*ca.* 407), but the cracks were already visible along which the final cleavages came.   Little over a half-century later the Western Empire was extinguished by Odoacer, the first barbarian king of Italy (476–490), its disappearance so complete that nothing of its greatness was left during the succeeding "Dark Ages" to the advent of Charlemagne.[132]

All agree that the immediate causes were the German barbarians in whose discord Tacitus, long before, had found the safety of the Empire. But by the third century they were no longer separate and feeble but were banded in powerful federations on a military and feudal basis—Allemanni, Franks, Goths, etc.—and near the close of the fourth were settled in great numbers below the Danube frontier in the Eastern provinces as allies (*foederati*), the year 376 marking the beginning of Rome's decline when Valens let the Visigoths settle there as refugees from the Huns.

[127] *C.Th.* XVI:2, 18; cf. XVI:2, 19.

[128] *Exkurse über römisches Recht* (Leipzig, 1880), p. 644f., quoted by Huttmann, *op. cit.,* pp. 181–82 and note.

[129] E.g. in *C.Th.* XVI:5, 46: *Gentiles quos vulgo paganos appellant.*

[130] See A. Güldenpenning, *Kaiser Theodosius der Grosse* (Halle, 1878); T. Hodgkin, *The Dynasty of Theodosius* (Oxford, 1899).   For his character and work, *C.M.H.,* I (Cambridge, 1911), 247–49.

[131] In the final paragraph of chap. lxxi.

[132] On the completeness of the disaster, see chap. i of Frantz Funck-Brentano's *The Middle Ages;* tr. from the fifth Paris ed. of 1922 by Elizabeth O'Neill (London, 1923).

But there has been no unanimity in rating the relative importance of the internal factors of decay. The problem has been approached from many angles according to the bent of the historian's erudition—political, social, military, economic and financial, religious and moral, agricultural and disease—all of which must have played their part in the debacle. Thus the causes of Rome's fall form the greatest puzzle of history since Gibbon found it "the natural and inevitable effect of immoderate greatness," and added that instead of inquiring why it was destroyed "we should rather be surprised that it had survived so long," since "the causes of destruction multiplied with the extent of conquest."

Even in antiquity there were theories why the Western Empire was dying. The later Greek and Roman rhetoricians liked to think the world was dying of old age—*mundus senescens*—the theory developed in our time among others by John W. Draper who emphasized the biological idea that political states like individual humans have their infancy, childhood, adolescence, maturity, old age, and death.[133] St. Cyprian, bishop of Carthage, more definitely explained the third century crisis as due to lack of rainfall, excessive heat and subsequent dearth of laborers, soldiers and sailors.[134]

In our time stress is usually laid on political and economic factors—bad administration, breakdown of authority and law, the gigantic bureaucracies instituted by Diocletian, unbalanced budgets for centuries, debased coinage, and taxation amounting to extortion so unbearable that Goldwin Smith long ago called the later Empire merely a "huge tax-gathering and barbarian fighting machine," though it is well known that similar economic phenomena have attended modern states which have recovered. But many other causes have also been given. Otto Seeck found the chief cause in "the loss of Roman blood through wars and celibacy."[135] Guglielmo Ferrero found it in "the interminable civil wars" caused by Rome's attempt to reconcile monarchy with a republican organization, the failure to establish an emperor succession, and other defects of Caesarism.[136] Michael Rostovtzeff has explained it by the growing antagonism between urban and rural populations and the consequent deliberate revolt of the semi-civilized peasant and soldier proletariate against the dominant bourgeoisie of the municipalities.[137] Vilpredo Pareto explained it rather as a combination of political, religious, moral and sociological causes.[138]

[133] In his *History of the Intellectual Development of Europe* (New York, 1867).

[134] *Epist. ad Demetrianum* 3: cf. his *De mortalitate* 25.

[135] *Die Geschichte des Untergangs der antiken Welt* (Berlin, 1897–1920), I, chap. iii, 240f.; and cf. VI, "Die Auflösung des Reiches." Similarly, Sir John R. Seeley found it in the dwindling population; *Roman Imperialism and Other Lectures and Essays* (Boston, 1871), Lecture 2, 37–74.

[136] *The Ruin of Ancient Civilization and the Triumph of Christianity*, tr. from the French and ed. by Lady Whitehead (New York and London, 1921).

[137] *The Social and Economic History of the Roman Empire* (Oxford, 1926) and cf. his "Decay of the Ancient World and its Economic Explanation," *Econ. Hist. Rev.*, II (1930), 197–214.

[138] *Traité de sociologie générale* (Lausanne, 1917–19), II, chap. xiii, "L'Equilibre social dans l'histoire"; tr. from Italian by P. Bovan.

Others, notably V. G. Simkhovitch, have given the failure of agriculture as the major cause.[139] Ellsworth Huntington and others have stressed the so-called "water-cycle of antiquity," i.e., the cyclic change in temperature and rainfall due to changes in solar radiation and magnetic activity as shown by dendro-chronology based on the rings of giant trees.[140] Some have found the cause of the decline of antiquity in the increase of malaria in Greece and Italy and consequent abandonment of the farms.[141] Recently Hans Zinsser, following the lead of Niebuhr, has emphasized as a "material if not decisive factor" the many epidemics which swept over the Roman world unchecked by sanitation and beyond political genius and military valor to halt. Between the plague of Nero's reign (after the fire of 64), which Tacitus mentions as extraordinarily destructive,[142] and that of Justinian, described as the worst in antiquity by Procopius, since it continued with intermissions from 541 to 590, once for four months during which ten thousand are said to have died daily in Byzantium alone, Zinsser lists nine such epidemics which demoralized social, political and military life.[143]

Among the first to seek the cause in Christianity was F. A. Lange who referred it to the preaching of the Gospel to the poor, a *"Religion der Underdrückten und der Sclaven, der Müheseligen und Beladenen."* [144] And Christianity must take its place as one of the major causes of Rome's decline. Religion was always the basis of the Roman State as it has been of every other since till its exclusion by the totalitarian governments of our time. While for over a millennium the chief external interest of the Graeco-Roman world was in politics, beneath this there was always a religion basis. Augustus had revitalized the civic cult largely in the interest of politics, and, despite the disfavor of Christian emperors, the cult kept some of its vitality even beyond the close of the fourth century. Commo-

---

[139] See his two essays, "Rome's Fall Reconsidered" and "Hay and History," in his *Toward the Understanding of Jesus and other Historical Essays* (New York, 1921).

[140] *Civilization and Climate* (3rd ed.; New Haven, 1924); *Climatic Changes : their Nature and Causes* (New Haven, 1922); and cf. J. Huxley, "Climate and History," *Saturday Review* (1930). Semitic scholars had long emphasized the migration of desert peoples from Arabia as the key to Israelite and Moslem conquests of southwestern Asia, though both historians and archaeologists no longer agree with Huntington's *Palestine and its Transformation* (Boston, 1911), whatever truth there may be in the progressive desiccation of western Asia which forced its population out, finally propelling the Germanic tribes on to the Roman frontiers and thus helping to destroy the Empire. See refutation by Sir C. L. Woolley and T. E. Lawrence, *The Wilderness of Zin* (New York, 1936), pp. 51f.

[141] E.g., W. H. S. Jones, *Malaria and Greek History* (Manchester, 1909, Victoria University Publications); *Malaria, a Neglected Factor in the History of Greece and Rome* (Cambridge, 1907); Ronald Ross, *Malaria in Greece* (Washington, 1909, Smithsonian Annual Report, 1908), pp. 697–710.

[142] *Annales* XVI:13 (*omne mortalium genus vis pestilentiae depopulabatur*); cf. Suetonius, *Life of Nero*, 39. While Tacitus regarded it as god-sent, Suetonius called it an accident of fortune. He adds that 30,000 deaths were registered in a single autumn in the temple of *Venus Libitina* (goddess of death; cf. Horace *Carm*. III, 30, 7). A contemporary physician, Aretaeus, 2:5, called it *cholera morbus*.

[143] *Rats, Lice and History* (Boston, 1935), pp. 128f. For this bubonic plague, see Procopius, *History of the Wars*, 2:22, 1–23, 21.

[144] In his *Gesch. des Materialismus* (Leipzig, 1887), p. 127; tr. by E. C. Thomas (London, 1892), I, 170.

dus, Septimius Severus, Elagabal, Aurelian, Diocletian, Constantine, Julian and Theodosius all sought a type of religion to bolster their rule. When Christianity entered Rome, Roman society was already deeply religious and its devotees constantly grew at the expense of paganism. Down to Constantine's time its pacific spirit had injured the State, its softening spirit subtilely infused into the army and government although Nietzsche's idea that the armies became so softened that they could not resist the barbarians is untenable since Rome was doomed before the frontiers were broken and her Germanized armies retained their valor and discipline to the end. It was rather the sectarian fights within the Church which broke down resistance and led to the entrance of barbarians within the frontiers, just as later dissensions in part were the cause of the Moslems entering the Eastern half of the Empire.

But Christianity played a more subtle role as a factor in the dissolution of Rome. As prosperity waned and national vigor declined men naturally turned to religion for solace and paid greater attention to the vision of another world of peace than to the turbulent affairs of this, which many believed was doomed. Thus an unconscious change from political allegiance to the State to spiritual allegiance to the Church with its promise of future happiness was gradually wrought. In this way Christianity first weakened and then undermined the Roman State. Tertullian affirmed that a Christian and a Caesar were contradictions in terms and that Christ had refused an earthly kingdom since it was impossible to serve two masters.[145] It was for this reason that he also said of his fellow-Christians that "for us nothing is more foreign than the commonwealth. We recognize but one universal commonwealth, the world." [146] A recent writer has remarked: "As the Church never saw the value of paganism and the greatness of Rome was due to the belief in polytheism, it could easily destroy it and Rome with it." [147] If then, as Dean Inge has said, "the Christian Church was the last great creative achievement of classical culture," [148] it unfortunately proved to be one of the contributing causes to the latter's downfall.

That Christianity was already the conqueror at the close of the fourth century is shown by Theodosius yielding to the rebuke of a churchman. It was left only for Justinian to close the pagan schools of philosophy and rhetoric in Athens and, in the words of Salomon Reinach, "the world was ripe for the Middle Ages."

[145] In his *Apologeticus* 21, and *De idolatria* 18–19, respectively.
[146] *Apol.* 38.
[147] Ed. Lucas White in *Why Rome Fell* (New York and London, 1927). On the subtle influence of religion and philosophy on the collapse of Rome, see A. Drews, *Plotin und der Untergang der antiken Weltanschauung* (Jena, 1907).
[148] In the *Legacy of Greece*, ed. by Sir R. W. Livingstone (Oxford, 1921), p. 30.

EPILOGUE

Out of the conflict of religions in the Roman Empire only two, both Asiatic in origin, have survived in Western civilization—Judaism and Christianity. In conclusion we add a brief account of their condition today fifteen and one-half centuries after the death of Theodosius the Great.

JUDAISM

Judaism throughout the centuries after the final impetus to the Diaspora by Hadrian has remained an ethnic faith, that of the Jews alone. Since they ceased to be a nation the Jews have lived among alien peoples and, in spite of persecution, have remained steadfast in their ancient religion. Their chief contribution to religion since antiquity has been their preservation of strict monotheism emphasizing, as no other people has done, the distinction between the human and divine in religion. In this respect they have surpassed both Islam and Unitarianism which give a higher reverence to Mohammed and Jesus respectively than the Jews have given to Moses, the founder of their religion and nation. While there were many different sects in ancient Judaism, and in the eighth century the Karaites or "Readers" arose at Bagdad and still exist in small communities in Southern Russia, Turkey, Egypt, and even Jerusalem—adherents to the "written" law of the Pentateuch who reject the traditional "oral" law of the Talmud and all rabbinical methods—these were all unimportant beside the central faith.

Through alien contacts in later centuries Judaism has undergone many changes. Its two great medieval representatives were Maimonides (Rabbi Moses ben Maimon) of Corduba, Fez, and Cairo (1135–1204), called "the Light of the West" and "the Second Moses"; and Gersonides (Levi ben-Gerson) of France (1288–1344). Maimonides, the greatest of Jewish philosophers and chief Jewish exponent of tolerance and rationalism, was the first to liberalize his fellow-Jews by condensing the dogmas of their religion into his "Thirteen Articles" of faith which included immortality with its promise of rewards and penalties and which were received into the synagogue ritual. His great work was the *Dalalat al-Ha'irin* published in Arabic during his exile in Egypt and translated into Hebrew as the *Moreh Nebukim,* i.e., *Guide of the Perplexed,* which influenced not only Jews but the Scholastic philosophy of the Church. From it the Church received its first true knowledge of the medieval Synagogue. Gersonides' great work *Milhamoth 'Adonai* or *The Wars of God* (1317–29), was modeled on that of Maimonides. It is a criticism of Jewish dogmas and the syncretism of Jewish orthodoxy and the Aristotelian system. Herein he discussed six philosophical problems on Aristotelian principles and so opposed to Maimonides: immortality, prophecy, God's omniscience and providence, the nature of the celestial spheres and the eternity of matter. But real liberalism came to the Jews long after the Renaissance through the labors of Moses Mendelssohn (1729–86) who initiated a Jewish Renaissance by championing their emancipation in two great works: *Jerusalem oder über religiöse Macht und Judenthum* (1783) and his more celebrated *Phaedon* (1767). The former was a survey of Judaism both in its religious and national aspects and a plea for freedom of conscience, "an irrefutable book" in the opinion of Kant, since it proclaimed non-interference by the State in the faith of its citizens. The *Phaedon,* an earlier work, based on Plato's dialogue on the same subject, comprehended all that could be urged in support of immortality.

In 1791 the French National Assembly, instigated by the revolutionary churchman Henri Gregoire who tried to reconcile Catholicism with modern conceptions of liberty, first gave political freedom to the Jews of France. Just before, on June 21, 1788, New Hampshire cast the enabling vote to ratify the Constitution of the United States in which all distinctions of creed are obliterated and all men are allowed freedom of worship according to their conscience in the two hundred and fifty or more religious bodies which now flourish in the United States. Not until three-quarters of a century later (1860) was the British Parliament opened to Jews. Today anti-Semitism reigns actively on the European continent, especially in Germany, Austria, Rumania and Russia, but nowhere in England or in the Americas.

The heart of ancient Judaism, belief in Yahweh and observance of the Mosaic law, has survived among the Jewish masses everywhere. Today, however, there is less compulsion about belief and it is difficult to tell whether the average modern Jew really believes as his ancestor did in Jesus' time. The educated Jews of today have no specific philosophy of their own, but follow the systems of the peoples among whom they live. All schools of thought have their Jewish followers and Darwin, Buechner, Haeckel, Spencer and Nietzsche are as eagerly read by free-thinking Jews as by free-thinking Christians. But the accusation that atheism is commoner among Jews than among Christians is ill-founded. Few present-day Jewish thinkers include atheism in their systems, and that of their last great philosopher, Spinoza (1632–77), though he said that no free personal God existed, which religiously might be construed as atheism, ended in pantheism and not in atheism. Jews everywhere still believe in the God of their fathers and in their prayers confess their faith in Moses' words (Deut. 6:4): "Hear, O Israel: the Lord our God is one Lord." Only recently in Eastern Europe atheism and hatred of religion have crept in along with socialistic ideas which reach Jewish writers through Yiddish literature and translations. Zionism bade fair to check such tendencies and was leading the Jewish people back to their faith in Yahweh's omnipotence and mercy.

The chief differences between present-day Orthodox and Reformed Jewry are concerned with the observance or non-observance of inherited practices or of those added to the ancient faith since the time of Isaac of

Fez in the eleventh century and the later Maimonides. Rationalism is the key-note of the Reformed Synagogue while the Orthodox Jews of Eastern Europe have remained hostile to the spirit of progress and lag behind their Western brothers because of their strict adherence to such tenets as the observance of the Sabbath and certain dietary restrictions far more tenaciously than orthodox Christians do to the observance of Sunday and the exactions of Lent. The Reformed Jews accept Maimonides' creed in the main, especially its emphasis on the unity, incorporeality, and om-niscience of God, on truth in the prophecies of Moses and the Hebrew prophets, and to a lesser extent on the belief in immortality and on the coming of a Messiah.[1] But they now reject the minutiae of ceremonial and follow instead Micah's teachings that Yahweh is pleased with right conduct rather than with burnt-offerings. Many no longer believe that the restoration of Jewish nationality in Palestine or elsewhere is an essen-tial of the coming Messianic era of universal peace and justice and thus have little interest in Zionism or in the Jewish Territorial Organization (*ITO*) started in 1905 by Israel Zangwill to establish a Jewish State in the East African Protectorate or elsewhere. But since the Second World War, Zionism has become strong.

In America the Reformed Jews have largely abandoned the taboos of the Pentateuch and Talmud for they have renounced a kosher, i.e., ritually clean diet, and openly eat pork, hold services at convenient times rather than on the Sabbath alone, and many regard Jesus as the climax of the prophetic teaching inaugurated by Amos, Hosea, and Isaiah and as the chief ethical figure of their race. Rabbis preach doctrines of salvation and good works similar to those of the Christian priests and make little ethical distinction between Jew and Christian. Jews even now leave the Syna-gogue for the Church as their ancestors did in Paul's day, albeit now, it may be, they are largely moved by social and business expediency. They are all justly proud of their history and "mission" wherein they believe that they surpass all others and some may still hope the Messiah in the form of uni-versal Jewish ideas will yet come.

Dispersed Jews have never felt at home in Central and Eastern Europe where the majority of them live. They have never known since pre-Christian Alexandrian times any prolonged period of freedom or security but have been restricted to ghettos and today are as little wanted as ever in the same areas of war-torn Europe. Thus far there seems to be little disposition to welcome them elsewhere in post-war economy. Many Jews have in consequence looked to Palestine as their only refuge, which before the Second World War had already accepted over a half million of their people as the result of the Balfour Declaration of 1917—more refugees than the entire world has welcomed since 1933. Through the redistribution of wasteland, intensification of agriculture, and modernization of industry, Palestine could support many more inhabitants despite threats of Arab

---

[1] See remarks in the *Union Prayer Book*, compiled by the Central Conference of American Rabbis (Cincinnati, 1890); and for Maimonides' creed, the *Orthodox Prayer Book* in prose and meter—the latter the work of Daniel Ben Judah Dayyan (1404).

interference.   But the British *White Paper* (1939) had limited immigration into Palestine to 25,000 annually in defiance of the Balfour Declaration and the present policy is to limit it to 1,500 a month, which has led to conflict between the Zionists in Palestine and the British occupational forces.   One thing seems certain: that the future responsibility of the Jews lies with their religious leaders, who as yet have shown no tendency toward urging their racial or religious assimilation to their neighbors, a tendency long ago sponsored by Maimonides and the logical solution of the Jewish problem.

CHRISTIANITY

Nor has Christianity, after the lapse of many centuries and despite the fact that it has obliterated many national boundaries and become the faith of many unrelated peoples, become a universal religion.   For it still belongs to Europe and its colonies in Asia, Africa, and the Americas. Sixty years ago Edward Freeman wrote: "Christianity has hardly anywhere taken firm and lasting root, except in those countries which either formed a part of the Roman Empire or learned their religion and civilization from it." [2]   The question is often raised why Christianity after its victory in the Roman Empire has since been confined almost entirely to Europe and its cultural offshoots, a question no less perplexing than the larger one of why all the great religions of the world have originated in Asia and none in Europe.

The answer to the first question, at least, is not to be found in any peculiarity of Christianity nor in any psychological difference between Europeans and non-Europeans.   In origin Christianity was Asiatic, its two founders and the disciples were Asiatics, and its sacred writings largely Semitic, the Old Testament in Hebrew with a fraction in Aramaic, the New Testament in Greek, though the Gospels may well have been translations from original Aramaic sources.   Moreover, certain peoples who have migrated into Europe in later times ultimately from Asia, e.g. the Magyars who settled Hungary about 895, were easily converted to Christianity. Something should be said, too, for Christian missionary efforts in eastern Asia and south and central Africa.   Furthermore, Christianity once had a strong hold in western Asia, in the Parthian and New Persian empires till the latter was overthrown by the Saracens in 641 at Nehavend.   The Armenians are said to have been converted in the early fourth century by St. Gregory, "the illuminator," priest and exarch of Great Armenia (302–332) and reputed founder of the Gregorian Armenian Church. [3]

Consequently, we must look elsewhere for a possible explanation of the problem and this we find in the great East Asiatic religions.   In

[2] *General Sketch* (1882), p. 100; cf. his *Chief Periods of European History* (London, 1886), pp. 67–68.

[3] We now know, however, that this, in part, fabulous figure did not begin their conversion, i.e., "illuminate" them, since they had been in part Christianized already by Syrian missionaries and that Gregory merely catholicized the country by influencing King Tiridates (238–314), whom he baptized, to get rid of the last vestiges of paganism.

Asia ethical and religious systems had long antedated Christianity, such as Confucianism and Taoism [4] in China, Brahmanism, Buddhism, and others in India. Even if commercial relations between the Mediterranean and the Far East had been greater in antiquity such firmly established systems would have ignored Christianity. Since the early Middle Ages, Islam which with Judaism has kept the godhead undivided in a way that Christianity has not—Moslems revere Isa (Jesus) as "the prophet of the Christians" and as a "Spirit of God" only—has formed a broad belt through central and south Asia and westward over North Africa to the Atlantic which in turn has resisted the advance of Christianity in both directions. Moreover, these Eastern systems, natural products of their environments, have met the religious needs of their peoples far better than Christianity could have done. Only in recent years the Japanese in seeking the adoption of a national religion rejected the claims of Christianity finding their native Shinto and borrowed Buddhism better suited to their needs. In religion, therefore, Europe and Asia-Africa have gone their separate ways as in all things else. Africa especially, apart from Egypt and the narrow fringe between the Sahara and the Mediterranean in Roman antiquity, has remained almost untouched by Christian culture down to our time.

The Greek Orthodox Church

Of the three main groups into which the once unified Church has been in the course of time divided the oldest is the Holy Orthodox Catholic Apostolic Church of the East, popularly known as the "Greek" or "Eastern" Church, which grew out of the primitive churches founded or exhorted by Paul and his fellow-missionaries, in which Greek was the language of the Scriptures and service. It claims uninterrupted succession from these churches and conformity with their doctrines. Without creeds in the Western sense it comprehends all the churches which accept the decrees of the first seven ecumenical councils as well as those developed out of these through missionary effort. Such are the Armenian and also certain autocephalous schismatic ones such as the Nestorian Chaldean, Syrian Jacobite, Egyptian Coptic and Abyssinian national Churches. These left the mother organization because of the Monophysite doctrine, debated at the Councils of Chalcedon (451) and Constantinople (553), a doctrine which they retained, i.e., the belief in the single nature of Christ whose humanity and divinity are fused.

By the seventh century Orthodox fundamental problems had been settled and their unconditional acceptance was demanded of its members; the Church thus early became crystallized and intellectual curiosity ceased. Furthermore, since it was centered in the Eastern capital, it easily became a department of the Byzantine State subject to its supervision and laws. Justinian in the sixth century proclaimed that Church and State were alike creations of God and that it was the latter's duty to direct the former, a basic principle of the Orthodox Church everywhere thereafter—as its re-

[4] Taoists are generally classed with Confucianists today.

cent difficulties in Russia have shown. But it never tried to usurp State functions as Rome did in the West even if its influence has at times controlled certain administrative policies. Nor did it secede from State supervision and found an invisible State—*imperium in imperio*—as Christianity did in the West, and certainly it never proclaimed that the secular government should be subject to it.

Following the division of the Empire begun at the death of Theodosius in 395—though the cleavage may be said to have been already underway when Constantine made Constantinople the capital—it was but natural that the Church of the Eastern half should gradually have become independent of the West both in organization and doctrine so that the name "Orthodox" came to include all churches ruled over by the four Eastern patriarchs. Only since the ninth century, however, have its bishops been called "ecumenical" patriarchs. While the Church of Rome in the West had effectively effaced national distinctions and had early brought all churches there under her jurisdiction and, since about 250, had used only Latin in her services, each of the thirteen different Churches of the East has used its own language, generally in its archaic form. While, then, the Church government of the West became monarchical, ruled from one center, it remained oligarchical in the East ruled from four main centers—Alexandria, Antioch, Jerusalem and Constantinople—each amenable to its sectional synod.

After the councils of Nicaea and Constantinople there was little further theological disputation in the West and Rome's many statesmanlike bishops gave the Roman Church a unique position. But the East was long torn by doctrinal dissensions. Theology there had developed out of Greek philosophy, the Greek Church Fathers being the successors of the Sophists, while in the West it had developed largely out of Roman law, the Latin Church Fathers being the successors of the Roman advocates.[4] In this way theological differences between East and West arose and the final division of the Church was inevitably hastened by the ever-expanding pretensions of Rome and intensified by political jealousies. This began at Philippopolis in 344 from which the Eastern bishops, summoned the year before by Constans to meet with those from the West at Serdica, withdrew and excommunicated the Roman Pope, Julius I (337–352), as well as Athanasius and many priests. The estrangement, thus begun, grew ever stronger down to the irrevocable schism of the eleventh century.

The later papacy, virtually abandoned by the Eastern Empire, took refuge with the Carolingian Franks in 754 and became almost forgotten in the East where its pretensions had long been opposed by the emperors and patriarchs of Constantinople. Rome had ever less contact with the Greeks, being rarely invited to councils and merely to help ratify decrees and then only on important occasions such as at the close of the debate on the use of images denounced by the "iconoclastic" Emperor Leo, the Isaurian, in the sixth century and the quarrel between the rivals Photius and Ignatius over

[4] See Dean A. P. Stanley, *Lectures on the History of the Eastern Church* (London, 1861; 2nd ed. 1873 and now in *Everyman's Library*), chap. i.

the patriarchate at Constantinople in the ninth when Pope Nicolaus I deposed Photius in 863 in a manner offensive to Eastern Church independence only to be excommunicated himself in turn. Finally, after many premonitions, the "Great Schism" was consummated in 1054 when Pope Leo IX and Patriarch Michael Cerularius mutually excommunicated one another.

The ostensible cause of the rupture, which occurred centuries before, was the insertion into the creed at the Third Council of Toledo in 589 of the words *filioque* in the doctrine of the procession of the Holy Spirit. This the Greeks regarded as wrong since it had been done neither at an ecumenical council nor after consultation with them. While the Western churches from the time of Tertullian had accepted the view that the Holy Spirit proceeded from both the Father and Son—the later argument of Augstine for the unity of the godhead—the Eastern Church relying on a passage in John (15:16) regarded the double procession from Father and Son as a degradation since both the Holy Spirit and the Son were subordinate to the Father who alone was the source of each. The Eastern position was best stated in the eighth century by John of Damascus, called *Chrysorrhoas* (gold-streaming) because of his eloquence, the most famous of Eastern theologians. He speaks of the Holy Spirit as "proceeding from the Father and communicated through the Son . . . and we do not speak of the Spirit as from the Son." [5] This alone, however, was too unimportant permanently to cleave the Church in twain and so the real causes lay deeper—the entire question of Roman pretensions to primacy, the limitation of the right of confirmation to bishops alone, priestly celibacy (since the Orthodox priest may marry once) and the use of unleavened bread at the Eucharist since the Orthodox use leavened bread dipped in wine.

Many attempts have been made since to heal the breach especially in the thirteenth and fifteenth centuries but the memory of the horror of the sack of Constantinople and division of its spoils among the Latins of the Fourth Crusade who, under Baldwin of Flanders, set up a Latin Empire there in 1204, was too poignant to be forgotten or forgiven. The last important effort was made in our time by Leo XIII whose note of reconciliation was answered by the patriarch of Constantinople in 1895 with the usual rehearsal of Roman theological innovations, such as the *filioque* clause, purgatory, immaculate conception (1854), and papal infallibility (1870).[6] Since 1054 the Romans have regarded the Greeks as cut off from the original Apostolic Church, while the latter claim that they alone have preserved its original doctrines. The issue is now too longstanding, the Roman Church too immovable in its pretensions and the Greek Church too apathetic to hope for unity. Only two Oriental churches, the Armenian, in part, and the Maronite of the Lebanon, have remained loyal to Rome. The latter, now numbering some 300,000 members in Syria, Pal-

---

[5] *Exposition of the Orthodox Faith*, I, chap. viii, pp. 6–11, tr. by S. D. F. Salmond in *Nicene and Post-Nicene Fathers*, 2nd Series, Vol. XIV (1898).

[6] For the Catholic view of attempts at reconciliation, see A. Fortescue, *The Orthodox Eastern Church* (London, 1916).

estine, Egypt, and Cyprus, and originally Monothelites, i.e., modified Monophysites, forms a military state. They submitted to Rome about 1182 and now are united with her although they retain certain privileges such as the use of Syriac in their litany and permission for the lower clergy to marry.

In these latter years the four patriarchates still function but in greatly reduced fashion. The patriarch of Constantinople, at one time the most exalted Eastern ecclesiastic, now acts with the permanent Holy Synod and a National Mixed Council which includes laymen. While once enjoying jurisdiction over Turkey in Europe, Anatolia, the Aegean Isles, etc., he is now under Turkish control and feeble. Similarly, the patriarch of Alexandria while still keeping his grandiloquent titles "Pope (*pappas*), father of fathers, pastor of pastors, archpriest of archpriests, thirteenth apostle and ecumenical judge" is now insignificant under Egyptian control. The patriarch of Antioch—since the loot of the old Syrian capital by the Egyptians in 1268 reduced to a small town, Antakia, of about twenty thousand inhabitants—was long under French control, and instead of ruling over twelve metropolitans and some two hundred and fifty bishops has only twenty sees. And the patriarch of Jerusalem whose office was created in 451 to take charge of Palestine, which theretofore had been a bishopric depending on the metropolitan of Caesarea, today is under British control and, because of the continuous strife between Jew and Arab, is the least important of all.

The Church of Russia was the largest and most important branch of the Orthodox Church from the ninth century down to the Lenin Revolution of 1917 when it contained perhaps five-sixths of the total membership of the Orthodox body. Founded in 892 its metropolitans, then under the patriarchs of Constantinople, lived at Kiev until 1320 when they removed to Moscow. In 1582 the patriarch Jeremiah raised Job, the forty-sixth metropolitan in succession, to the patriarchal dignity which made five Eastern patriarchs until 1700. Then Peter the Great ended the Muscovite patriarchate and in 1721 instituted instead the Holy Governing Synod which controlled the Church thereafter with a procurator to represent the czar. The Church was injured by the later czars especially through the encouragement of the Russification policy of Alexander III (1881–94) by the reactionary and brutal procurator of the Holy Synod, Pobédonostzef (1880–1907),[7] whom Mommsen called "the modern Torquemada." For he opposed all Western influences, a policy which led to religious persecution of non-Christians, especially Jews. Thus one writer has rightly said that "under the guise of protecting the Church, the State in reality had enslaved it." [8]

After the Lenin Revolution a "Great Council" was convened in August 1917 consisting of five hundred and fifty-five bishops and priests which replaced the old Holy Synod of Peter the Great. A patriarch was again installed in Moscow, the separation of Church and State agreed upon and

[7] See his *Reflections of a Russian Statesman*, tr. by R. C. Long (London, 1898).
[8] Ageyev, *The Christian East* (1920) (unavailable to the writer).

freedom of worship guaranteed. But when the Bolshevists got into power all was changed. For they were foes of religion and thought it had been used merely to drug the masses. They forbade religious instruction in schools and churches, broke up religious associations, abolished the right of the Church to hold property, confiscated all churches which were not self-supporting, destroyed some and transformed others into museums, and converted monasteries, from which the higher clergy are drawn, into lay institutions. They insulted, even killed, priests, monks, and nuns, though such atrocities were exaggerated as is natural when an established Church is divested of its property holdings, its state support, and its monopoly of education, in a word, when it is forced to become a religious institution only—its real grievance. While the reaction of 1919 mitigated some abuses, today there is no effective Church resistance to the Government even if the masses are still allowed to worship since they cannot be made irreligious. All Bolshevists (only a tiny fraction of the population but their masters) must, as is well known, take an oath of atheism.

The Hellenic Church was under the jurisdiction of the patriarch of Constantinople until the war of liberation from the Turks (1821–29). As the patriarch was then forced by the Sultan to oppose Greek aspirations to freedom, he was later repudiated and a Holy Synod of four bishops and a royal commissioner to represent the new Greek king was formed instead under the presidency of the metropolitan of Athens and a Council of the Synod both of which still function. Since the adoption of the Greek Constitution in 1827 there has been no proselytizing.

The ordinary Greek regards himself on historical grounds as alone Christian denying the title to Catholics and Protestants and even to members of the Bulgarian Church although the ritual of the latter is almost identical with his own. But the educated classes are not fanatical and some of the metropolitans have been noted for scholarship, e.g. Philotheus Bryennios of Seres and later of Nicomedia who was friendly to the Catholics and published the complete manuscripts of the Epistles of Clement (1875) and of the *Didaché* (1883) which he discovered in Constantinople in 1873. Unfortunately, the parish priests in Greece, as in Russia, are ignorant men and command little respect from their flocks. They have no social position, receive no salaries but are dependent on fees from christenings, weddings, and funerals. They recite the Bible from memory and preach no sermons. In the rural districts they are more pagan than Christian, their religion being a mixture of pagan and Christian folklore. Such ignorance seems strange since the Greeks of today pay much attention to education and the Hellenic Church is under the jurisdiction of the Ministry of Education and Ecclesiastical Affairs.

The educated Greek, even if sceptical, seldom leaves the Church, for during the centuries of Turkish enslavement it was the Church alone which preserved Greek nationality and, therefore, it is reverenced as a great social institution. That ignorance is the worst feature of the Greek Church was shown in 1903 by the effort of the Holy Synod under the influence of

Queen Olga, a Russian princess, to introduce a much-needed version of the Gospel in Romaic, i.e., modern Greek, in place of the ancient text which few priests or members understood. The populace, however, regarded the movement as pan-Slavic propaganda and mob outbreaks and even bloodshed continued till the attempt was given up. The Julian calendar was replaced by the Gregorian first on February 14, 1918, by the Bolshevists (except in the Russian Church, where it is retained) and later (on March 1, 1923) by the Greeks, so that Church festivals common to the Greek and Roman Churches which were formerly thirteen days apart are now generally celebrated simultaneously, although some Orthodox churches both in Europe and in the United States still celebrate their feast days according to the Julian calendar.

The Roman Catholic Church

Nearly one-half of Christendom belongs to the "Holy Catholic Apostolic Roman Church" popularly known as the "Catholic Church." We have already discussed the claim of the Roman bishops to primacy on the basis of the Petrine doctrine. Out of this grew the early trend of the bishops, who from the first were conscious of their special position in the capital city, toward monarchical rule already visible by the middle of the second century.[9] In the eighth century the bishop of Rome became a temporal prince through the donation of Pepin the Short, king of the Franks (751–768), confirmed by his son Charlemagne, which created a Papal State by conferring on Stephen II in 755 the Exarchate of Ravenna with the Pentapolis and Territories of Ferrara and Bologna, a strip of land taken from the Lombards, stretching across Italy to Rome. In this way the Pope became independent of the Eastern emperor, Constantine V. His temporal power with subsequent additions lasted over eleven centuries until 1870, when the Catholic possessions were joined to the kingdom of Italy under Victor Emmanuel I with Rome as its capital. Thereafter the Pope remained a self-imposed prisoner on Vatican Hill until Mussolini reunited Church and State by the Lateran Pact of February 11, 1929 which closed the so-called "Roman Question." By it Pius XI regained complete liberty as an independent sovereign for himself and his successors by the formation of the neutral State of "The City of the Vatican" which "will remain extraneous to the temporal competitions between other States" and "will only endeavor to fulfill its mission of peace if invited to do so," i.e., it will suffer no interference from the Italian government nor interfere in any diplomatic negotiation with any foreign country without the latter's express invitation. While, then, Stephen II was the first temporal head of the Roman Church, Pius IX was the last.

[9] H. Lietzmann, C.A.H., XII (1939), chap. xv, pp. 575f., traces it to Anicetus (ca. 157–ca. 167), tenth bishop from Peter, or even to Xystus (ca. 119–ca. 126), sixth in the succession, on the basis of Irenaeus (Adv. haer. 3:3, 3) who gives the first official list of bishops from Linus named by Peter to Eleutherus (?177–189), and of Eusebius H.E. V:24, 14. He shows that all early papal dates down to Pontianus (230–235) are guesses, even if the names be trustworthy.

On July 18, 1870, during the Twentieth Ecumenical Council held in the Vatican—December 8, 1869 to October 20, 1870—the pontificate of Pius IX (1846–77) reached the zenith of its astonishing innovations when the last great doctrine of the Roman Church became a dogma, the belief in the "Infallibility" of the Pope and "universality" of his episcopate. This meant that the Pope when pronouncing on religious or moral questions in the discharge of his duties, i.e., when speaking *ex cathedra,* because of the Apostolic authority vested in his office is free of error. Such a belief had been generally assumed at earlier councils but was now officially arrogated despite the fact it wounded reason by placing his pronouncements above the consensus of councils even, it might be, in matters of history. Of the five hundred and thirty-five bishops who could vote fifty remained absent and only two answered *non placet.* Since only the Pope can summon councils and preside—or name a substitute—and alone can determine the topics and order of the agenda the College of Cardinals is now reduced to the position of a Senate in a totalitarian state, for whatever it may advise must receive the papal confirmation. Since 1870, then, there has been no need of further Church councils and it is for this reason that it was said in the Introduction that the Roman Church is now spiritually an absolute monarchy. The chief appeal of the Reformation, liberty of individual interpretation of the Scriptures and denunciation of recent councils and popes, was intellectual in character; but the Church of Rome, despite its correction of certain abuses and its redefinition of doctrines in the pre-Reformation spirit at the Council of Trent (1545–63), still appeals to the emotions.

The last intellectual movement within the Roman Church was modernism, i.e., the assimilation of scientific criticism to the Scriptures. It arose during the latter years of the last century but crumbled almost before the century was out. Some two hundred years before the French biblical critic Richard Simon started the critical exegesis of the Scriptures with his *Histoire critique du Vieux Testament,* which was confiscated in France while in manuscript, but later was published in Holland (1685), followed by four additional works on the New Testament (1689–95). In the earlier work he critically examined the Hebrew text and reviewed the results of contemporary criticism, especially that concerning the authorship of the Pentateuch. But the spirit thus initiated lay dormant in France and first bore fruit in Germany in Strauss's *Leben Jesu* (1835) which, as already noted, started an era in the study of Christian origins. His influence first appeared in France in Renan's *Vie de Jésu* (1863) and again in the works of the Abbé L. Duchesne and in those of his greater pupil, Alfred Loisy, a well-trained Hebraist and Assyriologist who became the storm-center of modernism around the turn of the century and later the chief exponent of liberalism in the Roman Church. The publication by the rector of the *Institut catholique,* Monsignor d'Hulst, of a work attacking the infallibility of the Old Testament on historical and scientific grounds, a work influenced by Loisy, caused Leo XIII, perhaps the ablest of the popes since

Benedict XIV (1740–58), to reply with his encyclical *Providentissimus Deus* (1893) which reaffirmed the spirit of Trent.

Loisy's *L'Evangile et l'église* (1902) was an answer to v. Harnack's *Wesen des Christentums* (1900). The two had diametrically opposite ideas about the future of the Church. While the latter had the ultra-Protestant view that the "essence" of Christianity was the individual realization of God in the soul of man and that an organized Church was no longer needed since it had retrograded sadly from its early purity, Loisy spoke for the continued need of a Church organization with its hierarchy and governing machinery and for the sacraments ordained by God in order to bring God to the inner man by way of symbols. In 1903 in his *Le quatrième évangile* he went farther from the path of conservatism by denying all historical value to John's Gospel.

Leo's successor, the saintly Pius X (1903–14), in 1907 published a decree of the *Inquisition*—the present Congregation of the Holy Office concerned with heretical writings—beginning *Lamentabili sane,* which contained sixty-five propositions, some forty of which represented Loisy's ideas. His encyclical *Pascendi dominici gregis* published the same year—the longest but not the most enlightening of papal utterances [10]—was likewise directed against modernism, for it denounced all who, in disregard of the authority of the Holy See, maintained "the absurd doctrine that would make of the laity the factor of progress in the Church." Here again Loisy was meant and his answer was his *Simples reflexions sur l'encyclique Pascendi dominici gregis* (1907). On the publication of his *Les évangiles synoptiques* (1907 and 1908) he was excommunicated (March 7, 1908). Henceforth he ceased all attempts at reconciliation with Rome, put aside his clerical garb and became Professor of Religions in the Collège de France, whose management was now quite unlike what it was in the time of Renan, and Catholicism lost its ablest would-be interpreter.[11] Similar treatment was visited on Father George Tyrrell, the Irish theologian, who had entered the Roman Church through the influence of Cardinal Newman in 1879 and had joined the Society of Jesus in 1880, from which he was expelled in 1906 for modernism. Later, on criticizing the encyclical *Pascendi*,[12] he was virtually excommunicated but kept up his writings till his death in 1909.[13]

Enough has been said to show that the papacy has reaffirmed its control of the Catholic mind, has stopped the spirit of progress within the Church, forbidden its priests to express their ideas and the laity to read certain books.[14] The priests were compelled to sign the anti-modernist oath about

[10] See text and translation in *American Catholic Quarterly Review*, XXXII (1907), 683–730.

[11] See *My Duel with the Vatican: the Autobiography of a Catholic Modernist,* tr. by R. W. Boynton (New York, 1924).

[12] In his *Programme of Modernism; a Reply to the Encyclical of Pius X,* tr. from the Italian by L. Lilley (New York, 1908).

[13] See Alfred Loisy's tribute to him in his *George Tyrrell et Henri Bremond* (Paris, 1936). He was denied Roman Catholic burial and was buried by the Church of England in Storington, his Church having repudiated him both in life and death.

[14] Under Leo XIII, in 1897–1900, was published by decree of the Congregation of the Holy Office (developed from the former Congregation of the Roman Inquisition) a re-

such questions as original sin, the fate of non-believers hereafter, etc. While modernism, then, is outlawed, still there are modernists in the Roman Church and there will always be devout churchmen there who are actuated by the eternal search for truth. The modernist movement is sure to rise again in the ancient Church of the West which is now—despite modernistic tendencies in the present Pope, Pius XI, who is interested in the support of all scientific movements—the citadel of conservatism and illiberality.

The Protestant Churches

The spirit of liberalism excluded from the Orthodox Church through apathy and from the Roman Catholic through pronouncements of reactionary popes and councils is now best seen in the Protestant bodies whose membership totals nearly one-third of the Christian Church. Here a silent revolution in ideas has been going on for over a century in respect of the rational interpretation of the Bible and especially of the Old Testament. While the Orthodox and Roman churches are still devoted to the belief that the Old Testament has equal inspirational value with the New, the Protestants in a graduated scale from the least intellectual, i.e., most literal in their interpretation, to the so-called "broad" churches are honeycombed with the idea that this collection of heterogeneous writings is not from cover to cover the inspired "Word of God."

Until 1859 when Darwin's *On the Origin of Species by Means of Natural Selection* appeared—in which he propounded the theory of biological evolution which, with the necessary additions and corrections made since, is generally accepted in principle in place of the older doctrines of the fixity and immutability of species—little dissent had been heard from the traditional notion of creation and biblical chronology made authoritative two centuries before by James Ussher, archbishop of Armagh in Ireland (1625–40). He taught that God, i.e., Yahweh, created mankind in 4004 B.C. when the first human pair appeared in the Garden and transgressed the divine law, since which event the race has been in need of a mediator between it and God.[15]   It was not until 1938 that the archbishops of Canterbury and York repudiated such uncritical notions officially, when they endorsed the idea that the first eleven chapters of Genesis which contain the accounts of the Creation, the Deluge, etc. were unhistorical. The movement toward a rational viewpoint in the Church in harmony with astronomy, geology, paleontology, physics, biology, anthropology, archaeol-

vised *Index librorum prohibitorum* or official list of books forbidden Catholics, by ecclesiastical authority, to read or possess. It is a part of the *Constitutio officiorum* of forty-nine articles. A fifth edition was published in 1911 by order of Pius X. The earliest such *Index* in the modern sense was published by the Inquisition under Paul IV in 1557 and 1559. The ancient *Index* ascribed to Pope Gelasius I (462–496) was different, as is shown by its title, *Notitia librorum apocryphorum qui non recipiuntur.*

[15] *Annales Veteris et Novi Testamenti* (1650–54). Here (in *Chronologia sacra*) he dated the Deluge, 2348; Abraham, 1996–1821; and the Exodus, 1491 B.C. Such dates were inserted in the margin of "reference" editions of the A.V. by an unknown hand.

ogy, ancient history, and especially recent knowledge gained from cuneiform documents found in Sumeria and Mesopotamia, has been slow both
in Britain and America.

A cross-section of present-day Protestant thinking was afforded during
the sesquicentennial meeting of the General Assembly of the Presbyterian
Church in the United States (whose membership numbers about two million) held in Philadelphia in May, 1938. This was a survey of views held
by a representative group of five hundred ministers in active service in the
Baptist, Congregational, Episcopal, Evangelical, Lutheran, Methodist, and
Presbyterian churches. The analysis showed that thirteen per cent rejected the distinguishing doctrine of Christianity, the Trinity; twenty-eight
per cent the Scriptural account of Creation; thirty-eight per cent did not
believe in special revelation; twenty-eight per cent rejected prophecy; fifty-
five per cent held that the Bible contains myth and legend; eighteen per
cent did not believe in the Virgin-birth of Christ; twenty-four per cent did
not believe in the Atonement; twelve per cent did not believe in the bodily
Resurrection of Christ; thirty-four per cent did not believe in future punishment; thirty-three per cent rejected the resurrection of the body; and
twenty-seven per cent did not believe that our Lord will come again. We
quote from one of the ministers present:

> More appalling yet is the unbelief indicated in a survey among 200 students of
> five representative theological seminaries of the Protestant Church in America.
> There 91% said they do not believe in the plenary inspiration of the Scriptures,
> and they are the ministers of tomorrow.[16]

Such statistics from the liberal standpoint should be compared with those
compiled from a survey of the beliefs of scientists a quarter-century ago by
Professor James K. Leuba.[17] He found that of "the greater men of science"
thirty-four and eight-tenths per cent of the physicists believed in God and
forty per cent in immortality; of the biologists sixteen and nine-tenths per
cent and twenty-five and four-tenths per cent respectively; of the historians
thirty-two and nine-tenths per cent and thirty-five and three-tenths per cent;
of the sociologists nineteen and four-tenths per cent and twenty-seven and
one-tenth per cent; and of the psychologists forty-three and two-tenths per
cent and eight and eight-tenths per cent. Such statistics reflect the present
state in America of the endless conflict between theology and science.

All agree that the First World War injured Christianity more than any
preceding one and more than all the scoffers from Lucian to Voltaire, a
war ending in incredible losses of men and treasure.[18] The Orthodox
Church was the worst sufferer for in Russia in consequence of the Revolu-

16 See *Philadelphia Inquirer*, May 30, 1938, p. 7.
17 In his *The Belief in God and Immortality* (Chicago and London, 1921), Pt. 2, chap.
ix, pp. 218f.
18 *Fortune* (Dec. 1939) gave the total casualties as 37,514,636, which included 8,543,515
slain and 21,219,452 wounded, i.e., 57.6% of the whole number mobilized or 65,058,840.
Besides there were about 9,000,000 deaths from flood, famine, disease, air-raids, and sink-
ings at sea.

tion of 1917 it is only a shadow of its former size, the Eastern Church now being confined mainly to southeastern Europe and the eastern Mediterranean sea-board. The injury to the Western churches, Roman and Protestant, besides actual losses in membership was more insidious, since their priests on both sides of the conflict vied with one another behind the lines —for hatred is seldom found in the trenches—in bringing down God's wrath on the enemy in the true Hebraic style of Joshua, oblivious that God is indivisible and not national like Yahweh.[19] With the opening of the Second World War in September 1939 the same un-Christian spirit was again displayed by Church leaders in England and America [20] and continued throughout the war.

How great the injury to the Church through the Second World War will prove to be it is too early to say. We know the thirty-point program of the proposed National Church of the National Socialists in Germany, now happily futile, prepared by Dr. Rosenberg, chief anti-religious polemicist of the party, and released January 2, 1942, which was almost a complete reversal of Christianity. It was to be based on the removal of all the Jewish elements from Christianity. All churches in the Reich were to be turned over to the new cult, although without any compulsion to accept it. The new church was to have neither pastors, chaplains, nor orders, only "national orators," i.e., state officials to speak at evening services much like the "traveling disciples" of early Christianity. *Mein Kampf* was to replace the Bible on every altar with a sword at its right and the Swastika replacing the Cross at the left. Sins were held to be irrevocable without remission through prayer and the baptism of children in the name of the Trinity replaced by the parents' oath that they were pure Aryan. Marriage was no longer to be regarded as a sacrament, but a civic ceremony only, as in Russia, consummated by an oath of fidelity; and the only national festival the anniversary of the foundation of the new church. But there is no need of discussing further this already forgotten attempt to destroy Christianity.

Friedrich Nietzsche in his last book, his autobiography *Ecce Homo* (1888), prophesied that as the result of his onslaughts on Christianity and democracy both would disappear in the present century. A half-century later the prophecy was fulfilled in part since a large part of Europe even before the outbreak of the Second World War had renounced both, Russia by Bolshevik decree, Germany by her Nazi decrees, accompanied by the worst persecution of Jews and Christians since Torquemada. Nietzsche further maintained, relying on Hegelian reasoning, that war produced greater benefits than the Christian rule of love, a doctrine utterly disproved by the fate that has overtaken his countrymen at the close of the Second World War. But long before the civilized world had tacitly neglected

[19] See R. H. Abrams, *Preachers Present Arms: a Study of War-time Attitudes and Activities of the Churches and the Clergy in the United States 1914–18* (Philadelphia, 1933).

[20] See e.g. accounts in *New York Herald Tribune*, Feb. 1 and 2, 1940.

Christian ethics because they were incompatible with war and standing armies. Today, as in Constantine's time, it is difficult to gauge the influence of Christianity, to separate those who conform without belief from those who believe without conforming. Many basic beliefs, notably immortality, now seem largely inoperative since many people act as if they expect no future judgment. And yet Christianity has been long taught in the public schools everywhere—except in the French "schools without God"—and we know that education is the only solution of human ills and nowhere is it needed more than in religion.

Despite its shortcomings in belief and practice Christianity is doubtless the best religion yet known with its teaching of an omnipotent God who shows a father's solicitude for his creatures, a Son the ideal of tolerance with his message of human brotherhood and the Golden Rule, and—at least in the Orthodox and Catholic Churches—a Mother the ideal of motherhood. Its influence on softening human nature, however, will always be differently appraised. One writer has worded his belief thus:

It may be truly said that the simple record of [Jesus'] three short years of active life has done more to regenerate and to soften mankind than all the disquisitions of philosophers and all the exhortations of moralists. . . . Amid all the sins and failings, amid all the priestcraft and persecution and fanaticism that have defaced the Church, it has preserved, in the character and example of its Founder, an enduring principle of regeneration.[21]

But while the Church claims Christianity is the unique revelation of God's will and laws of conduct and that the birth of Christ launched a momentous change in world-morality, and despite the fact that it has been taught from millions of pulpits over a period of two millennia other writers have affirmed that it has done little to regenerate mankind—barring examples of outstanding individuals. They point out that man still shows the same aggressive spirit collectively in ruling subject peoples, in humiliating defeated enemies, and in exploiting the poor, and individually in his relations with his fellow-man. We quote from the words of two such pessimistic writers, Bertrand Russell, now Fellow at Cambridge University, and C. E. M. Joad, Professor of Philosophy in the University of London. The former says:

You will find as you look around the world that every single bit of progress in humane feeling, every improvement in the criminal law, every step toward the diminution of war, every step toward the better treatment of the colored races, every mitigation of slavery, every moral progress that there has been in the world, has been consistently opposed by the organized churches of the world.[22]

21 W. E. H. Lecky, *European Morals*, II, 9.
22 See his brochure, *Has Religion Made Useful Contributions to Civilization?* (London, 1930). Mr. Russell in his letter of Nov. 6, 1943 granting the writer permission to quote this passage says that "further study has made me consider it an overstatement, though I still think it is a first approximation to the truth since the thirteenth century."

The latter in speaking of Christian cruelty says:

More killing, starving, imprisoning and torturing have been done in the name of Christ, who bade his followers love one another, than in the name of any other creed or cause. Christians have been intolerant as much as, perhaps more than, the followers of any other creed. . . .[23]

He adds that the Church has accepted imperialism, capitalism, slavery, war, imprisonment, and torture in Christ's name and has completely ignored his pacifism; and that the story of Christianity shows that it has been disgraced by atrocities which have no parallel in other religions—such as the destruction of the Albigenses in Southern France in 1208 because of their revolt from Rome, one of the bloodiest wars of extermination, instigated by Pope Innocent III, the Spanish Inquisition, the Thirty Years War of the seventeenth century caused by friction between Protestants and Catholics in the Holy Roman Empire, and many others.

Christianity has shared with all other great religions the fate of organization although its appeal, like that of all others, is essentially individualistic. It has developed into a dogmatic system with an authoritative body of doctrine and ritual, things which Jesus would have held as trivial. William Ellery Channing, leader of Unitarian thought in his day (1780–1842), once said that "an established Church is the tomb of intelligence," and Dean Stanley (1815–81) of the English "Broad Church" movement that "all confessions and similar doctrines, if taken as final expressions of absolute truth, are misleading." But organized Christianity is here to stay and the only question is whether it, when cleared of "the silt of time," i.e., nonessential doctrines and beliefs which still cling to it like barnacles to a ship, can redeem the world.

Unitarianism

Such an attempt has been made especially in England and America by the Unitarians, strictly a non-Christian sect since they revere Jesus as a human being rather than as Christ,[24] and have labored for the last two centuries to present Jesus' message in harmony with the experience of history and science. The Unitarian belief is very old reaching back to the second century, since Tertullian—who first introduced the name *trinitas*—says that in his day (*ca.* 200), i.e., long before the Church became officially trinitarian, "the common people think of Christ as man," a position taken by the "Monarchians" of his day and, with modifications, by the followers of Arius at Nicaea and centuries later by the Socinians of Italy. As a definite movement in modern times Unitarianism may be said to have started with Servetus who was burned at the stake at the instigation of Calvin in 1553 for the heretical opinions expressed in his *De trinitatis erroribus* (1531 and 1532) and *Christianismi restitutio* (1553). In

[23] *God and Evil* (London, 1942), pp. 330–31.
[24] They are classified in the *United States Religious Census* as unevangelical, and generally as non-Christian by the Evangelical churches, definitely so in 1905 at the organization of the Federation of Christian Churches of America.

England between 1551 and 1612 nine persons were martyred for holding the belief in the unity of the godhead. The name "Unitarian" first appears, however, in a decree of the Diet of Transylvania in 1600 and Transylvanian churches officially used it instead of Arian by 1638. As a Church it began in England (*ca.* 1773) but the doctrine was first taught in the West Church of Boston in 1747 and was accepted by King's Chapel there in 1782. Joseph Priestly, the famous physicist who discovered oxygen, came to America in 1794 and organized the first two Unitarian churches in Pennsylvania, one at his home in Northumberland and the other in Philadelphia in 1796. Today the name is extended to mean all who stand for simple monotheism rather than tritheism.

Here is a religion without creed or official theology, possessing only statements of faith which are neither final nor authoritative, and without any doctrinal test for admission. The Unitarians assert that neither Jesus, the Apostles, nor the early Church were cramped by such restrictions, which they believe merely multiply persecutions and hamper free-thought. While differing in individual views collectively as an institution they assert that the Christian Church is a human institution and stands for the unipersonality of God the Father, the harmony of religion and reason, and complete freedom of thought. To them Jesus was not "conceived of the Holy Ghost and born of the Virgin Mary," which merely makes him another mythological figure so prominent in other ancient religions and an imaginary being of theologians, but a normal human being who differs from other men only in degree, one who taught men to worship God and not him. They renounce all theological speculation about him—his incarnation, deity, mediation, and the popular Pauline idea that he died as an atoning sacrifice for men, for he is a leader rather than a savior, nor do they think of salvation as a means of escaping the consequences of sin since a man must reap what he sows with no escape. They believe that inspiration has been confined to no period nor people but that revelation is progressive and that the Bible is merely its repository in the past, a sacred but not an infallibly inspired book. Nor do they deny value to other religions for they believe that God did not choose any one people as intermediary between him and us and so follow Symmachus' plea already quoted that "the Great Mystery cannot be approached by one road" alone. They show little interest in a hereafter, though professing to hope for it, but have little idea what or where it may be. They share with the Universalists—who arose in England in 1750 and in America in 1770—the conviction that hell, if it exists, is not eternal but that all finally will be saved. They believe further that the purpose of religion is not to prepare for a life to come, but to inspire mankind to live righteously here.

Still Unitarianism with its rational program though it has included many of our foremost Americans—twenty out of seventy-two in the New York University Hall of Fame—remains a small sect. In the United States it has only three hundred and fifty-two active churches and a membership of only sixty-three thousand six hundred and forty-nine or only one-tenth of one per cent of Protestantism,[25] and about the same number in England. If this be any indication—though these numbers include only professed Unitarians—of what rationalism may accomplish in Christianity with the warmth of emotionalism renounced—which led Lyman Beecher to call it "the icy system"—the outlook is not encouraging. It shows clearly that the belief that Jesus was the only begotten son of God sent here to save mankind cannot be taken from Christianity, for it has been its main attraction since the time of Paul. Still, many Christians both in and out of the Church agree that there is need now as never before of a reformation in Church beliefs whereby outworn Old World ideas of man, God, and the universe may be modified, puritanical opposition to intellectual progress be removed, and our lagging spiritual outlook be brought into harmony with our material advance.

FUTURE OF CHRISTIANITY

Since the Dantesque picture of life and the hereafter which epitomized the mental horizon of an era, followed by that of Milton, our outlook over the physical universe has vastly expanded. Ever since Copernicus just four centuries ago demonstrated scientifically the heliocentric explanation of our solar system there has been a tendency to throw off such ancient shackles and to conceive of God in terms worthy of the creator and ruler of a vast universe undreamed of in Jesus' day. For it was Copernicus' glory that he made the Sun the ruler of our system and the earth its satellite, the Sun whose vastness befits the dignity of a celestial ruler with a mass equal to three hundred and thirty-four thousand earths all in one, maintained in mysterious majesty at a mean distance of some ninety-three million miles. Today, however, we know that this, the central body of our system, is only one of the smallest of the myriads of suns which stud the sky even though, because of its relative proximity, it seems the largest; and that it wheels on its axis from west to east, the term of its rotation, as calculated from the spots which cross its surface and from spectroscopic observations, about twenty-five times that of the earth, and that, as Sir William Herschel showed in 1783, it is moving with great velocity through the heavens in a vast orbit.

All this has lowered man from his exalted position at the center of the universe so great that it requires four hours for light to reach Neptune and an incomprehensible time to reach the stars beyond, the nearest of which, Alpha Centauri, is four and three-tenths light years away, and light travels one hundred and eighty-three thousand three hundred and thirty miles or over seven times around the earth in a second! For it has reduced man to

[25] These data are taken from the *American Unitarian Year Book*, 1941–42. In *Builders of America*, by E. Huntington and L. F. Whiting (New York, 1927), there is a table (p. 195) of Unitarians listed in the then current *Who's Who in America* which shows that they headed the list of religionists with twelve hundred and eighty-eight insertions, followed by the Universalists with four hundred and eleven, Episcopalians with one hundred and seventy-four, and other denominations in a descending scale. See also G. W. Cooke, *Unitarianism in America: Its Origin and History* (Boston, 1902).

a mere speck of matter on a tiny fragment of an endless cosmic machine whose immutable motions go on forever. Copernicus' discoveries began to raise the question, whether man is, after all, the final aim of creation; whether the countless other suns have planetary systems similar to ours on which similar beings dwell; or whether our system may be, as recently suggested by Sir James Jeans, unique, an abnormality or freak, the result of an initial disruption caused by an accidental near-collision of another sun with ours which by its approach raised immense gaseous tides on the latter's surface out of which the planets became crystallized into matter, an occurrence which not one in many millions of suns might undergo.

Such questions remain and will remain unanswered, but they must affect our idea of God. Whether Christianity, still preached as in the time of Paul in the spirit of emotionalism and faith alone, can be transformed into a religion which meets the spirit of our enlightened age remains to be seen. Today men are more perplexed than ever by the mysteries of life and death which surround us. The advance of science accumulates doubts since it is dynamic while our religion remains almost static. But, however slow any change in the latter may be, we know that whenever in the past science and theology have clashed the former in the end was ever the victor. Thus a higher form of our religion, which neither its defenders nor assailants have yet visioned, must be in the making to bring it into harmony with the scientific trend of our day. Great numbers of the intelligentsia remain outside the Church and the number is increasing. Only by modernizing Church beliefs can we hope to bring them back again within its influence.

EXCURSUSES

Excursus I

THE ORIGIN OF CHRISTMAS

THE most widespread myth in Christendom is that of Christmas. Those who take the Bethlehem birth-story as history readily accept the traditional date of Christ's birthday.[1] But all branches of the Church agree that no data exist for determining the day, month, or year of the event, nor was such a festival celebrated in Apostolic or early post-Apostolic times. It does not appear in the festival lists of Tertullian or Irenaeus who both died in the early third century. The Nativity may have been celebrated in the early Eastern churches along with Epiphany on January sixth as it still is in the Armenian Church. There is evidence, however, that in the West December twenty-fifth was not accepted by the Church until the middle of the fourth century when it borrowed the *dies natalis invicti solis,* "birthday of the unconquered Sun," a festival long known to the ancient world from Mithraism. The change from January sixth (Epiphany) to December twenty-fifth (Christmas), if the two were originally celebrated together, was made in the pontificate of Liberius (352–366) in the reign of Constantius (337–361), specifically in 353.

Early Christian writers were interested more in the spiritual birth of Christ, i.e., his "manifestation to the Gentiles" or Epiphany, than in his corporeal birth though here again neither the day, month, nor year is known. Birthdays were not generally celebrated among Semites even if the older Israelites gave fantastic life-spans to many Old Testament characters which still excite our wonder. Keeping such holidays was rather an Aryan custom. Herodotus (1:133) says that it was the one day that every Persian honored most and it was celebrated by both Greeks and Romans, especially by the latter during the early Empire when the oft discredited *natalicia* (natal entertainments) are mentioned by various Augustan writers,[2] when patrons received gifts from their clients in honor of their "Genius." We learn from Josephus[3] that the Emperor Titus after the fall of Jerusalem celebrated the eighteenth birthday of his brother Domitian with great pomp when over twenty-five hundred Jewish captives were slain in fights with beasts or with one another, and that later at Berytus (Beirut) he celebrated the sixty-first birthday of his father with still greater pomp.

Uncertainty about Jesus' birthday in the early third century is reflected in a disputed passage of the presbyter Hippolytus, who was banished to Sardinia by Maximin in 235, and in an authentic statement of Clement of Alexandria. While the former favored January second, the learned Clem-

---

[1] Old English *Cristes maesse,* the earliest appearance of the name, in 1038.
[2] See Ovid *Tristia* 3:12, 2 and 5:5, 1; Martial *Epigr.* 8:64, 4; etc.
[3] *Jewish War* 7:3, 1 (37–40).

ent [4] of Alexandria enumerates several dates given by the Alexandrian chronographers, notably the twenty-fifth of the Egyptian month *Pachon* (May twentieth) in the twenty-eighth year of Augustus and the twenty-fourth or twenty-fifth of *Pharmuthi* (April eighteenth or nineteenth) of the year A.D. 1, although he favored May twentieth. This shows that no Church festival in honor of the day was established before the middle of the third century. Origen at that time in a sermon [5] denounced the idea of keeping Jesus' birthday like that of a Pharaoh and said that only sinners such as Herod were so honored. Arnobius later similarly ridiculed giving birthdays to "gods." [6] A Latin treatise, *De pascha computus* [7] (of *ca.* 243), placed Jesus' birth on March twenty-first since that was the supposed day on which God created the Sun (Gen. 1:14–19), thus typifying the "Sun of righteousness" as Malachi (4:2) called the expected Messiah. A century before Polycarp, martyred in Smyrna in 155, gave the same date for the birth and baptism placing it on a Wednesday because of the creation of the Sun on that day. [8]

The widely-held belief of the early Church that Jesus' baptism marked his spiritual birth when he was adopted as "Son of God" magnified Epiphany and caused indifference about his physical birth. [9] Clement (*l. c.*) tells us that the Alexandrian Gnostic Basilides, who lived in the reign of Hadrian (117–138), and his followers thus early celebrated the baptism—which they believed occurred in the fifteenth year of Tiberius, i.e., A.D. 28 on the eleventh or fifteenth of the month *Tybi* (January sixth or tenth), but we cannot say whether they celebrated the Nativity with it.

The first authentic record of December twenty-fifth as the "Festival of the Nativity" is found in the Roman Church calendar of Furius Dionysius Philocalus compiled in 353–354, though probably a rewriting of an older one of about 336. It begins with a civil calendar of pagan festivals, consuls and bishops, the latter from Peter to Liberius, and for December twenty-fifth gives *N[atalis] Invicti* (birthday of [Mithra] unconquered). In an accompanying *Martyrologium* or list of martyrs arranged according to the dates of their deaths we find at the head of the list the entry *Christus natus est VIII Kal. Jan.* (December twenty-fifth) in the consulship of Lentulus and Piso, i.e., 1 B.C., and his death *VIII Kal. Aprilis* (March twenty-fourth) in the consulship of Tiberius and Silvanus, i.e., A.D. 30. [10]

[4] *Stromateis* 1:21, 147; Migne, *Patrologia Graeca*, VIII, 88. Cited hereafter as *P.G.*

[5] In *Lev. hom.* VIII; *P.G.*, XII, 495.

[6] *Adversus nationes* 1–7 (beginning of the fourth century); 7:32; Migne, *Patrologia Latina*, V, 1264. Cited hereafter as *P.L.*

[7] *P.L.*, IV, 963f.

[8] Fragment of an Armenian treatise by Ananias of Shirak.

[9] The Feast of the Epiphany on January sixth commemorated Christ's baptism and the marriage at Cana where he performed his first miracle and, since the fifth century in the West, also the appearance of the Magi at Bethlehem, his first "manifestation" to the Gentiles.

[10] This calendar and one of Polemius Sylvius dating over a century later (448–449)—the latter a miscellany like a modern almanac—are published on facing pages in *C.I.L.*, I (1863), 334–57, *P.L.*, XIII, 675f. (*Martyrologium,* pp. 687f.); J. B. Lightfoot, "The Liberian Catalogue" in *The Apostolic Fathers* (2nd ed.; London and New York, 1890), I, 243f.

The extension of the new festival eastward was slow. Epiphanius of Cyprus at the close of the fourth century still maintained that January sixth was the "birthday" and November eighth the baptism of Christ,[11] and the contemporary converted Jew, Ephraem Syrus, who wrote hymns on Epiphany, says the birth-festival was thirteen days after the winter solstice or January sixth. After being approved by the Roman Church and Constantius in 353–354 we find it accepted by part of the church community of Antioch in 375–376 and by the rest of it, through the influence of a sermon delivered there by Chrysostom, ten years later; in Cappadocia by 383; at Constantinople, through the influence of Gregory Nazianzen, in 378–381; and in Alexandria between 400 and 432. At Jerusalem, a double festival, the birth by a procession to Bethlehem and the baptism by a procession to the Jordan, was celebrated January sixth at least until the middle of the sixth century, as we learn from Cosmas Indicopleustes, Egyptian monk and navigator (*P.G.*, LXXXVIII, 147). The Armenian Church has never accepted it but continues to celebrate both birth and baptism on January sixth oblivious, however, of the fact that this is also a pagan date when the sacred waters were blessed by the priests of both Osiris and Dionysus. While Valentinian II (375–392) in his list of holidays included Sunday and Easter [12] Honorius later extended the law by closing theaters and circuses also on Christmas and Epiphany [13] and Justinian in 534 forbade all toil on Christmas day.[14]

St. Chrysostom, in his sermon at Antioch on December 30, 385 (or 386) in which he exhorted all Antiochenes to accept the new date, said that December twenty-fifth in the West had been known "from Thrace to Cadiz from the beginning." While all agree, then, that the festival on December twenty-fifth passed from Rome to the East the learned world still differs about the history of both festivals in Rome and the East. While H. Usener [15] has maintained that the Festival of the Nativity was celebrated early both East and West on January sixth but was changed in Rome to December twenty-fifth under Liberius in 353–354, leaving Epiphany for January sixth, others, following L. Duchesne,[16] believe that January sixth was the Eastern date from the beginning and December twenty-fifth the Western, the two being later combined into one.

Many Christians opposed the mixing of the birthdays of the Sun (Mithra) and Jesus (Christ). Thus Tertullian [17] said that Sol was not the Christian God and Augustine [18] two centuries later called it "a diabolical doctrine" to identify the two and exhorted the Christians to celebrate

[11] *Panarion* 51:27; *P.G.*, XLI, 935.

[12] *C.Th.*, XI:8, 19.

[13] *C.Th.*, XV:5, 2; XI:8, 20, 23–25.

[14] *Cod. Just.* 3:12, 6.

[15] "Das Weihnachtsfest" in his *Religionsgeschichtliche Untersuchungen* (Bonn, 1889), pp. 1f.

[16] In his *Origines du culte chrétien* (3rd ed.; Paris, 1889), tr. by M. L. McLure as *Christian Worship: Its Origin and Evolution* (5th ed.; London, 1919).

[17] *Apol.* 10.

[18] *Tractatus* 34:2; *P.L.*, XXXV, 1652.

Christmas not because of the Sun but of Christ who made it. Leo the Great (440–461) in a sermon [19] denounced solar survivals, and the Armenians called the Romans "Sun-worshipers" in derision.

Thus there is ample evidence that the origin of Christmas is found in pagan heliolatry which, as we saw in chapter vii, culminated at Rome under Aurelian in 374. For centuries the ancients had mistaken December twenty-fifth for December twenty-first as the winter solstice (*bruma* in Latin) [20] a mistake perpetuated in the Julian calendar of 46 B.C. but corrected in the Gregorian of 1582. Mithraists and Northern sun-worshippers generally had used it as the birthday of the sun, i.e., the time when the days began to lengthen and the solar heat to increase. The Christian adoption of the date is only one of many examples of the Church custom already noted of tolerating and absorbing pagan customs as it spread over pagan lands. Contributing causes to the choice of December twenty-fifth are not difficult to find. Thus Constantine had named the Mithraic Sunday as a public holiday in 321 which the Church had already taken as its sacred day. This, along with the influence of the Manichaeans who identified the Sun with the "Son of God," helped the Christians to join the two and their birthdays. Moreover, on the belief that Gabriel's annunciation to Joseph occurred on March twenty-fifth, December twenty-fifth was felt to be an appropriate date for the birth of Christ.

Many pagan customs have survived in our Christmas-tide, Roman from the South and Teutonic from the North. Without doubt Christmas inherited its spirit of mirth and jollity from the great Roman festival of the *Saturnalia*. This was instituted, in popular belief, in honor of Saturn, an early divine king of Italy under whom Italy enjoyed a Golden Age of plenty, prosperity, and justice. It was held in December after the close of vintage and harvest, the prototype of the English "Harvest Home" and our "Thanksgiving," a period given over to pleasure, merriment, and license with special indulgences extended to slaves who, relieved of toil, could wear the *pilleus* or cap of freedom, enjoy license of speech, and sit at banquet in their masters' places as guests.[21] During the Republic it lasted one day only, December seventeenth, under Augustus three days (seventeenth to nineteenth), and under the later Empire seven (seventeenth to twenty-third). Certain features of it reappear in such customs as Christmas card-playing on Christmas eve, a reminiscence of gambling allowed by the Roman aediles, and in the exchange of presents. But most of the features of the *Saturnalia* have descended rather to the Italian carnival—popularly from Latin *carne vale* (farewell, meat)—held during the three or four days before

---

[19] 27:4; *P.L.*, LIV, 218.

[20] For *brevima*, cf. *brevissimus dies*, Lucretius 5:746, and Varro *De lingua latina* 6:8. The solstice festival, *Brumalia,* is mentioned by Philocalus and Sylvius as celebrated on November twenty-fourth but it seems to have culminated on December twenty-fifth; Servius *Comm. in Georg.* (of Vergil) 1:2, and see *C.I.L.*, 1, 2; 287.

[21] Described by Macrobius, fourth-century grammarian, in his *Saturnalia* 1–7, a discussion held (during the festival) on myth and history, supposedly at the house of Vettius Praetextatus.

Lent, and its offshoots elsewhere. Some of the inherited features are its mimicry and mummery, masquerading and feasting, its use of the conical fools' cap (*pilleus*), and of confetti (originally grains of wheat and barley). Even the *cerei* or wax-tapers given to the wealthy Roman patron by his poorer clients are retained in the *moccoletti* of the Roman carnival. The exchange of presents—*strenae* (cf. French *étrennes*)—as "omens" at New Years reappear in Christmas presents which Tertullian called "idolatrous." [22]

Apart, however, from the jollification and presents most of the features of our Christmas have a northern origin especially in the ancient Yule feast known to us from Icelandic sagas and early Anglo-Saxon celebrations. [23] Procopius, sixth-century Byzantine historian, mentions a festival on Thule—an isle north of Scotland discovered by Pytheas of Massilia near the middle of the fourth century B.C.—in honor of the return of the Sun; [24] and still later the Venerable Bede in describing one in England says: [25]

The ancient peoples of the Angli [i.e. before their conversion in 597] began the year on December 25 when we now celebrate the birthday of the Lord; and the very night which is now so holy to us, they called in their tongue *Modranecht* . . . by reason, we suspect, of the ceremonies which in that night-long vigil they performed.

The Icelandic sagas tell of the *Julblot,* a mid-winter sacrifice for good crops and prosperity in honor of Frey, Scandinavian god of fertility, sunshine, and prosperity. The Teutons added the belief that during Yuletide people were menaced by demons of the air and of the lower world who then roamed about. [26] Houses were cleaned, baking and brewing done and in Sweden a table was set for such nocturnal visitors when the family was at church. In England churches and houses are decked with mistletoe (*visum album*), a ceremonial plant believed by the Celtic Druids, if found hanging to oak-trees, to have magical powers of healing, of which our custom of "kissing" beneath a sprig of it is a survival.

In Germany evergreen branches were first used as decorations out of which the *Weichnachtsbaum* or "Christmas Tree" was developed. The latter is first mentioned at Strasbourg in 1605 but became general in the eighteenth century over German lands and reached Scandinavia in the nine-

[22] *De idolatria* 14. *Strenae* are frequently mentioned by Suetonius in his *Lives* (e.g. Augustus 57; Tiberius 34; Caligula 42). Cf. the old essay of J. P. Thompson, "Christmas and the Saturnalia," *Bibl. Sacra,* XII (1855), 144f.

[23] The origin of the word "Yule" is uncertain but it is connected with old Norse *jol,* Icelandic *iol* (a December festival), Anglo-Saxon *geol,* and English "jolly." Bede in *De temporum ratione,* 4, derived it from *Giuli,* a corruption of the names of the two successive months one before the other after the solstice meaning "rejoicing at the year's end."

[24] *Gothic War* (of Justinian) 6:15, 14.

[25] *Op. cit.* 13.

[26] This idea survives in the festival of All Souls on November second, on which night the souls not yet purified at death can be helped by the prayers of the faithful on earth, *Commemoratio omnium fidelium defunctorum,* first observed by Odilo, abbot of Cluny, in the eleventh century and later by the Church, now revived in Anglo-Catholic and Continental Protestant churches.

teenth.   Princess Helene of Mecklenburg is said to have introduced it into France in 1840 and Albert, Prince Consort of Victoria, into England the same year.   This was also the year when the custom of sending Christmas greeting-cards arose in England, a custom brought to America in 1842. Such greetings had their origin in the ancient custom seen on papyrus letters from Graeco-Roman Egypt.   Paul used them in his letters, e.g. "Grace to you and peace from God the Father."   It was also a Roman custom for we find such greetings as *si valetis gaudeo* and the abbreviation *S.D.* (*Salutem dixit*) and many similar ones in Cicero's letters.   The Christmas tree reached America earlier than England or France having been brought here by the Moravian religious sect from Moravia, Bohemia, and eastern Germany.   At first only evergreen boughs were used as decorations (*Putz*) as in earlier Germany, but later the whole tree was brought indoors.   The first Moravian Christmas Eve celebration was held at Bethlehem, Pennsylvania, December 24, 1741 in a log building which is still standing.[27]

Another more recent addition to Christmas is Santa Claus, the popular form of the name of the semi-legendary St. Nicholas whose cult is now widespread both East and West, but whose history is obscure.   He is supposed to have been a bishop of Myra in Lycia in faraway Asia Minor who was imprisoned and tortured under Diocletian at the beginning of the fourth century.   He has become patron saint of Russia and protector of virgins, children, sailors, merchants, and even robbers.   His day, December sixth, was long celebrated in the Low Countries and along the Rhine, in Belgium and Holland, the sixth, rather than the twenty-fifth, is the real day of jollity.   His bones were brought to Bari in South Italy in the eleventh century where his tomb became the center of popular pilgrimages. During the past two centuries his customs have become merged in those of Christmas.   Dutch colonists brought them to New York—Santa Claus being the American corruption of the Dutch form of St. Nicholas—especially his character of gift-bearer to children which is now transferred to Christmas.[28]

In 1644 English Puritans protested against Christmas jollity and caused Parliament to make Christmas a fast and market day when shops were open.   Christmas delicacies such as mince pies and plum puddings were condemned as well as the "wassail bowl" from whose beverage—a concoction of ale, sugar and spices—healths were drunk.   The protest caused some bloodshed but at the Restoration Charles II revived the merriment although some Scotch dissenters still call Yule-tide "Fools'-tide."   Today Christmas is the most joyous Church festival bringing "good tidings of great joy" along with its ancient customs to all Christian lands including Jews and non-church-goers, a welcome relief from the general somberness of Christianity.

[27] See George E. Nitzsche, "The Christmas Putz of the Pennsylvania Germans," *Penna. German Folklore Society Magazine,* VI (1942).

[28] On coming to America his white horse, on which he rode over the housetops and showered gifts down the chimneys, was exchanged for reindeer as we see in the popular poem of Clement Moore, "'Twas the Night before Christmas" written in 1822, in which he makes St. Nick a jolly elf who rides "in a miniature sleigh drawn by eight tiny reindeer."

Nor can we recover the year of Jesus' birth beyond the general impression that it took place near the close of Herod's reign. Most Christians erroneously believe that the Christian era starts with his birth. This idea was the result of a work of the Scythian abbot, Dionysius Exiguus (the "Little," either because of his stature or humility), which he composed in Rome in the early sixth century, the *Cyclus paschalis* or "Easter-table" in which in 532 he added five years to the ninety-five-year table arranged by Cyril of Alexandria in 436. Thus, he introduced into the Roman Church the Alexandrian Easter computation which had been used in the East since Nicaea. He numbered the years not from the era of Diocletian (284) the "persecutor" but from the "Incarnation of the Lord" which he dated with others March twenty-fifth and his birth, therefore, December twenty-fifth of the Roman year 754 A.U.C.,[29] i.e., 1 B.C. The era made its way slowly after its unofficial acceptance in Rome and Italy in 533, reaching Gaul at the end of the century and England in the eighth and came into general use under the Carolingians in the latter century. Charlemagne was the first king to adopt it and Adrian I the first Pope (in 781). Dionysius based his reckoning on two passages of Eusebius [30] who, in turn, based his on the Gospels: in one case having Jesus born in Bethlehem in the forty-second year of Augustus, i.e., 1 B.C. (dating from the latter's first consulship in 43 B.C.) when Eusebius wrongly says Quirinius made his census, and in the other when Jesus was "beginning to be about thirty years old" which brought his birth also to Augustus' forty-second year. The following year was the *annus Domini*—the beginning of our era. Clement of Alexandria had already given the same date [31] but his predecessors Irenaeus and Tertullian had placed the birth in 751 A.U.C., i.e., 3 B.C.[32] Neither date can be reconciled with Matthew who says (2:1) that Jesus was born in Herod's reign, and the census of Quirinius placed it in a worse plight than the Gospels had done.

Rationalizing attempts have been made to subject the "Star of Bethlehem," which Matthew (2:9) says guided the Magi to Bethlehem at Herod's command, to astronomical conditions but these have yielded nothing. Because of its evident brightness some have referred the star to certain planetary conjunctions, notably to that of Jupiter and Saturn in Pisces on June 28, 7 B.C., or to a greater one of these with Mars in Aries a year later. Such an attempt fails, if for no other reason, because the approach of two or three planets would not have been near enough to mistake them for one with the naked eye. Others have conjectured that the "Star" was a new one which appeared in the sky at Jesus' birth. Since the discovery of Tycho Brahe's *Nova Cassiopeiae,* November 11, 1572, which then flared into brilliancy and vanished eighteen months later,[33] the suggestion has

[29] Although many dates were assigned by Roman writers to the foundation of Rome, 753 B.C. became the conventional one.

[30] *H.E.* 1:5, 1 and 1:10, 1.

[31] *Stromateis* 1.

[32] Irenaeus *Adv. haer.* 3:25; Tertullian *Adv. Judaeos* 8.

[33] *De nova stella* (Copenhagen, 1572; facsimile, 1901).

been made that it may have been a variable over a long period, even though for long afterwards no star appeared in that vicinity exceeding the twelfth or thirteenth magnitude. In the middle of the thirteenth century a bright star was also reported in that part of the heavens which, combined with a vague notice of a similar appearance three centuries before, led some to connect it with the star of 1572, the interval between them being about three hundred and ten to three hundred and fifteen years. According to such reckoning five such intervals backward might reach near to the birth of Jesus, in one case to 3 B.C. Kepler observed a bright new star September 30, 1604, which remained visible for seventeen months [34] and he wrote articles about 1613 to show that Jesus' birth took place about March, 6 B.C.

It is a well-known phenomenon that bright stars temporarily flame as the result, perhaps, of collisions but all such data are too indefinite for the drawing of historical conclusions. It is curious how the myth of the "Star of Bethlehem" still holds our attention, since as late as February 19, 1942, at a Conference held in Pueblo, Mexico, Dr. Cecilia H. Payne-Gaposhkin of Harvard University explained it as, possibly, such a *nova*. But for such a "star" to move (Matt. 2:9) "till it came and stood over where the young child was" is obviously too absurd to connect it with any star. Thus the "Star of Bethlehem" is in the same category as the story of Joshua at Jericho in the Old Testament.

St. Jerome [35] speaks of a grove of Adonis in Bethlehem; and Ammianus (22:9–14) says a bright star appeared over Antioch to greet the Emperor Julian when he passed through the Syrian capital in 363 on his way to Mesopotamia. This may have been merely the "morning star" Venus whose rising was the signal for opening the festival of Adonis. If, then, we insist on a historical background for the "Star of Bethlehem" it may have been Venus which guided the Magi to Bethlehem which, though not the birthplace of Jesus, was a center of the Phoenician cult of Adonis.[36]

---

[34] *De stella nova in pede Serpentarii* (Prague, 1606). The "Serpent" was once part of the ancient constellation Ophiucus, but is now separate.

[35] *Ep.* LVIII, 3; *P.L.*, XXII, 581; cf. Sir J. G. Frazer, *Adonis, Attis and Osiris*, p. 215.

[36] On Christmas, see K. Lake, *E.R.E.*, III (1910), 601–08, and E. Lehmann on Christmas customs, *ibid.*, III, 608–10; G. N. Newman in Schaff-Herzog, *op. cit.*, III (1909), 47–48; C. Martindale in *Catholic Encyclopaedia*, I (1908), 325–28; R. H. Schauffler, *Christmas, its Origin, Celebration and Significance* (New York, 1907).

Excursus II

SUNDAY OBSERVANCE

ONE of the examples noted in the text to show Jesus' rebellion against the ritualism of Judaism and the idea that the law was an end in itself was his opposition to the rigorous observance of the Sabbath. On one occasion (John 5:18) he ran the risk of losing his life at the hands of the enraged Jews on that account and he stressed his protest by saying (Mark 2:27-28): "The sabbath was made for man, and not man for the sabbath: so that the Son of man is lord even of the sabbath."

Little can be adduced from the New Testament to show any worship of the Sabbath and little for that of Sunday with which today it is often confused. While Sunday as a day of worship arose in Paul's churches the Jewish tendency toward keeping the Sabbath gradually became a sign of Judaizing like circumcision. This we see in Paul's words (Col. 2:16): "Let no man therefore judge you . . . or in respect of a feast day . . . or a sabbath day," and in the words of Ignatius.[1] Modern Christians who talk of keeping Sunday as a "holy" day, as in the still extant "Blue Laws" of colonial America, should know that as a "holy" day of rest and cessation from labor and amusements Sunday was unknown to Jesus and that Paul regarded it as merely a convenient day for Christian meetings. It formed no tenet of the primitive Church and became "sacred" only in course of time. Outside the Church its observance was legalized for the Roman Empire through a series of decrees starting with the famous one of Constantine in 321, an edict due to his political and social policies rather than, as Eusebius thought,[2] to religious ones. For he took the day not because of the Christian custom of meeting then to commemorate the Resurrection but from "the venerable day of the Sun" (Mithra), and especially in order to give to Roman slaves respite from labor which their Semitic brothers had enjoyed for centuries. So much confusion in identifying Sunday and the Sabbath has been inherited by Britain and America through Puritan influence that it seems well to recapitulate the well-known facts.

In the primitive Church the Christians naturally regarded all days alike as belonging to the Lord. Origen says [3] "to the perfect Christian all days are the Lord's," and St. Chrysostom over a century later said "the entire time is a festival with Christians because of the excellency of the good things which have been ours." Still later the Church historian Socrates remarks that "the Apostles had no thought of appointing festival days, only of promoting a life of blessedness and piety." But as the Jewish element in the Church waned the Christians came to feel the need of a fixed day for

[1] In his letter to the Magnesians (4). Composed 110–117.
[2] *Life of Constantine*, 4:18–21.
[3] *Contra Celsum* 8:22; *P.G.*, 11, 1550.

meetings to replace the Sabbath. Then Sunday, like other pagan festivals such as Christmas, came gradually into being, first as a fit day for worship and later one for rest.

We preface our account of Sunday with the Old-Testament attitude toward the Sabbath. When the Israelites reached Canaan they found there the Babylonian week,[4] which originally was an astrological invention, and stressed its seventh day as particularly appropriate, the Hebrew *Shabath*, "day of rest," which was incorporated into the Decalog (Exod. 20:8).[5] We meet "the seventh day" first in Genesis (2:3) as the day on which Yahweh rested at the close of creation. In early days it was so strictly observed by the Israelites that no work could be done, not even a fire be kindled on pain of death (Exod. 35:2, 3; cf. 31:4).[6] The prophets Ezekiel (23:38) and Deutero-Isaiah (56:2) denounced its profanation and Nehemiah, part restorer of the national faith after becoming Persian governor of Judaea in 444 (13:15–19), did likewise. After the Captivity it was regarded as unlawful to engage an enemy on the Sabbath, a scruple which cost the Jews dearly in the time of the Maccabees (I Macc. 2:34–38) and against the Romans who took advantage of the taboo at the sieges of Jerusalem by Pompey in 63 B.C. and by Titus in A.D. 70. During the Empire, however, the Jews found their scruple convenient in obtaining exemption from military service.

By Jesus' time the Jews were keeping the ancient day as a definite sign of their nationality. By then the scribes had formulated thirty-nine rules listing what sorts of labor were prohibited on that day. Thus, according to the rabbinical view, when the disciples plucked ears of corn on the Sabbath (Matt. 12:1; Mark 2:23; Luke 6:1) they violated rule No. 3; and when Jesus healed the sick man, in the chapter of John cited above (5:5–10), he broke another according to which no sick person should receive medical aid unless his life were in danger. But Jesus omitted the Fourth Commandment and Paul was also silent about its observance since he did not denounce its violators and followed Jesus in omitting it in his list of commandments (Rom. 13:9). He evidently regarded the observance of the Sabbath as a superstition. Thus his churches renounced the Sabbath and used it merely for preaching to Jews and Greeks (Acts 18:4). The Ebionites, who meticulously accepted the written law, observed both the Sabbath like other Jewish customs and also Sunday, the latter on which to commemorate the Resurrection.[7] Socrates says (6:8) that in the time of Theodosius II (408–450)

[4] Archaeological discoveries in Northern Babylonia have shown that the Akkadians, long before the time of Abraham, had divided time into weeks of seven days named from the Sun, Moon and five known planets. On the seventh day, *Sabatu* (rest day), all labor was unlawful.

[5] Its present form goes back, perhaps, to the Exile though a simpler one had existed long before.

[6] In Numbers (15:32–36), a man found gathering sticks in the wilderness on the Sabbath was brought before Moses and Aaron, imprisoned, and later, at the Lord's command, slain.

[7] Eusebius *H.E.* 3:27, 5.

churches at Constantinople worshiped both days. Curiously, today business houses there, such as banks, are closed three days a week, on Saturday for the Jews, Sunday for the Christians, and Monday for the Moslems.

As for the new day Sunday in the New Testament Paul (I Cor. 16:2) urged the Corinthians to set aside funds for charity "upon the first day of the week." In Acts (20:7) he is represented as preaching at Troas "upon the first day of the week, when we were gathered together to break bread," words which seem to point to a customary day for communion thus early. The Fourth Gospel (20:19 and 26) represents Jesus as reappearing to his friends on "the first day of the week" and "after eight days" respectively. In Revelation (1:10) we first hear Sunday called "the Lord's day"—in Greek *Kyriaké*. The Pauline author of Hebrews (10:25) speaks of "not forsaking the assembling of ourselves together, as the custom of some is," words which may refer to Sunday. Thus by later Apostolic times the custom of meeting on a fixed day for Christian worship had developed, Sunday being regarded as the best because it commemorated the Resurrection—as we may see from the apocryphal Epistle of Barnabas (15) of the end of the first century where we read "we keep the eighth day for rejoicing in which Jesus also rose from the dead"—and also because it was the day on which God started creation (Gen. 1:1–5).

The idea of the Christians meeting on a "fixed day" (*die stato*) first appears explicitly in a pagan writer, Pliny, in his letter to Trajan and then a little later in the letter of Ignatius, bishop of Antioch martyred under Trajan. Here Ignatius contrasted "the Lord's Day" with the Sabbath since he speaks of the converts from Judaism as "no longer observing Sabbaths, but fashioning their lives after the Lord's Day on which our life also rose through him." In the second-century *Didaché* (14) Christians are advised: "On the Lord's own day gather yourselves together and break bread and give thanks." Justin Martyr who died about 163 is the first churchman to mention "the day of the Sun" and the Sabbath together,[8] and in the same century St. Dionysius of Corinth in a letter to Bishop Soter (168–176) of Rome says: "Truly we observed the holy day of the Lord and read out your letter."[9] About the same time, in the reign of Marcus Aurelius, Melito, bishop of Sardis,[10] wrote a treatise "On the Lord's Day," which unfortunately is lost.

Irenaeus,[11] who says that the Jews did away with the Sabbath, is the first to refer to the tendency toward making Sunday a day of rest rather than of Christian worship since he says the Church forbade harvesting that day; and Tertullian[12] advised Christians to abstain from all labor of anxiety on the Lord's Day, even business, and again[13] first *called* Sunday a day

[8] *Apol.* 1:67.
[9] Quoted by Eusebius *H.E.* 4:25, 11.
[10] Eusebius *ibid.* 4:26, 2.
[11] In his *Adv. haereses.*
[12] *Ad Judaeos* (composed after 208).
[13] *Ad nationes* 1:13; cf. *Apol.* 16.

of rest, i.e. a holy day, although the Church did not sanction the idea as yet that it in any way replaced the Sabbath. Thus by the close of the second and the beginning of the third century Sunday as a day of rest had replaced it as a day of worship.

We are indebted to Justin Martyr (*l. c.*) for our earliest description of a Church service at Rome "on the day of the Sun." While earlier meetings had been short to accommodate slaves and the poor by his time they lasted two hours:

And on the day called Sunday, all who live in cities or in the country gather together to one place, and the memoirs of the apostles or the writings of the prophets are read, as long a time as time permits; then, when the reader has ceased, the president verbally instructs [i.e., the sermon], and exhorts to the imitation of these good things. Then [beginning the second part of the service] we all rise together and pray, and, as we before said, when our prayer is ended, bread and wine and water are brought, and the president in like manner offers prayers and thanksgiving, according to his ability, and the people assent, saying amen; and there is a distribution to each and a participation of that over which thanks have been given, and to those who are absent a portion is sent by the deacons. . . .

But Sunday is the day on which we all hold our common assembly, because it is the first day on which God, having wrought a change in the darkness and matter, made the world; and Jesus Christ our Savior on the same day rose from the dead. For he was crucified on the day before that of Saturn [a circumlocution for Friday, *dies Veneris,* as Justin being a Christian abhorred the pagan Venus]: and on the day after that of Saturn, which is the day of the sun [Sunday] having appeared to his apostles and disciples. . . .

Here Justin naturally uses *dies solis* rather than *dies dominica* for Sunday, for the latter was used generally only after the Empire became Christian.[14] At the Council of Illiberri (Elvira in Spain) at the beginning of the fourth century the Lord's day was first made compulsory for Church attendance, the penalty for remaining away on three successive Sundays being excommunication.

Parallel to the Church movement outlined but independent of it another had been developing in the State which after an obscure past culminated in Constantine's decree of 321 when the observance of the "day of the Sun" was imposed on the Empire, a decree marking an epoch in the history of Sunday as the beginning of both civil and later of ecclesiastical legislation. Now *dies Solis,* sacred in various solar cults and notably in Mithraism, was to play a role as the Christian Sunday as Christmas did a little later. We quote the edict:

All judges and city-people and all tradesmen must rest upon the venerable day of the Sun, but let those dwelling in the country freely and with full liberty attend to the culture of their fields, since it frequently happens that no other day is so fit

[14] The Greek Church still uses "Lord's Day" (*Kyriaké*), but Western Churches use derivatives of *dies dominica* (e.g. French, *Dimanche;* Italian, *Domenica*), while in Teutonic lands and England, Sunday is still used.

for the sowing of grain or planting of vines.   Hence the favorable time should not be allowed to pass lest the provisions of heaven be lost.[15]

This is the "parent" Sunday law making it a day of rest and release from labor.   For from this day to the present there have been decrees about the observance of Sunday which have profoundly influenced European and American society.   When the Church became a part of State under the Christian emperors Sunday observance was enforced by civil statutes and later, when the Empire was past, the Church in the hands of the papacy enforced it by ecclesiastical, and also influenced it by civil enactments. The emperors after Constantine made Sunday observance more stringent but in no case was their legislation based on the Old Testament.   For Augustine said: "the Sabbath signifies rest, Sunday the Resurrection." Many such decrees are found in Justinian's code of 534—laws providing for manumission of slaves on Sunday, cessation of business and amusements, and even the Emperor's birthday if it fell on a Sunday had to be postponed. At the Third Synod of Aureliani (Orléans) in 538 rural work was forbidden but the restriction against preparing meals and similar work on Sunday was regarded as a superstition.   After Justinian's death in 565 various *epistolae decretales* were passed by the popes about Sunday.   One of Gregory I (590–604) forbade men "to yoke oxen or to perform any other work, except for approved reasons," while another of Gregory II (715–731) said: "We decree that all Sundays be observed from vespers to vespers and that all unlawful work be abstained from." [16]   He thus exempted necessary labor such as concerned perishable goods and then only if part of the profit from its sale were given to the Church for charity.

Charlemagne at Aquisgranum (Aachen) in 788 decreed that all ordinary labor on the Lord's Day be forbidden since it was against the Fourth Commandment, especially labor in the field or vineyard which Constantine had exempted.   Thus there could be no ploughing, reaping, grass-cutting, fence-setting, tree-felling or root-digging, and all quarriers, house-builders, gardeners, and hunters must attend Church, and the use only of sacred vessels and provisions, and the holding of burials were allowed on Sunday. Moreover, women could not sew, weave, embroider, spin or beat flax, wash clothes or sheep on that day, for all must go to mass and praise God.[17]   In 813 as emperor he decreed that "all servile labor must be abstained from." From his time onward, then, the idea of substituting Sunday for the Sabbath began, for all his decrees were based on the Old Testament command to keep the Sabbath day holy, and throughout the succeeding Middle Ages the Old Testament became the basis for Sunday observance.   In the Eastern Empire Leo III "the Isaurian" (717–740) and Leo VI "the Sage" (886–911) also prohibited agricultural labor on Sunday, the latter by a statute (No.

[15] *Cod. Justin.* Bk. III, Tit. XII, 3 (*de feriis*); text and tr. in P. Schaff, *History of the Christian Church* (New York, 1888–1910), III, 380, n. 1.

[16] From the beginning to the seventeenth century Sunday, like the Sabbath, extended from sundown to sundown but since then from midnight to midnight.

[17] From J. I. Mombert, *A History of Charles the Great* (New York, 1888), p. 319.

LIV) which thus, like the statutes of Charlemagne, abolished Constantine's exemptions. But the Church neither then nor since has ever identified officially Sunday and the Sabbath but has merely quoted the Fourth Commandment as sanctioning that a day of rest and relaxation from work should be kept each week.

The Reformers of the sixteenth century, though they believed in the Old Testament, were nevertheless, on the basis of the teachings of Jesus and Paul, against rigid Sunday observance. Luther (1483–1546) as we see from his *Table Talk* denounced those who kept Sunday as a "holy day" and advised people rather to feast and dance on that day, a custom still kept up in Germany. Zwingli, his Swiss contemporary (1484–1531), said: "It is lawful on the Lord's Day after the divine service for any man to push his labors." In Luther's *Larger Catechism* he taught that one day was no better than any other, but that it was well that one be set aside and for convenience's sake this should be Sunday. Melanchthon protested against the "Sabbath superstition." [18] Thus the Reformation stood for the original idea of Sunday rather than for the Sabbath.

But the Scotch Calvinists and other Puritan sects [19] because of their strict adherence to the Old Testament returned to the idea of the Jewish Sabbath. Their repression culminated in a book written by a Scotch clergyman,[20] in which he claimed for Sunday all the authority of the Sabbath, a thesis which started a century of empty controversy. The first reply to it was the *Book of Sports for Sunday* issued by James I in 1617 and republished by Charles I in 1633. Here we read that: "no lawful recreation shall be barred to my good people which does not tend to the breach of the laws of my kingdom and the established canons." It lists dancing, archery, leaping, vaulting, Whitsun ales, May Poles, and games, and bars only bull- and bear-baiting and bowling. But in 1625 a law forbade people to leave their parish on Sunday in quest of amusements and in 1644 James' book was burned by Parliament and the Puritan Sunday was again in force. Still later acts barred all Sunday pleasures, even walking, but these were revoked by Charles II.

However, in 1676, Puritan ascendancy again appeared in a law, the most severe of its kind in England, which forbade tradesmen, artisans and laborers to carry on business on Sunday under penalty of a fine or, on its default, of two hours in the public stocks. This law has never been repealed and so remains the law of England although its provisions have been modified since to obviate inconvenience, notably by the law of 1871 which forbade prosecution on the ground of the original penalties but with serious restrictions.

The law of 1676 was the general law of the American colonies down to the Revolution for it formed the basis of all subsequent colonial Sunday

[18] In article 28 of the *Augsburg Confession* of June 25, 1530—whose "unaltered" form containing Luther's ideas became the creed of the Lutheran Church.

[19] The name "Puritan" was first used of themselves by the Anabaptists in 1564.

[20] Nicholas Bound's *Sabbathum Veteris et Novi Testamenti* published in 1595.

laws. The first one was passed by Virginia in 1617 whereby the penalty for failure to keep Sunday sacred and to attend Church was a tobacco fine. Later the United States became the first of all countries to separate completely Church and State through the influence of Thomas Jefferson and so no general law has been passed to regulate Sunday observance since religious liberty is the main safeguard of the Constitution. Therefore such restrictions were made by the individual states. The first Sunday law after the Revolution was passed by New York in 1788 and Pennsylvania passed one in 1794. The latter, only after repeated attempts, since the power of the clergy's opposition is so strong, was partly repealed in 1933.[21]

On the continent of Europe today there is great freedom in reference to Sunday observance in strong contrast with America and Britain, and especially Scotland where even restaurants are closed. The refusal here of churchgoers to work or play on that day—or let others do so—is amazing in view of the history of Sunday as here outlined. Clergymen do not hesitate to read the Mosaic commandment to their congregations though they must know that Jesus abolished the Jewish Sabbath and knew nothing of Sunday. This is another example of the influence still exerted over the Christian Church by the Old Testament.

Constantine's law did much good in its own and later Roman times for it helped the slaves and the poor. Curiously, while Christians were ready thus early to follow his decree about Sunday, which mitigated the evils of slavery, they neither then, when slaves could be tortured without redress, nor since have ever as a body raised an effective protest against slavery, the great blot on ancient civilization extended into the nineteenth century. The Old Testament had inculcated kindness to bondsmen (Deut. 15:12f.; 23:15–16), but the beautiful sentiment which can be read on our Liberty Bell, "Proclaim liberty throughout all the land unto all the inhabitants thereof," in its context (Lev. 25:10) was no call to liberty in any general sense but merely the freeing of slaves in "the fiftieth year" of jubilee. The pre-Christian Essenes and the Theraputae of Alexandria, perhaps a branch of the former,[22] a radical offshoot of pre-Christian Judaism prominent in the first century, stand alone in civilized antiquity in refusing to keep slaves. While the early Church regarded slaves as *spiritu fratres religione conservi*—"brothers in spirit, fellow-slaves in religion"—to use Lactantius' phrase—and held manumission a holy act, it made no effort to extirpate the evil. In the Middle Ages the Church tried to free Christian slaves from the Moslems and to improve the condition of negro ones who had been introduced into Europe by the Portuguese in 1442, a traffic later sponsored by Pope Paul III (1534–49) who confirmed the right of both clergy and laity to own them. It is to the honor of the Pennsylvania Quakers who, urged on by humanitarian and religious motives, were able first to prohibit the slave-trade from their state in 1696. In the following century

---

[21] Since that date certain amusements such as baseball and, in 1937, moving pictures have been allowed during certain hours. Still, there is no dispensation of liquor, not even of beer, allowed on Sunday in America's second largest commonwealth.

[22] Described by Philo alone in his *De vita contemplativa*.

the British House of Commons rejected the plea of David Hartley (who died in 1757) "that the slave-trade is contrary to the laws of God and the rights of man." Here again it was the English Quakers who formed the first anti-slavery Society in 1783 which, in conjunction with others formed later, was the prelude to the emancipation of slaves which began in Denmark in 1792 and ended in the United States when President Lincoln in 1862 proclaimed, in the midst of a civil war, that the slaves "are and henceforward shall be free." [23]

[23] On Sunday, see M. J. Glazebroock in Hasting's *E.R.E.*, III (1925), 103–11; R. E. Prime, "Sunday Legislation," in Schaff-Herzog, *op. cit.*, XI (1911), 146–151; W. L. Wardle in *Encycl. Britannica* (11th ed.), XIX, 787–89.

WAS ST. PETER IN ROME?

ONE of the most widely-extended and, to judge from the results of its acceptance, most important traditions of the early Church is that the Apostle Peter sometime after his miraculous escape from prison in Jerusalem (Acts 12:1–19) during the persecution of Herod Agrippa I, last native king of Judaea (41–44), went to Rome where he collaborated with Paul in founding the Church which still bears his name, acted as its first bishop and died a martyr's death on a cross under Nero. While most Protestant scholars have denied the tradition (with the Reformation its denial became almost a dogma) the Roman Church has ever thrown the weight of its authority into its acceptance. Thus J. P. Kirsch has called the Roman sojourn "an indisputably established historical fact," though how long or when Peter was there or the date of his death is admittedly unknown.[1] On the other hand, P. W. Schmiedel sums up his detailed study of the problem by affirming that on the basis of the New Testament, the Church Fathers, and the *Acta Petri,* "our decision must therefore decidedly be that Peter never was in Rome at all"[2] and that the belief in Church circles began only about 160–170 in connection with Peter's supposed controversies with Simon Magus who was supposed to have been in Rome.

After his escape from prison Peter left Jerusalem and "went to another place" (Acts 12:17) but his final appearance in Acts (15:7–11) connects him years later with the first "Apostolic Council" at Jerusalem in 51 or 52 where with Paul he championed a liberal policy toward the Gentiles. Of his life thereafter we are in almost complete darkness beyond his ministry recounted in the disputed I Peter and the Roman tradition which formed around him, and which continuously accumulated unhistorical details even if it may have contained a germ of truth. The tradition of his Roman sojourn is well-known having been worked out by many scholars, both Catholic and Protestant, and may be repeated here in barest outline.

The first certain mention of it is by Dionysius, Bishop of Corinth (*ca.* 170). In a letter addressed to the Roman Church in the time of Bishop Soter (166–174) thanking it for aid he says: "You bound together the foundations of the Romans and Corinthians by Peter and Paul, for both of them taught together in our Corinth and were our founders, and together also taught in Italy in the same place [Rome] and were martyred at the same time."[3] This statement about founding the Corinthian Church is

[1] *Catholic Encyclopedia* (New York, 1911), II, 748.
[2] *Encyclopedia Biblica* (New York and London), IV (1903), 4608 (Analysis, pp. 4589–4627B), "Life Outside Palestine; and Death."
[3] Quoted by Eusebius *H.E.* 2:25, 8.

irreconcilable with the accounts in Acts (18:1–18) and I Cor. (3:10–15 and 4:15), and evidently rests upon Paul's saying (*ibid.* 1:12 and 3:22) that there was a "Cephas" party there. A better witness is Irenaeus, bishop of Lugdunum in Gaul (177f.), who speaks of the church "founded and constituted at Rome by the two very glorious apostles Peter and Paul," and again says that the "Apostolic succession has been preserved continuously by those [faithful men] who exist everywhere." [4] Here the Greek text ends and the Latin is in dispute. He names the bishops down to Eleutherus in his day (174–186) and adds that Mark was interpreter to Peter which agrees with the statement in I Peter (5:13) where the unknown author mentions "Mark, my son."

Near the close of the century Clement of Alexandria, then head of the catechetical school there (190–203), in connection with the composition of Mark's Gospel in his *Hypotyposes* or accounts of the canonical Scriptures, states, on the basis of being told by "older presbyters," that "after Peter had publicly preached the word at Rome . . . Mark . . . set down these discourses in writing." [5] At the close of the same century the apocryphal *Acta Petri* and the almost contemporaneous *Acta Petri et Pauli* also tell the story of Peter's later labors and death in Rome in great detail. At the beginning of the third century, although the tradition gains nothing by later repetition, Tertullian says [6] that "Peter equalled the suffering of his master," i.e., death by crucifixion, and that Paul "was crowned with death," i.e., by beheading. In still another work,[7] he also alludes to Peter's crucifixion in Rome.

Caius, a Roman presbyter who lived during the episcopate of Zephyrinus (198–217), in his polemic against the Montanist Proclus says [8] that he "can point out the trophies of the apostles who founded this (Roman) Church" on the Vatican and the Ostian Way respectively. . . . Here "trophies" (*tropaea*) means "places of martyrdom" rather than "graves" as Eusebius thought. This statement is, however, of little importance since the relics of the two apostles were not buried at the sites he mentions till after his time, Peter's in St. Peter's basilica—said to have been founded by Constantine at the request of Pope Sylvester—after 354 and Paul's, according to the *Depositio martyrum* connected with Philocalus' calendar of 353–354, as early as 258 (to avoid depredation during Valerian's persecution) on the road to Ostia and later in 354 in the same basilica. In 258 Peter's remains, according to the same *depositio,* were taken *ad catacumbas* on the Appian Way (near the church of San Sebastiano erected there in the fourth century), but Paul's relics were not buried by the Ostian Way in Caius' time, and Peter's should already have been transferred to the catacombs if by Caius' time they rested on the Vatican. There were both Jewish and Christian graves in the catacombs.

4 *Adv. haer.* 3:1, 12 and 3:3, 2.
5 Quoted by Eusebius *H.E.* 6:14, 6f.
6 *De praescriptione adv. haereticos* 36.
7 Tertullian *De Scorpiace* 15.
8 Quoted by Eusebius *H.E.* 2:25, 6–7.

In the middle of the third century Origen [9] says Peter was crucified "head downwards having himself desired to suffer in this way" and that Paul suffered martyrdom under Nero. Hippolytus in his *Philosophumena* (composed *ca.* 235) mentions Peter's polemic against Simon Magus in Rome. Finally, Eusebius assembled all that was known about the supposed sojourn of Peter in Rome in his two works; the *Chronicon* (1), an epitome of universal history down to 325, and in his *Church History;* the former dates Paul's death in the thirteenth or fourteenth year of Nero, i.e., 67 or 68, a date later followed by Jerome [10] although this is three years too late for Nero's persecution; in the latter the passage in which he speaks of Caius—he says: "It is related that in his [Nero's] time Paul was beheaded in Rome itself and that Peter likewise was crucified, and the title of "Peter and Paul," which is still given to the cemeteries there, confirms the story." [11] In the *Chronicon* he also speaks of Peter's Roman bishopric as lasting for twenty-five years (A.D. 42–67), and makes him co-founder with Paul of the Roman church. Lactantius who died in 346, in his disputed *De mortibus persecutorum,* repeats the story of Peter's crucifixion and Paul's beheading. Prudentius, the Christian poet who died *ca.* 400, in his *Peristephanon* says the two were martyred on the same day in Rome, but one year apart, the tradition followed by St. Augustine.[12] Nor should we omit the statement in Theodosius' decree of 380 that "a pious belief from Peter to the present declares that the holy Peter was delivered to the Romans," [13] i.e., to death in Rome.

St. Jerome in summing up Peter's later activity (*op. cit.*) says that he after serving as bishop of Antioch and laboring in Asia Minor came to Rome in the second year of Claudius, i.e., 42, to oppose Simon Magus (even if there is no proof that the latter ever was there), the tradition begun by the author of the *Acta Petri* (190). The supposed proof of Simon's presence in Rome, first maintained in the *Apology* of Justin Martyr,[14] rests on a misunderstanding of an inscription to the archaic Sabine deity Semo Sancus, god of oaths and good faith in social life, identified by the Romans with Hercules and with Dius Fidius, a surname of Jupiter as god of faith, as if it were in honor of the sorcerer.[15] Jerome repeats the tradition that Peter was bishop for a quarter of a century and that he was crucified "head downward" in the last year of Nero, 68, and was buried on Vatican Hill, i.e., in the Church of St. Peter. S. W. Gilmore [16] has shown the various

[9] In Vol. III of his *Comm. in Genesim* 2:24A, quoted by Eusebius *H.E.* 3:1, 2. Also in *Acta Petri* 84; and *Acta Petri et Pauli* 81.

[10] In his *De viris illustribus* 14.

[11] Eusebius *H.E.* 2:25, 5.

[12] *Sermo* 28 (*De Sanctis*).

[13] *C.Th.* XVI:1–2.

[14] 1, chap. 26 (cf. 56); followed by Irenaeus *Adv. haer.* 1, 20, and Tertullian *Apol.* 13.

[15] See *Nicene and Post-Nicene Fathers*, 2nd Series (New York, 1890–1900), I, 114, n. 11. Justin says a statue was set up to Simon on the Tiber Island inscribed *Simoni Deo Sancto;* the recovered inscription, however, reads *Semoni Sanco deo Fidio sacrum*—and so has nothing to do with Simon; see *C.I.L.*, VI, 1 (1876), 567.

[16] In Schaff-Herzog, *op. cit.*, VIII, 452; cf. Schmieder, l. c., pp. 4590f.

traditions on which these later statements rest: his bishopric at Antioch on Galatians 2:11f.; his being in Asia Minor on I Peter 1:1; his crucifixion on the literal understanding of the passage in John (21:15) to be discussed; his burial on the Vatican from the wrong statement of Caius; his twenty-five years bishopric on Justin whose work, composed about 150, first brought Peter into relation to Simon Magus; and further confusion on bringing the two apostles together which led to the belief that they founded the Roman church and labored together until their simultaneous deaths.[17]

The silence of various writers and especially of those of the earlier period speaks against the tradition just outlined. Paul in his *Epistle to the Romans* composed *ca.* 59 says nothing of Peter in Rome nor of his supervision of the church there but speaks of the faith of the Roman church (1:8) as already "proclaimed throughout the whole world." None of the later letters which he is supposed to have written during his Roman imprisonment 61–63 mentions Peter, neither Philippians, probably written there (1:13 and 4:22), Philemon, nor II Timothy, the latter expressly dated at Rome (1:8, 16 f. and 2:9). In the latter he mentions Mark and other co-workers, but not Peter. Nor is the latter mentioned in Colossians or Ephesians, if these were written in Rome rather than during his imprisonment in Caesarea. While in Ephesians there is no indication of the place of writing, Colossians mentions other co-workers of Paul in Rome (1:1 and 7; 4:7, 10, 12), but again nothing of Peter.

In the text it was stated that most critics condemn I Peter as non-Petrine. It speaks of Peter's labors in Pontus, Galatia, Cappadocia, Asia and Bithynia and is signed at Babylon, "She [the church] that is in Babylon . . . saluteth thee," which most critics have identified with Rome since Rome is so called in Revelation (17:5 "mother of the harlots and of the abominations of the earth"; 18:2, 10, 21, etc.). But when we reflect that Rome could not have been so called till after Nero's persecution and that, if the Epistle were composed by Peter before that date, Babylon would not have meant Rome and, if after it, all connection with Peter's authorship disappears, it seems inescapable that Babylon and not Rome was meant. Diodorus whose *General History* comes down to 21 B.C. expressly tells us (2:9, 9) that in his time "some small part [of Babylon] is occupied, though most is ploughed land" and this condition must have continued through the first and second Christian centuries for it is in harmony with the apocryphal *Acta Petri* at the end of the second which recounts Peter's labors in Babylonia. Indeed, the latter seems to have been his most important field for there were many Jews in Babylon and elsewhere in Babylonia ever since the Exile and among them doubtless many Greek-Jews.

[17] Various dates for Peter's crucifixion have been given: 64 by Harnack in *Gesch. der altchristlichen Litteratur bis Eusebius* (Leipzig, 1893), II (Chronologie, 1, 240); 64–68 by the cautious Duchesne in *Early History of the Christian Church*, tr. by C. Jenkins (New York, 1909–24); while Sir William Ramsay, who dates I Peter in 80, places his death in the reign of Titus (79–81) in his *The Church in the Roman Empire* (London, 1893) and other works.

Some have even started the tradition of Peter's Roman sojourn with Clement, the traditional third bishop of Rome after Peter (?91–100). But in the First of his two Epistles to the Corinthians (composed 95–97) [18] in connection with some dispute which led to the dismissal of several presbyters there he merely speaks (5:1 and 6:1) of "those who contended in the days nearest to us" and how Peter, having endured many tortures, "went to the glorious place which was his due," and how Paul "showed the way to the prize of endurance." In reference to the Neronian victims he also says: "To these men with their holy lives was gathered a great multitude of the chosen who . . . offered among us the fairest example in their endurance." He thus alludes to Peter's martyrdom but says nothing of *where* it occurred. And Ignatius, in his Epistle to the Romans [19] (composed *ca.* 110–117) merely says: "I do not order you as did Peter and Paul" (4:3) but this is also no proof of Peter's presence in Rome. Papias, bishop of Hierapolis (*ca.* 130–140), also tells us that Mark accompanied Peter as interpreter, but not necessarily to Rome.[20] The author of the Shepherd of Hermas, an apocalypse produced in Rome (*ca.* 148, or a little earlier), says nothing of either apostle having been in Rome and Justin Martyr in the middle of the century says nothing of Peter though much of Simon Magus.

Lastly, we mention the misunderstood prophecy about the manner of Peter's death in John (21:18) in which Jesus is supposed to have told Peter how he should finally glorify God:

Verily, verily, I say unto you, when thou wast young, thou girdedst thyself, and walkedst whither thou wouldst; but when thou shalt be old, thou shalt stretch forth thy hands and another shall gird thee and carry thee whither thou wouldst not.

This passage, if not like the preceding verses 15–17 a late interpolation perhaps in the interest of the growing tradition of Peter's martyrdom, to an ordinary reader merely foretells in figurative language the helplessness of old age but it has been twisted into meaning Peter's crucifixion. Tertullian who first speaks explicitly of his crucifixion says *Petrus passioni Domenicae adsequitur,* and Origen a half century later was the first, apart from apocryphal sources, to say he was crucified "head downwards." Some have imagined that these words mean that he was impaled "by the head," the same words appearing in another work of Eusebius.[21] But Jerome makes the meaning perfectly clear by his words *"affixus cruci martyrio coronatus est capite ad terram verso et in sublime pedibus elevatis."* As a reason for such an unusual position on the cross Origen, quoted above, says

---

[18] It disappeared from the Western Church in the fifth century but was rediscovered in the *Codex Alexandrinus* and published by Patrick Young (Oxford, 1633). In 1873, Bryennios discovered a manuscript of 1055 in the Jerusalem Monastery of the Holy Sepulchre in the Greek quarter of Constantinople and published it in 1875. A Syriac version dated 1169 is in the Cambridge University Library, and was published in 1876 by B. L. Bensly, and a third-century Latin version in 1894 by D. Morin, tr. by K. Lake in *Apostolic Fathers, L.C.L.* (1919 and 1917), Vol. I, dated between A.D. 75 and 110.

[19] Tr. by K. Lake, *op. cit.,* I, 225f.

[20] Quoted by Eusebius *H.E.* 3:39, 15.

[21] *Demonstratio evangelica* 3:11bc.

that Peter desired so to die, but Jerome adds that he felt himself unworthy
to die like his master. There is little indication, however, that this "upside-
down" position on the cross was really used in the Apostolic Age though
Eusebius tells [22] us that it was later employed in Tyre and Palestine during
Diocletian's persecution.[23]

We have found the tradition of Peter's sojourn and martyrdom at Rome
and his supervision over its church late and untrustworthy, beginning actually with Dionysius and Irenaeus and continuing to our time. Here,
then, there can be no question of an "established historical fact," but one
of inference based on faith alone. Peter could not have been in Rome
during Paul's imprisonment where, according to the final words of Acts
(28:30–31), Paul dwelt two years in his own hired house. Nor could he
have been there between his own imprisonment and the Jerusalem Council
(42–52) at which he attended and remained for some time afterward in
Antioch. If at any time, then, it must have been in the short period before Paul's arrival, though Peter's labors in Asia Minor and Babylonia take
up some of that interval. He may possibly have been in Rome after Paul's
death, but there is no proof that he was martyred there though there is indication enough of his crucifixion somewhere else, probably in an unknown
place during his missionary travels. Thus, an episcopate of twenty-five
years is impossible and this is not stressed by those who believe in his Roman residence. As for helping to found the Roman church Peter could
have had nothing to do with it beyond, possibly, his influence exerted from
Palestine on its foundation in the early reign of Claudius or even earlier.
Moreover, as there was no monarchical bishop of Rome till well into the
second century, if he were bishop rather than apostle he could not thus
early have passed his office on to a successor. The order of "apostolic succession" was of later origin, first developed in Irenaeus. But Irenaeus,[24]
who died about 202, and Eusebius,[25] who wrote in the early fourth century, seem to have regarded Linus and not Peter as the first Roman bishop
although they speak of Peter as founder. Thus Irenaeus says that "the
blessed apostle, then, having founded and built up the church, committed
in the hands of Linus the office of the episcopate."

Moreover, as Bishop Lightfoot long ago remarked: [26] "If there was any
primacy at the time it was the primacy not of Peter but of Paul, for Paul
was the foremost figure of the Apostolic Age." Peter is first definitely
named as first Roman bishop, in letters of St. Cyprian [27] who was beheaded
in Carthage in 258, and officially in Liberius' catalogue of 353–354. Still
the learned world is divided on the question of Peter's Roman sojourn.
While most scholars have opposed it from Baur (1831) and Paulus (1828)

[22] *H.E.* 18:8, 1.

[23] It was in this position that Giotto in 1299 painted Peter for Cardinal Stephanaschi
on the panel of the High Altar in St. Peter's church in Rome.

[24] *Op. cit.* 3:3, 3.

[25] *H.E.* 3:2, 21.

[26] *Apostolic Fathers* (London, 1885–90), II, Pt. 1, p. 490.

[27] LV:8; LIX:14.

to Schmieder (1903) others have supported it from Hilgenfeld (1872) and Joannes Delitzsch (1874) to Harnack and Kirsch.

Thus the claim of the Roman Church to universal authority based on the fulfillment of the words of Jesus to Peter (Matt. 16:18–19; cf. John 21: 15–17) has little historical basis. But whatever evidence there may be for the claim, interpreted authoritatively by the Catholic Church in its own interest, has been believed by myriads of good Catholics down to our time. These will have little patience with the negative results of the evidence outlined. When they journey to Rome they will lend eager belief to the local traditions of Peter's presence there. They will visit his prison, the upper chamber of the *Tullianum* on the lower slope of the Capitoline above the Forum beneath the tiny church of San Giuseppe dei Falagnami, the prison known in the Middle Ages as the Mamertine because of a statue of Mars nearby, and since the fifteenth century as San Pietro in Carcere. Here they will be shown the pillar to which the apostle was chained and the fountain which he caused miraculously to flow to obtain water with which to baptize his guards who were later reverenced as saints. They will visit the church of San Pietro in Vincoli built in 442 as a receptacle for Peter's chains then presented by Leo I to Eudoxia, the wife of Valentinian III, and the site of his crucifixion in San Pietro Montorio—erected since 1476—on the Janiculum. In the court of the latter's monastery is the circular Tempietto built from Bramante's designs (1499–1502) with an opening in the floor of the lower chapel disclosing the very hole in which the cross was fixed and the bronze chair enclosing the original on which the apostle is believed to have sat. And, lastly, he will see the bronze sarcophagus beneath the High Altar of St. Peter's church, transferred from Ad Catacumbas on the Appian Way—whither it had been brought in 258 as already related—first to the Lateran and finally here.

If all this be idle tradition, it is tradition too solidified in the Catholic heart ever to be destroyed. For nowhere has the spirit of the Greek proverb "Opinions are stronger than the works of the hands" been more potent than in Rome.

INDEX